MILES MORALES

THE CLONE SAGA

Saladin Ahmed
WRITER

Natacha Bustos (#22) & Carmen Carnero (#23-28)
ARTISTS

David Curiel
COLOR ARTIST

--- "BIG-TIME BUZZKILL" ---

Cody Ziglar
STORY

Natacha Bustos
ART

Rachelle Rosenberg
COLORS

VC's Cory Petit
LETTERER

Taurin Clarke
COVER ART

**Lindsey Cohick &
Shannon Andrews Ballesteros**
ASSISTANT EDITORS

Nick Lowe
EXECUTIVE EDITOR

SPIDER-MAN CREATED BY **Stan Lee & Steve Ditko**

COLLECTION EDITOR **DANIEL KIRCHHOFFER**
ASSISTANT MANAGING EDITOR **MAIA LOY**
ASSISTANT MANAGING EDITOR **LISA MONTALBANO**
SENIOR EDITOR, SPECIAL PROJECTS **JENNIFER GRÜNWALD**
VP, PRODUCTION & SPECIAL PROJECTS **JEFF YOUNGQUIST**
BOOK DESIGNERS **SARAH SPADACCINI** WITH **JAY BOWEN**
SVP PRINT, SALES & MARKETING **DAVID GABRIEL**
EDITOR IN CHIEF **C.B. CEBULSKI**

MILES MORALES VOL. 5: THE CLONE SAGA. Contains material originally published in magazine form as MILES MORALES: SPIDER-MAN (2018) #22-28. First printing 2021. ISBN 978-1-302-92601-4. Published by MARVEL WORLDWIDE, INC., a subsidiary of MARVEL ENTERTAINMENT, LLC. OFFICE OF PUBLICATION: 1290 Avenue of the Americas, New York, NY 10104. © 2021 MARVEL No similarity between any of the names, characters, persons, and/or institutions in this magazine with those of any living or dead person or institution is intended, and any such similarity which may exist is purely coincidental. Printed in Canada. KEVIN FEIGE, Chief Creative Officer; DAN BUCKLEY, President, Marvel Entertainment; JOE QUESADA, EVP & Creative Director; DAVID BOGART, Associate Publisher & SVP of Talent Affairs; TOM BREVOORT, VP, Executive Editor; NICK LOWE, Executive Editor, VP of Content, Digital Publishing; DAVID GABRIEL, VP of Print & Digital Publishing; JEFF YOUNGQUIST, VP of Production & Special Projects; ALEX MORALES, Director of Publishing Operations; DAN EDINGTON, Managing Editor; RICKEY PURDIN, Director of Talent Relations; JENNIFER GRÜNWALD, Senior Editor, Special Projects; SUSAN CRESPI, Production Manager; STAN LEE, Chairman Emeritus. For information regarding advertising in Marvel Comics or on Marvel.com, please contact Vit DeBellis, Custom Solutions & Integrated Advertising Manager, at vdebellis@marvel.com. For Marvel subscription inquiries, please call 888-511-5480. Manufactured between 7/23/2021 and 8/24/2021 by SOLISCO PRINTERS, SCOTT, QC, CANADA.

10 9 8 7 6 5 4 3 2 1

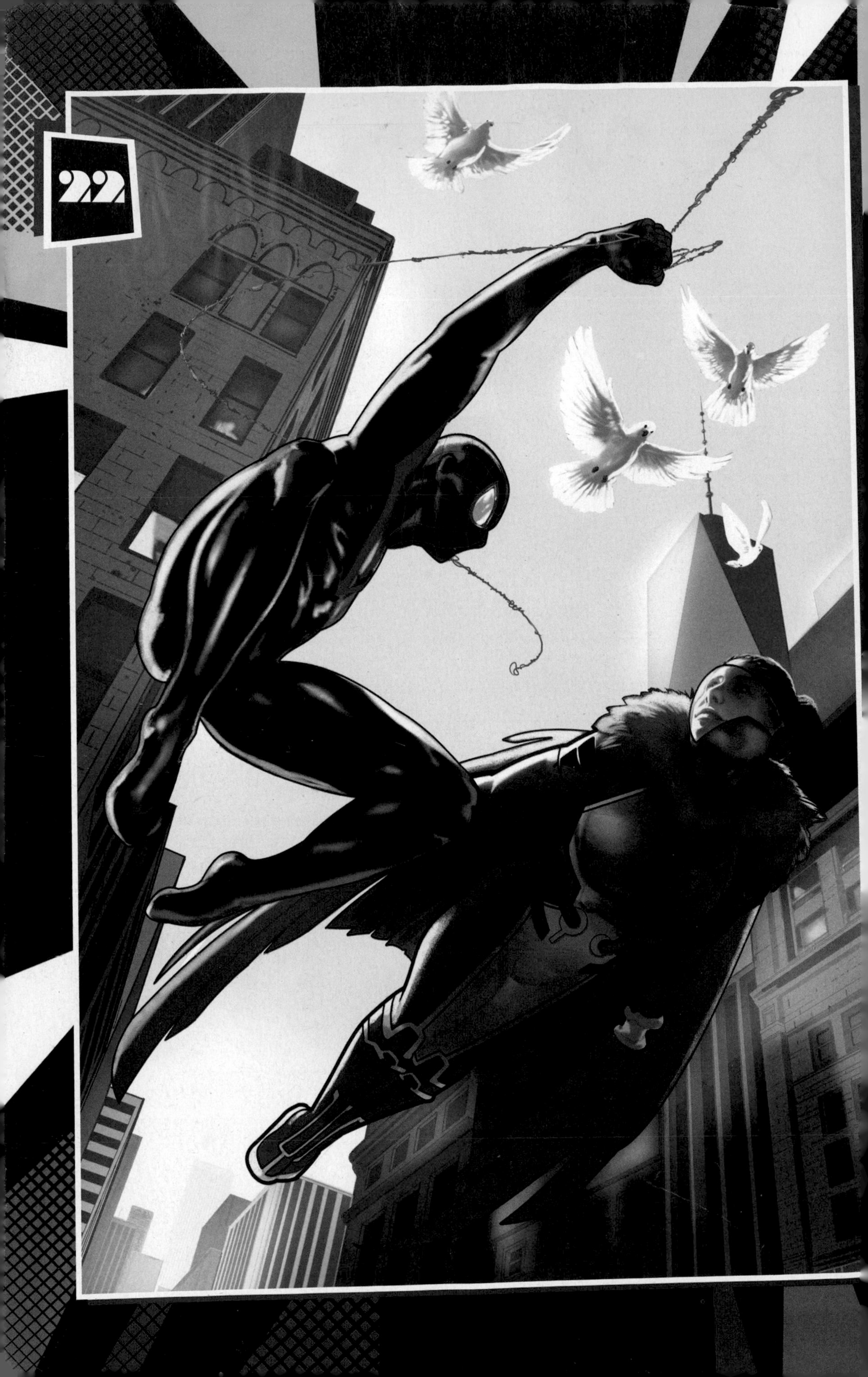
22

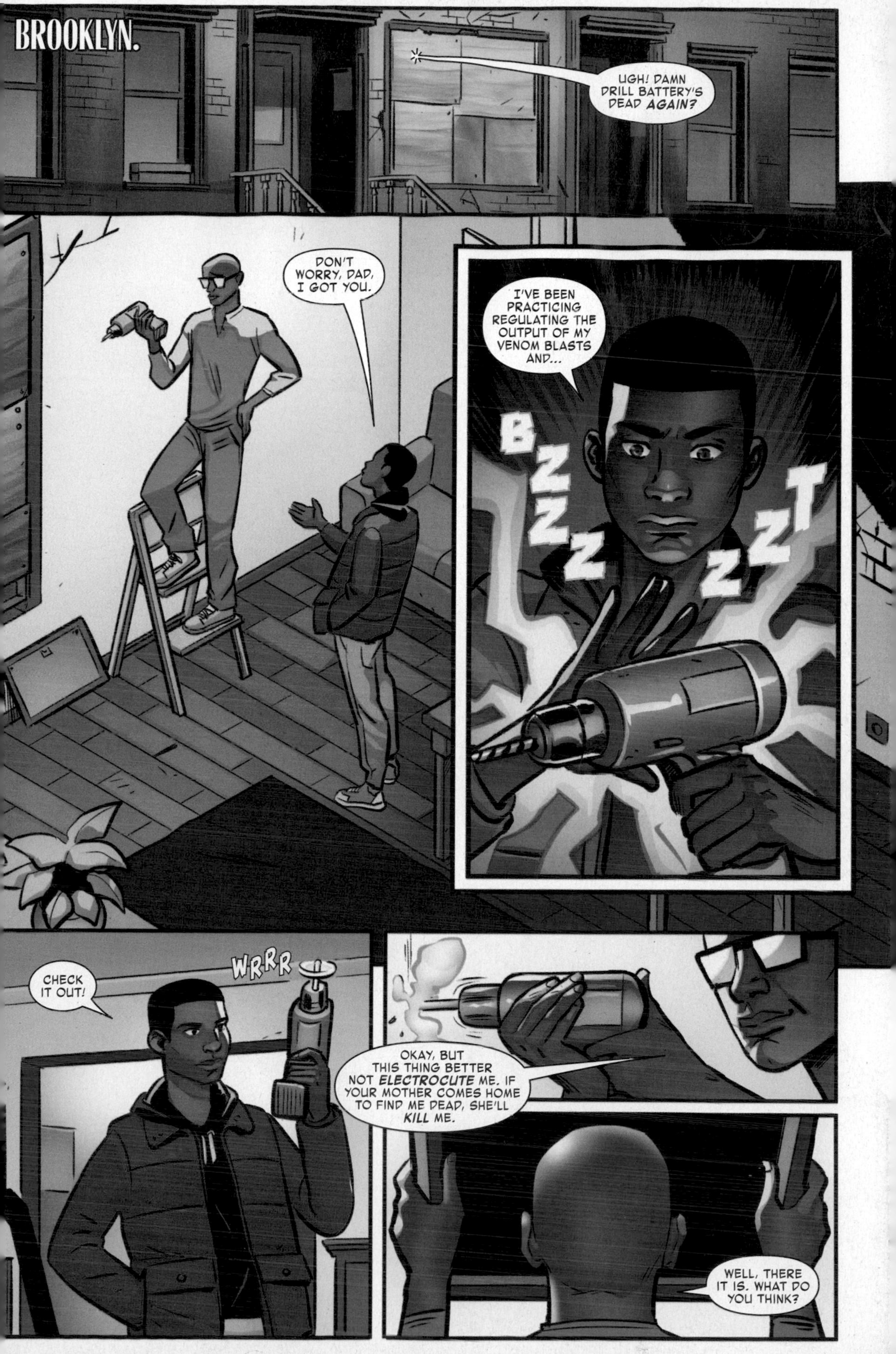
BROOKLYN.
UGH! DAMN DRILL BATTERY'S DEAD AGAIN?
DON'T WORRY, DAD, I GOT YOU.
I'VE BEEN PRACTICING REGULATING THE OUTPUT OF MY VENOM BLASTS AND...
BZZZZZZT
WRRR
CHECK IT OUT!
OKAY, BUT THIS THING BETTER NOT ELECTROCUTE ME. IF YOUR MOTHER COMES HOME TO FIND ME DEAD, SHE'LL KILL ME.
WELL, THERE IT IS. WHAT DO YOU THINK?

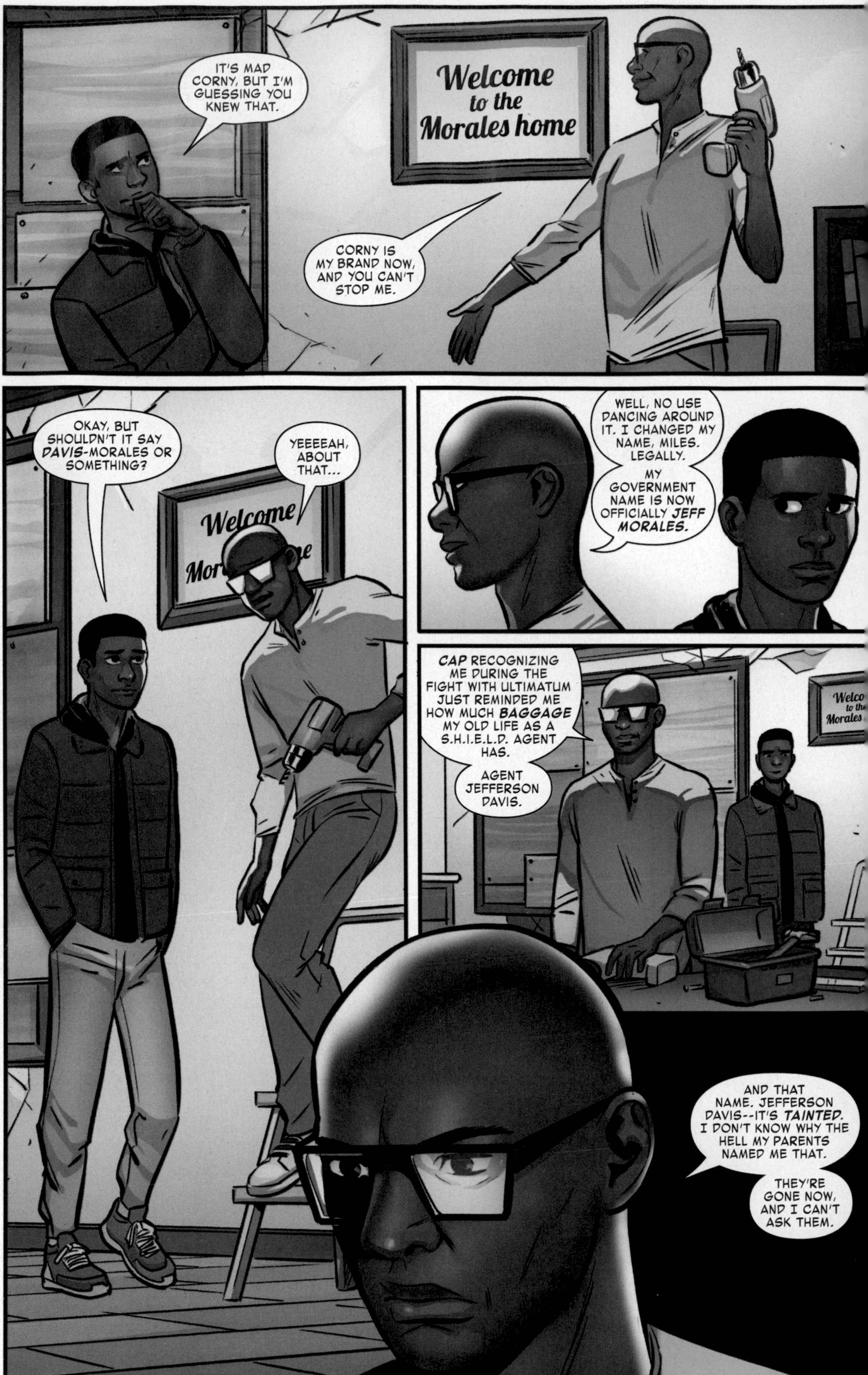
IT'S MAD CORNY, BUT I'M GUESSING YOU KNEW THAT.
Welcome to the Morales home
CORNY IS MY BRAND NOW, AND YOU CAN'T STOP ME.
OKAY, BUT SHOULDN'T IT SAY DAVIS-MORALES OR SOMETHING?
YEEEEAH, ABOUT THAT...
WELL, NO USE DANCING AROUND IT. I CHANGED MY NAME, MILES. LEGALLY.
MY GOVERNMENT NAME IS NOW OFFICIALLY JEFF MORALES.
CAP RECOGNIZING ME DURING THE FIGHT WITH ULTIMATUM JUST REMINDED ME HOW MUCH BAGGAGE MY OLD LIFE AS A S.H.I.E.L.D. AGENT HAS.
AGENT JEFFERSON DAVIS.
AND THAT NAME. JEFFERSON DAVIS--IT'S TAINTED. I DON'T KNOW WHY THE HELL MY PARENTS NAMED ME THAT.
THEY'RE GONE NOW, AND I CAN'T ASK THEM.

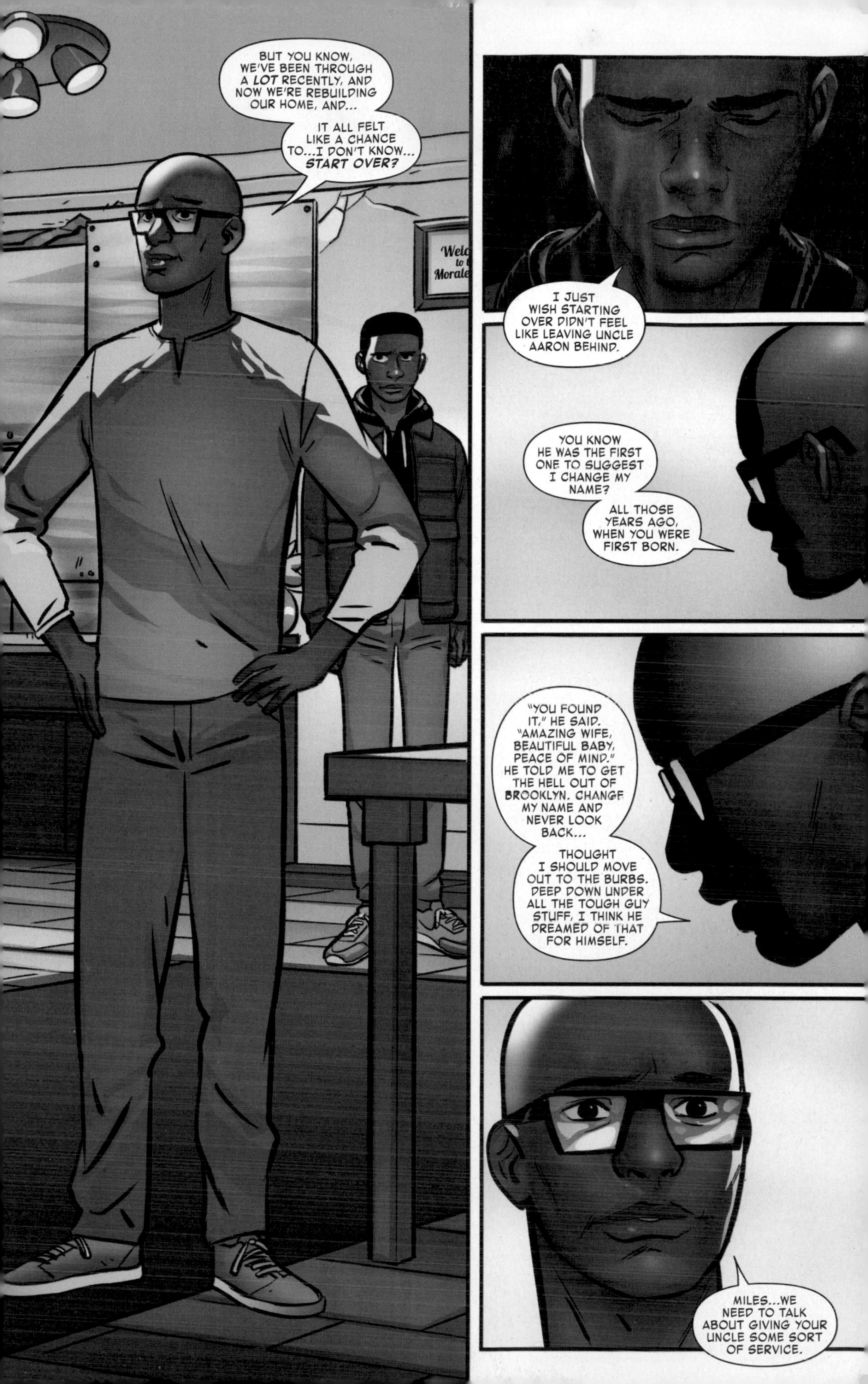
BUT YOU KNOW, WE'VE BEEN THROUGH A *LOT* RECENTLY, AND NOW WE'RE REBUILDING OUR HOME, AND...
IT ALL FELT LIKE A CHANCE TO...I DON'T KNOW... *START OVER?*
Welc to t Morale
I JUST WISH STARTING OVER DIDN'T FEEL LIKE LEAVING UNCLE AARON BEHIND.
YOU KNOW HE WAS THE FIRST ONE TO SUGGEST I CHANGE MY NAME?
ALL THOSE YEARS AGO, WHEN YOU WERE FIRST BORN.
"YOU FOUND IT," HE SAID. "AMAZING WIFE, BEAUTIFUL BABY, PEACE OF MIND." HE TOLD ME TO GET THE HELL OUT OF BROOKLYN. CHANGE MY NAME AND NEVER LOOK BACK...
THOUGHT I SHOULD MOVE OUT TO THE BURBS. DEEP DOWN UNDER ALL THE TOUGH GUY STUFF, I THINK HE DREAMED OF THAT FOR HIMSELF.
MILES...WE NEED TO TALK ABOUT GIVING YOUR UNCLE SOME SORT OF SERVICE.

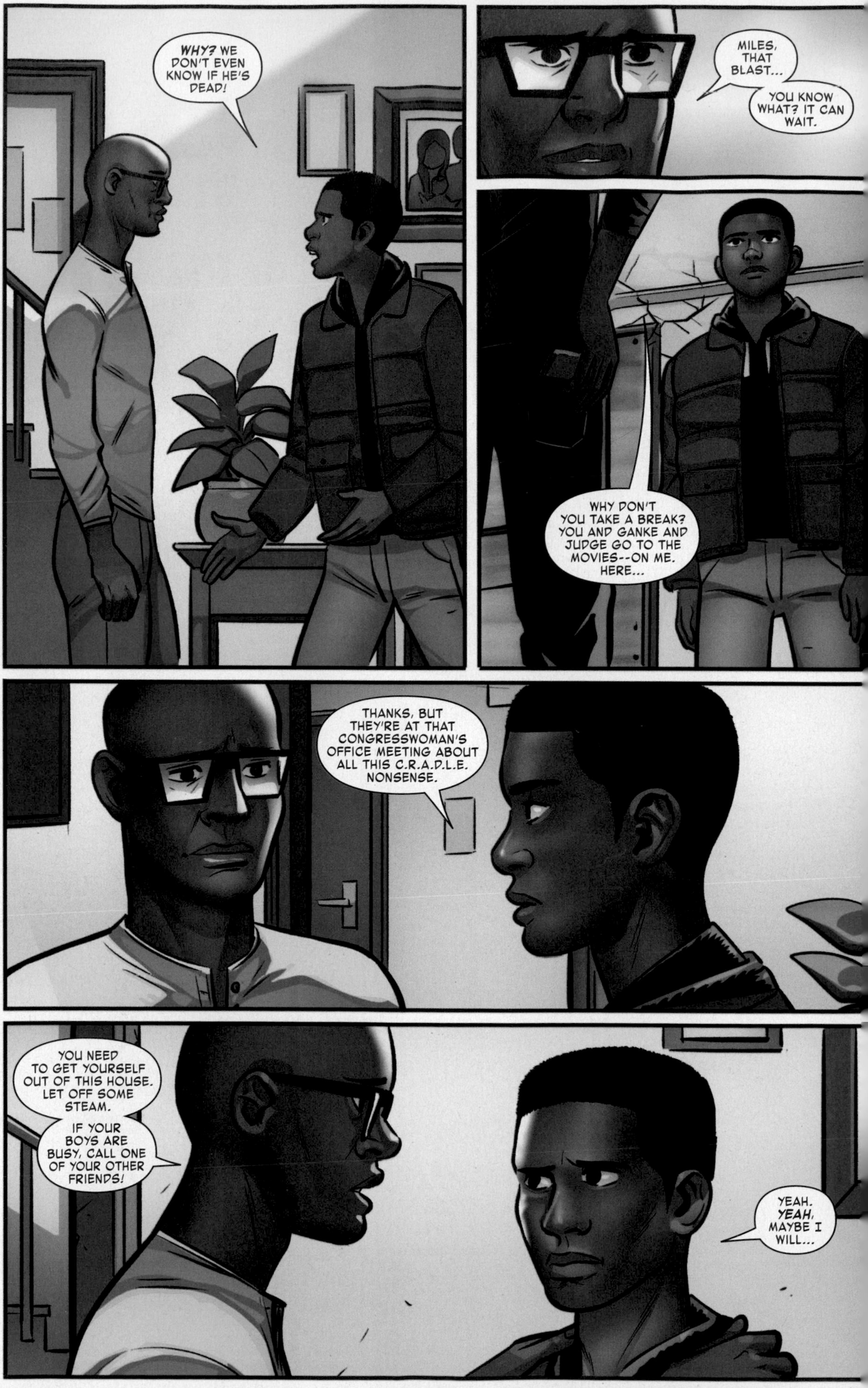
WHY? WE DON'T EVEN KNOW IF HE'S DEAD!
MILES, THAT BLAST...
YOU KNOW WHAT? IT CAN WAIT.
WHY DON'T YOU TAKE A BREAK? YOU AND GANKE AND JUDGE GO TO THE MOVIES--ON ME. HERE...
THANKS, BUT THEY'RE AT THAT CONGRESSWOMAN'S OFFICE MEETING ABOUT ALL THIS C.R.A.D.L.E. NONSENSE.
YOU NEED TO GET YOURSELF OUT OF THIS HOUSE. LET OFF SOME STEAM.
IF YOUR BOYS ARE BUSY, CALL ONE OF YOUR OTHER FRIENDS!
YEAH. *YEAH*, MAYBE I WILL...

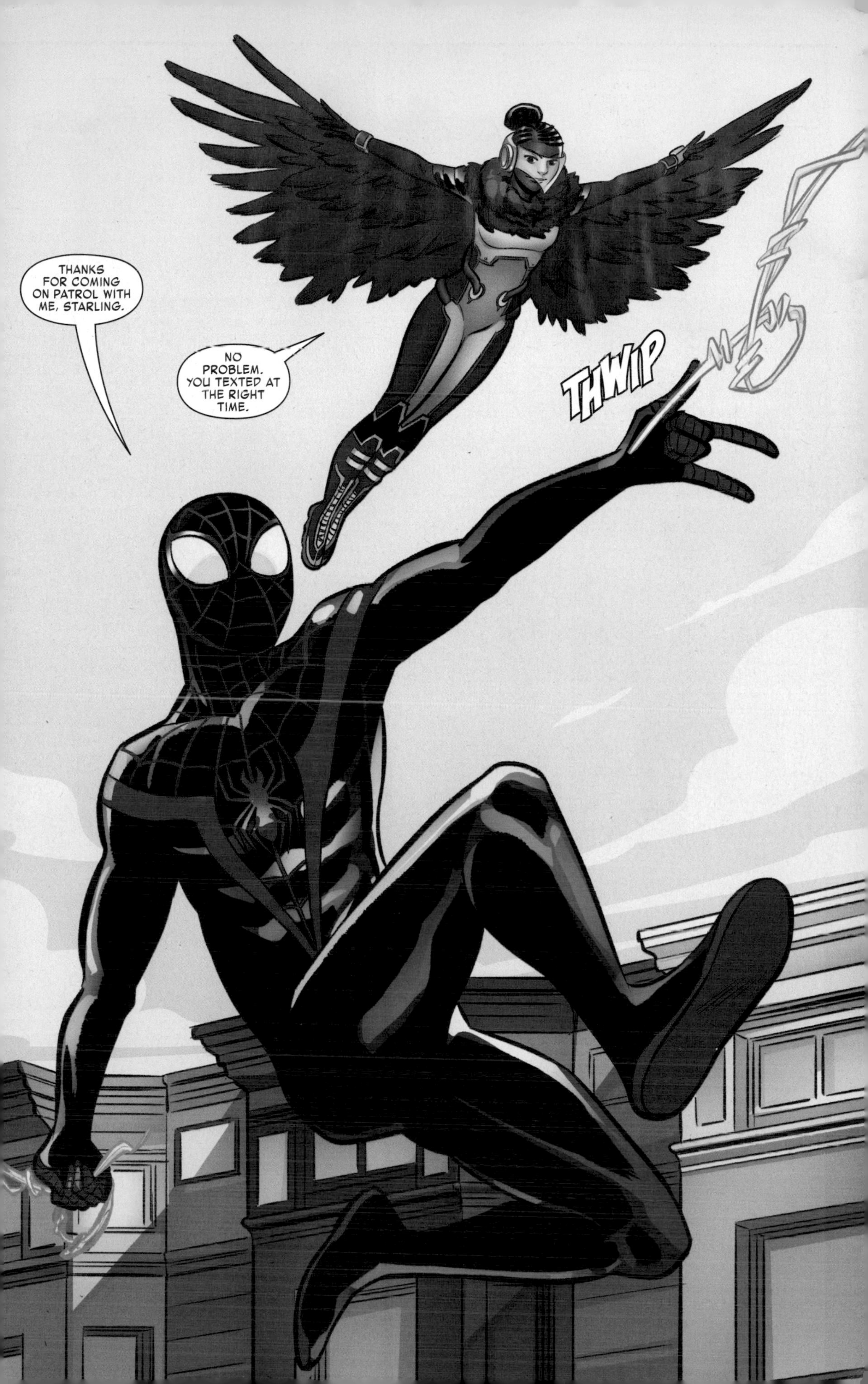
THANKS FOR COMING ON PATROL WITH ME, STARLING.
NO PROBLEM. YOU TEXTED AT THE RIGHT TIME.
THWIP

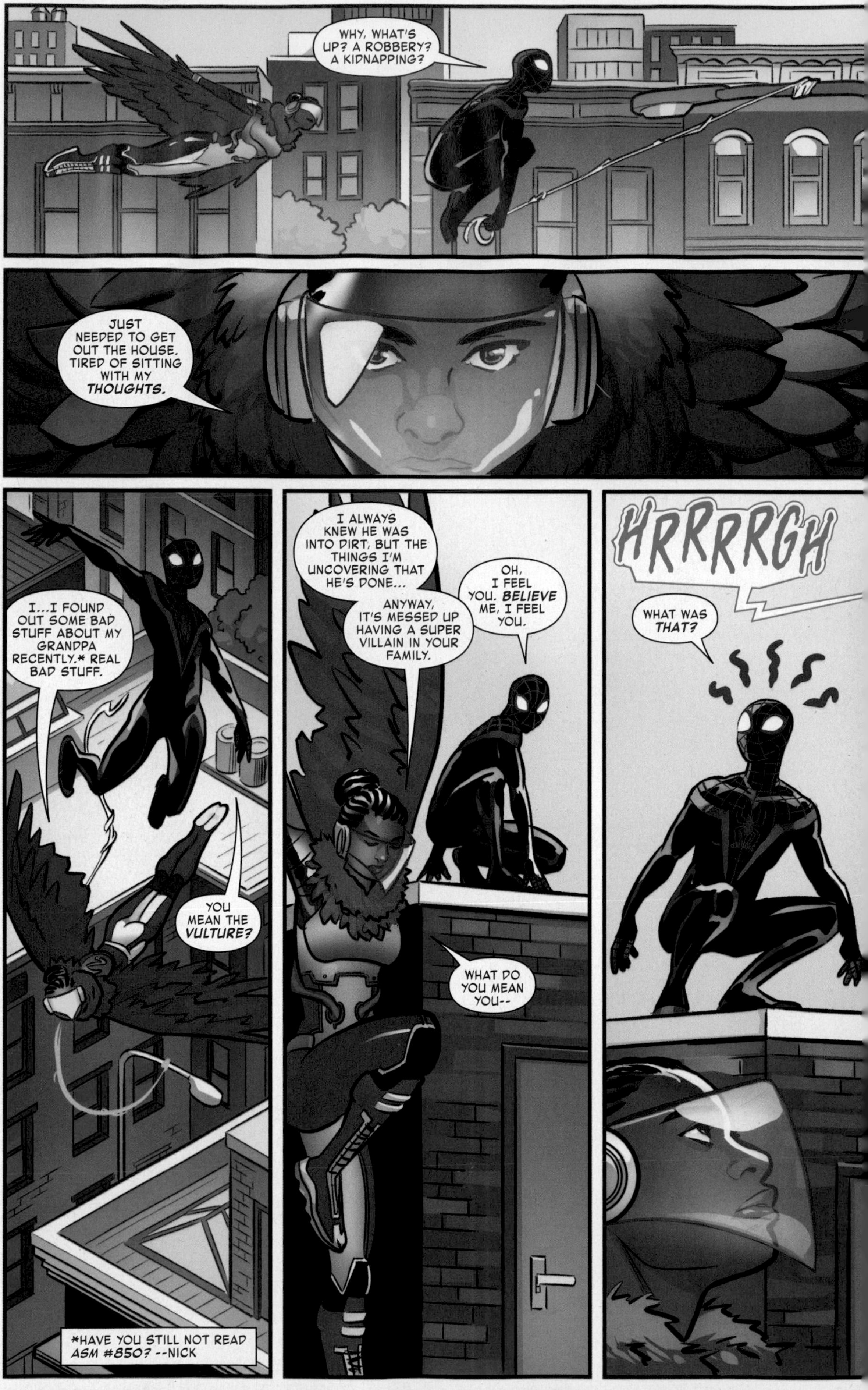
WHY, WHAT'S UP? A ROBBERY? A KIDNAPPING?
JUST NEEDED TO GET OUT THE HOUSE. TIRED OF SITTING WITH MY THOUGHTS.
I...I FOUND OUT SOME BAD STUFF ABOUT MY GRANDPA RECENTLY.* REAL BAD STUFF.
YOU MEAN THE VULTURE?
*HAVE YOU STILL NOT READ ASM #850? --NICK
I ALWAYS KNEW HE WAS INTO DIRT, BUT THE THINGS I'M UNCOVERING THAT HE'S DONE...
ANYWAY, IT'S MESSED UP HAVING A SUPER VILLAIN IN YOUR FAMILY.
OH, I FEEL YOU. BELIEVE ME, I FEEL YOU.
WHAT DO YOU MEAN YOU--
HRRRRGH
WHAT WAS THAT?

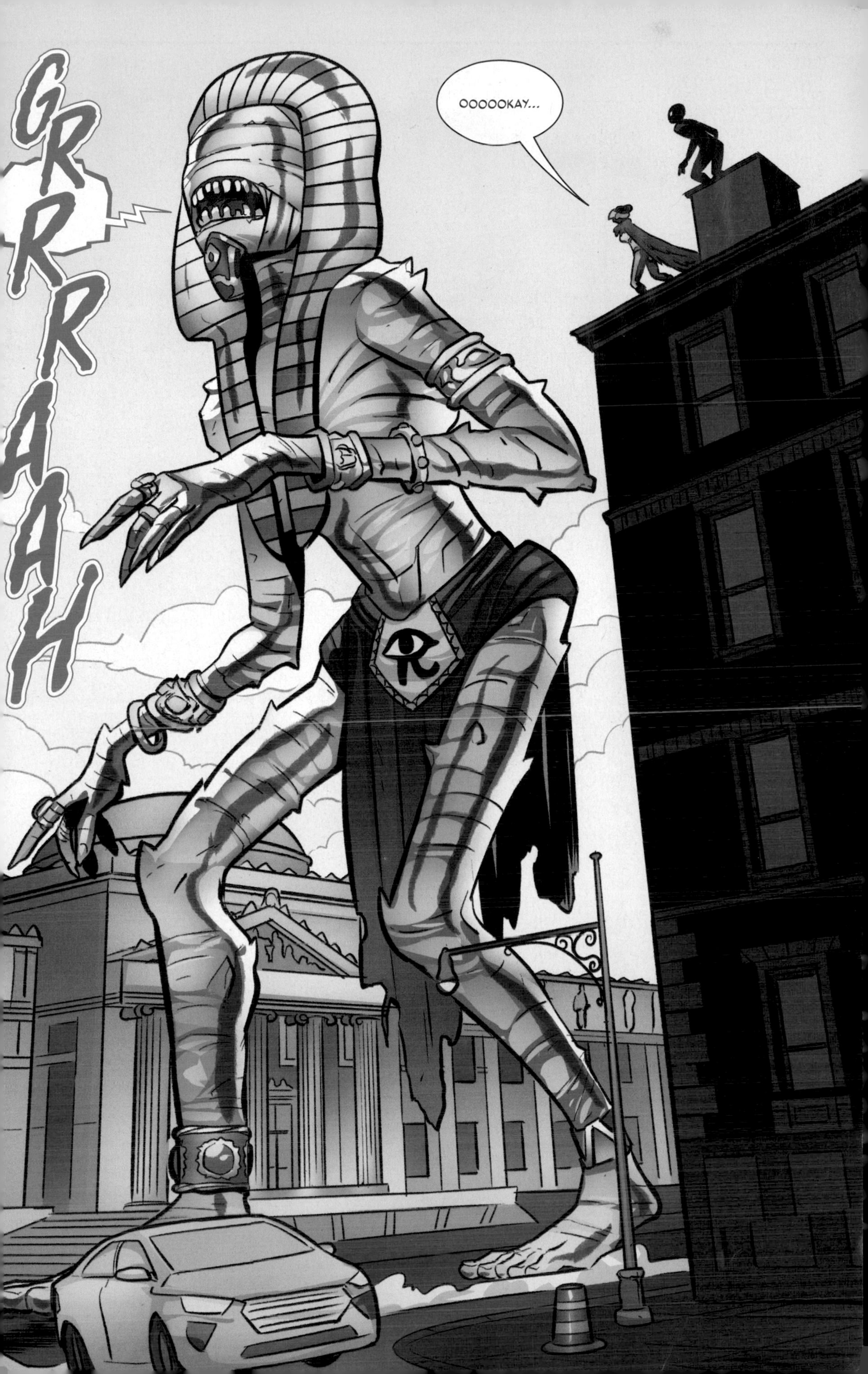
GRRRAAAH
OOOOOKAY...

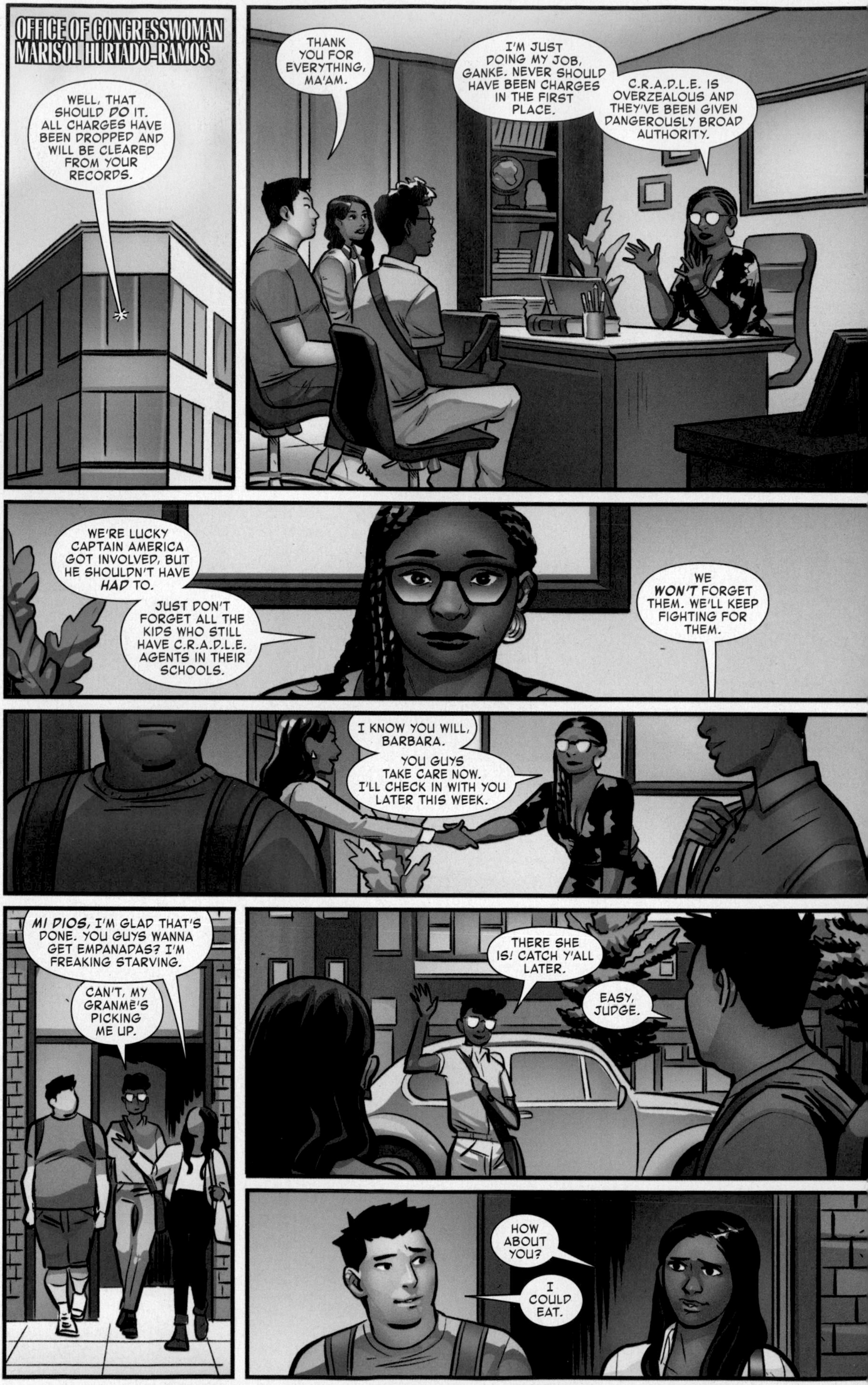
OFFICE OF CONGRESSWOMAN MARISOL HURTADO-RAMOS.
WELL, THAT SHOULD DO IT. ALL CHARGES HAVE BEEN DROPPED AND WILL BE CLEARED FROM YOUR RECORDS.
THANK YOU FOR EVERYTHING, MA'AM.
I'M JUST DOING MY JOB, GANKE. NEVER SHOULD HAVE BEEN CHARGES IN THE FIRST PLACE.
C.R.A.D.L.E. IS OVERZEALOUS AND THEY'VE BEEN GIVEN DANGEROUSLY BROAD AUTHORITY.
WE'RE LUCKY CAPTAIN AMERICA GOT INVOLVED, BUT HE SHOULDN'T HAVE HAD TO.
JUST DON'T FORGET ALL THE KIDS WHO STILL HAVE C.R.A.D.L.E. AGENTS IN THEIR SCHOOLS.
WE WON'T FORGET THEM. WE'LL KEEP FIGHTING FOR THEM.
I KNOW YOU WILL, BARBARA.
YOU GUYS TAKE CARE NOW. I'LL CHECK IN WITH YOU LATER THIS WEEK.
MI DIOS, I'M GLAD THAT'S DONE. YOU GUYS WANNA GET EMPANADAS? I'M FREAKING STARVING.
CAN'T, MY GRANMÈ'S PICKING ME UP.
THERE SHE IS! CATCH Y'ALL LATER.
EASY, JUDGE.
HOW ABOUT YOU?
I COULD EAT.

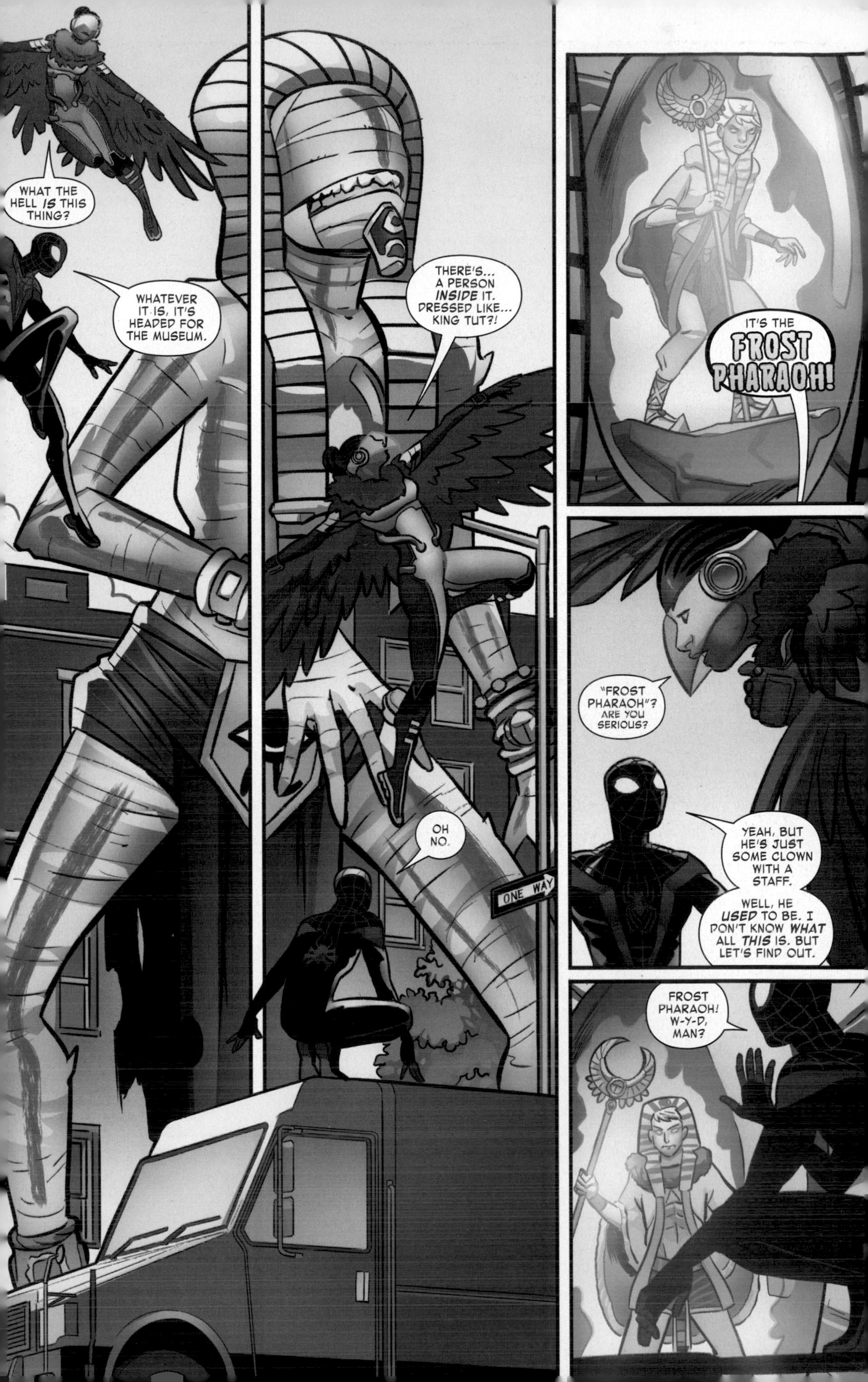
WHAT THE HELL *IS* THIS THING?
WHATEVER IT IS, IT'S HEADED FOR THE MUSEUM.
THERE'S... A PERSON *INSIDE* IT. DRESSED LIKE... KING TUT?!
OH NO.
ONE WAY
IT'S THE FROST PHARAOH!
"FROST PHARAOH"? ARE YOU SERIOUS?
YEAH, BUT HE'S JUST SOME CLOWN WITH A STAFF.
WELL, HE *USED* TO BE. I DON'T KNOW *WHAT* ALL *THIS* IS. BUT LET'S FIND OUT.
FROST PHARAOH! W-Y-D, MAN?

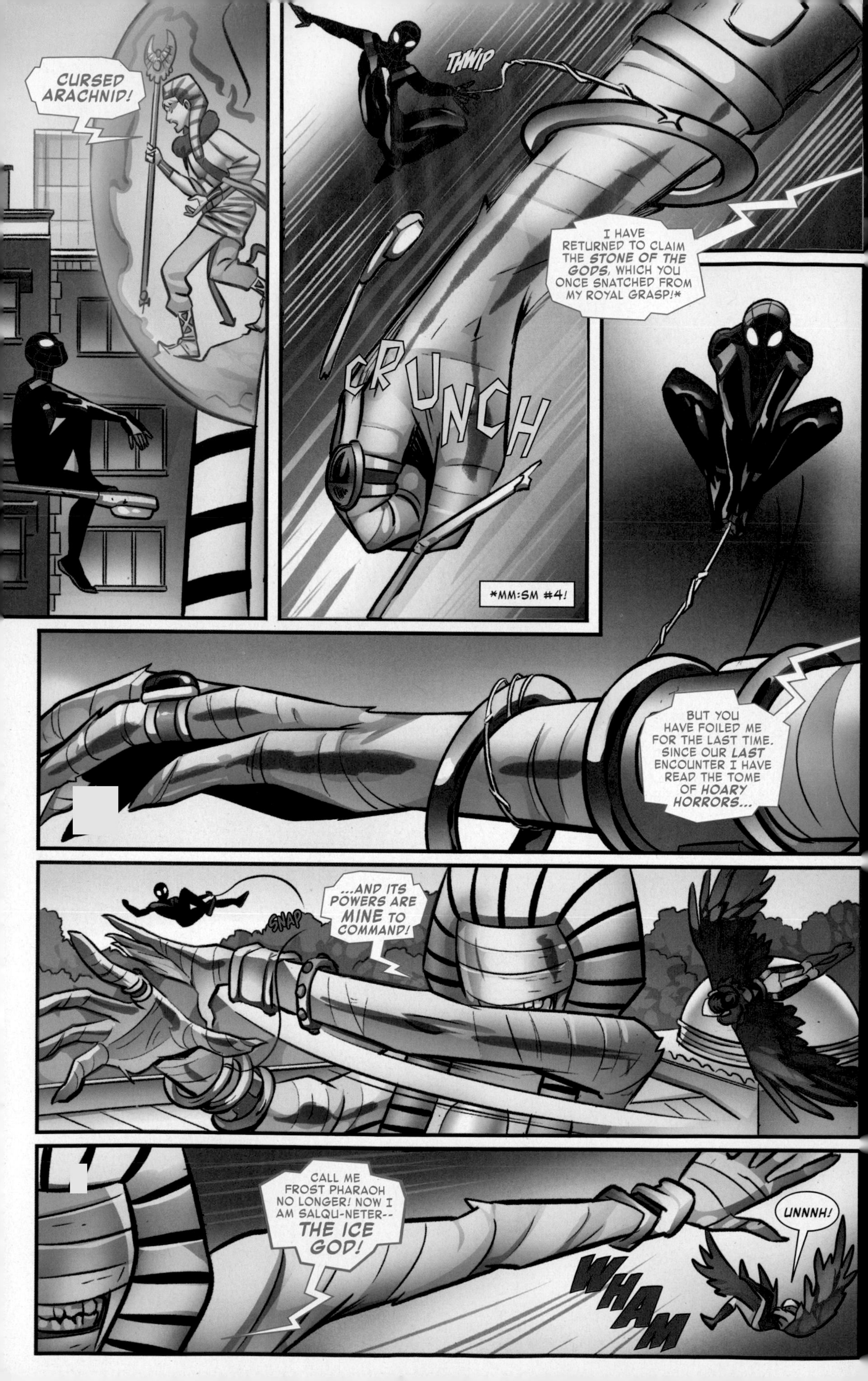
CURSED ARACHNID!
THWIP
I HAVE RETURNED TO CLAIM THE STONE OF THE GODS, WHICH YOU ONCE SNATCHED FROM MY ROYAL GRASP!*
CRUNCH
*MM:SM #4!
BUT YOU HAVE FOILED ME FOR THE LAST TIME. SINCE OUR LAST ENCOUNTER I HAVE READ THE TOME OF HOARY HORRORS...
SNAP
...AND ITS POWERS ARE MINE TO COMMAND!
CALL ME FROST PHARAOH NO LONGER! NOW I AM SALQU-NETER-- THE ICE GOD!
UNNNH!
WHAM

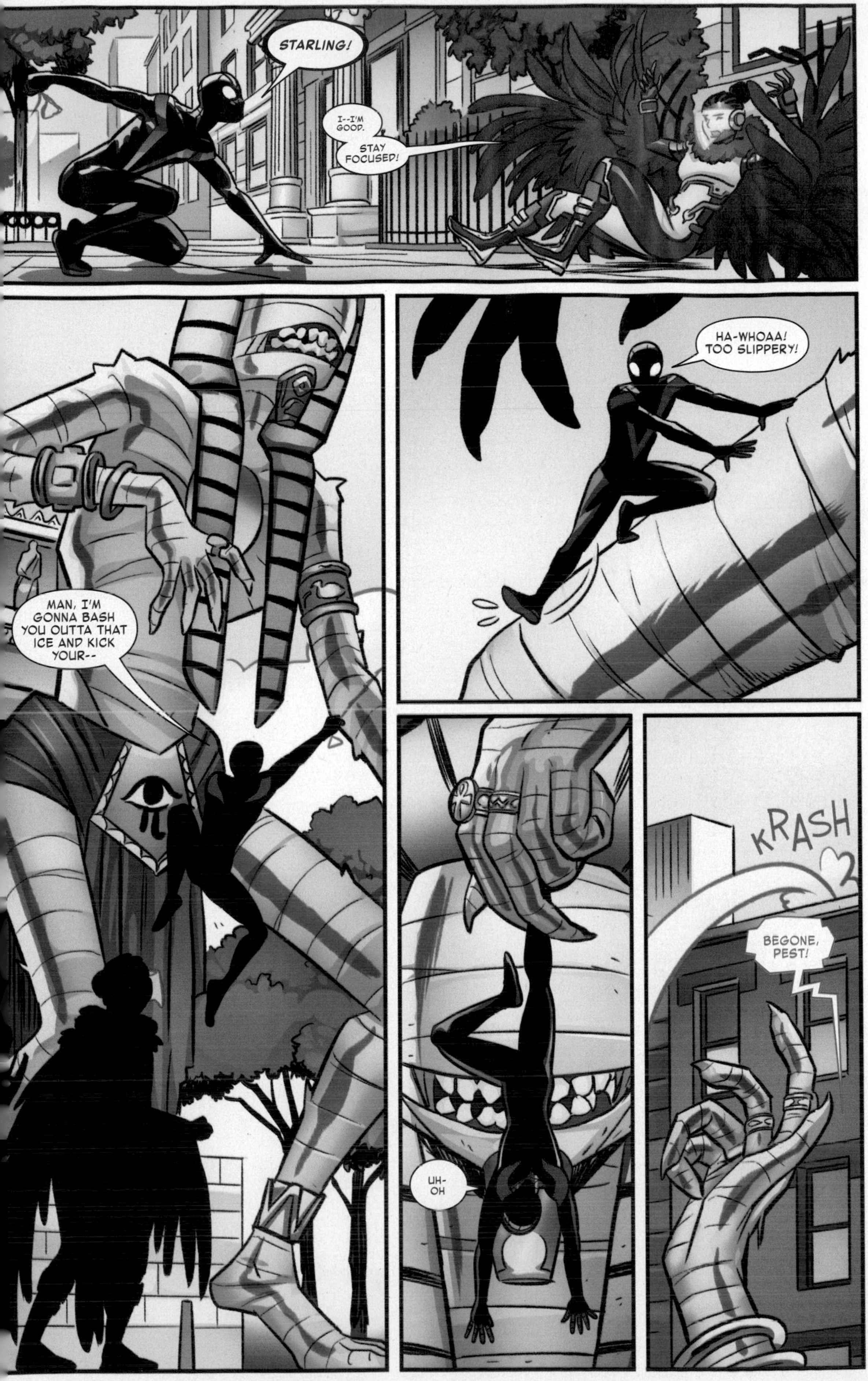
STARLING!
I--I'M GOOD.
STAY FOCUSED!
MAN, I'M GONNA BASH YOU OUTTA THAT ICE AND KICK YOUR--
HA-WHOAA! TOO SLIPPERY!
UH-OH
KRASH
BEGONE, PEST!

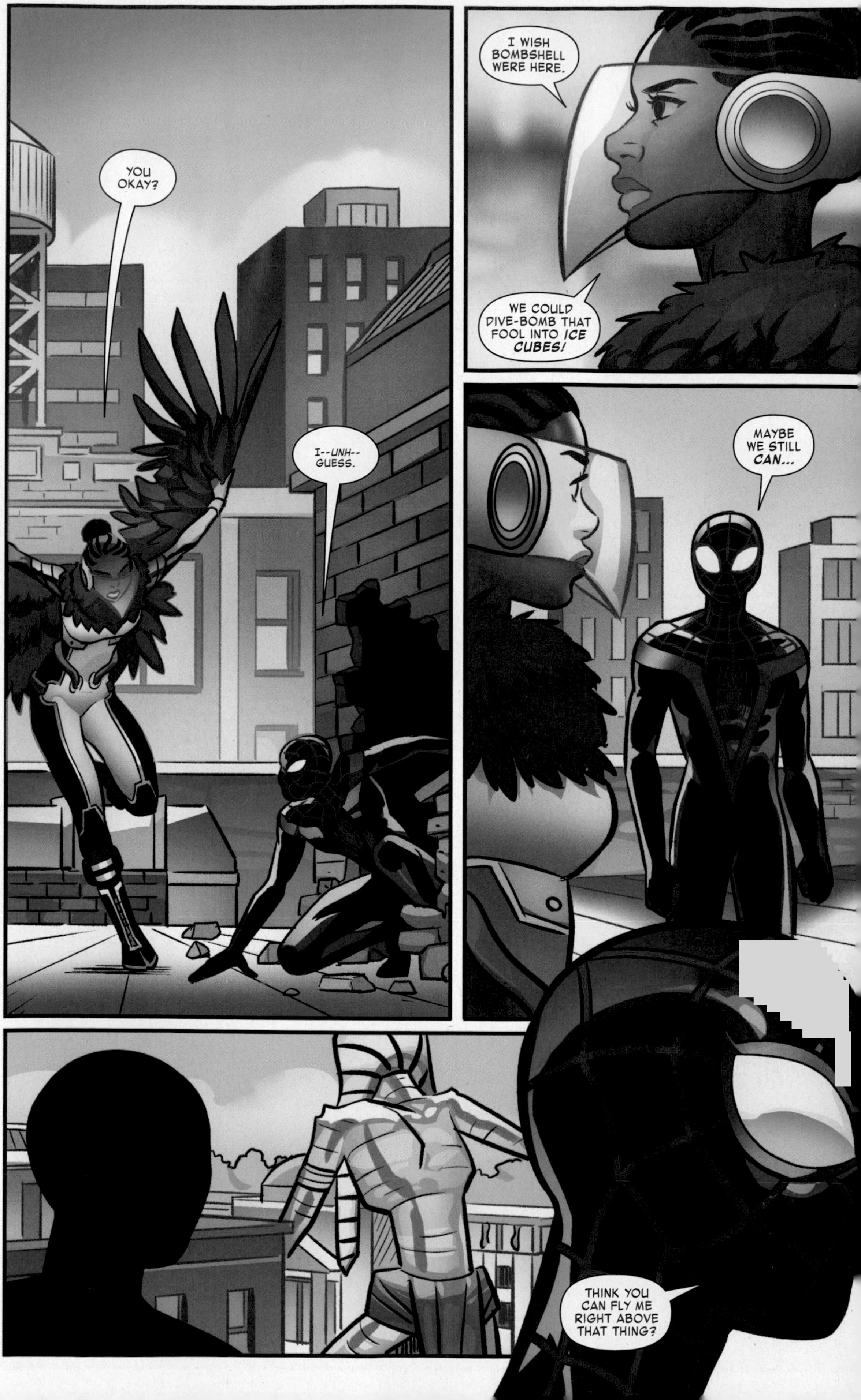
YOU OKAY?
I--UNH-- GUESS.
I WISH BOMBSHELL WERE HERE.
WE COULD DIVE-BOMB THAT FOOL INTO ICE CUBES!
MAYBE WE STILL CAN...
THINK YOU CAN FLY ME RIGHT ABOVE THAT THING?

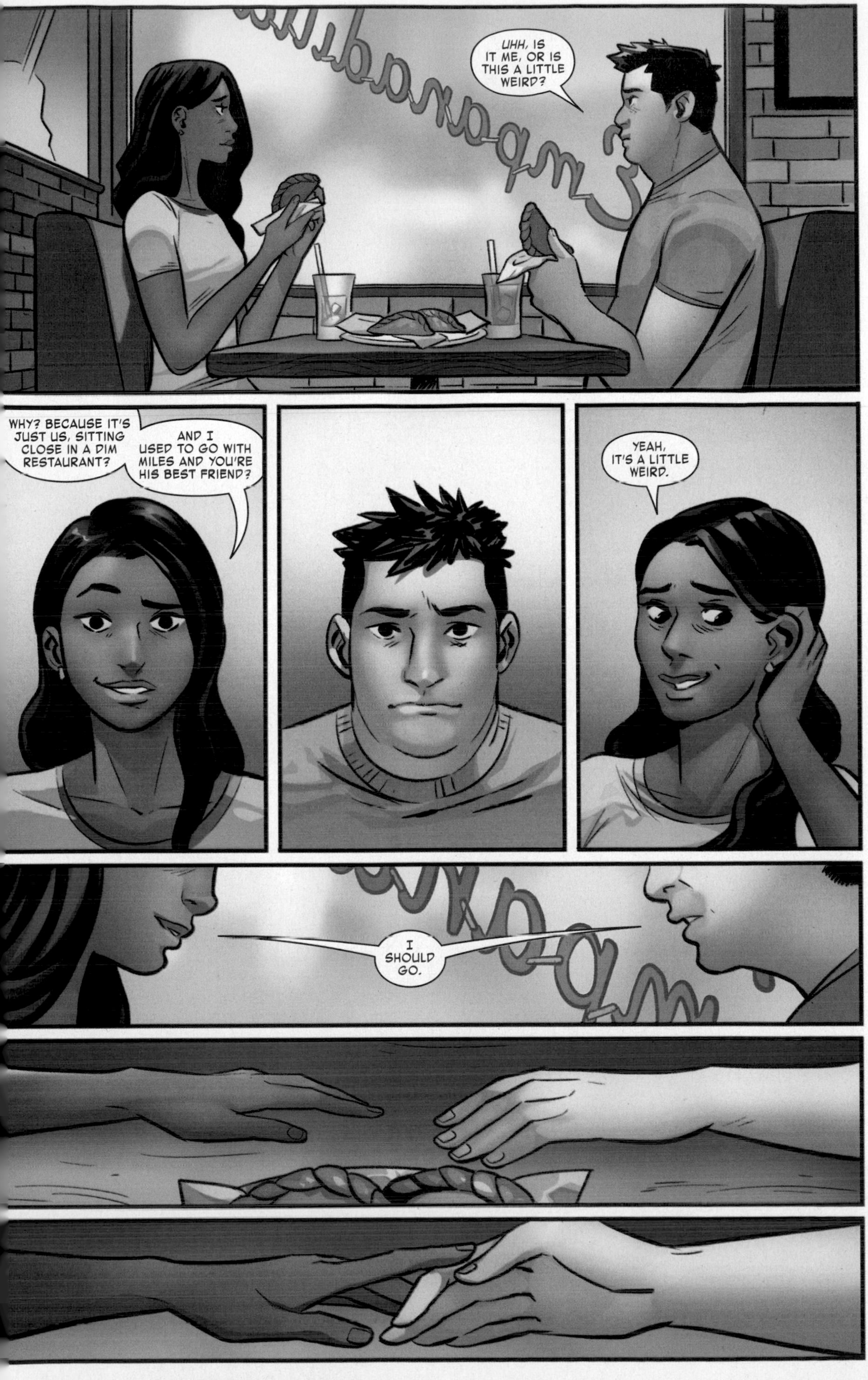
UHH, IS IT ME, OR IS THIS A LITTLE WEIRD?
WHY? BECAUSE IT'S JUST US, SITTING CLOSE IN A DIM RESTAURANT?
AND I USED TO GO WITH MILES AND YOU'RE HIS BEST FRIEND?
YEAH, IT'S A LITTLE WEIRD.
I SHOULD GO.

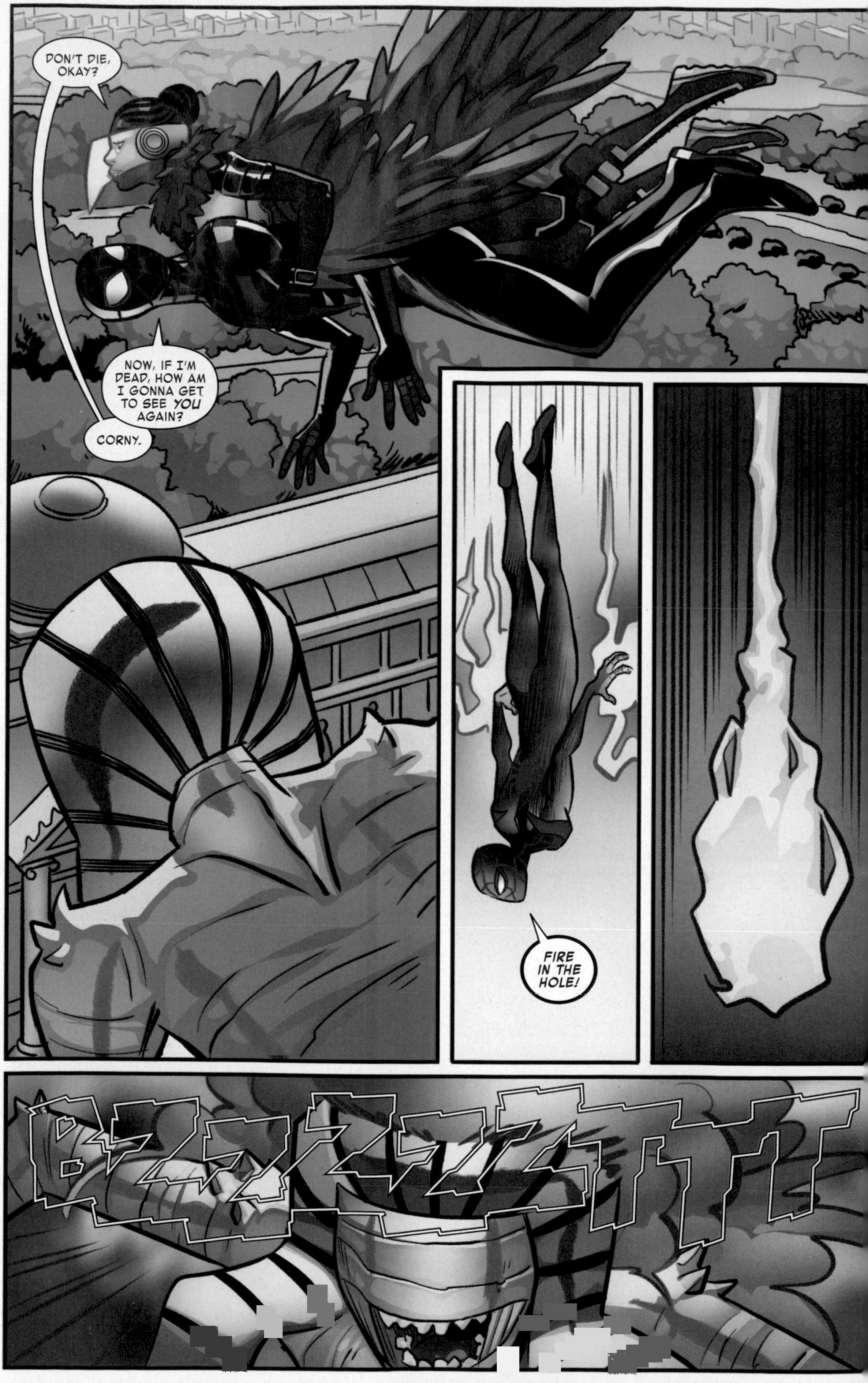

DON'T DIE, OKAY?
NOW, IF I'M DEAD, HOW AM I GONNA GET TO SEE *YOU* AGAIN?
CORNY.
FIRE IN THE HOLE!

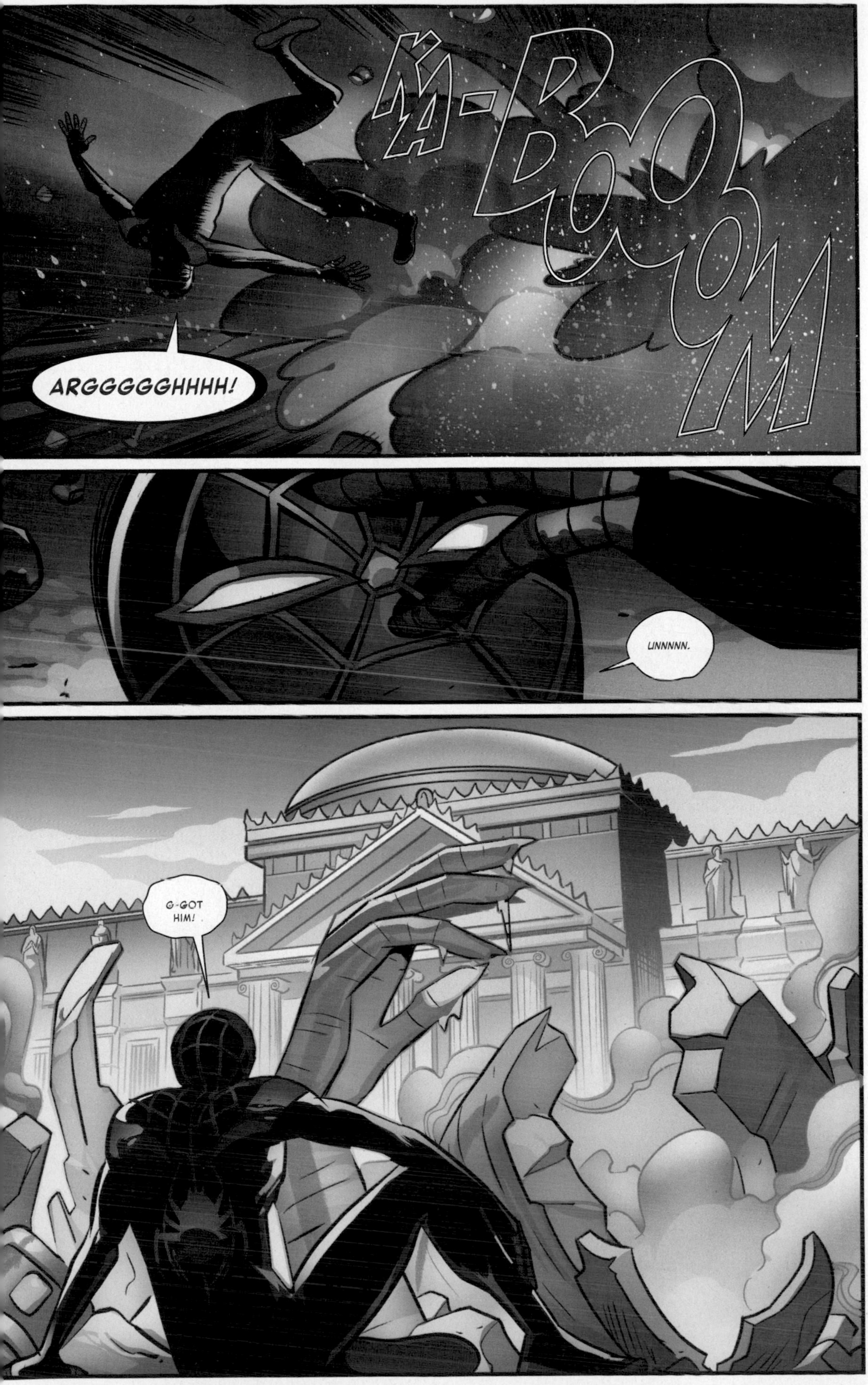
KA-BOOOOM
ARGGGGGHHHH!
UNNNNN.
G-GOT HIM!

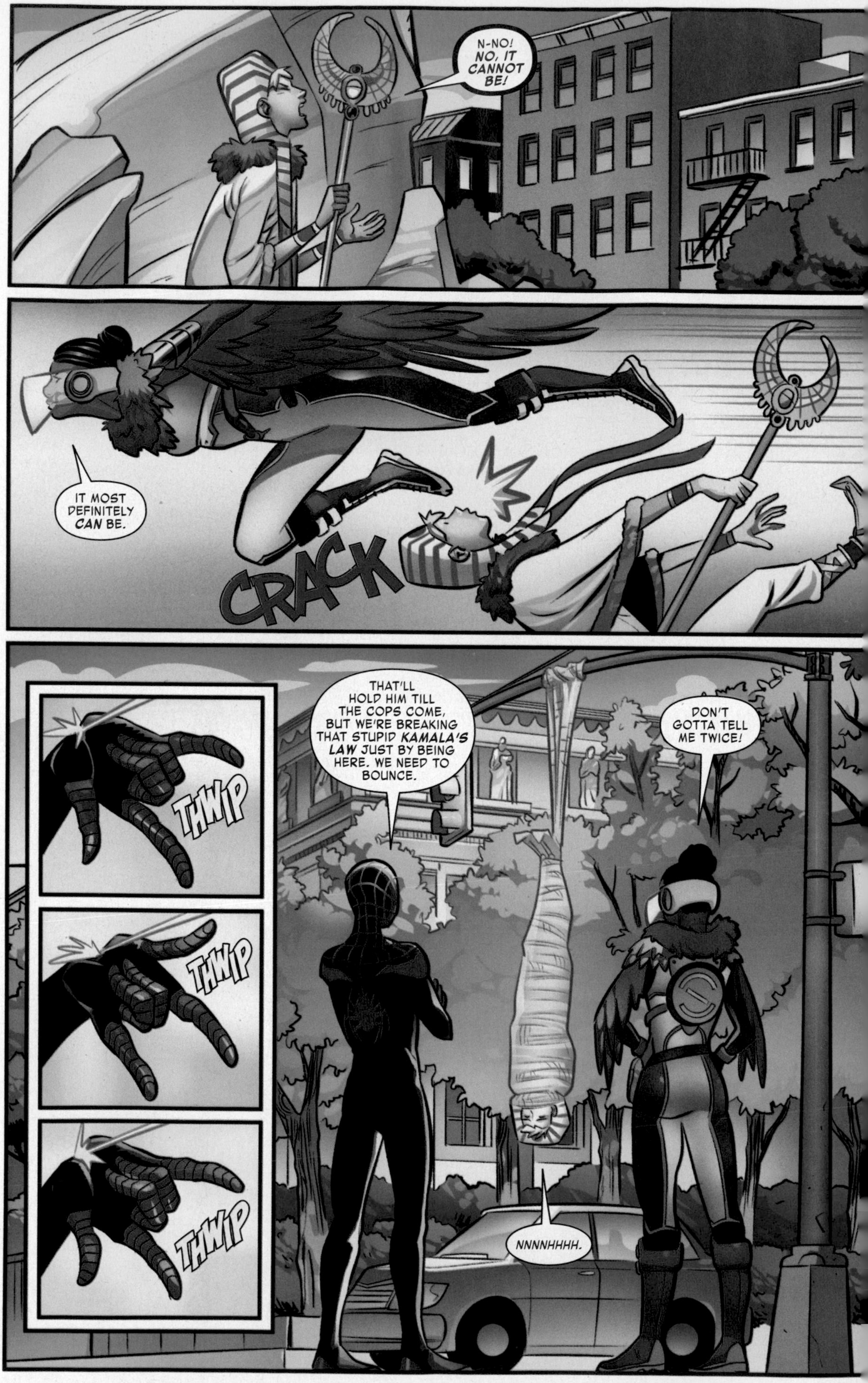
N-NO! NO, IT CANNOT BE!
IT MOST DEFINITELY CAN BE.
CRACK
THWIP
THWIP
THWIP
THAT'LL HOLD HIM TILL THE COPS COME, BUT WE'RE BREAKING THAT STUPID KAMALA'S LAW JUST BY BEING HERE. WE NEED TO BOUNCE.
DON'T GOTTA TELL ME TWICE!
NNNNHHHH.

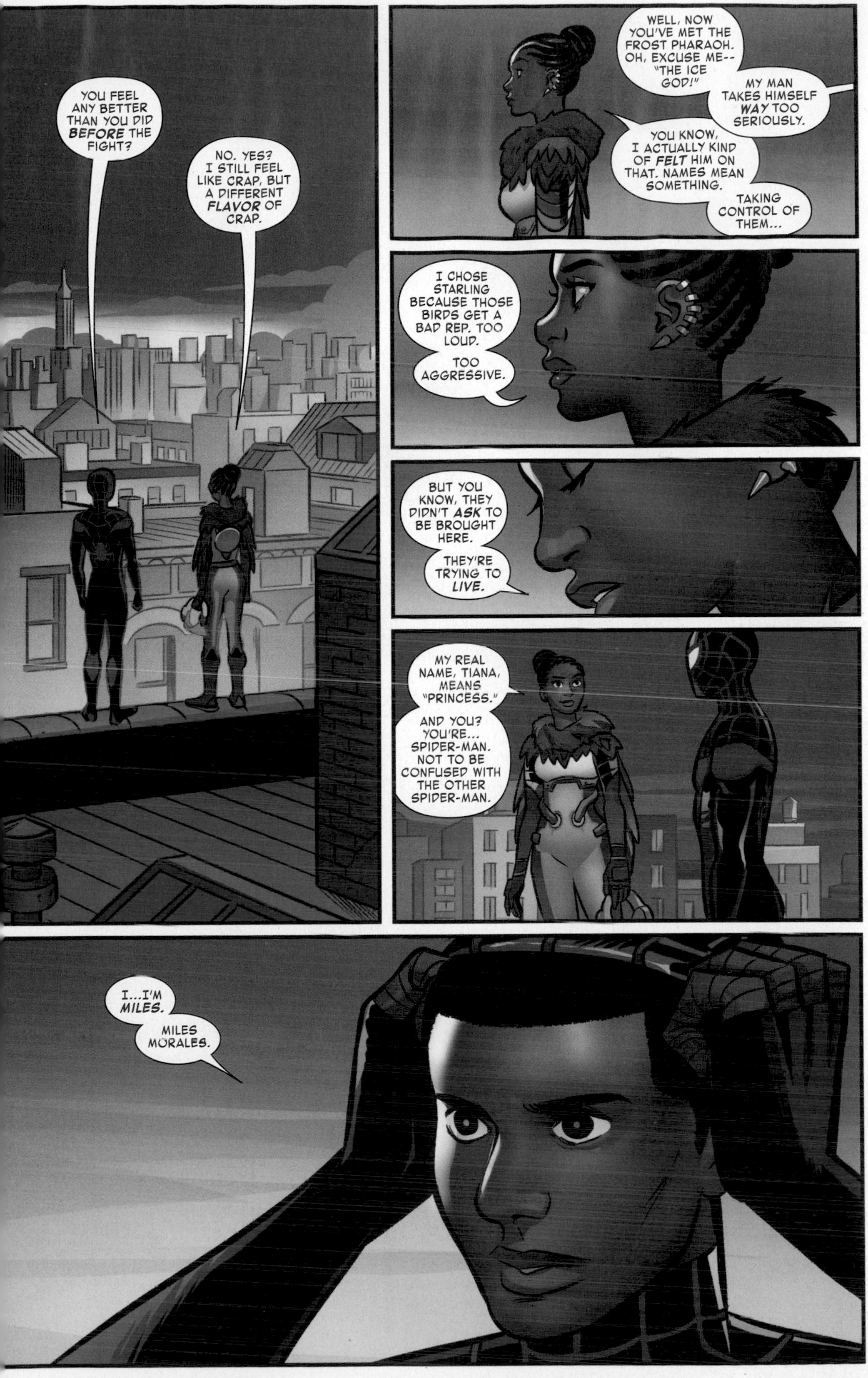
YOU FEEL ANY BETTER THAN YOU DID BEFORE THE FIGHT?
NO. YES? I STILL FEEL LIKE CRAP, BUT A DIFFERENT FLAVOR OF CRAP.
WELL, NOW YOU'VE MET THE FROST PHARAOH. OH, EXCUSE ME-- "THE ICE GOD!"
MY MAN TAKES HIMSELF WAY TOO SERIOUSLY.
YOU KNOW, I ACTUALLY KIND OF FELT HIM ON THAT. NAMES MEAN SOMETHING.
TAKING CONTROL OF THEM...
I CHOSE STARLING BECAUSE THOSE BIRDS GET A BAD REP. TOO LOUD.
TOO AGGRESSIVE.
BUT YOU KNOW, THEY DIDN'T ASK TO BE BROUGHT HERE.
THEY'RE TRYING TO LIVE.
MY REAL NAME, TIANA, MEANS "PRINCESS."
AND YOU? YOU'RE... SPIDER-MAN. NOT TO BE CONFUSED WITH THE OTHER SPIDER-MAN.
I...I'M MILES.
MILES MORALES.

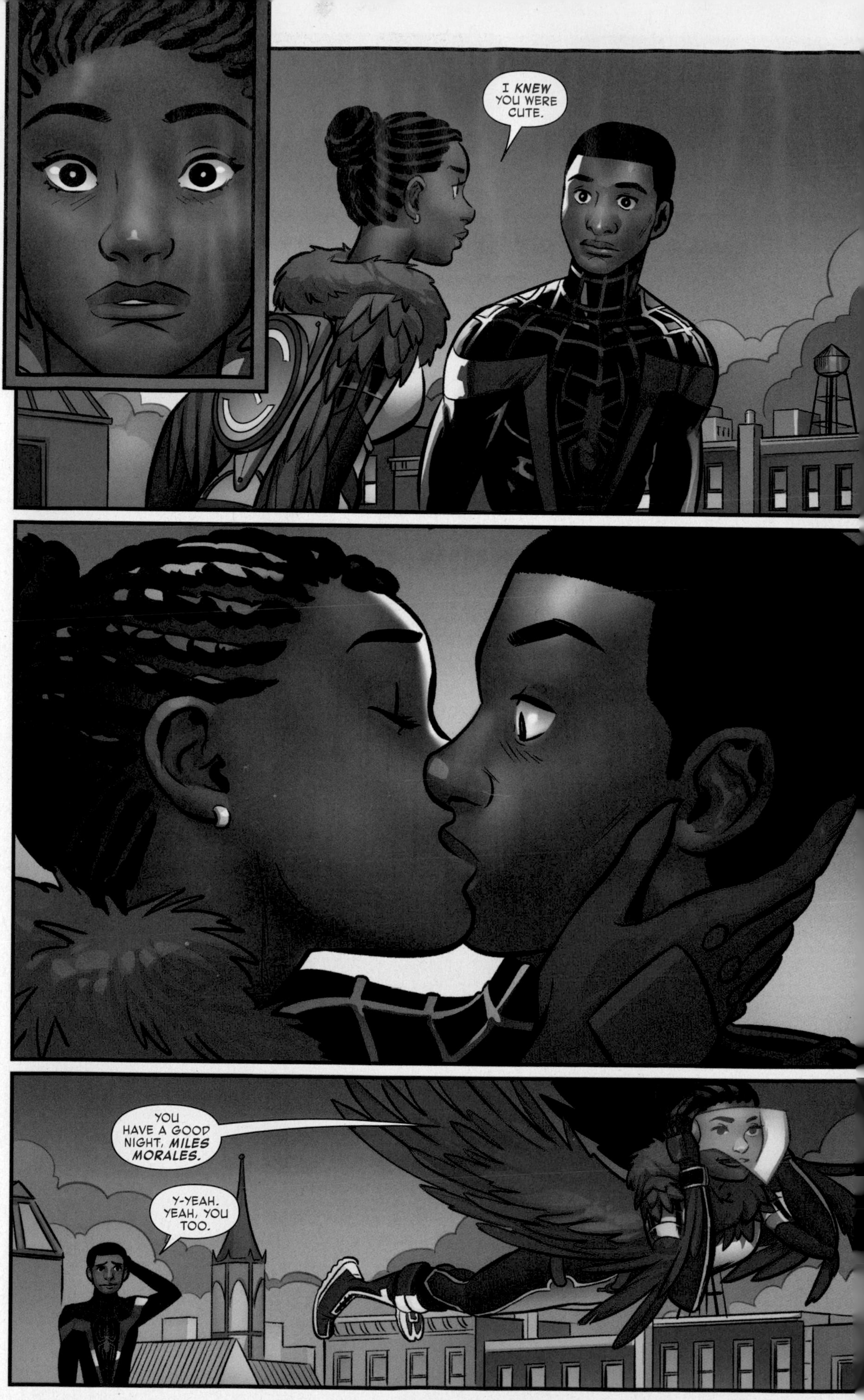
I KNEW YOU WERE CUTE.
YOU HAVE A GOOD NIGHT, MILES MORALES.
Y-YEAH. YEAH, YOU TOO.

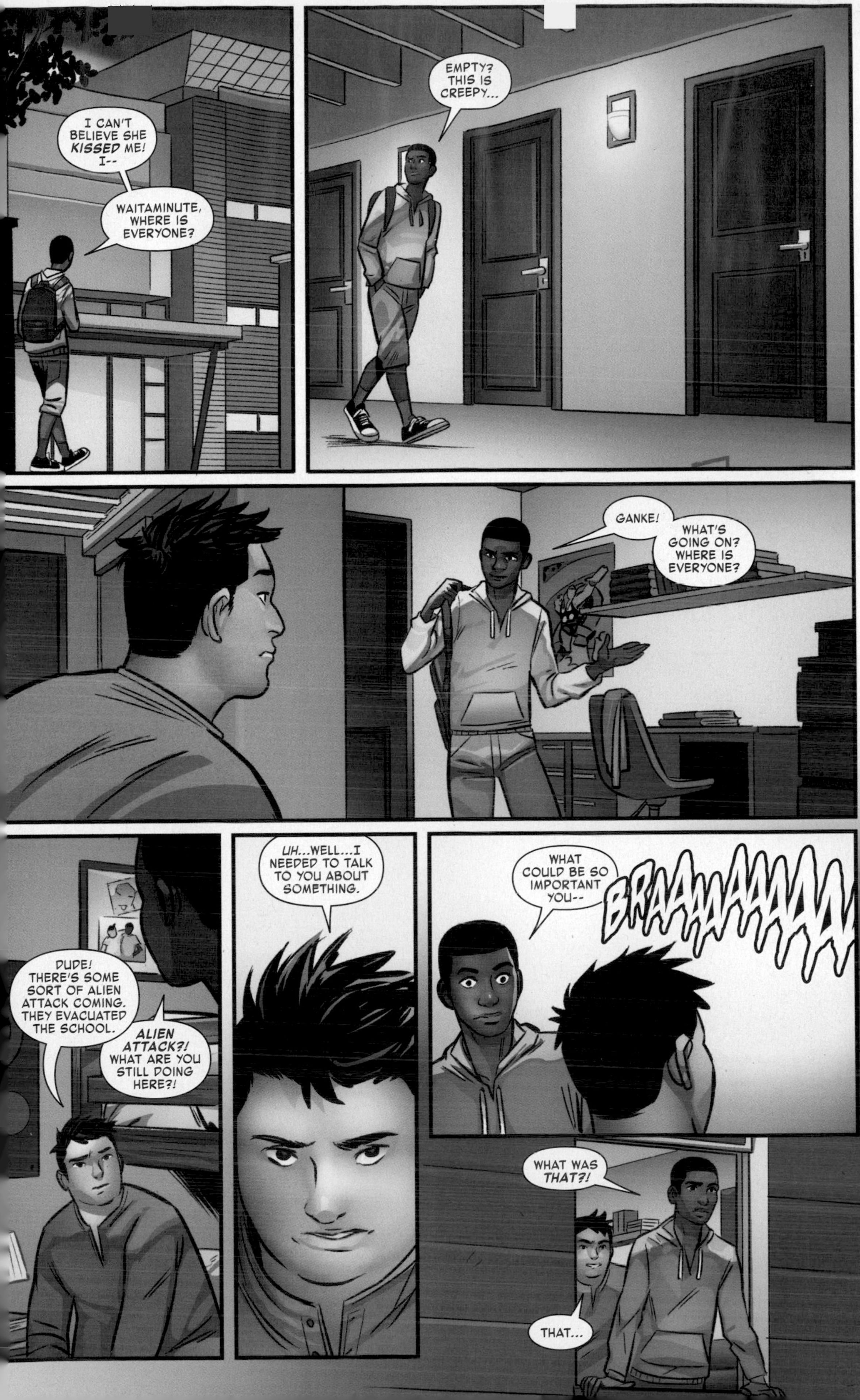
I CAN'T BELIEVE SHE KISSED ME! I--
WAITAMINUTE, WHERE IS EVERYONE?
EMPTY? THIS IS CREEPY...
GANKE!
WHAT'S GOING ON? WHERE IS EVERYONE?
DUDE! THERE'S SOME SORT OF ALIEN ATTACK COMING. THEY EVACUATED THE SCHOOL.
ALIEN ATTACK?! WHAT ARE YOU STILL DOING HERE?!
UH...WELL...I NEEDED TO TALK TO YOU ABOUT SOMETHING.
WHAT COULD BE SO IMPORTANT YOU--
BRAAAAAAAA
WHAT WAS THAT?!
THAT...

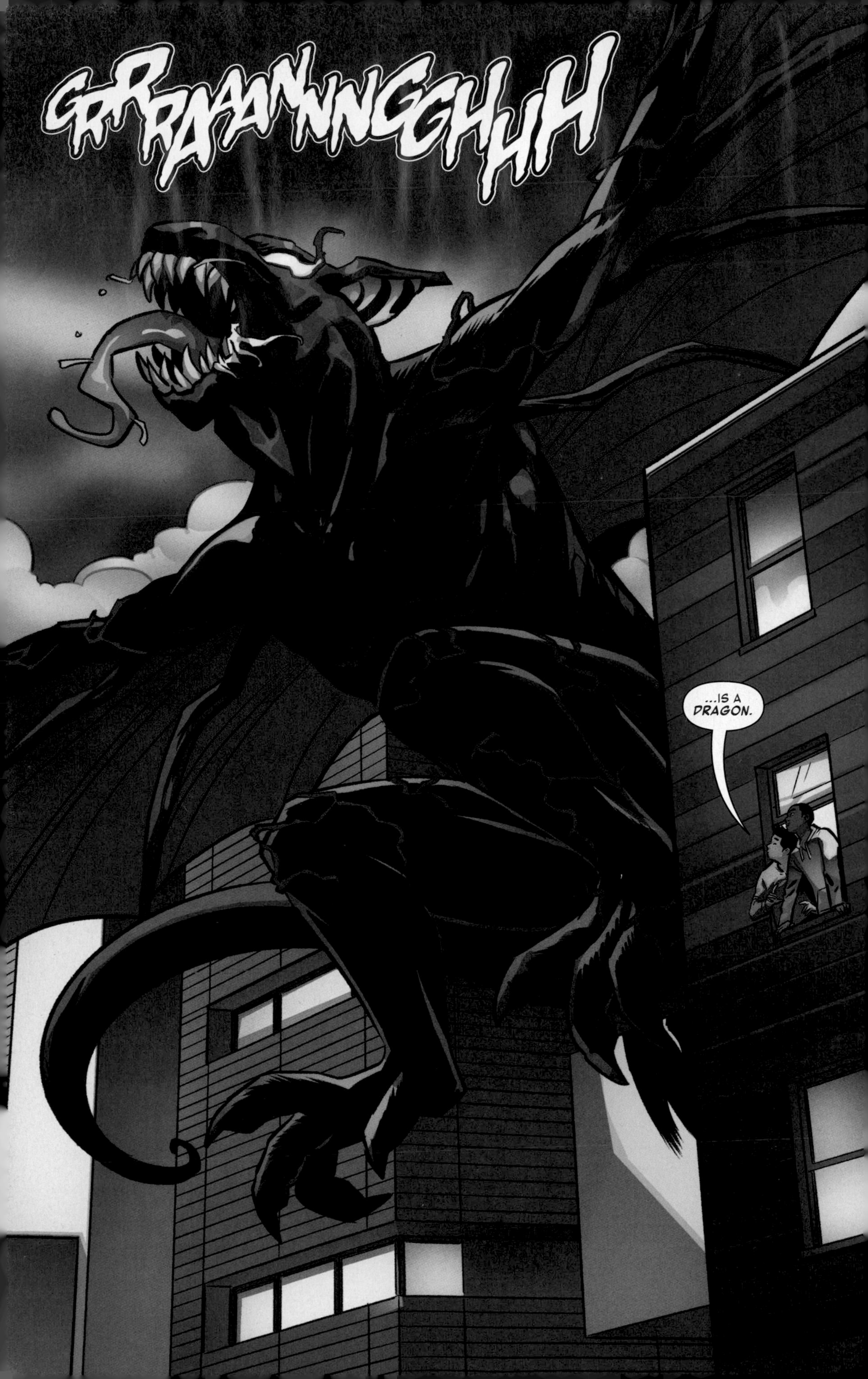
GRRRAAANNNGGHHH
...IS A DRAGON.

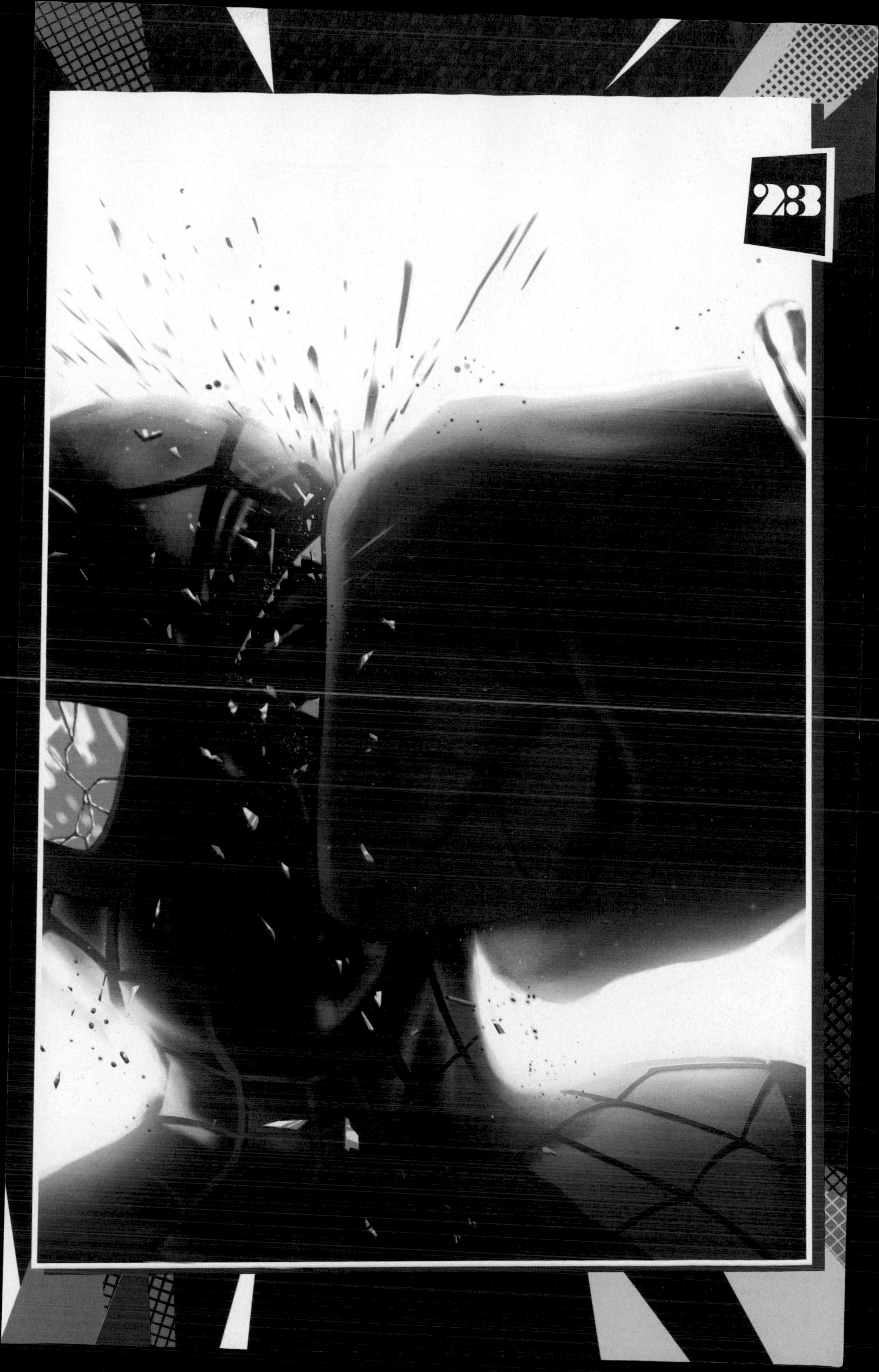
23

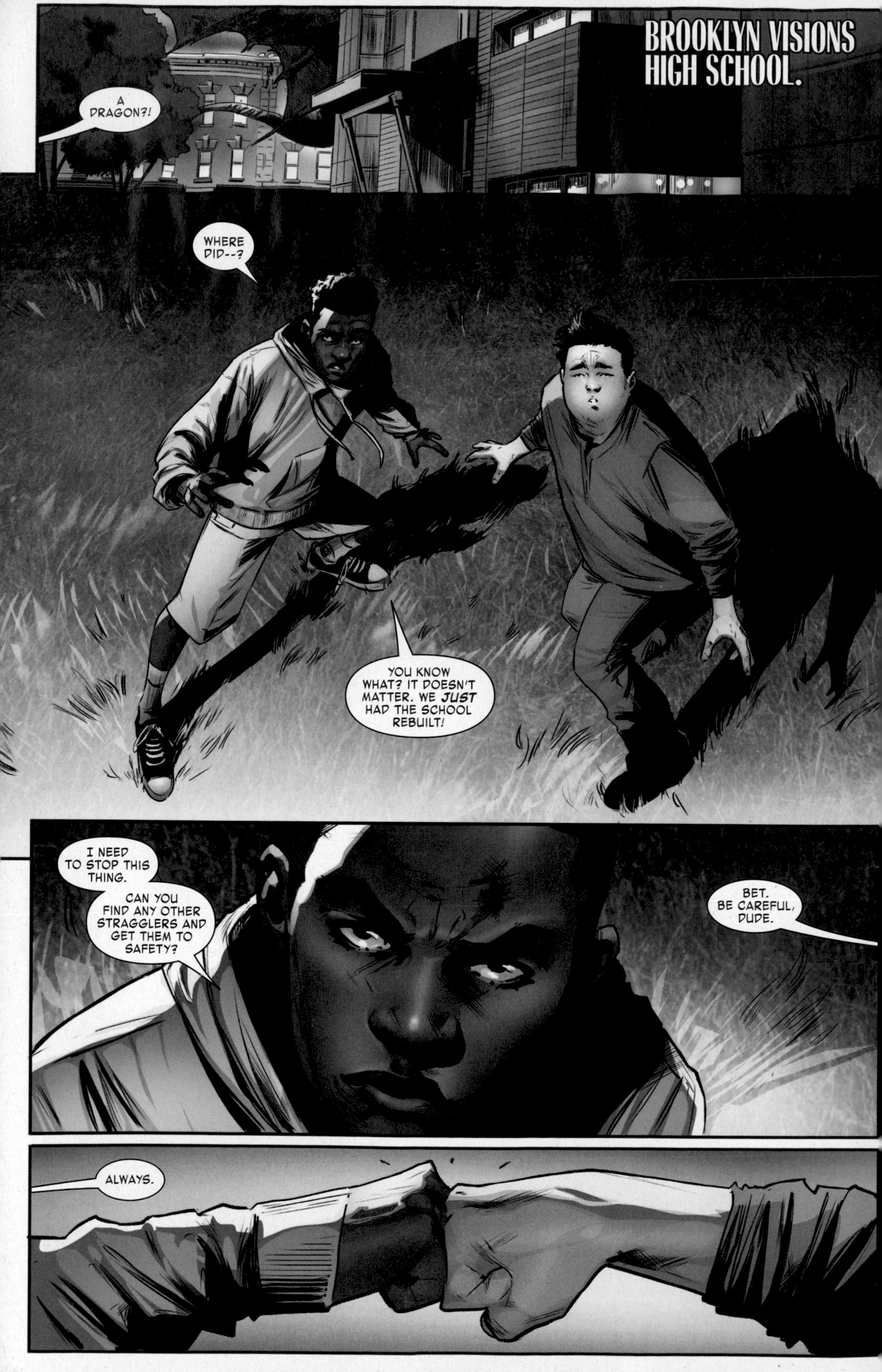
BROOKLYN VISIONS HIGH SCHOOL.
A DRAGON?!
WHERE DID--?
YOU KNOW WHAT? IT DOESN'T MATTER. WE JUST HAD THE SCHOOL REBUILT!
I NEED TO STOP THIS THING.
CAN YOU FIND ANY OTHER STRAGGLERS AND GET THEM TO SAFETY?
BET. BE CAREFUL, DUDE.
ALWAYS.

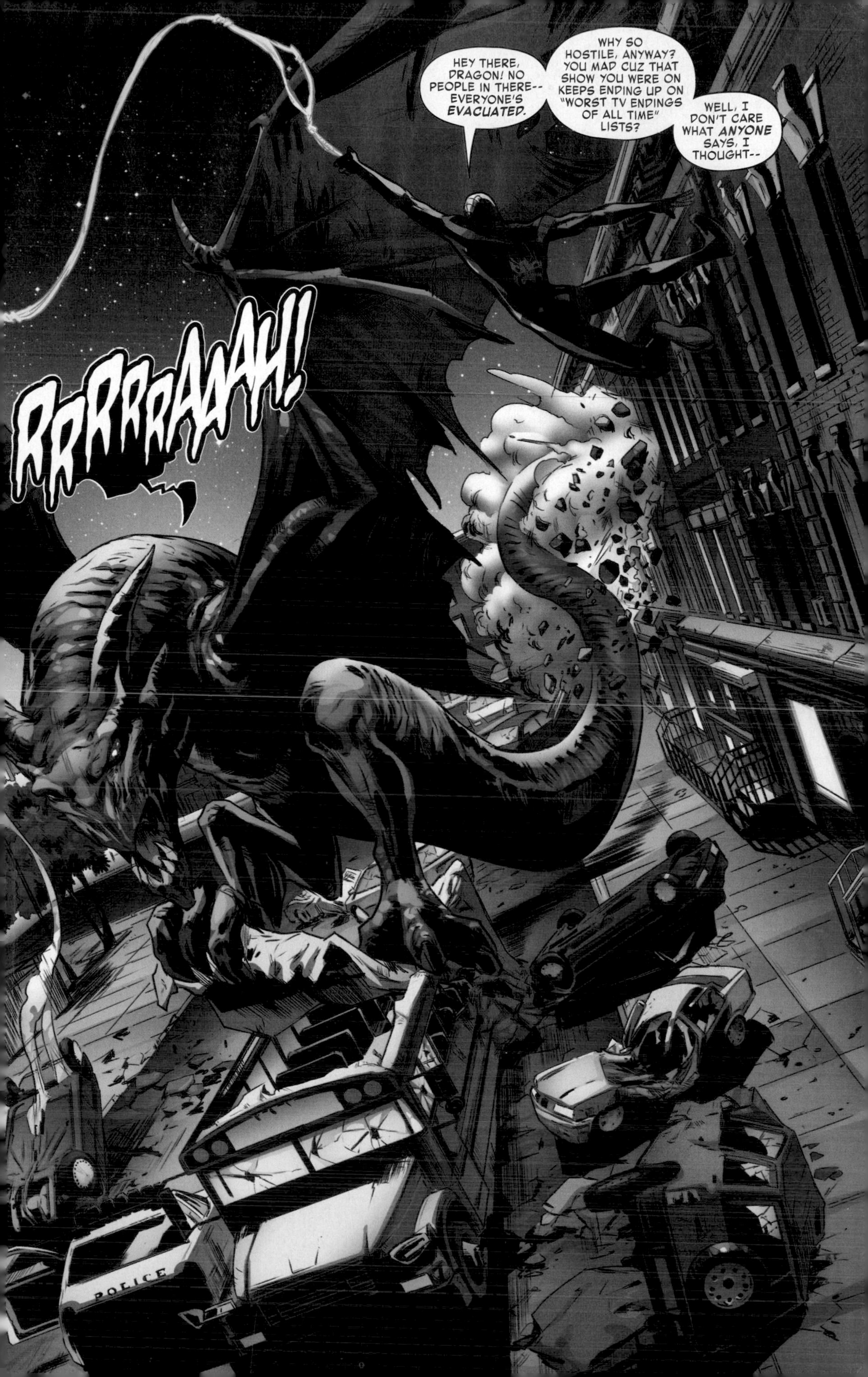
HEY THERE, DRAGON! NO PEOPLE IN THERE-- EVERYONE'S *EVACUATED.*
WHY SO HOSTILE, ANYWAY? YOU MAD CUZ THAT SHOW YOU WERE ON KEEPS ENDING UP ON "WORST TV ENDINGS OF ALL TIME" LISTS?
WELL, I DON'T CARE WHAT *ANYONE* SAYS, I THOUGHT--
RRRRRAAAH!
POLICE

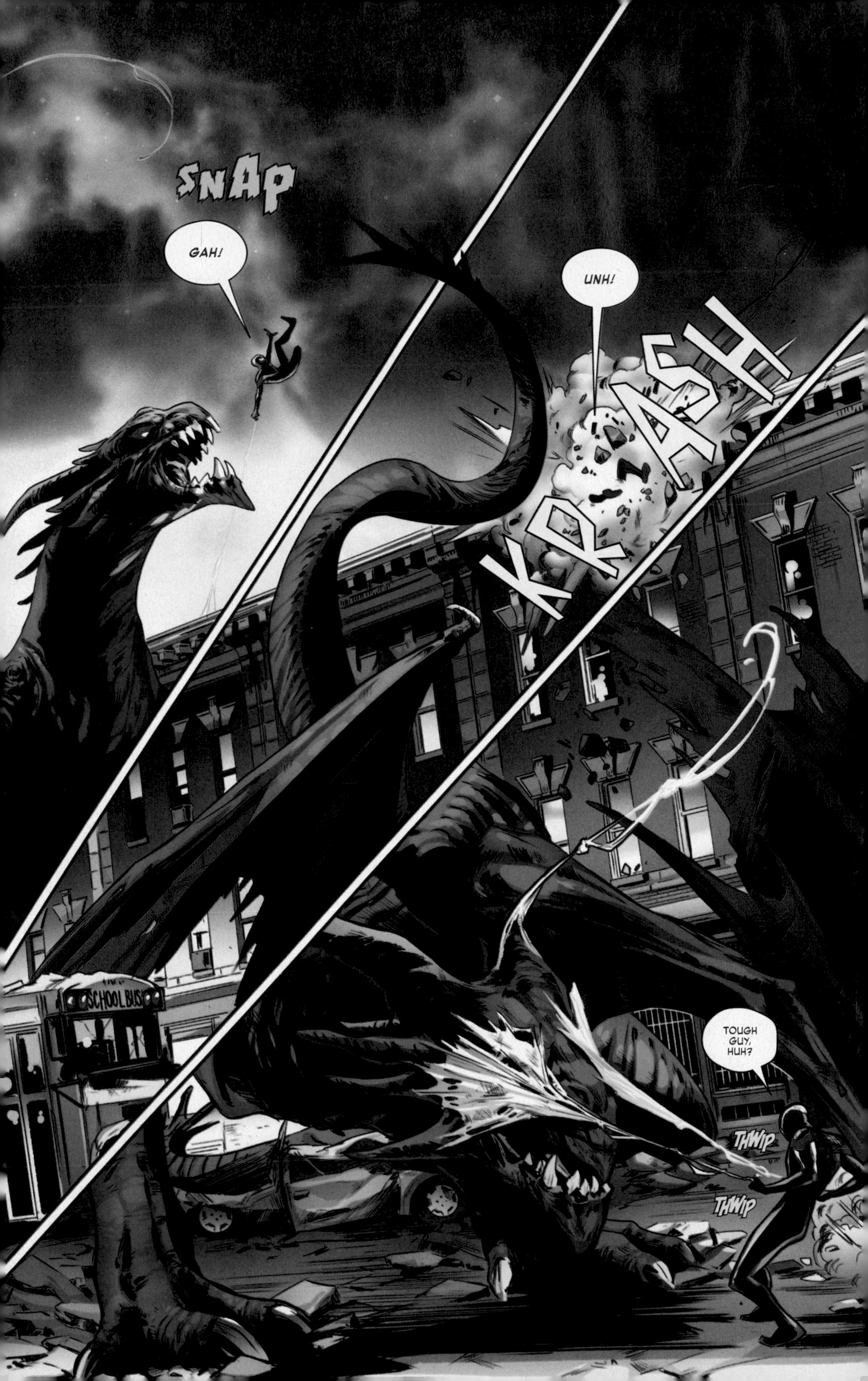
SNAP
GAH!
UNH!
KRASH
SCHOOL BUS
TOUGH GUY, HUH?
THWIP
THWIP

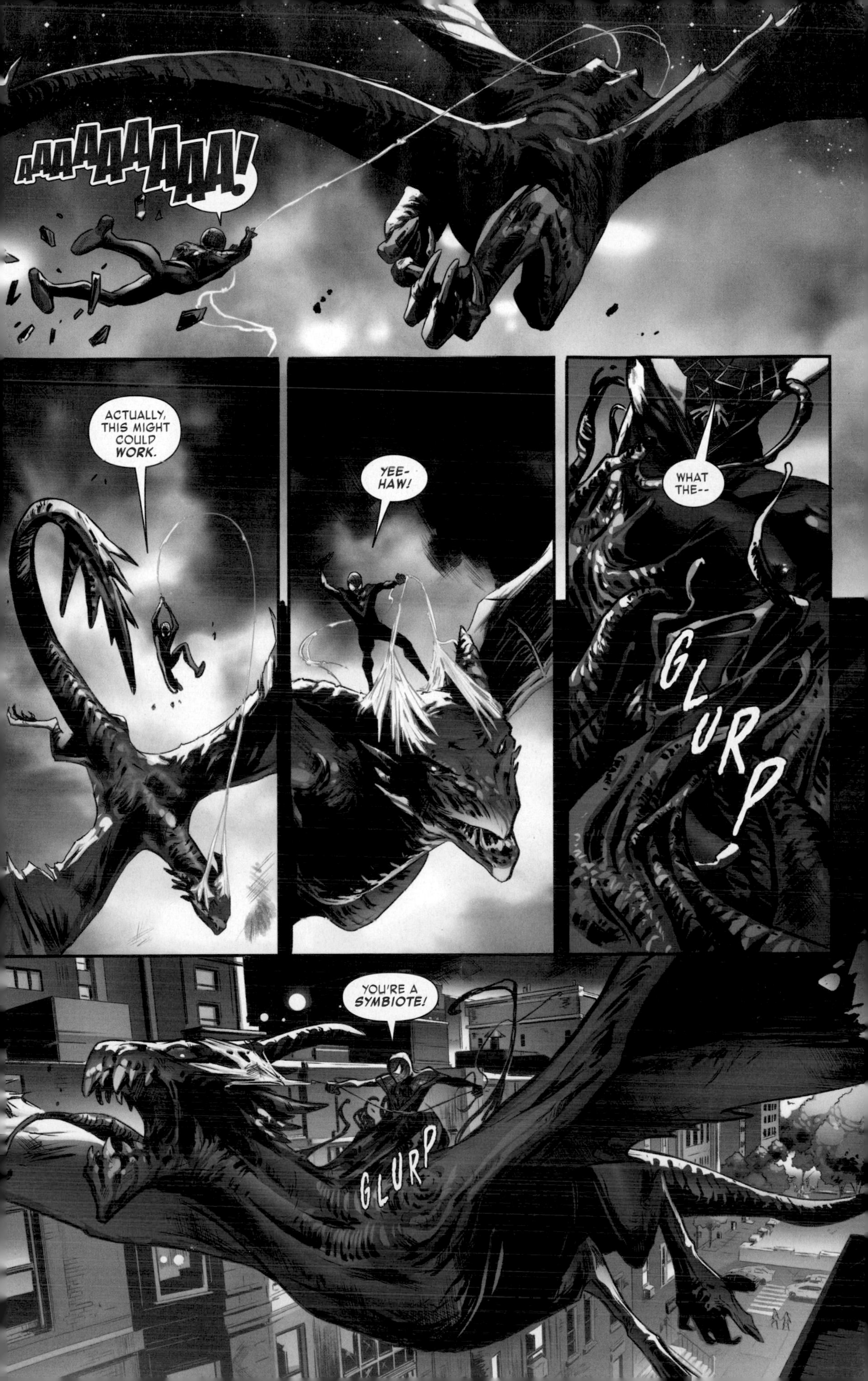
AAAAAAAAAAA!
ACTUALLY, THIS MIGHT COULD WORK.
YEE-HAW!
WHAT THE--
GLURP
YOU'RE A SYMBIOTE!
GLURP

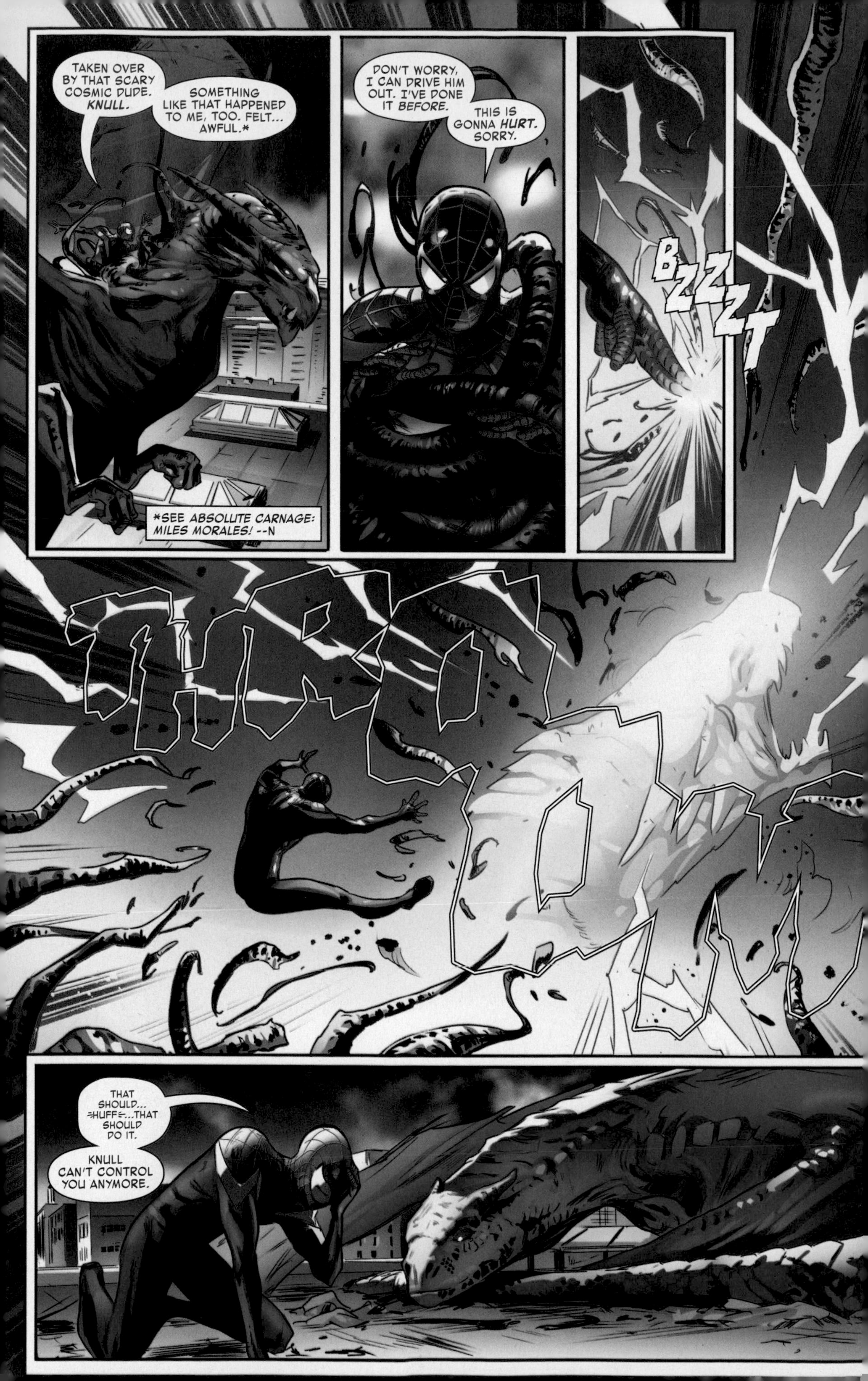
TAKEN OVER BY THAT SCARY COSMIC DUDE. KNULL.
SOMETHING LIKE THAT HAPPENED TO ME, TOO. FELT... AWFUL.*
*SEE ABSOLUTE CARNAGE: MILES MORALES! --N
DON'T WORRY, I CAN DRIVE HIM OUT. I'VE DONE IT BEFORE.
THIS IS GONNA HURT. SORRY.
BZZZZT
THAT SHOULD... =HUFF=...THAT SHOULD DO IT.
KNULL CAN'T CONTROL YOU ANYMORE.

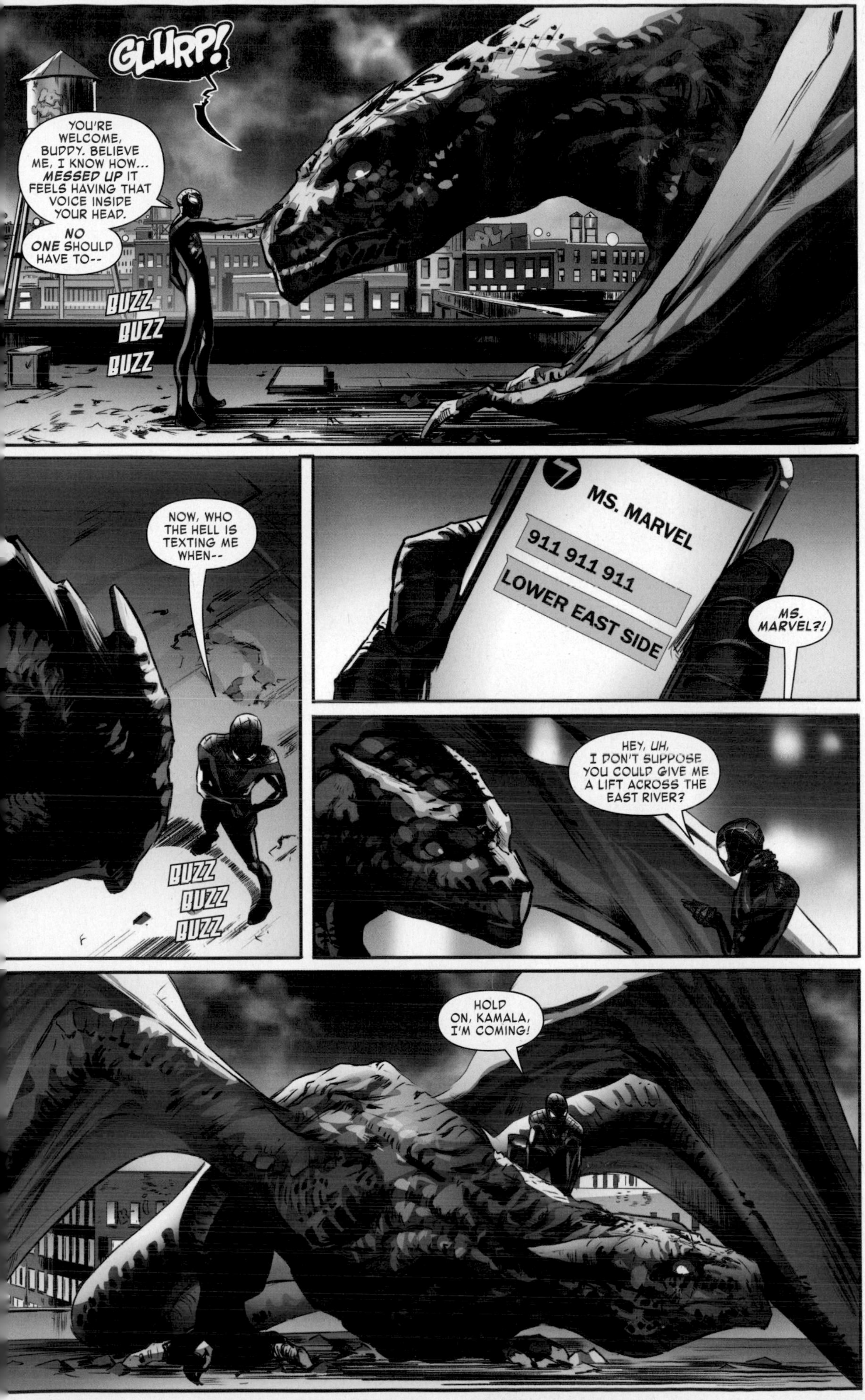
GLURP!
YOU'RE WELCOME, BUDDY. BELIEVE ME, I KNOW HOW... MESSED UP IT FEELS HAVING THAT VOICE INSIDE YOUR HEAD.
NO ONE SHOULD HAVE TO--
BUZZ
BUZZ
BUZZ
NOW, WHO THE HELL IS TEXTING ME WHEN--
BUZZ
BUZZ
BUZZ
MS. MARVEL
911 911 911
LOWER EAST SIDE
MS. MARVEL?!
HEY, UH, I DON'T SUPPOSE YOU COULD GIVE ME A LIFT ACROSS THE EAST RIVER?
HOLD ON, KAMALA, I'M COMING!

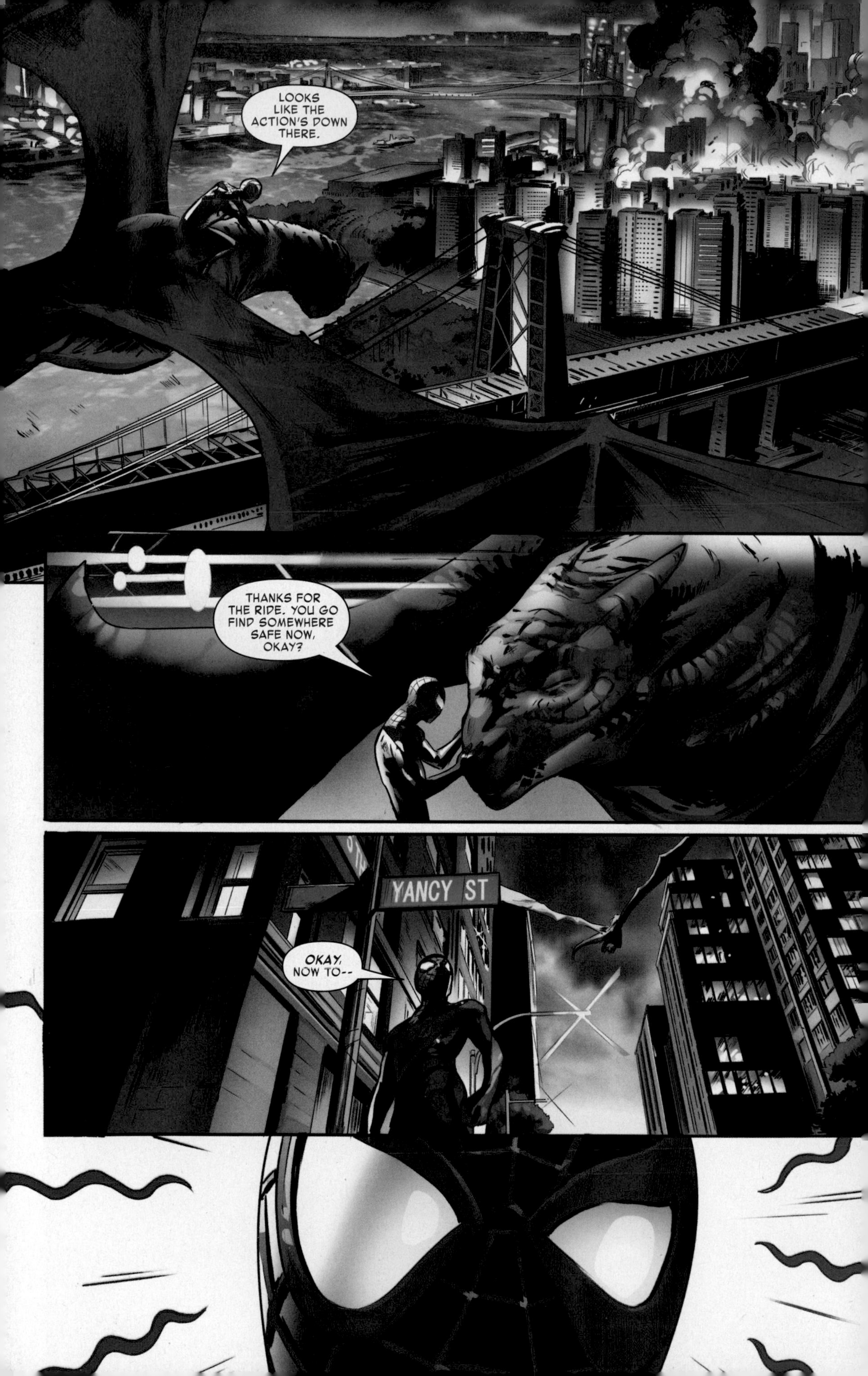
LOOKS LIKE THE ACTION'S DOWN THERE.
THANKS FOR THE RIDE. YOU GO FIND SOMEWHERE SAFE NOW, OKAY?
YANCY ST
OKAY, NOW TO--

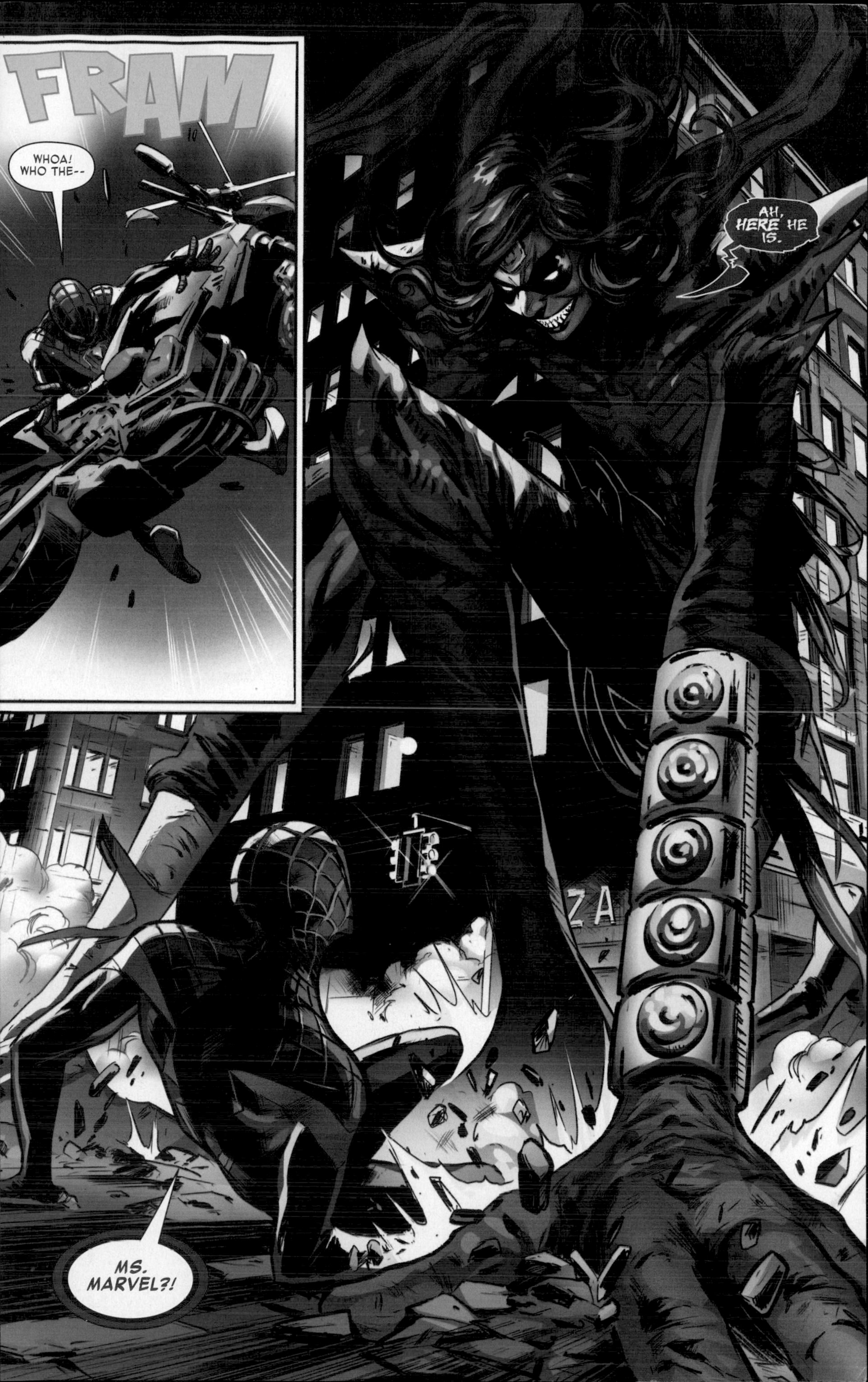
FRAM
WHOA! WHO THE--
AH, HERE HE IS.
ZA
MS. MARVEL?!

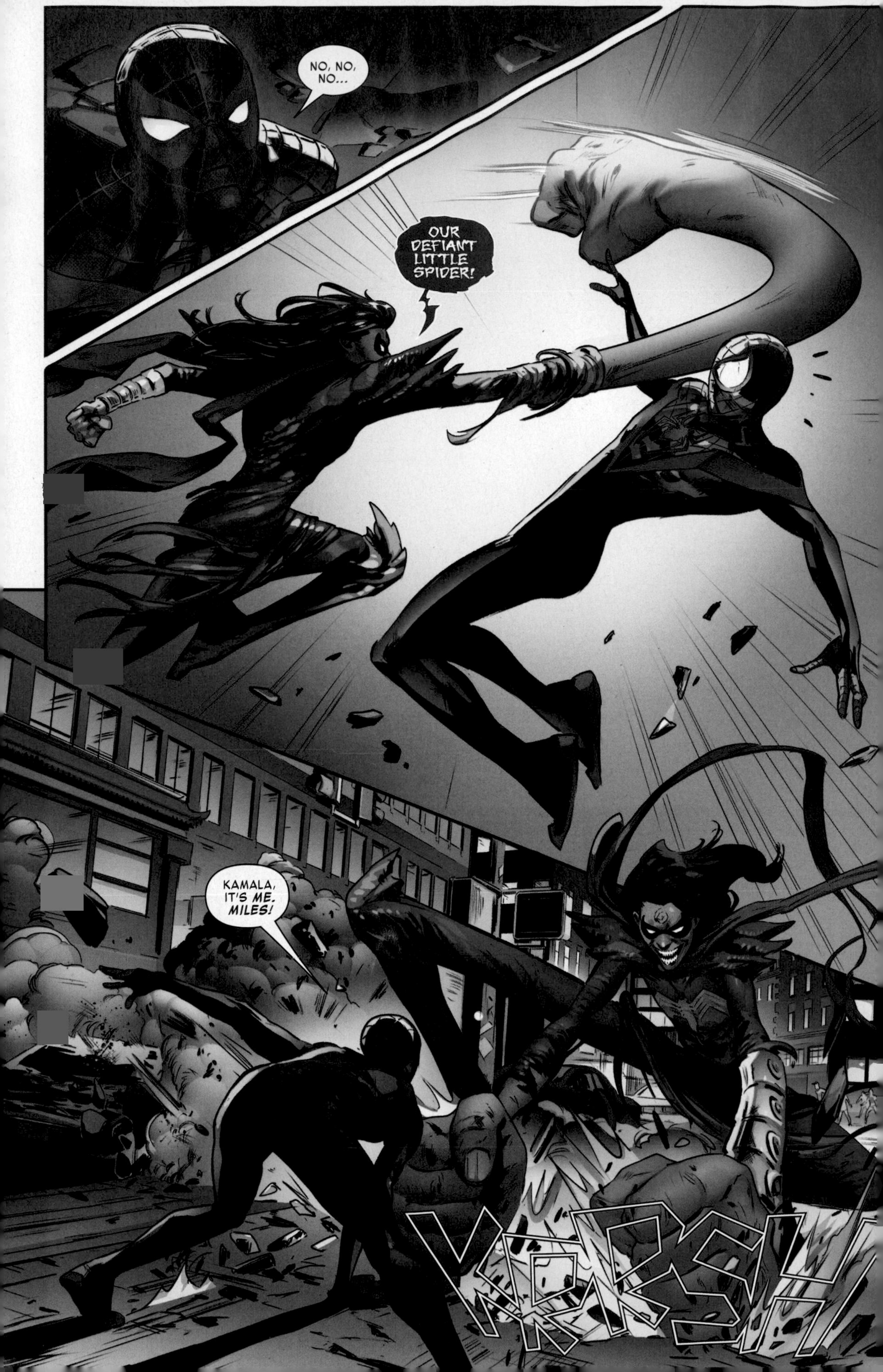
NO, NO, NO...
OUR DEFIANT LITTLE SPIDER!
KAMALA, IT'S ME. MILES!

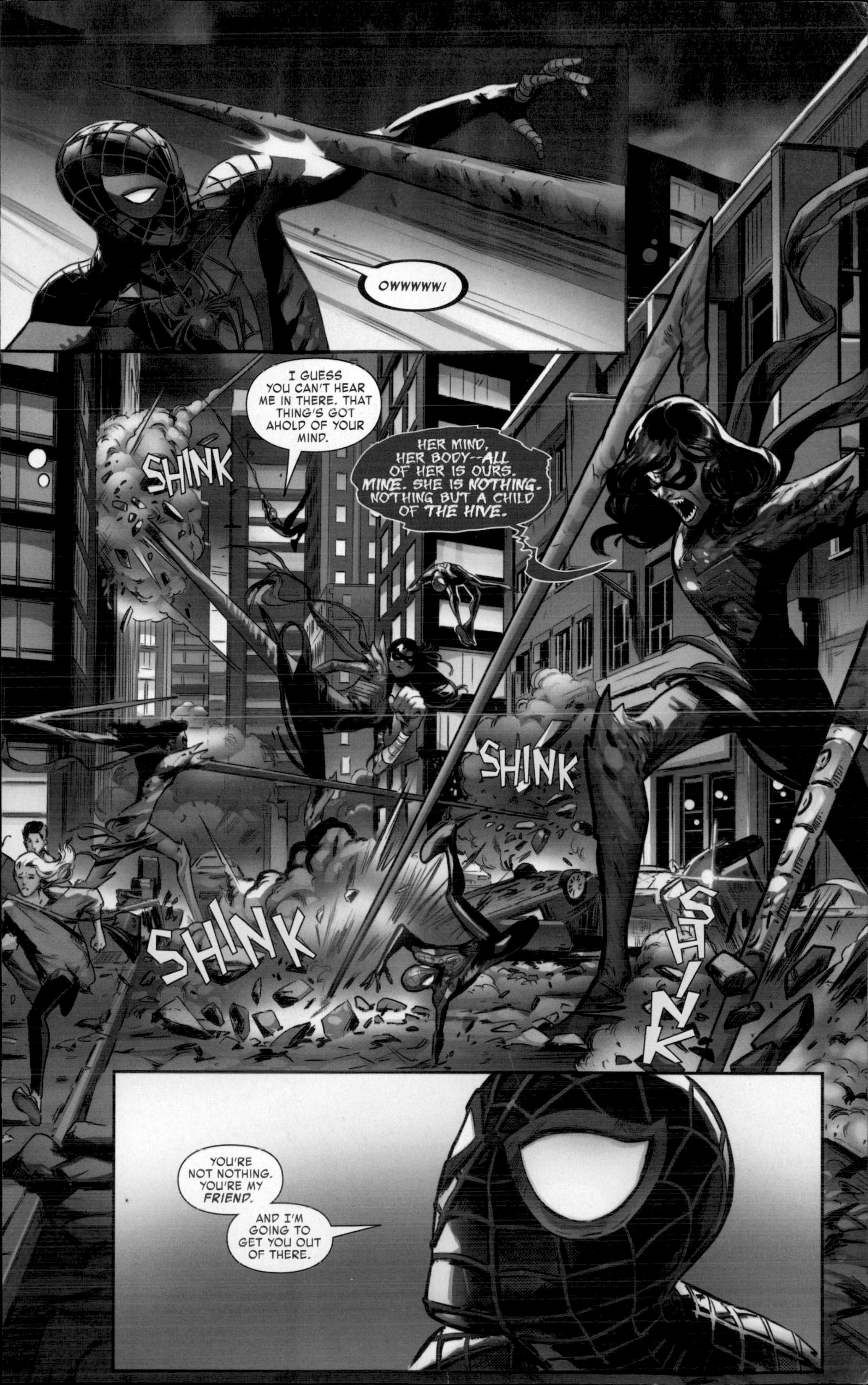

OWWWWW!
I GUESS YOU CAN'T HEAR ME IN THERE. THAT THING'S GOT AHOLD OF YOUR MIND.
SHINK
HER MIND, HER BODY--ALL OF HER IS OURS. MINE. SHE IS NOTHING. NOTHING BUT A CHILD OF THE HIVE.
SHINK
SHINK
SHINK
YOU'RE NOT NOTHING. YOU'RE MY FRIEND.
AND I'M GOING TO GET YOU OUT OF THERE.

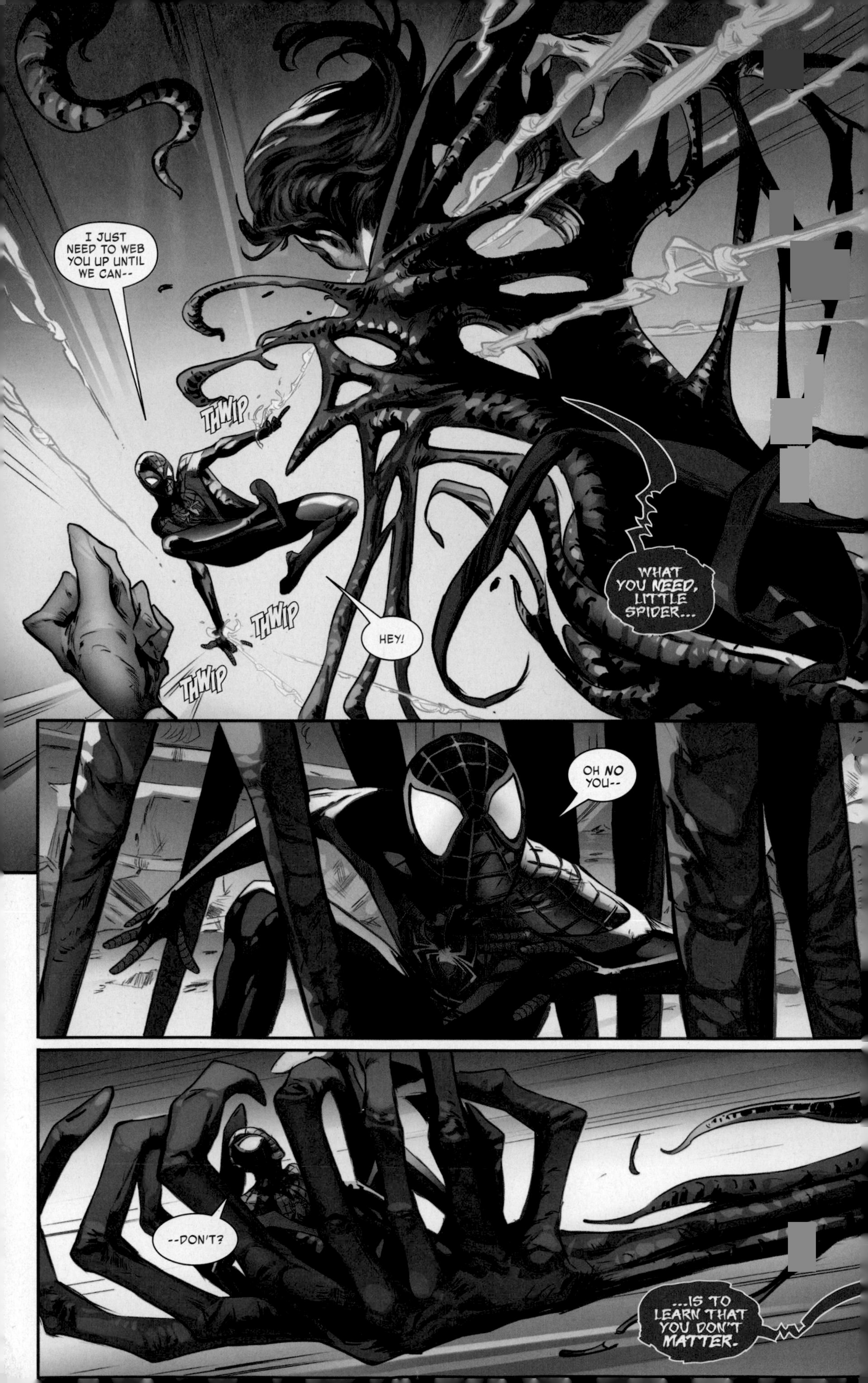

I JUST NEED TO WEB YOU UP UNTIL WE CAN--
THWIP
THWIP
THWIP
HEY!
WHAT YOU NEED, LITTLE SPIDER...
OH NO YOU--
--DON'T?
...IS TO LEARN THAT YOU DON'T MATTER.

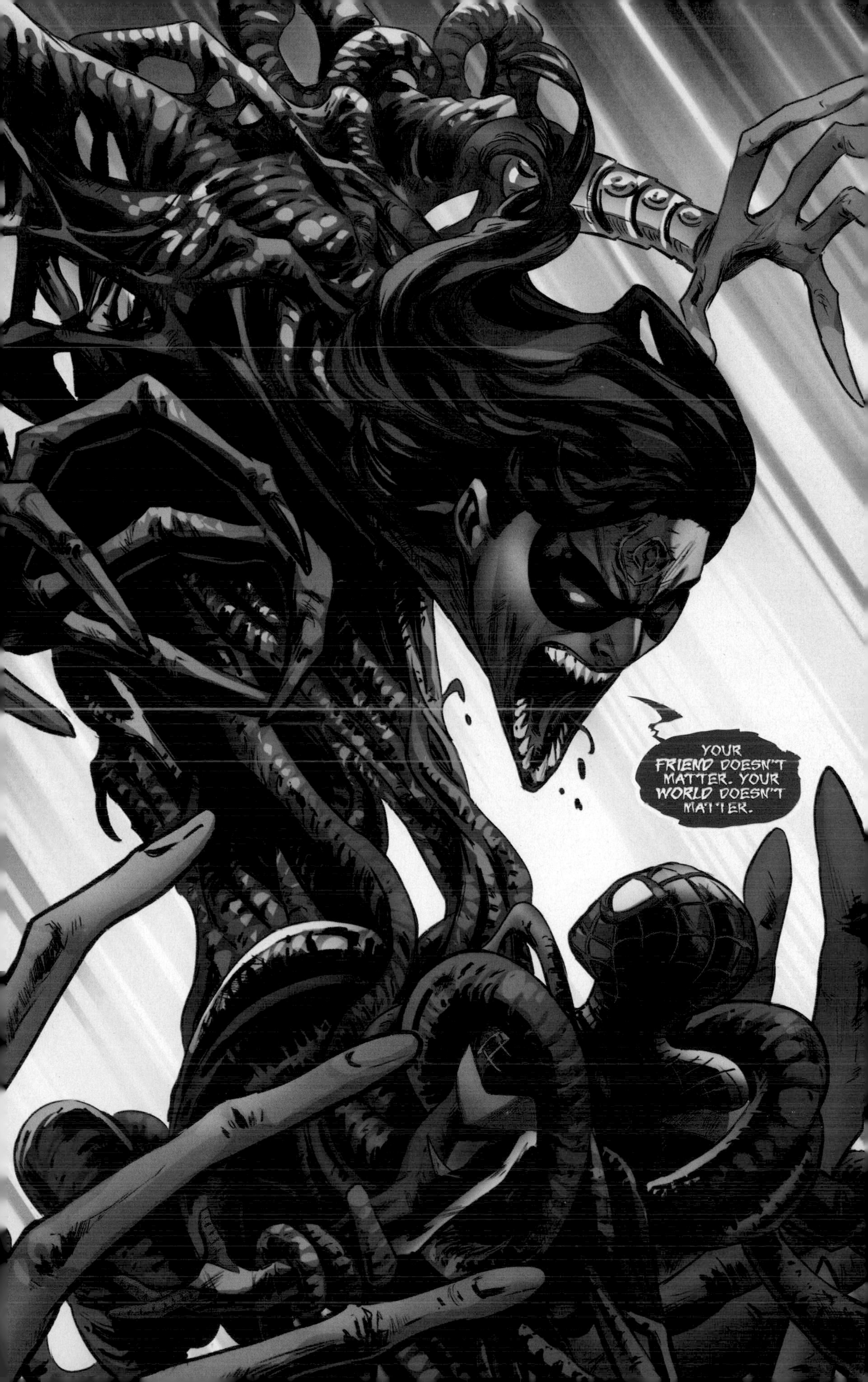
YOUR FRIEND DOESN'T MATTER. YOUR WORLD DOESN'T MATTER.

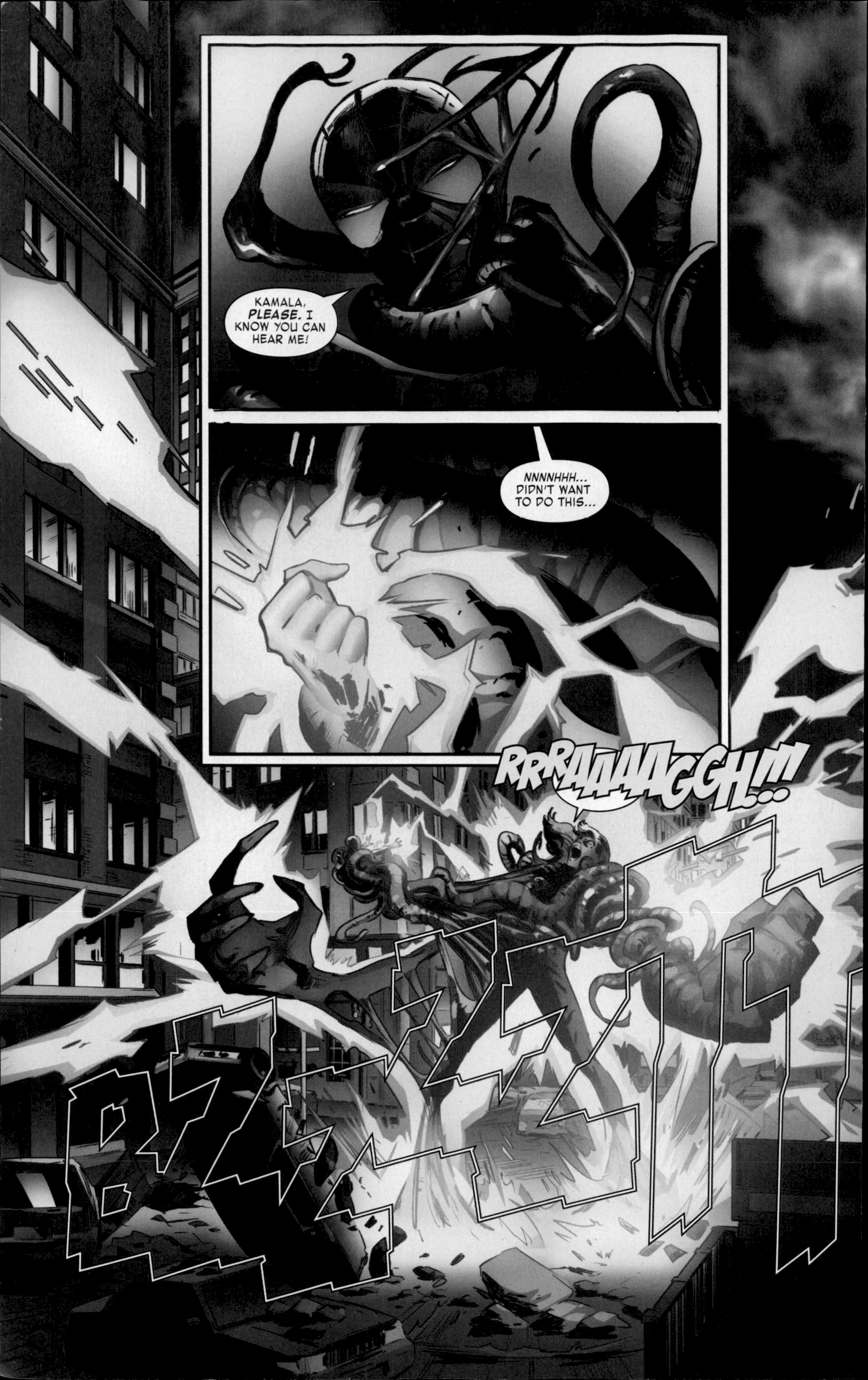

KAMALA, *PLEASE.* I KNOW YOU CAN HEAR ME!
NNNNHHH... DIDN'T WANT TO DO THIS...
RRRAAAAAGGH!!!

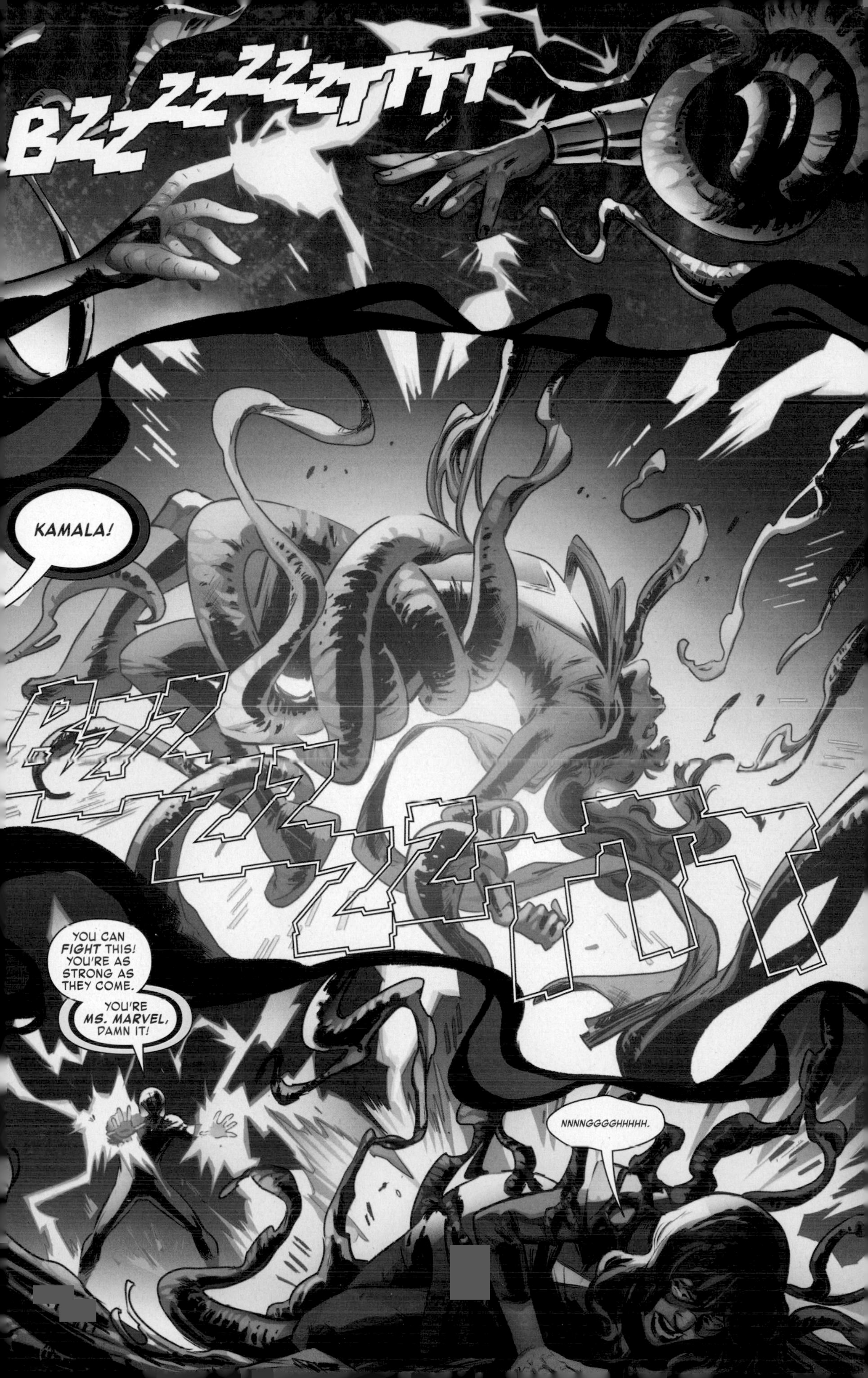
BZZZZZZTTTT
KAMALA!
YOU CAN FIGHT THIS! YOU'RE AS STRONG AS THEY COME.
YOU'RE MS. MARVEL, DAMN IT!
NNNNGGGGHHHHH.

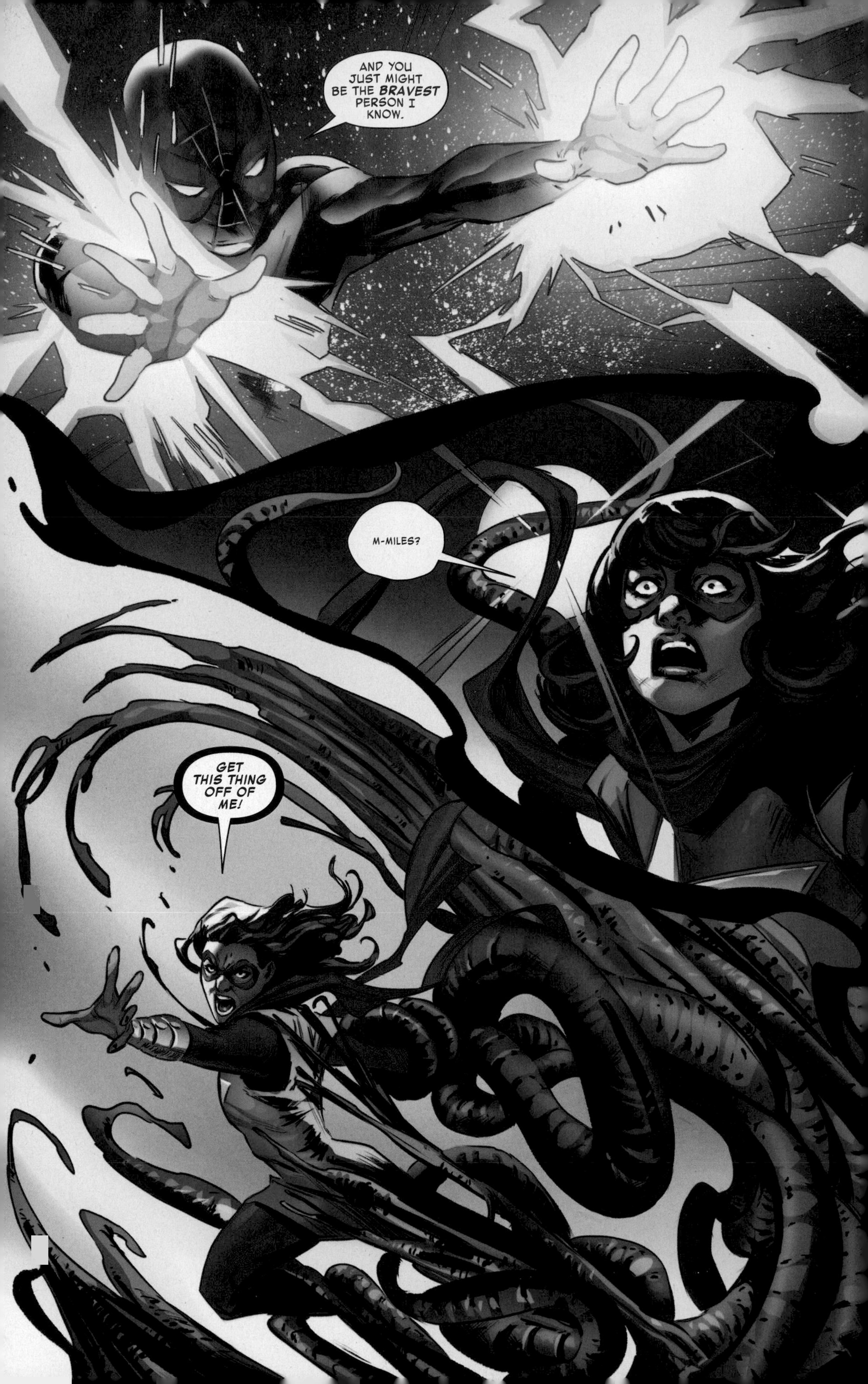
AND YOU JUST MIGHT BE THE BRAVEST PERSON I KNOW.
M-MILES?
GET THIS THING OFF OF ME!

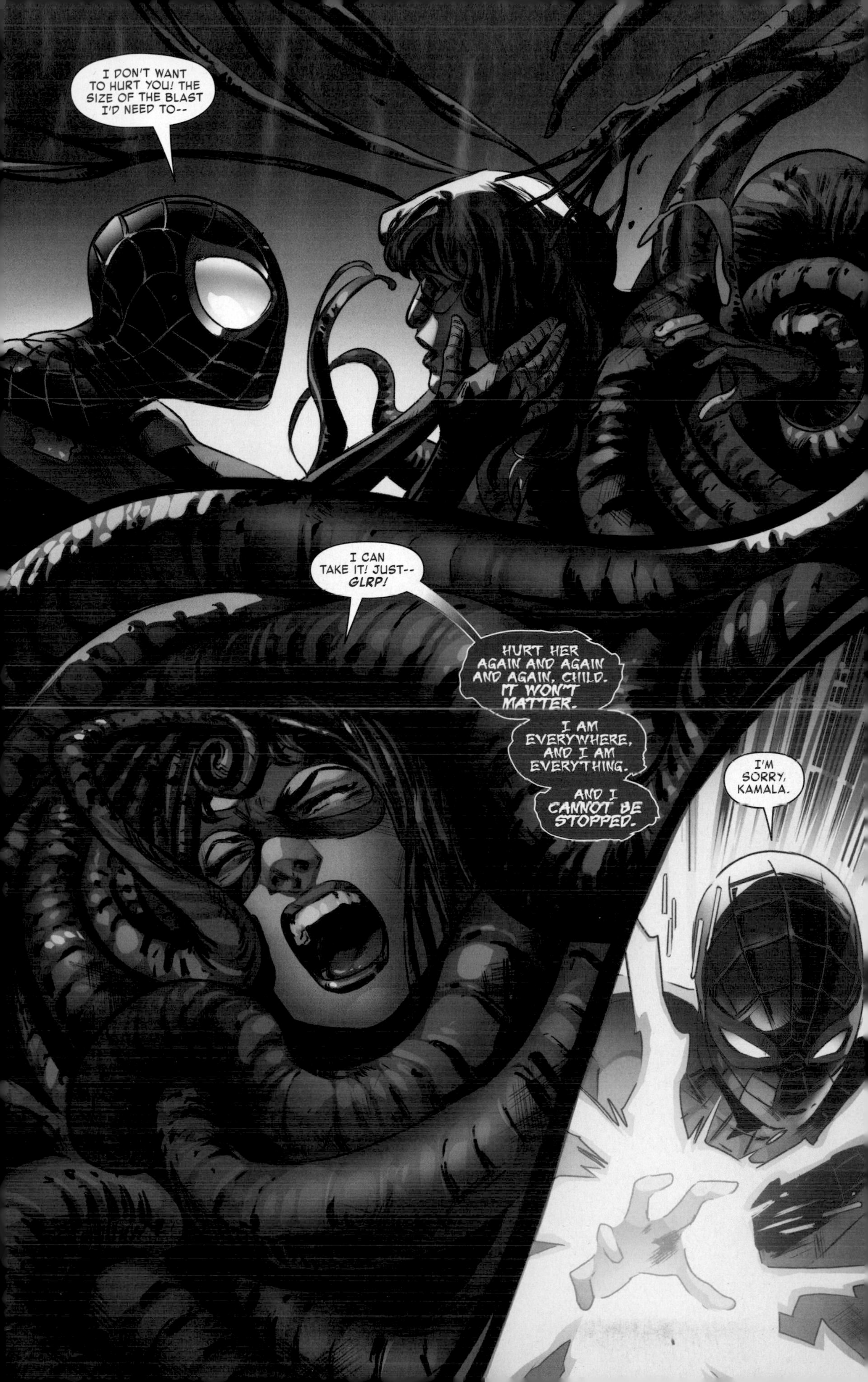
I DON'T WANT TO HURT YOU! THE SIZE OF THE BLAST I'D NEED TO--
I CAN TAKE IT! JUST-- GLRP!
HURT HER AGAIN AND AGAIN AND AGAIN, CHILD. IT WON'T MATTER.
I AM EVERYWHERE, AND I AM EVERYTHING.
AND I CANNOT BE STOPPED.
I'M SORRY, KAMALA.

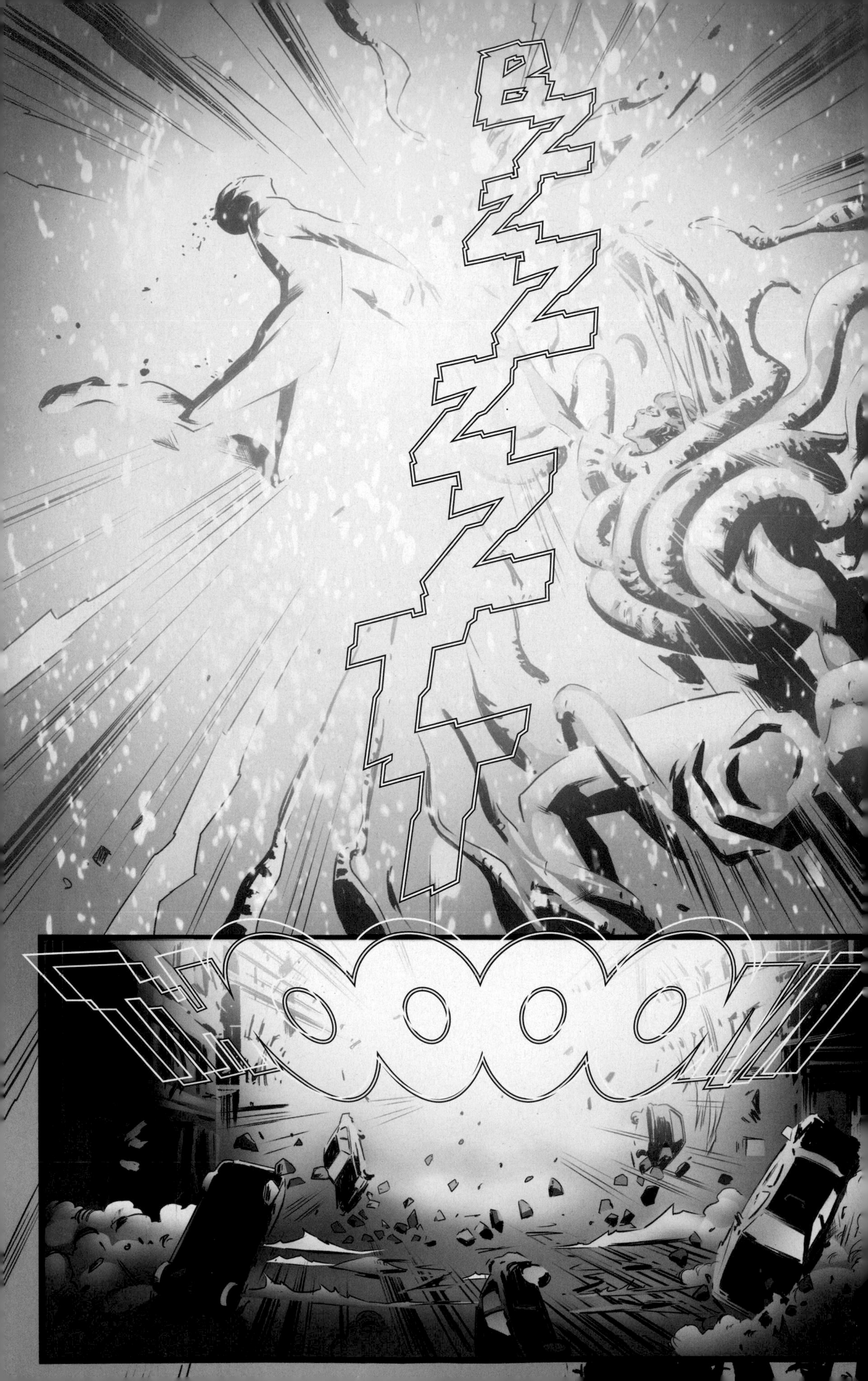
BZZZZT
THOOOOM

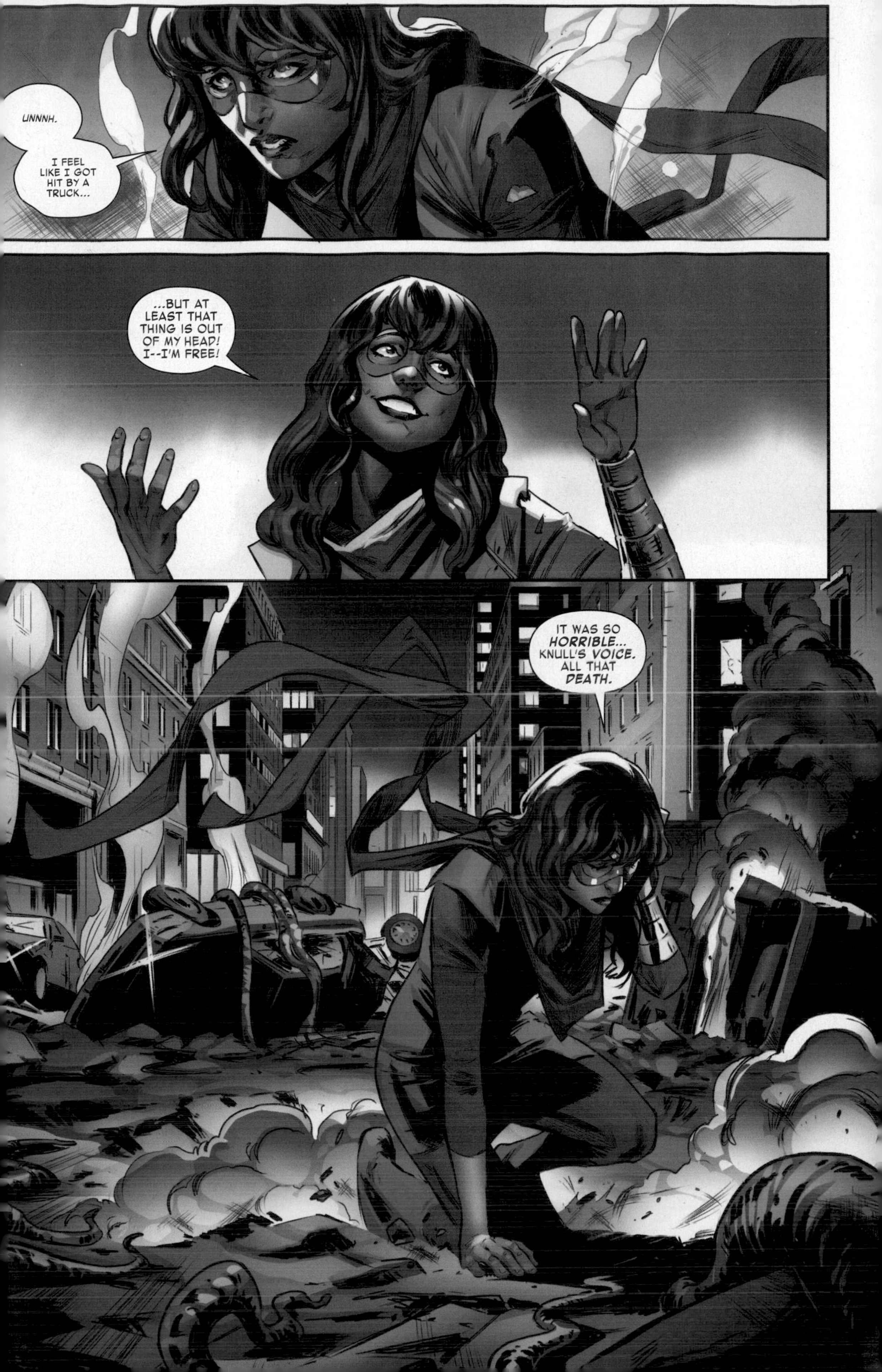
UNNNH.
I FEEL LIKE I GOT HIT BY A TRUCK...
...BUT AT LEAST THAT THING IS OUT OF MY HEAD! I--I'M FREE!
IT WAS SO HORRIBLE... KNULL'S VOICE. ALL THAT DEATH.

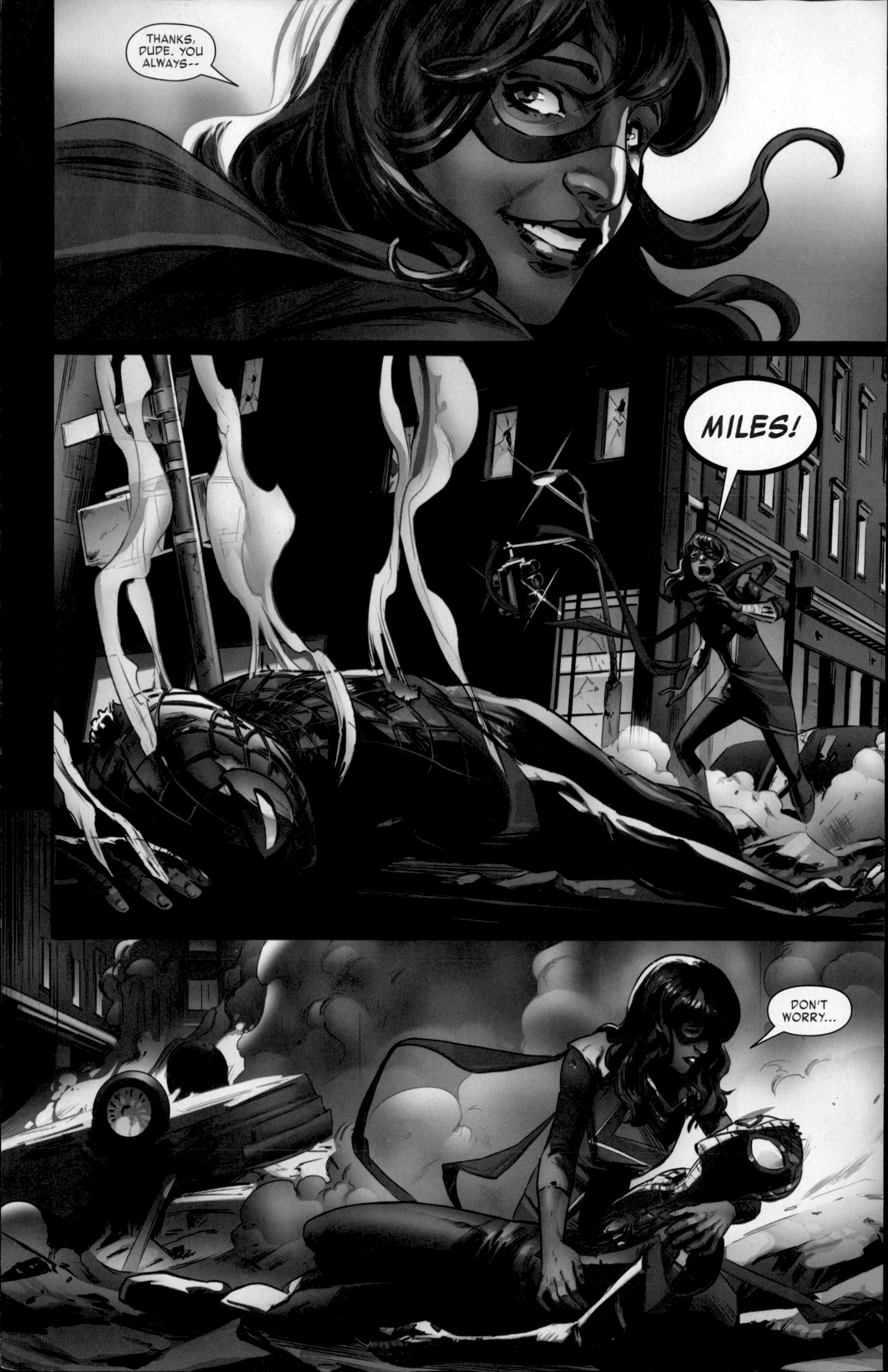
THANKS, DUDE. YOU ALWAYS--
MILES!
DON'T WORRY...

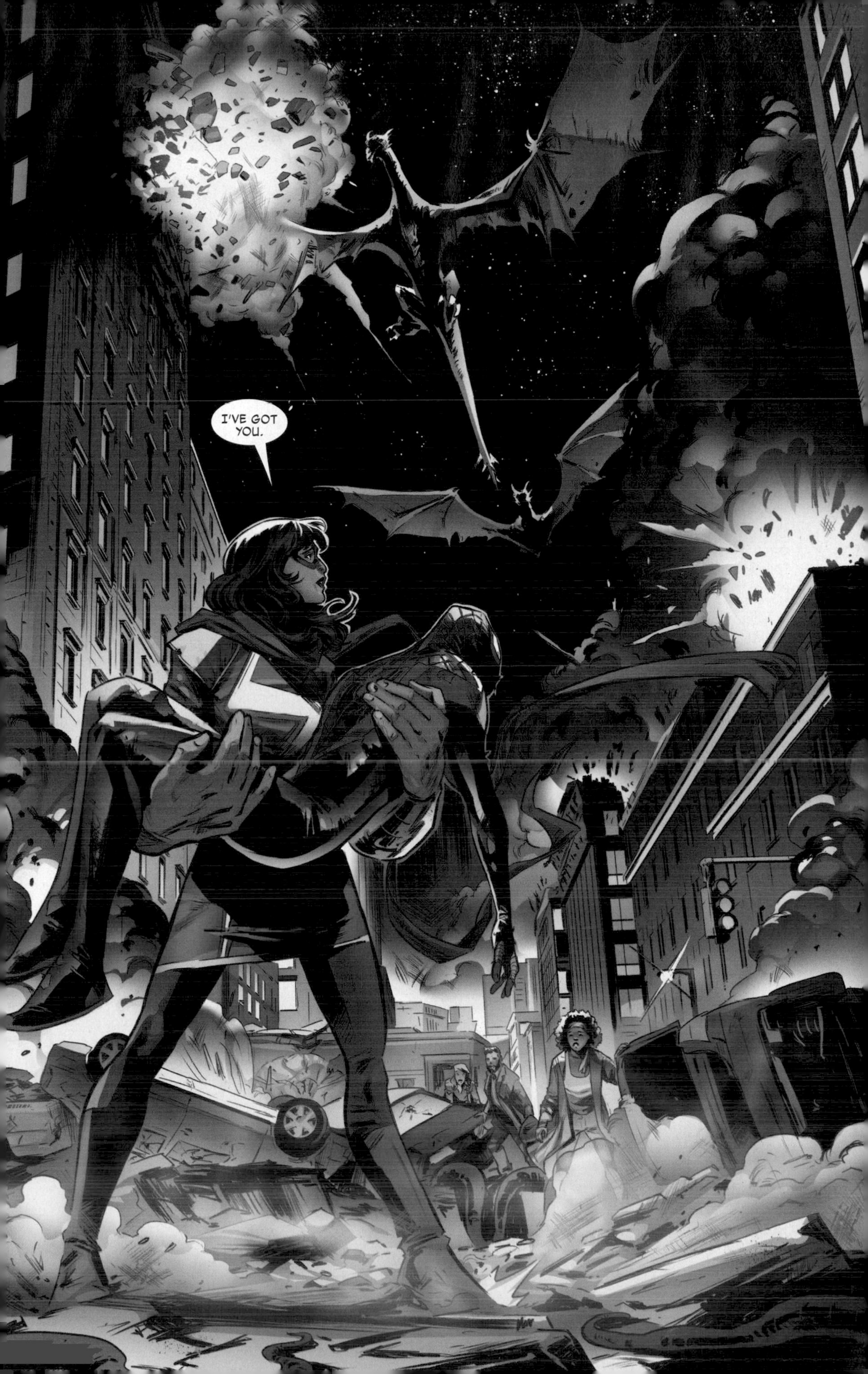
I'VE GOT YOU.

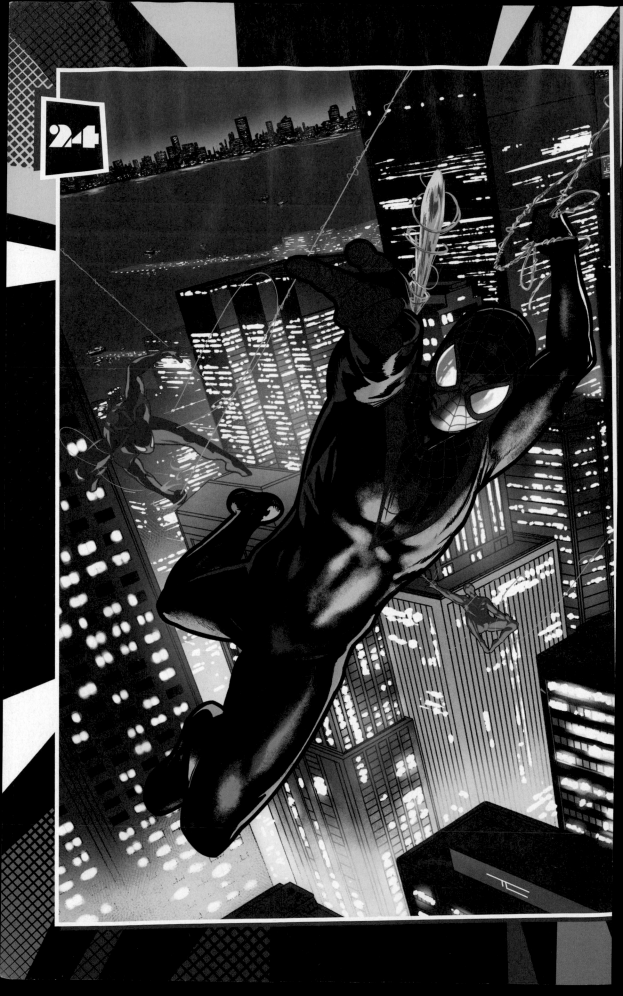

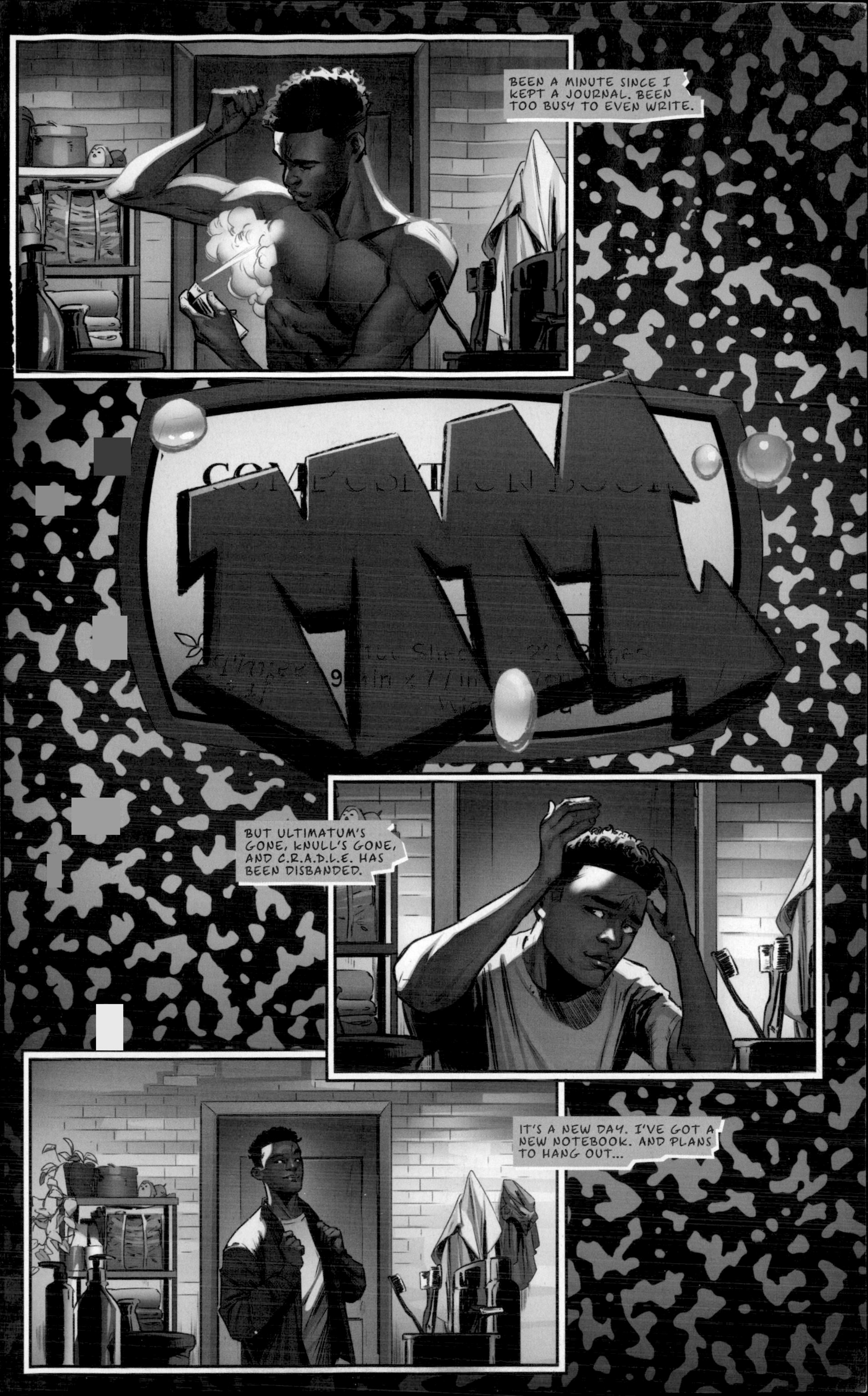
BEEN A MINUTE SINCE I KEPT A JOURNAL. BEEN TOO BUSY TO EVEN WRITE.
BUT ULTIMATUM'S GONE, KNULL'S GONE, AND C.R.A.D.L.E. HAS BEEN DISBANDED.
IT'S A NEW DAY. I'VE GOT A NEW NOTEBOOK. AND PLANS TO HANG OUT...

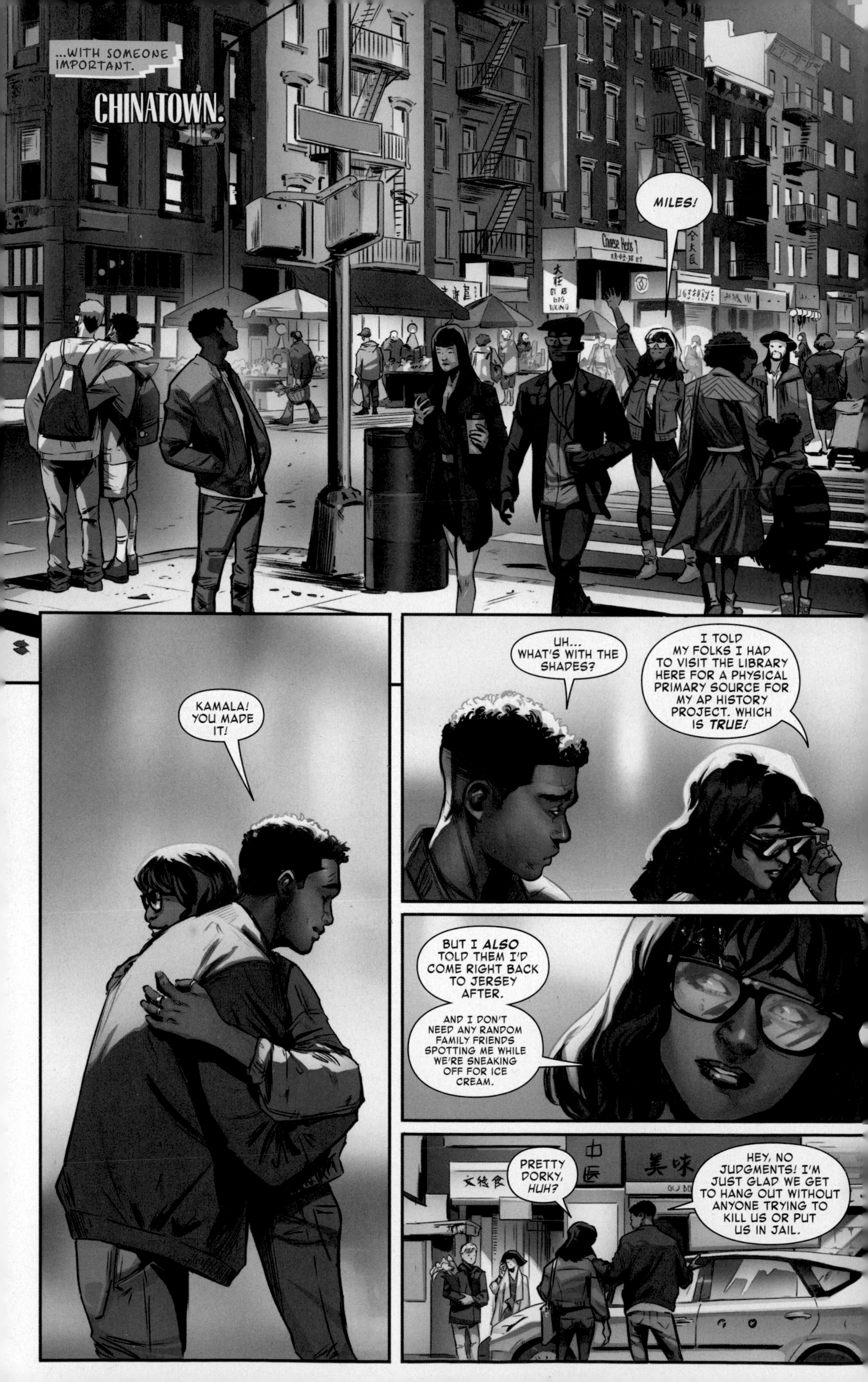
...WITH SOMEONE IMPORTANT.
CHINATOWN.
MILES!
KAMALA! YOU MADE IT!
UH... WHAT'S WITH THE SHADES?
I TOLD MY FOLKS I HAD TO VISIT THE LIBRARY HERE FOR A PHYSICAL PRIMARY SOURCE FOR MY AP HISTORY PROJECT. WHICH IS TRUE!
BUT I ALSO TOLD THEM I'D COME RIGHT BACK TO JERSEY AFTER.
AND I DON'T NEED ANY RANDOM FAMILY FRIENDS SPOTTING ME WHILE WE'RE SNEAKING OFF FOR ICE CREAM.
PRETTY DORKY, HUH?
HEY, NO JUDGMENTS! I'M JUST GLAD WE GET TO HANG OUT WITHOUT ANYONE TRYING TO KILL US OR PUT US IN JAIL.

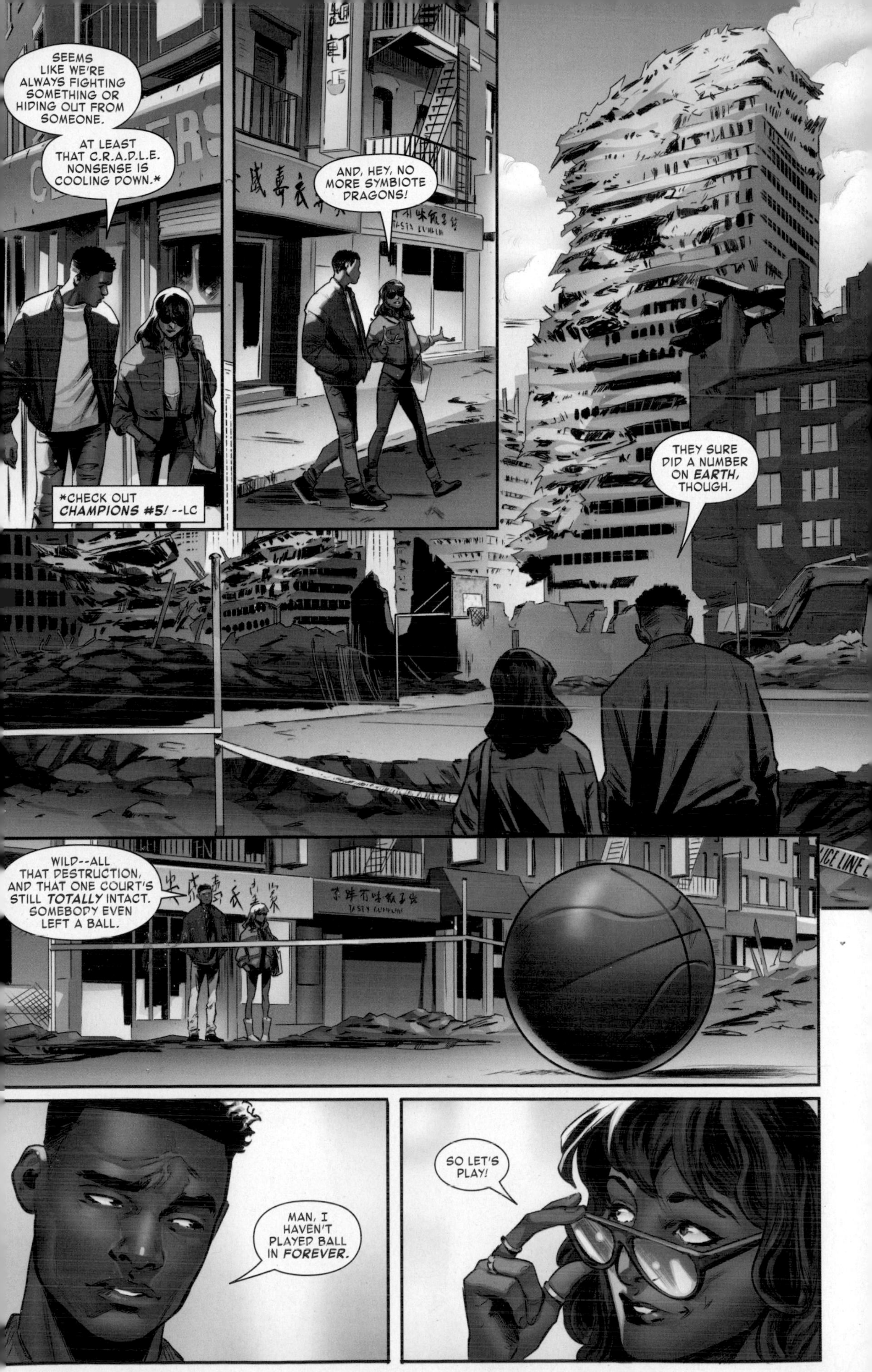
SEEMS LIKE WE'RE ALWAYS FIGHTING SOMETHING OR HIDING OUT FROM SOMEONE.
AT LEAST THAT C.R.A.D.L.E. NONSENSE IS COOLING DOWN.*
*CHECK OUT CHAMPIONS #5! --LC
AND, HEY, NO MORE SYMBIOTE DRAGONS!
THEY SURE DID A NUMBER ON EARTH, THOUGH.
WILD--ALL THAT DESTRUCTION, AND THAT ONE COURT'S STILL TOTALLY INTACT. SOMEBODY EVEN LEFT A BALL.
MAN, I HAVEN'T PLAYED BALL IN FOREVER.
SO LET'S PLAY!

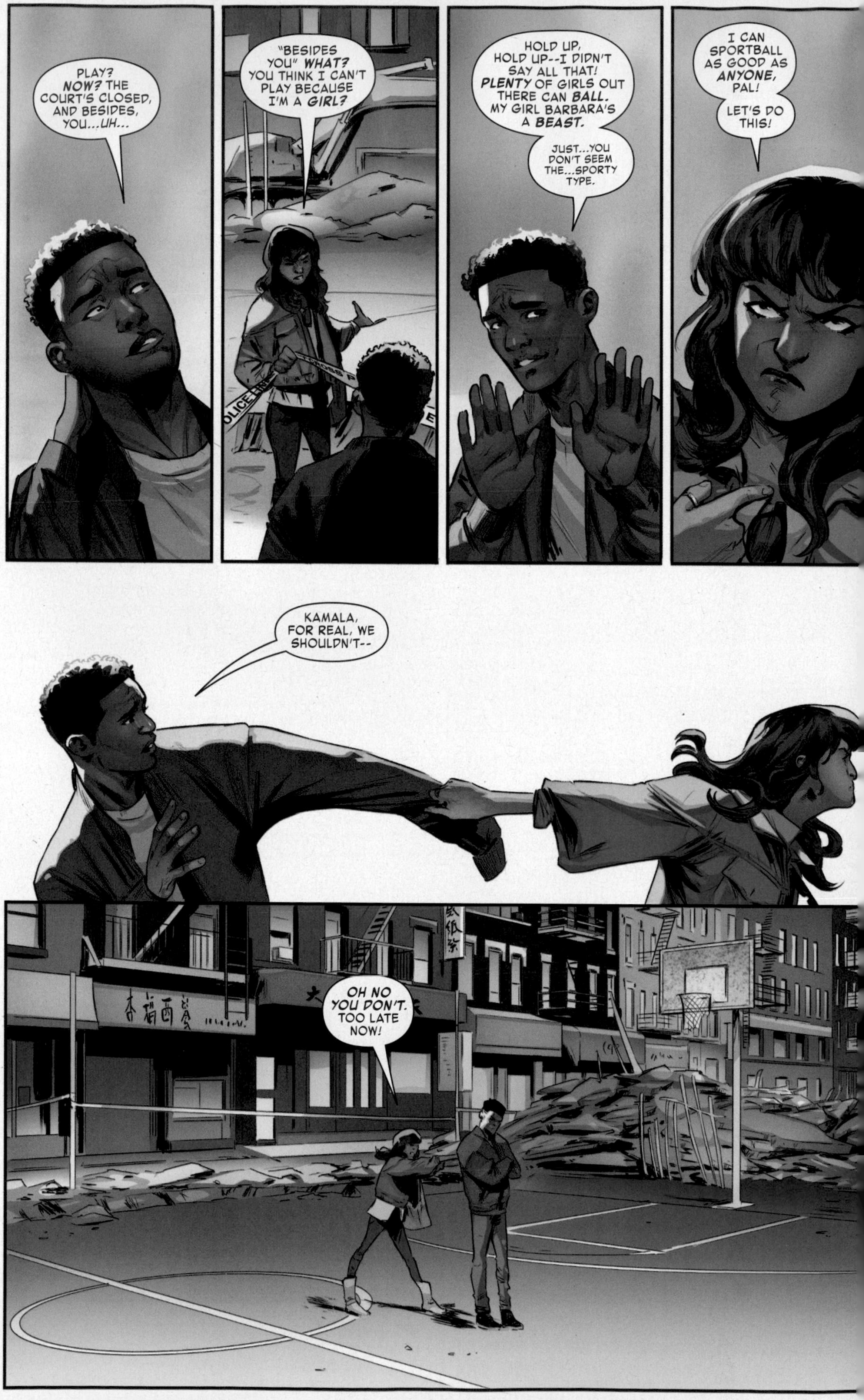
PLAY? NOW? THE COURT'S CLOSED, AND BESIDES, YOU...UH...
"BESIDES YOU" WHAT? YOU THINK I CAN'T PLAY BECAUSE I'M A GIRL?
HOLD UP, HOLD UP--I DIDN'T SAY ALL THAT! PLENTY OF GIRLS OUT THERE CAN BALL. MY GIRL BARBARA'S A BEAST.
JUST...YOU DON'T SEEM THE...SPORTY TYPE.
I CAN SPORTBALL AS GOOD AS ANYONE, PAL!
LET'S DO THIS!
KAMALA, FOR REAL, WE SHOULDN'T--
OH NO YOU DON'T. TOO LATE NOW!

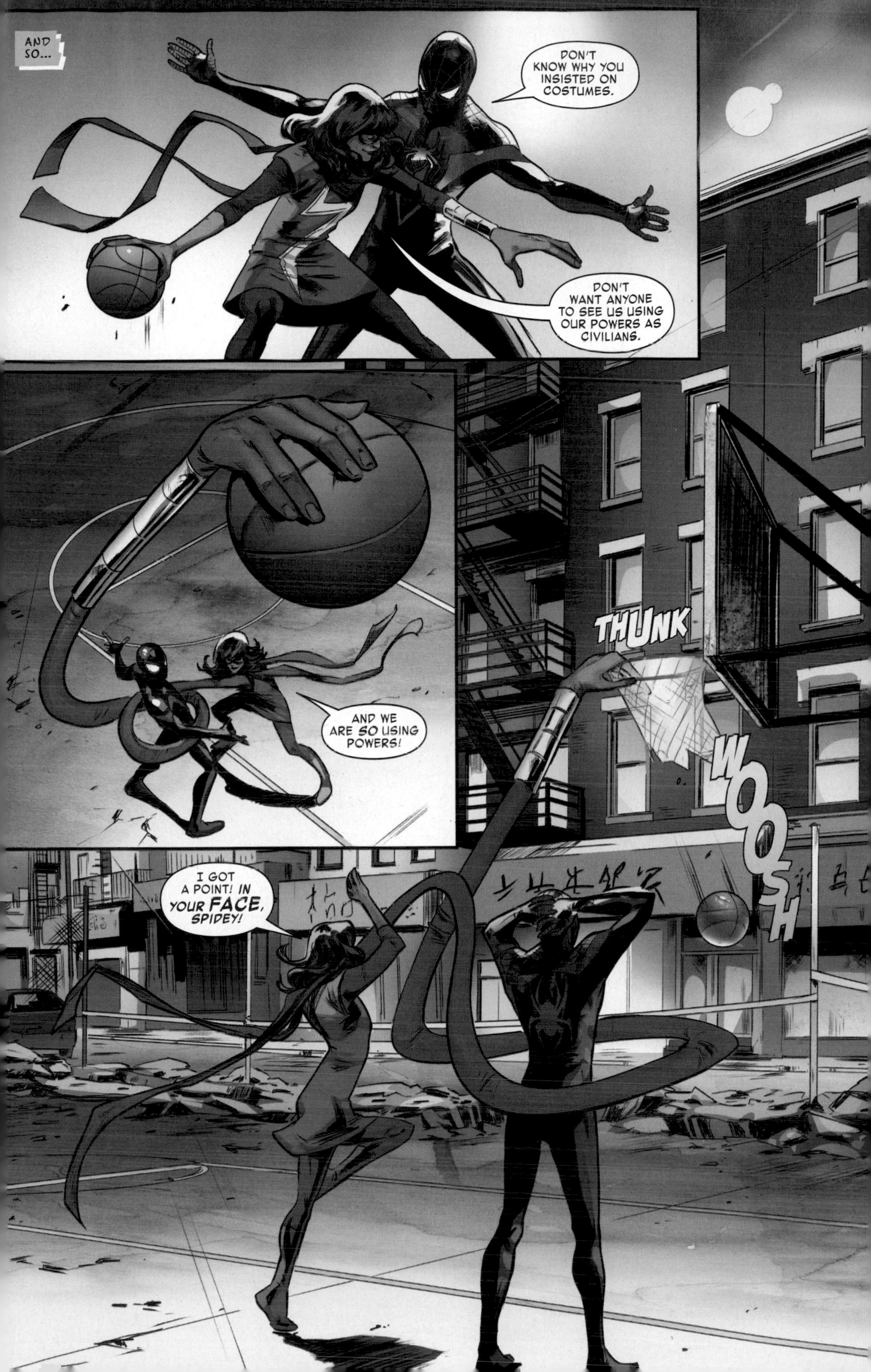
AND SO...
DON'T KNOW WHY YOU INSISTED ON COSTUMES.
DON'T WANT ANYONE TO SEE US USING OUR POWERS AS CIVILIANS.
AND WE ARE SO USING POWERS!
THUNK
WOOSH
I GOT A POINT! IN YOUR FACE, SPIDEY!

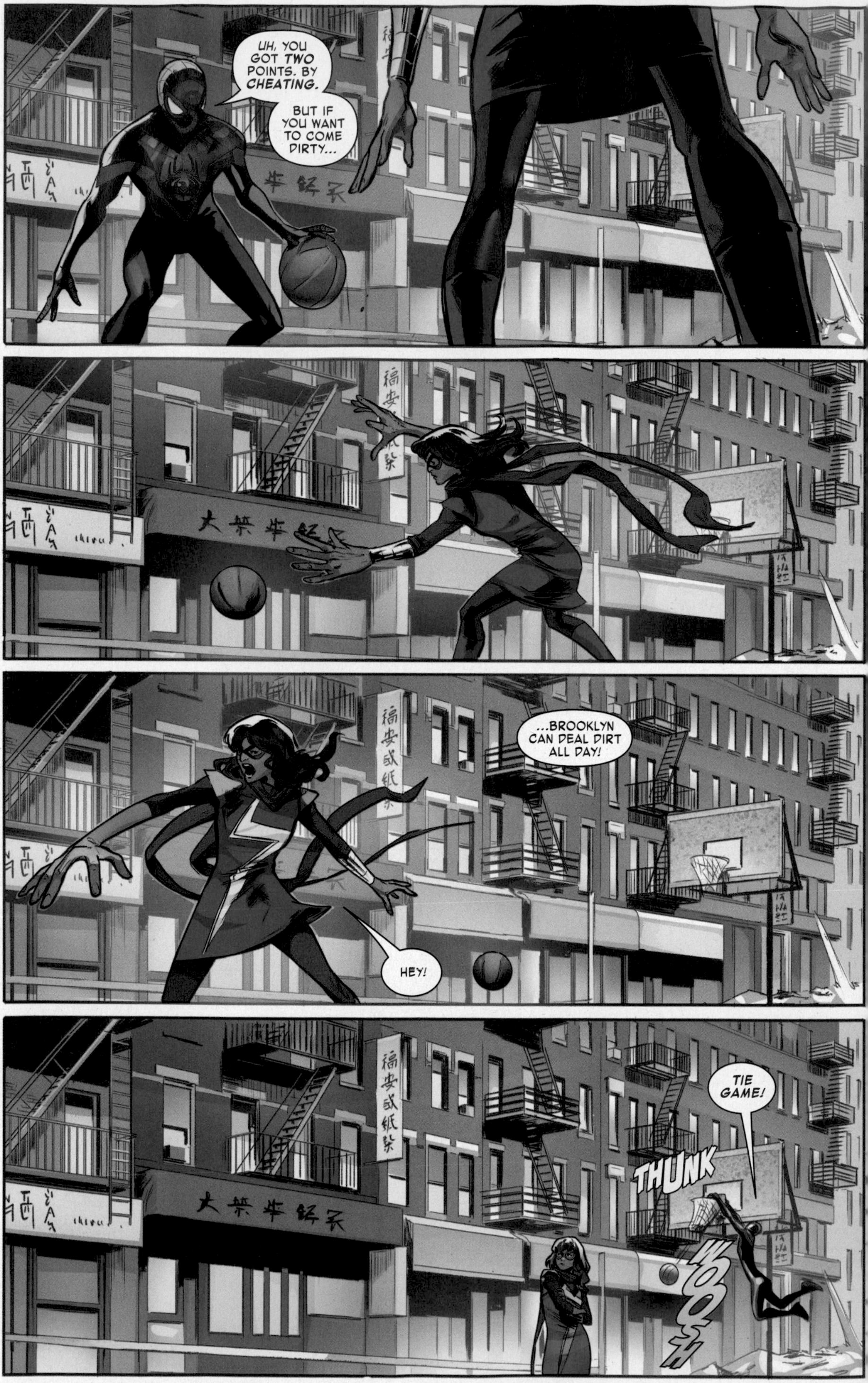
UH, YOU GOT TWO POINTS. BY CHEATING.
BUT IF YOU WANT TO COME DIRTY...
...BROOKLYN CAN DEAL DIRT ALL DAY!
HEY!
TIE GAME!
THUNK
WOOOSH

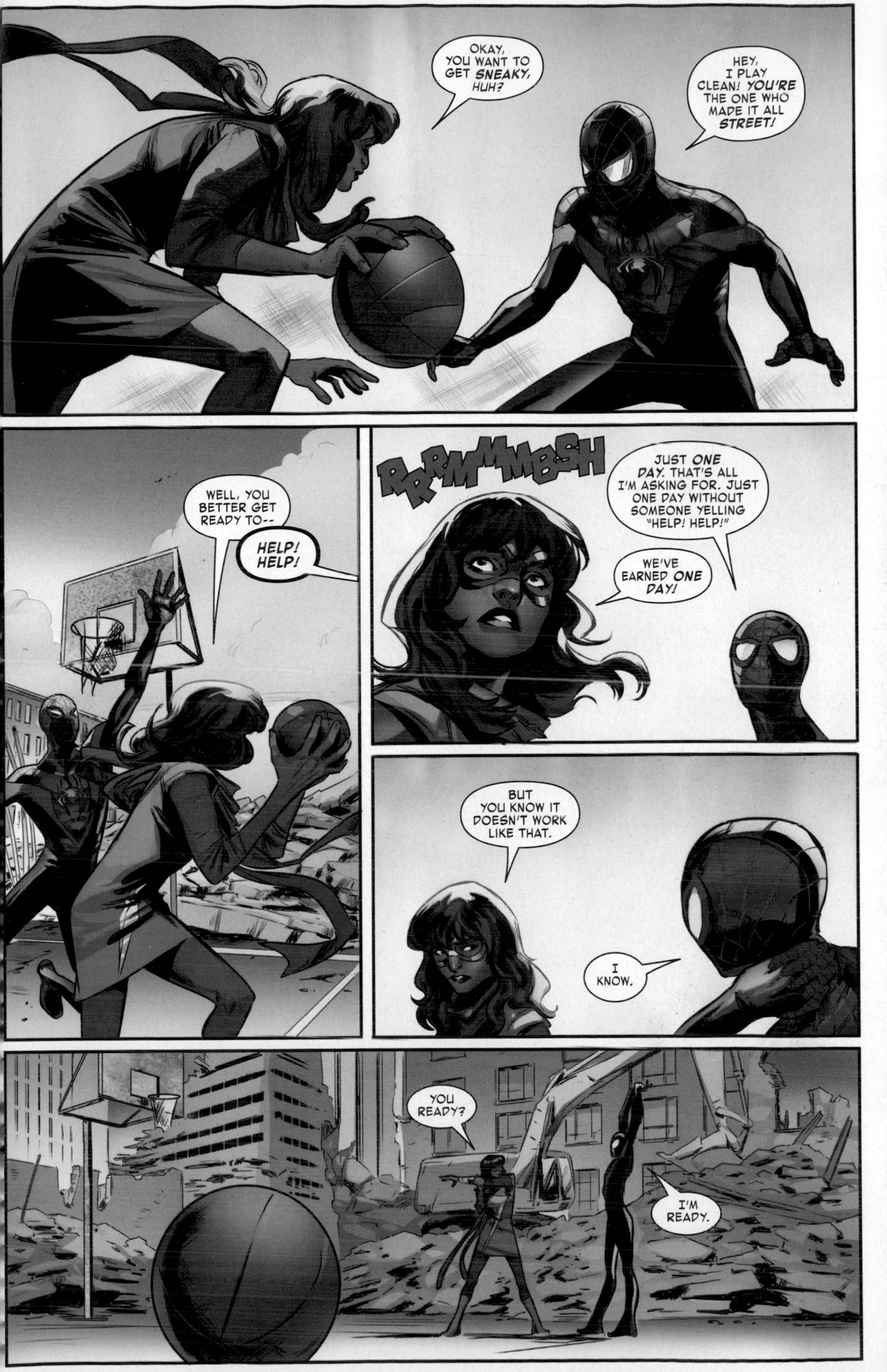
OKAY, YOU WANT TO GET SNEAKY, HUH?
HEY, I PLAY CLEAN! YOU'RE THE ONE WHO MADE IT ALL STREET!
WELL, YOU BETTER GET READY TO--
HELP! HELP!
RRRMMMBSH
JUST ONE DAY. THAT'S ALL I'M ASKING FOR. JUST ONE DAY WITHOUT SOMEONE YELLING "HELP! HELP!"
WE'VE EARNED ONE DAY!
BUT YOU KNOW IT DOESN'T WORK LIKE THAT.
I KNOW.
YOU READY?
I'M READY.

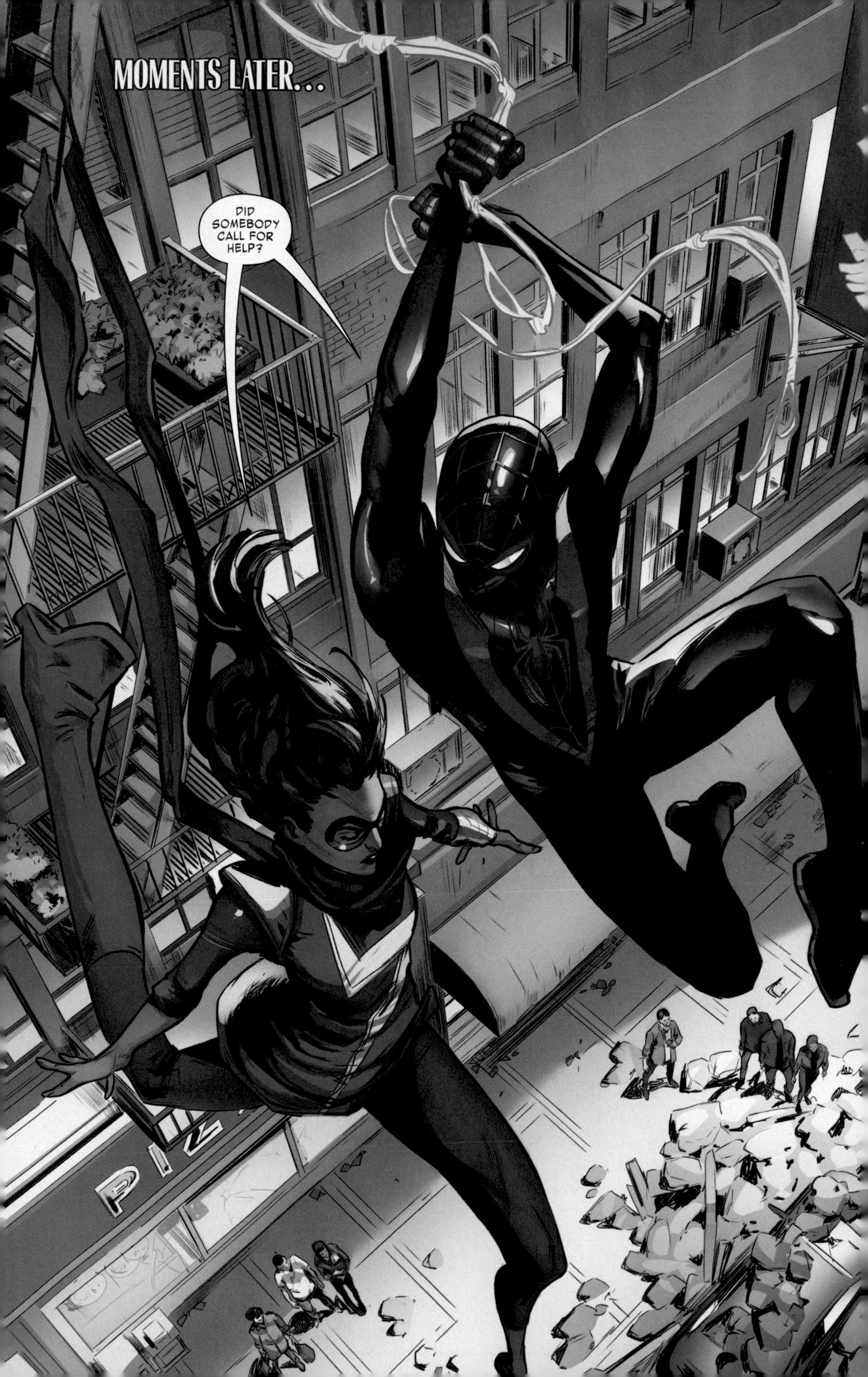
MOMENTS LATER...
DID SOMEBODY CALL FOR HELP?

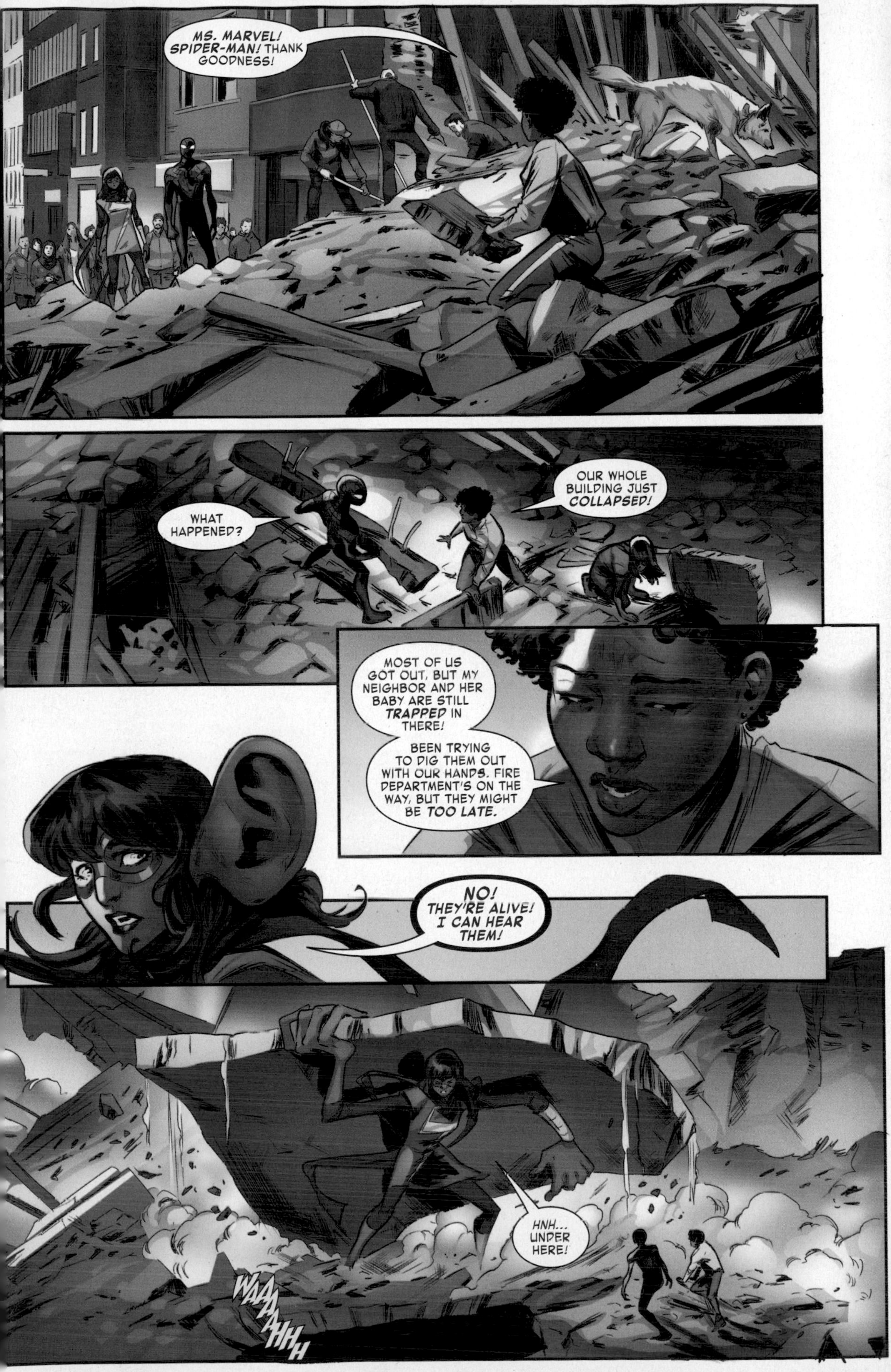
MS. MARVEL! SPIDER-MAN! THANK GOODNESS!
WHAT HAPPENED?
OUR WHOLE BUILDING JUST COLLAPSED!
MOST OF US GOT OUT, BUT MY NEIGHBOR AND HER BABY ARE STILL TRAPPED IN THERE!
BEEN TRYING TO DIG THEM OUT WITH OUR HANDS. FIRE DEPARTMENT'S ON THE WAY, BUT THEY MIGHT BE TOO LATE.
NO! THEY'RE ALIVE! I CAN HEAR THEM!
HNH... UNDER HERE!
WAAAAHHH

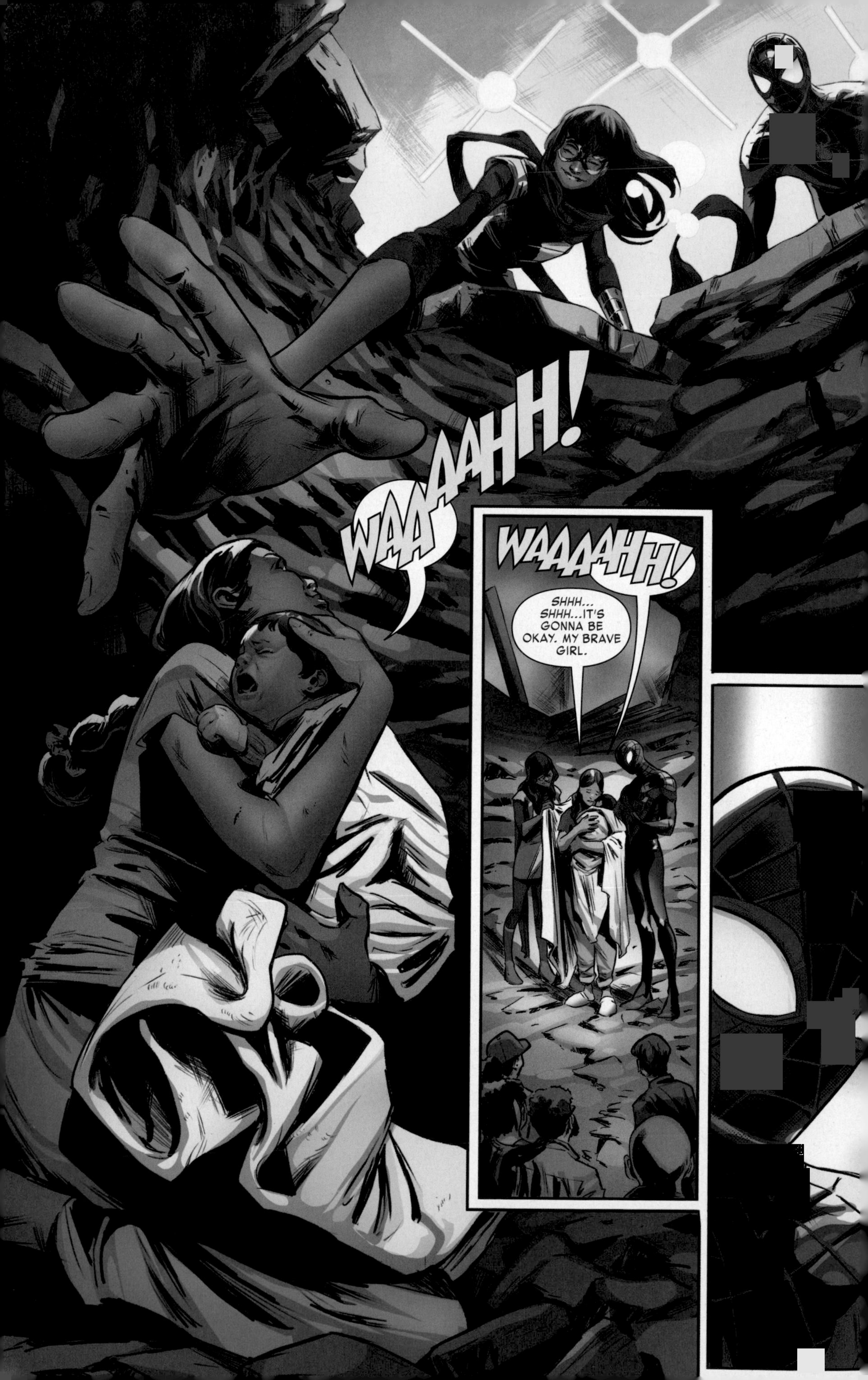
WAAAAHH!
WAAAAHH!
SHHH... SHHH...IT'S GONNA BE OKAY. MY BRAVE GIRL.

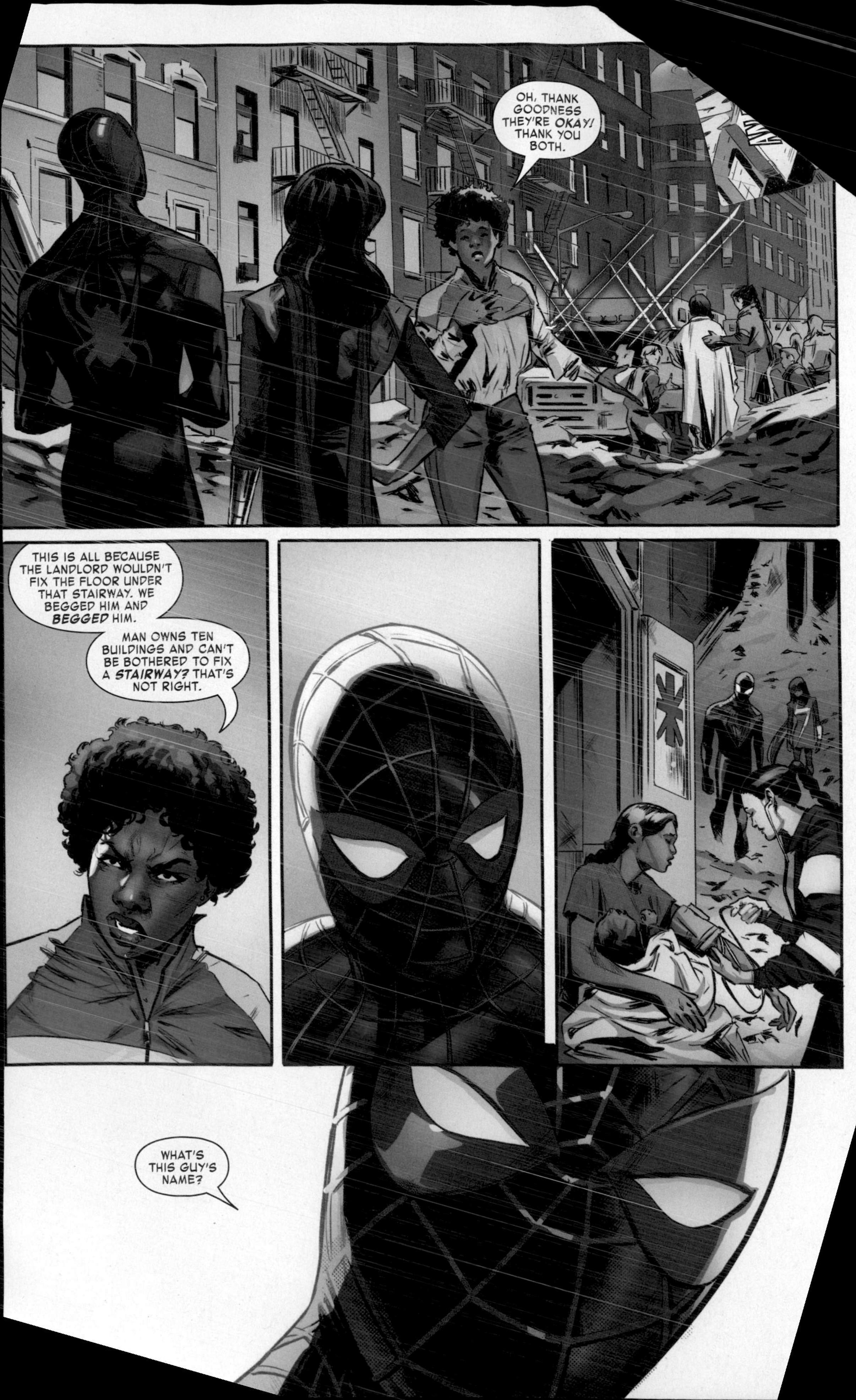
OH, THANK GOODNESS THEY'RE OKAY! THANK YOU BOTH.
THIS IS ALL BECAUSE THE LANDLORD WOULDN'T FIX THE FLOOR UNDER THAT STAIRWAY. WE BEGGED HIM AND BEGGED HIM.
MAN OWNS TEN BUILDINGS AND CAN'T BE BOTHERED TO FIX A STAIRWAY? THAT'S NOT RIGHT.
WHAT'S THIS GUY'S NAME?

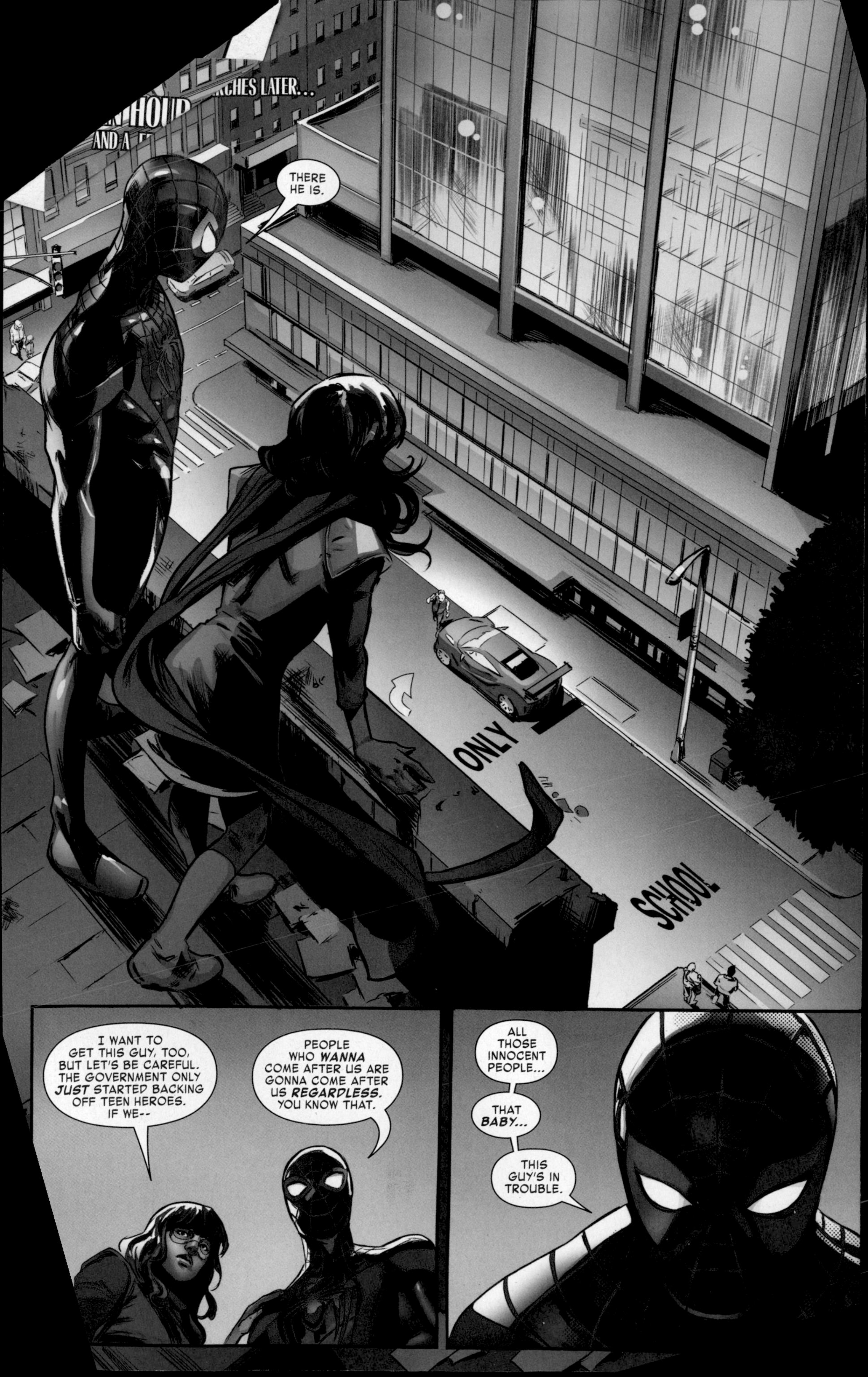
HOUR
AND A
CHES LATER...
THERE HE IS.
ONLY
SCHOO!
I WANT TO GET THIS GUY, TOO, BUT LET'S BE CAREFUL. THE GOVERNMENT ONLY JUST STARTED BACKING OFF TEEN HEROES. IF WE--
PEOPLE WHO WANNA COME AFTER US ARE GONNA COME AFTER US REGARDLESS. YOU KNOW THAT.
ALL THOSE INNOCENT PEOPLE...
THAT BABY...
THIS GUY'S IN TROUBLE.

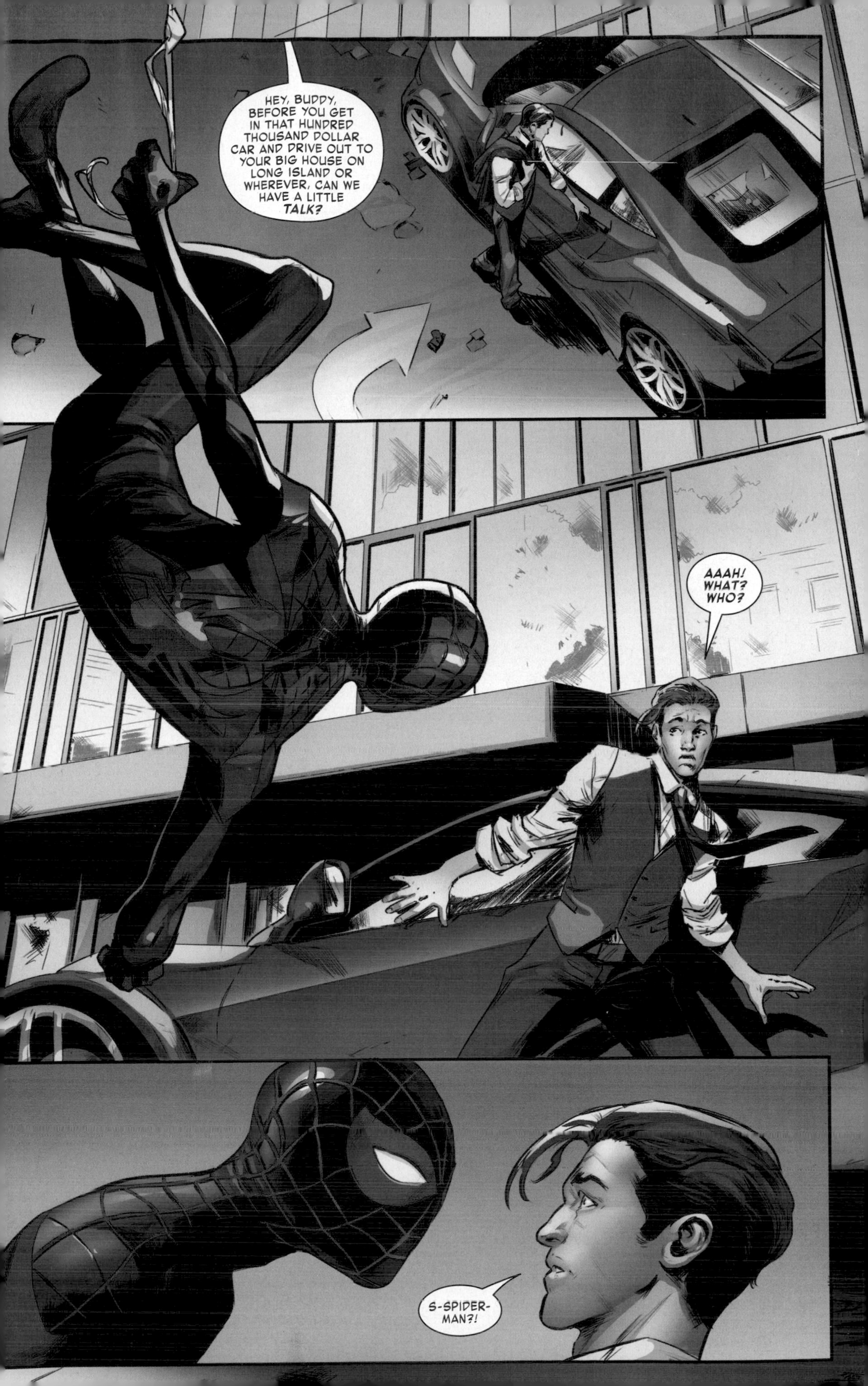
HEY, BUDDY, BEFORE YOU GET IN THAT HUNDRED THOUSAND DOLLAR CAR AND DRIVE OUT TO YOUR BIG HOUSE ON LONG ISLAND OR WHEREVER, CAN WE HAVE A LITTLE *TALK?*
AAAH! WHAT? WHO?
S-SPIDER-MAN?!

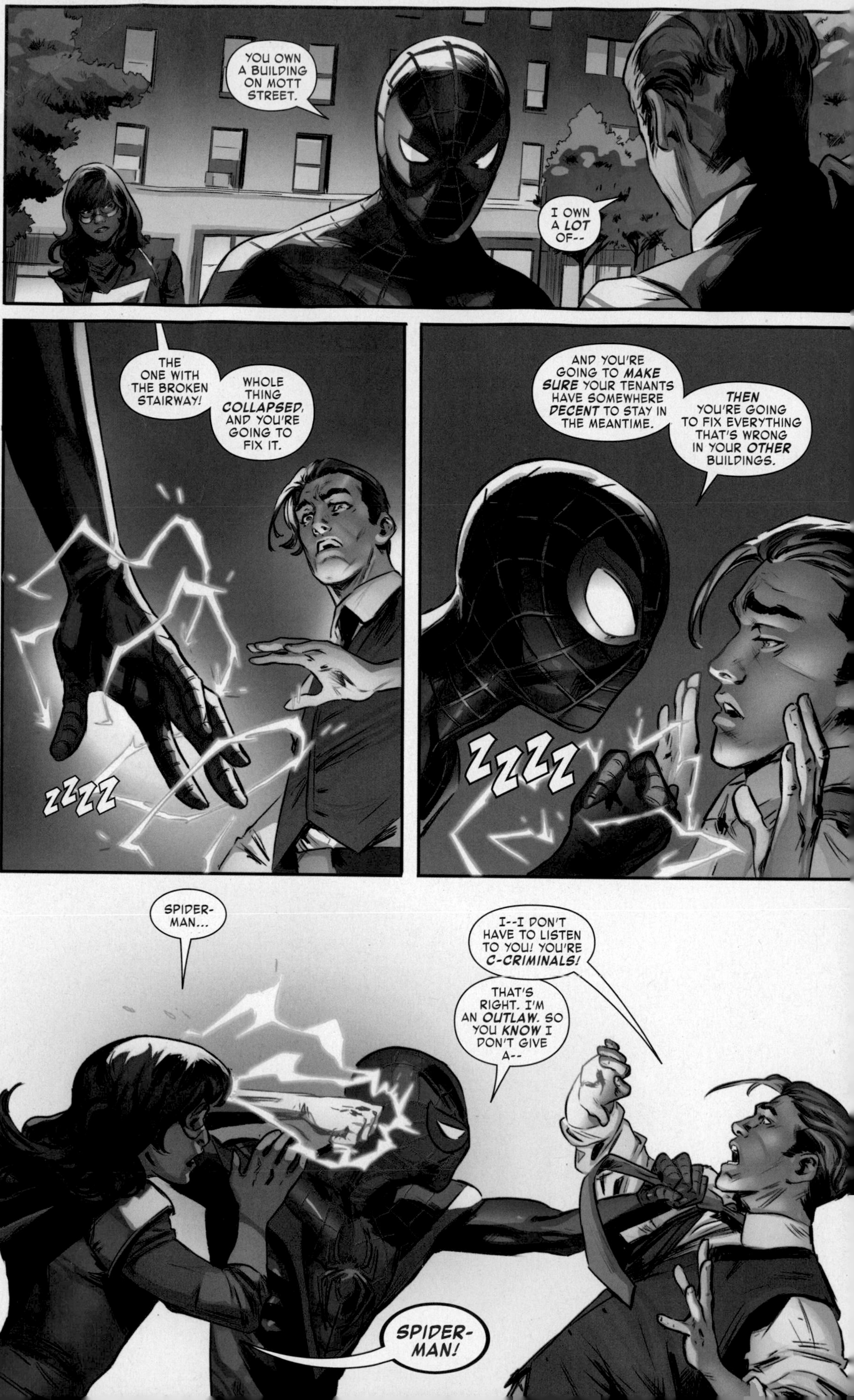
YOU OWN A BUILDING ON MOTT STREET.
I OWN A LOT OF--
THE ONE WITH THE BROKEN STAIRWAY!
WHOLE THING COLLAPSED, AND YOU'RE GOING TO FIX IT.
ZZZZ
AND YOU'RE GOING TO MAKE SURE YOUR TENANTS HAVE SOMEWHERE DECENT TO STAY IN THE MEANTIME.
THEN YOU'RE GOING TO FIX EVERYTHING THAT'S WRONG IN YOUR OTHER BUILDINGS.
ZZZZ
SPIDER-MAN...
I--I DON'T HAVE TO LISTEN TO YOU! YOU'RE C-CRIMINALS!
THAT'S RIGHT. I'M AN OUTLAW. SO YOU KNOW I DON'T GIVE A--
SPIDER-MAN!

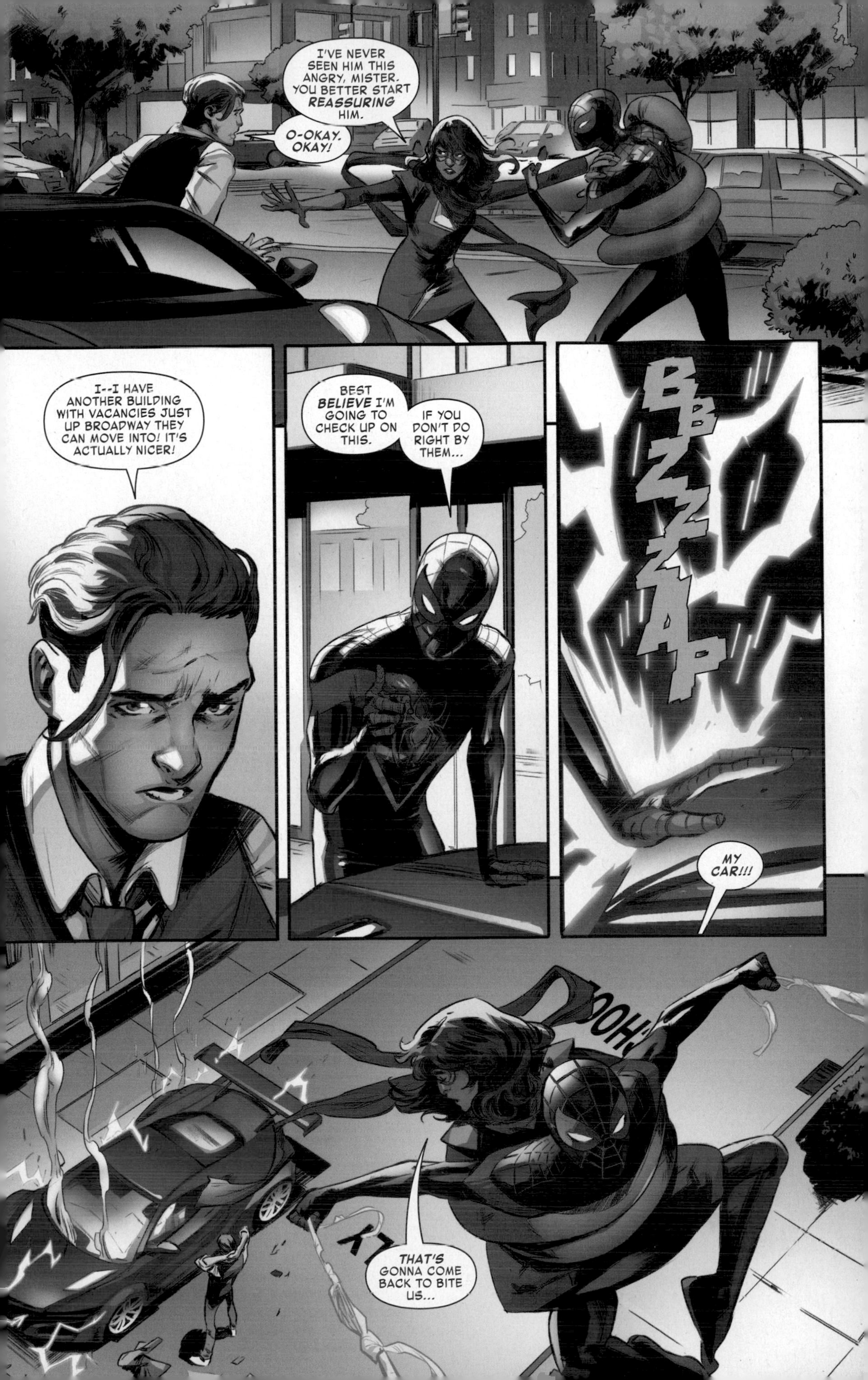
I'VE NEVER SEEN HIM THIS ANGRY, MISTER. YOU BETTER START *REASSURING* HIM.
O-OKAY. OKAY!
I--I HAVE ANOTHER BUILDING WITH VACANCIES JUST UP BROADWAY THEY CAN MOVE INTO! IT'S ACTUALLY NICER!
BEST *BELIEVE* I'M GOING TO CHECK UP ON THIS.
IF YOU DON'T DO RIGHT BY THEM...
BBZZZAP
MY CAR!!!
THAT'S GONNA COME BACK TO BITE US...

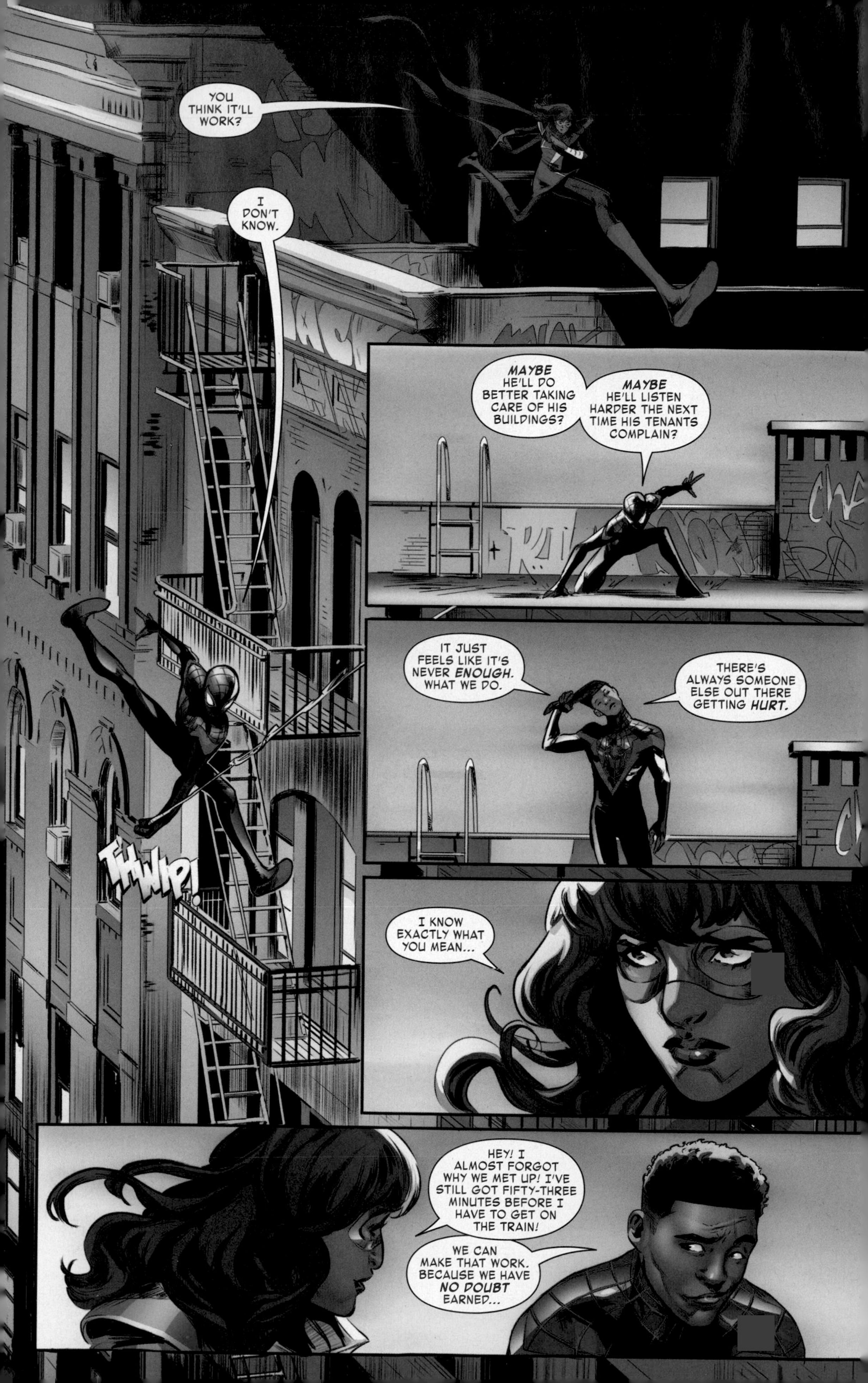

YOU THINK IT'LL WORK?
I DON'T KNOW.
THWIP!
MAYBE HE'LL DO BETTER TAKING CARE OF HIS BUILDINGS?
MAYBE HE'LL LISTEN HARDER THE NEXT TIME HIS TENANTS COMPLAIN?
IT JUST FEELS LIKE IT'S NEVER ENOUGH. WHAT WE DO.
THERE'S ALWAYS SOMEONE ELSE OUT THERE GETTING HURT.
I KNOW EXACTLY WHAT YOU MEAN...
HEY! I ALMOST FORGOT WHY WE MET UP! I'VE STILL GOT FIFTY-THREE MINUTES BEFORE I HAVE TO GET ON THE TRAIN!
WE CAN MAKE THAT WORK. BECAUSE WE HAVE NO DOUBT EARNED...

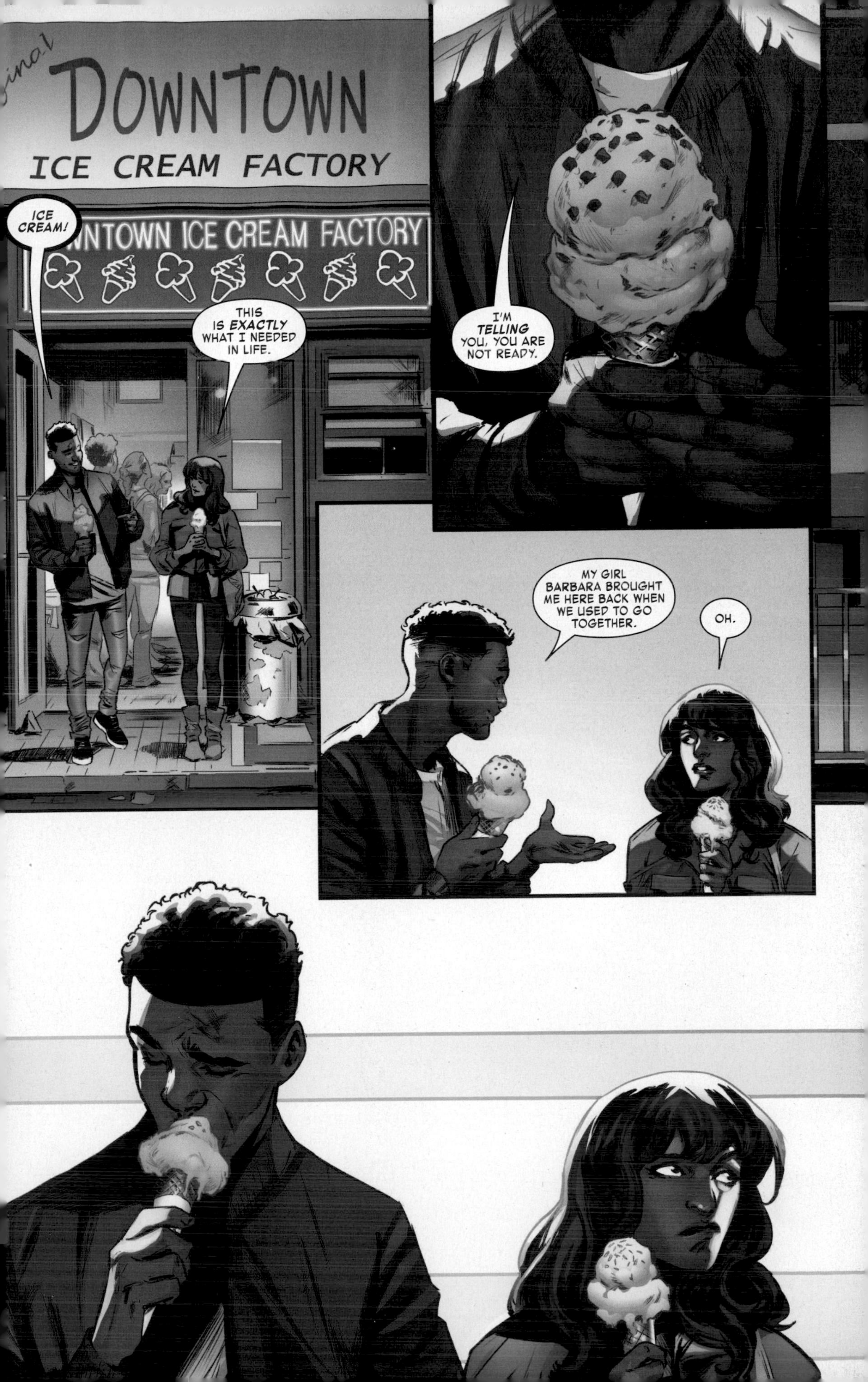

DOWNTOWN
ICE CREAM FACTORY
ICE CREAM!
WNTOWN ICE CREAM FACTORY
THIS IS EXACTLY WHAT I NEEDED IN LIFE.
I'M TELLING YOU, YOU ARE NOT READY.
MY GIRL BARBARA BROUGHT ME HERE BACK WHEN WE USED TO GO TOGETHER.
OH.

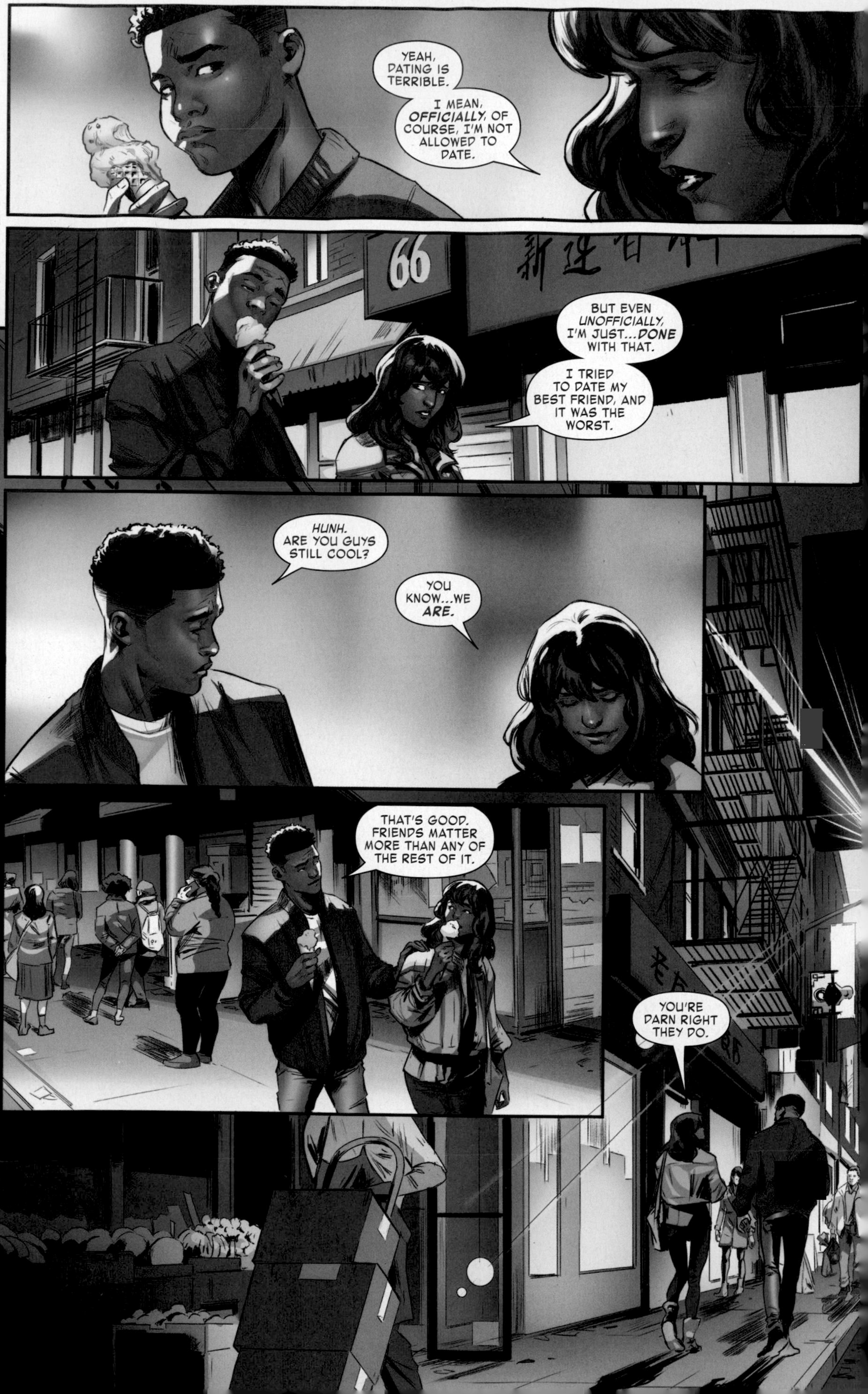

YEAH, DATING IS TERRIBLE.
I MEAN, OFFICIALLY, OF COURSE, I'M NOT ALLOWED TO DATE.
66
BUT EVEN UNOFFICIALLY, I'M JUST...DONE WITH THAT.
I TRIED TO DATE MY BEST FRIEND, AND IT WAS THE WORST.
HUNH. ARE YOU GUYS STILL COOL?
YOU KNOW...WE ARE.
THAT'S GOOD. FRIENDS MATTER MORE THAN ANY OF THE REST OF IT.
YOU'RE DARN RIGHT THEY DO.

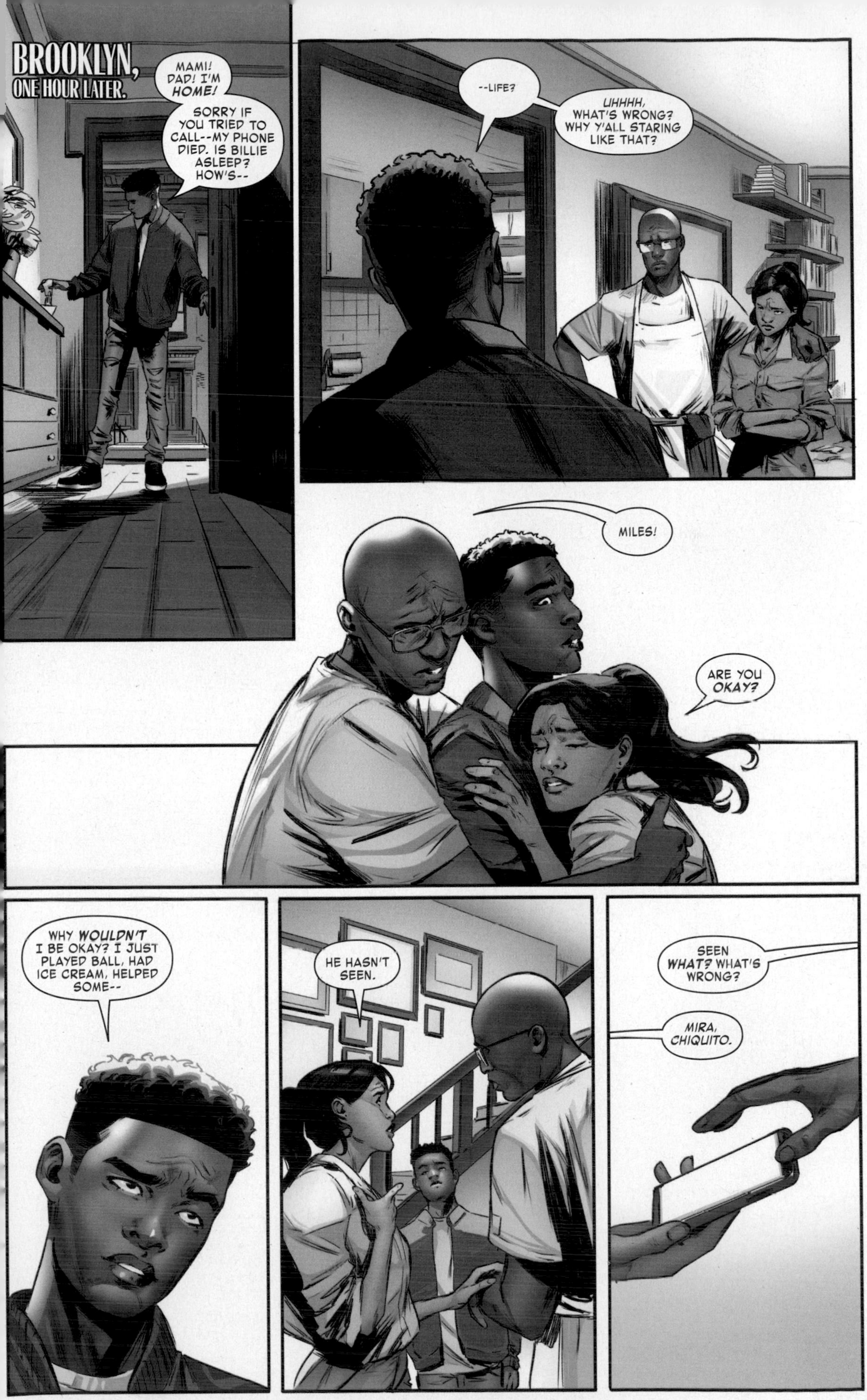
BROOKLYN, ONE HOUR LATER.
MAMI! DAD! I'M HOME!
SORRY IF YOU TRIED TO CALL--MY PHONE DIED. IS BILLIE ASLEEP? HOW'S--
--LIFE?
UHHHH, WHAT'S WRONG? WHY Y'ALL STARING LIKE THAT?
MILES!
ARE YOU OKAY?
WHY WOULDN'T I BE OKAY? I JUST PLAYED BALL, HAD ICE CREAM, HELPED SOME--
HE HASN'T SEEN.
SEEN WHAT? WHAT'S WRONG?
MIRA, CHIQUITO.

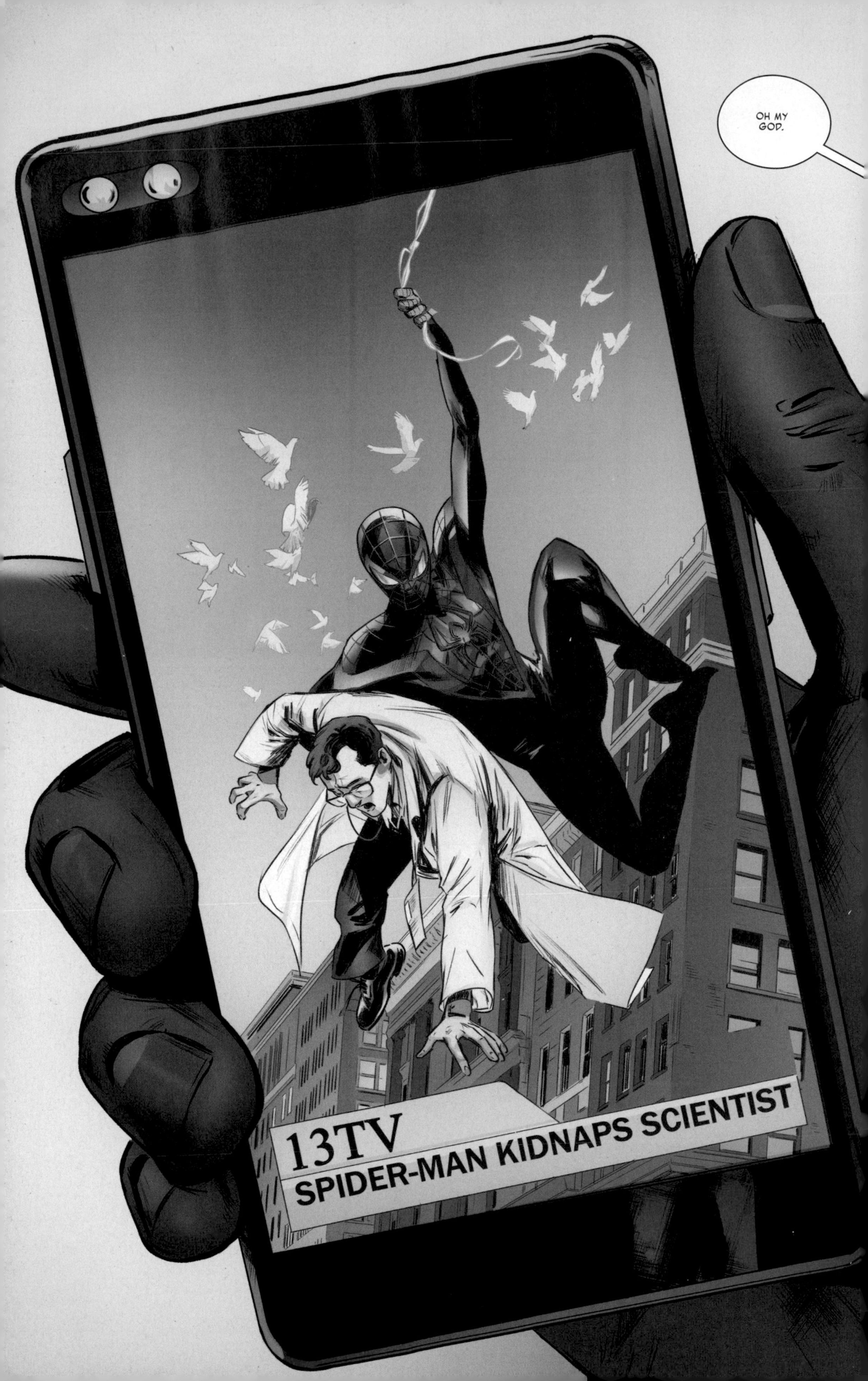
OH MY GOD.
13TV
SPIDER-MAN KIDNAPS SCIENTIST

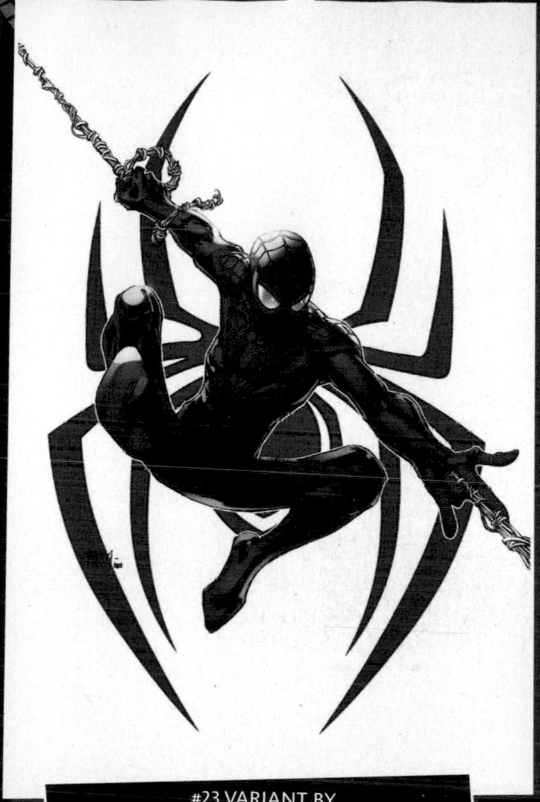

#23 VARIANT BY
DAVID FINCH & FRANK D'ARMATA

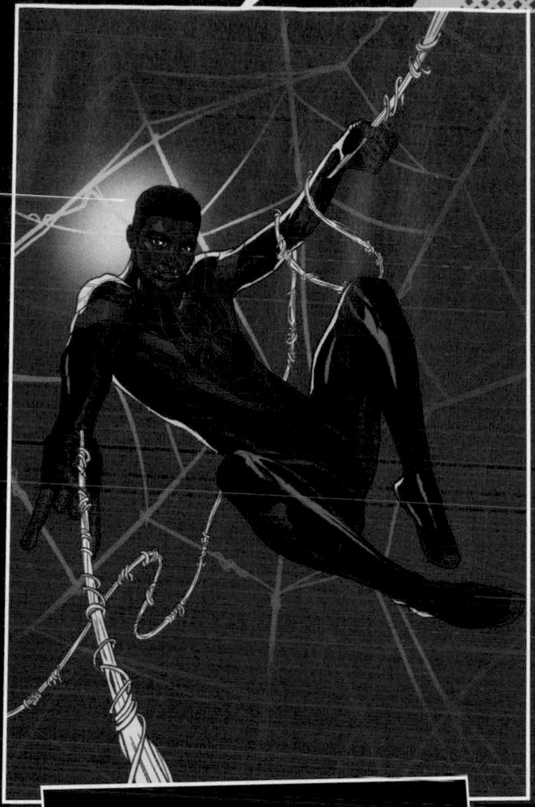

#23 BLACK HISTORY MONTH VARIANT BY
ERNANDA SOUZA

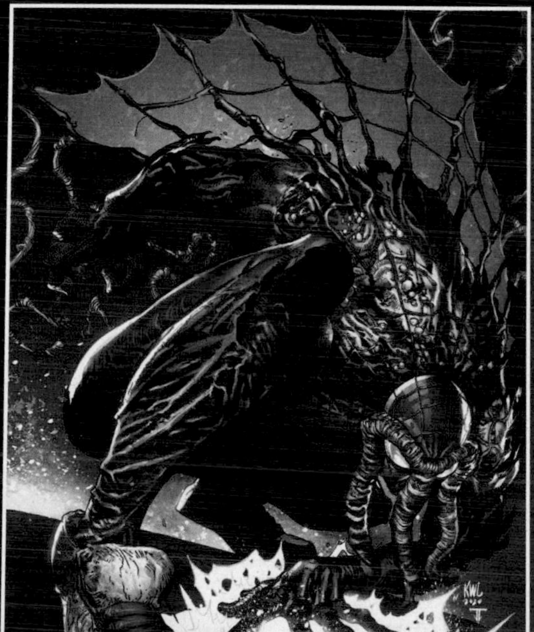

#24 MAN-THING 50TH ANNIVERSARY VARIANT BY
KEN LASHLEY & JUAN FERNANDEZ

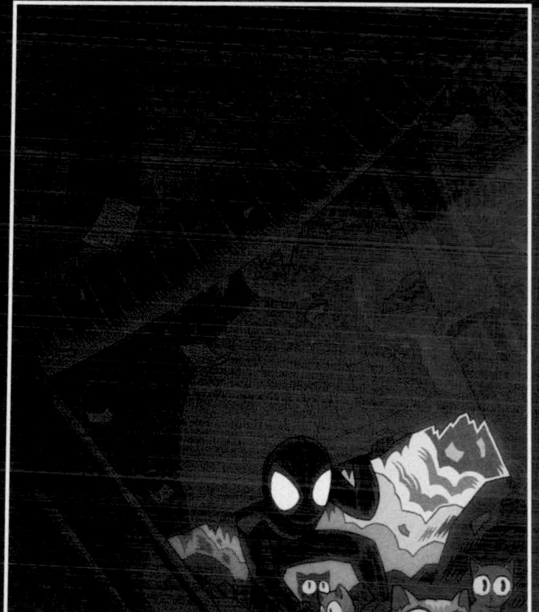

#25 VARIANT BY
DAN HIPP

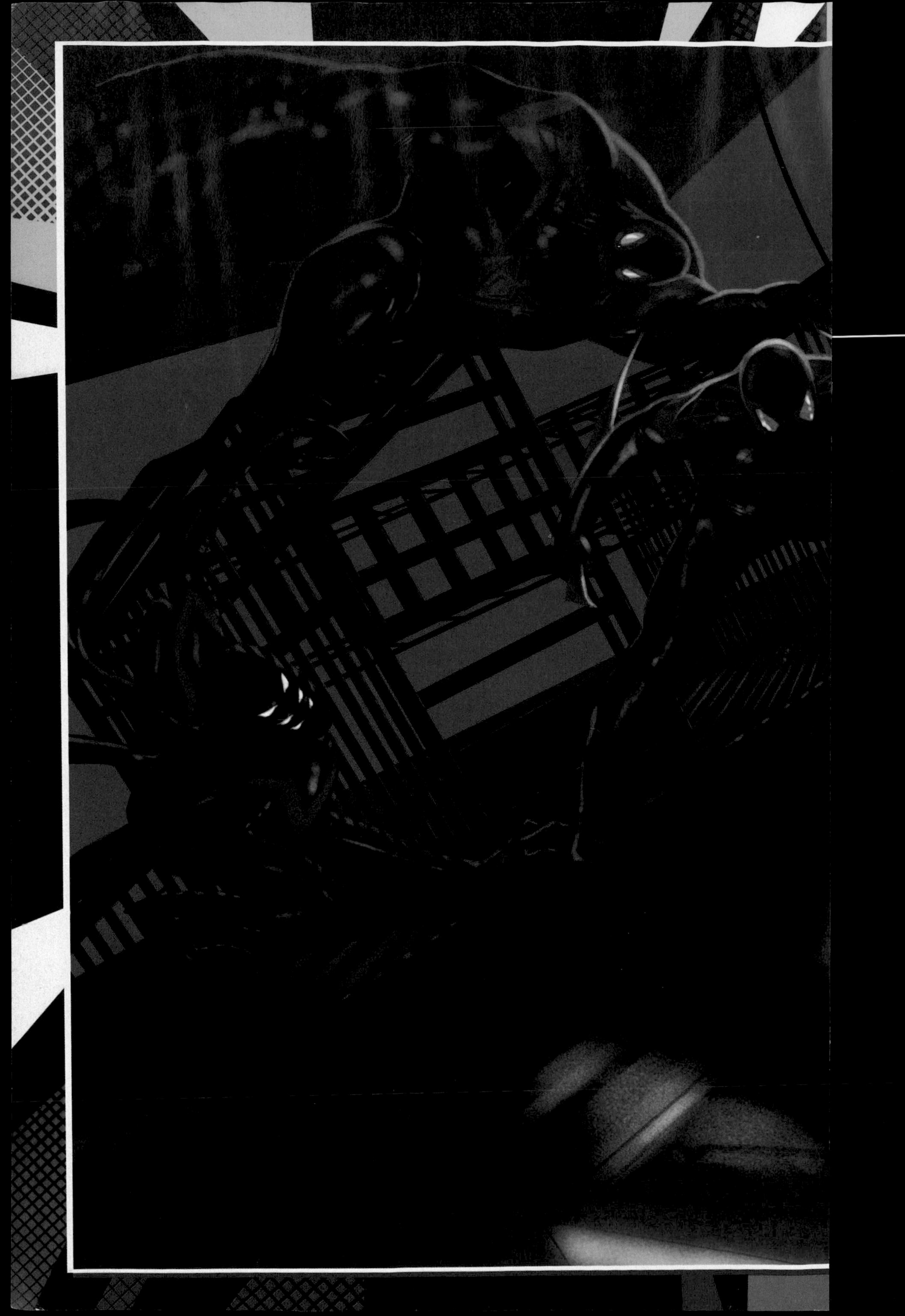

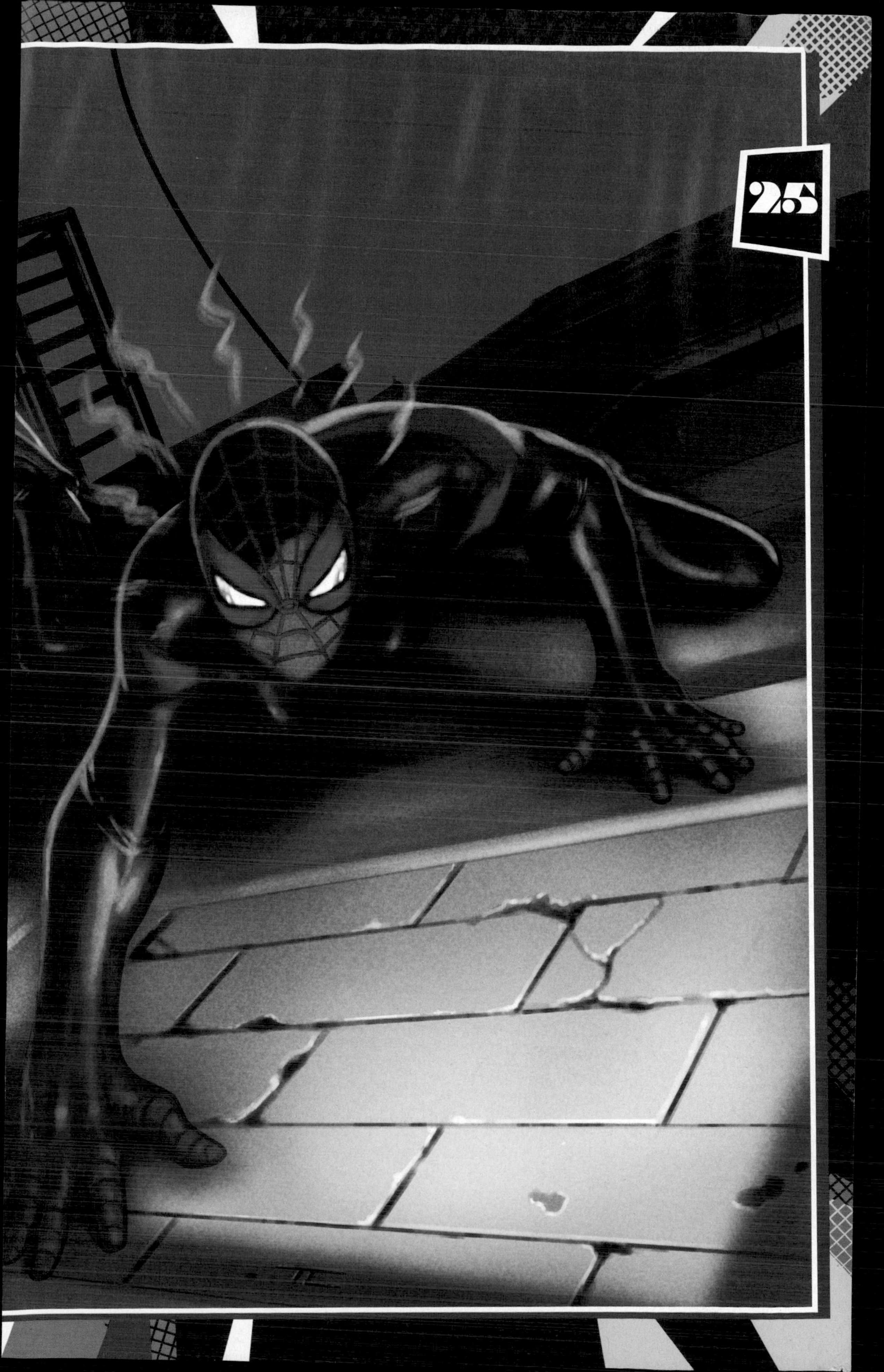
25

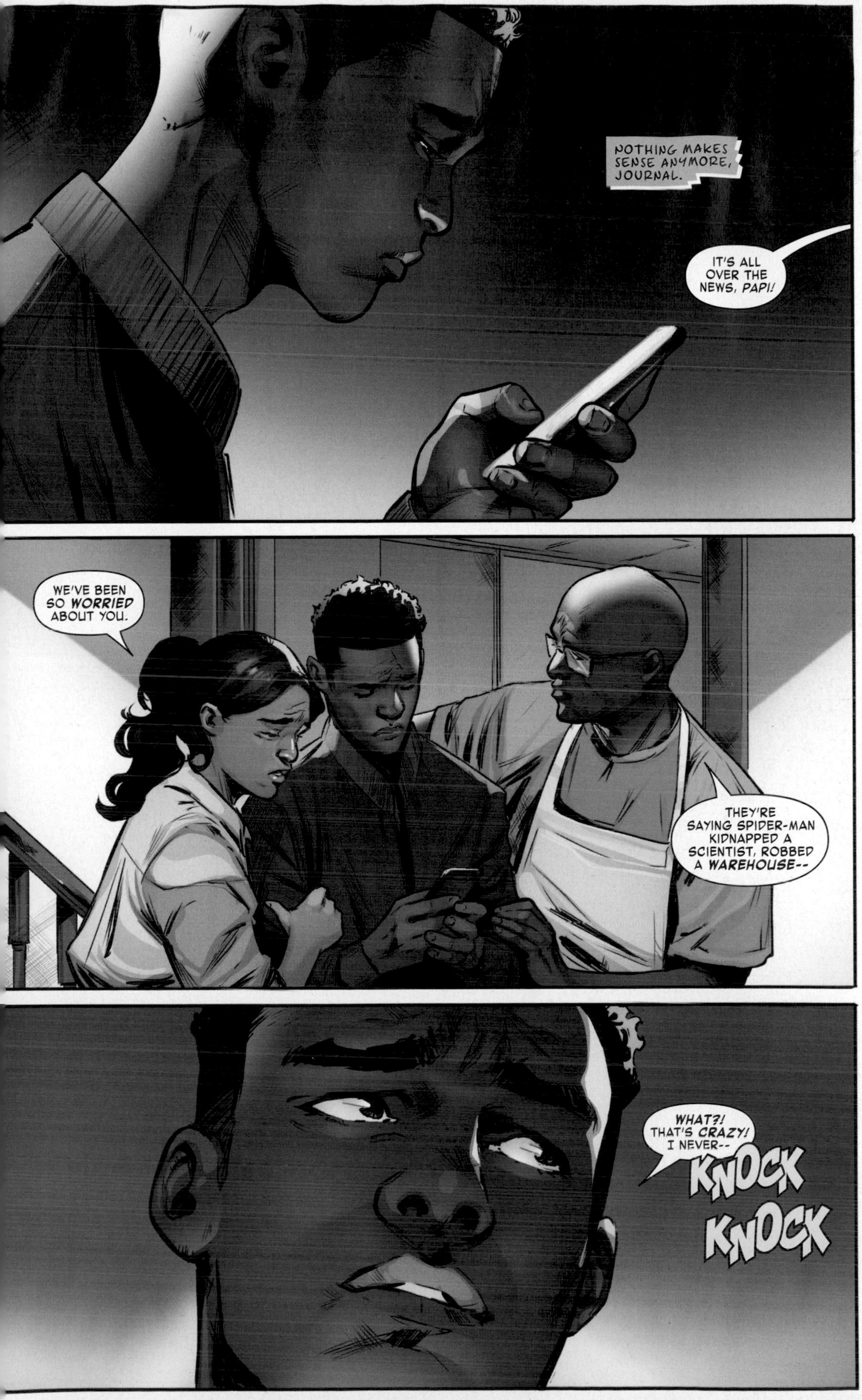
NOTHING MAKES SENSE ANYMORE, JOURNAL.
IT'S ALL OVER THE NEWS, PAPI!
WE'VE BEEN SO WORRIED ABOUT YOU.
THEY'RE SAYING SPIDER-MAN KIDNAPPED A SCIENTIST, ROBBED A WAREHOUSE--
WHAT?! THAT'S CRAZY! I NEVER--
KNOCK
KNOCK

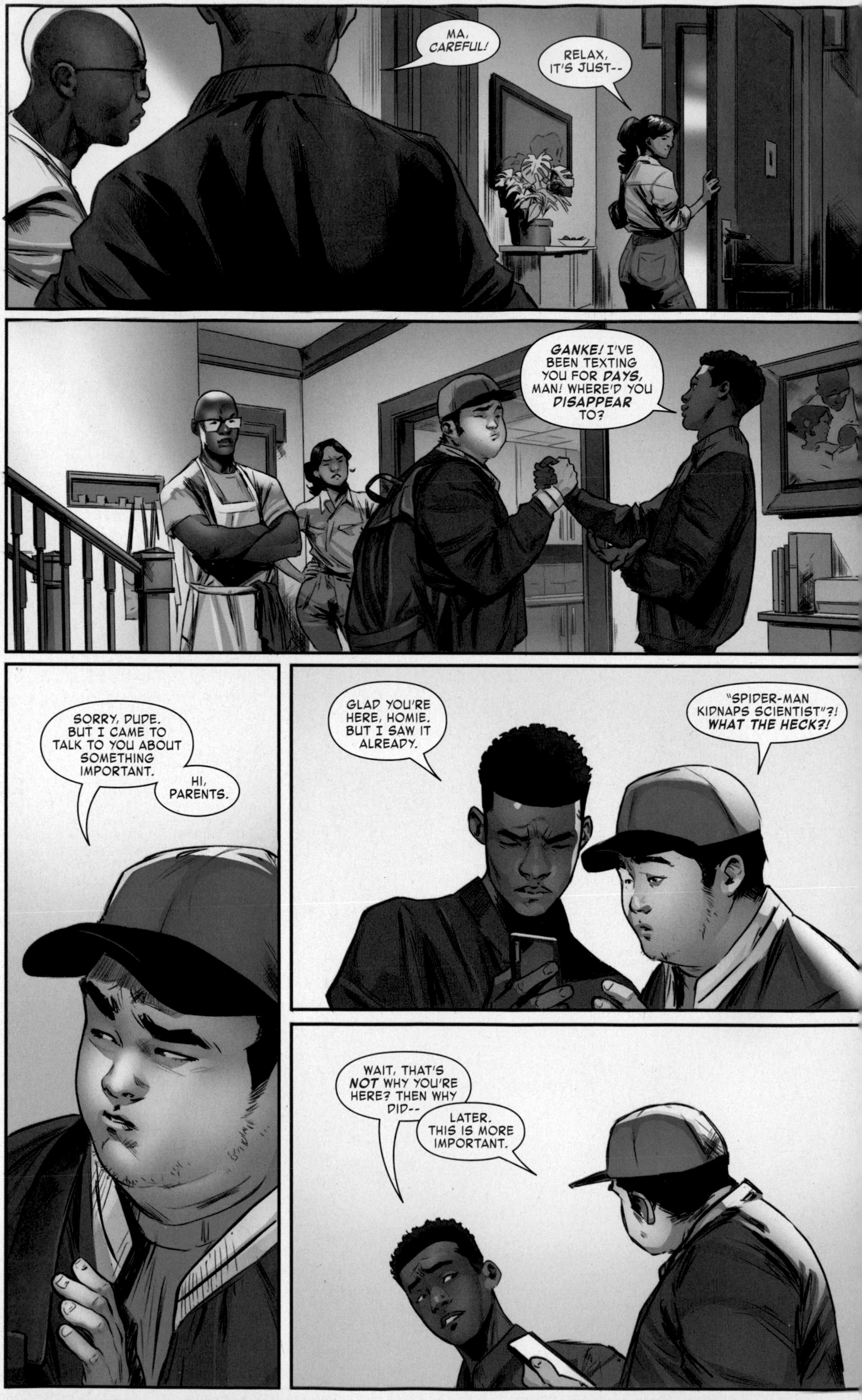

MA, CAREFUL!
RELAX, IT'S JUST--
GANKE! I'VE BEEN TEXTING YOU FOR DAYS, MAN! WHERE'D YOU DISAPPEAR TO?
SORRY, DUDE. BUT I CAME TO TALK TO YOU ABOUT SOMETHING IMPORTANT.
HI, PARENTS.
GLAD YOU'RE HERE, HOMIE. BUT I SAW IT ALREADY.
"SPIDER-MAN KIDNAPS SCIENTIST"?! WHAT THE HECK?!
WAIT, THAT'S NOT WHY YOU'RE HERE? THEN WHY DID--
LATER. THIS IS MORE IMPORTANT.

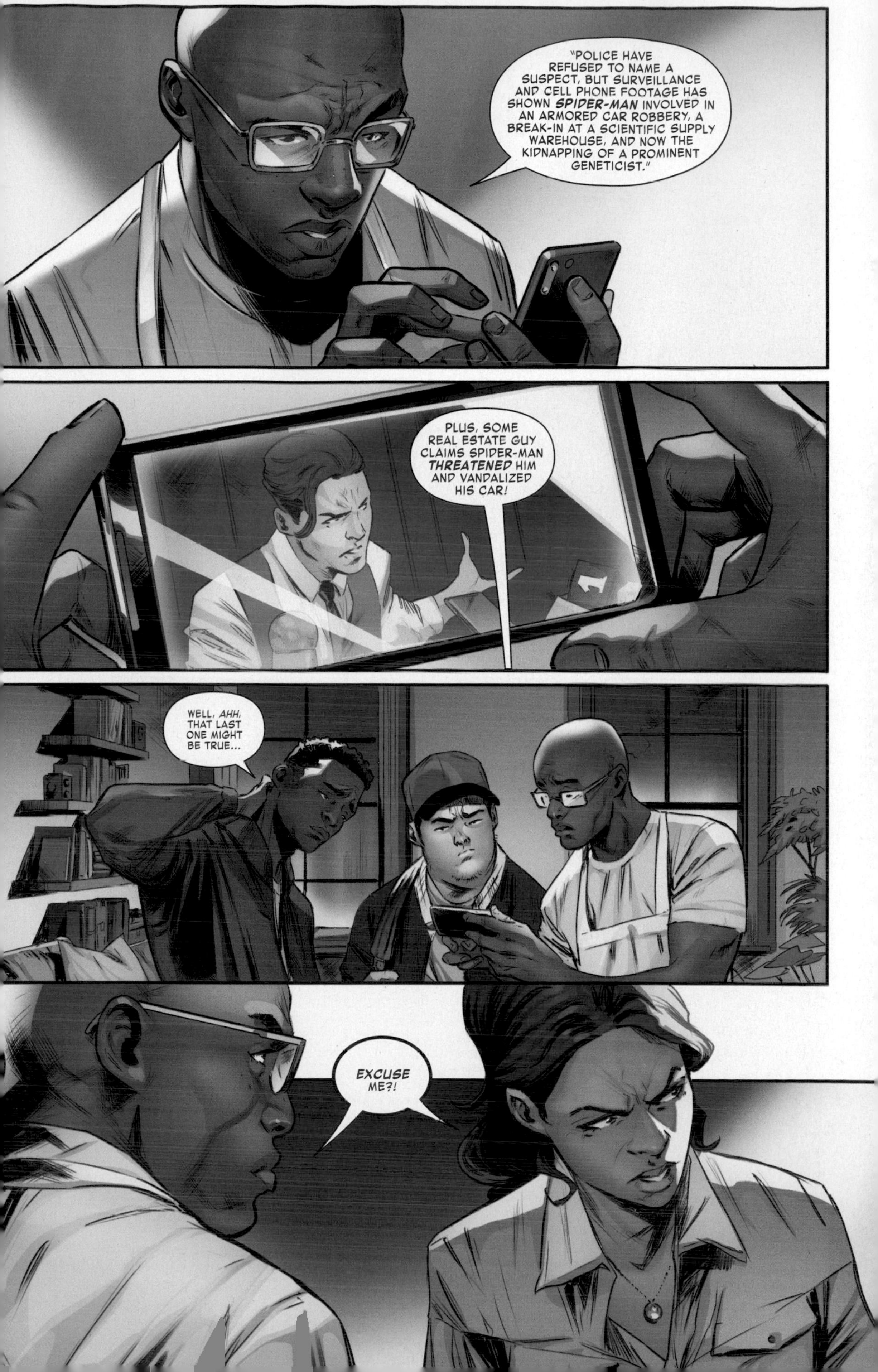
"POLICE HAVE REFUSED TO NAME A SUSPECT, BUT SURVEILLANCE AND CELL PHONE FOOTAGE HAS SHOWN SPIDER-MAN INVOLVED IN AN ARMORED CAR ROBBERY, A BREAK-IN AT A SCIENTIFIC SUPPLY WAREHOUSE, AND NOW THE KIDNAPPING OF A PROMINENT GENETICIST."
PLUS, SOME REAL ESTATE GUY CLAIMS SPIDER-MAN THREATENED HIM AND VANDALIZED HIS CAR!
WELL, AHH, THAT LAST ONE MIGHT BE TRUE...
EXCUSE ME?!

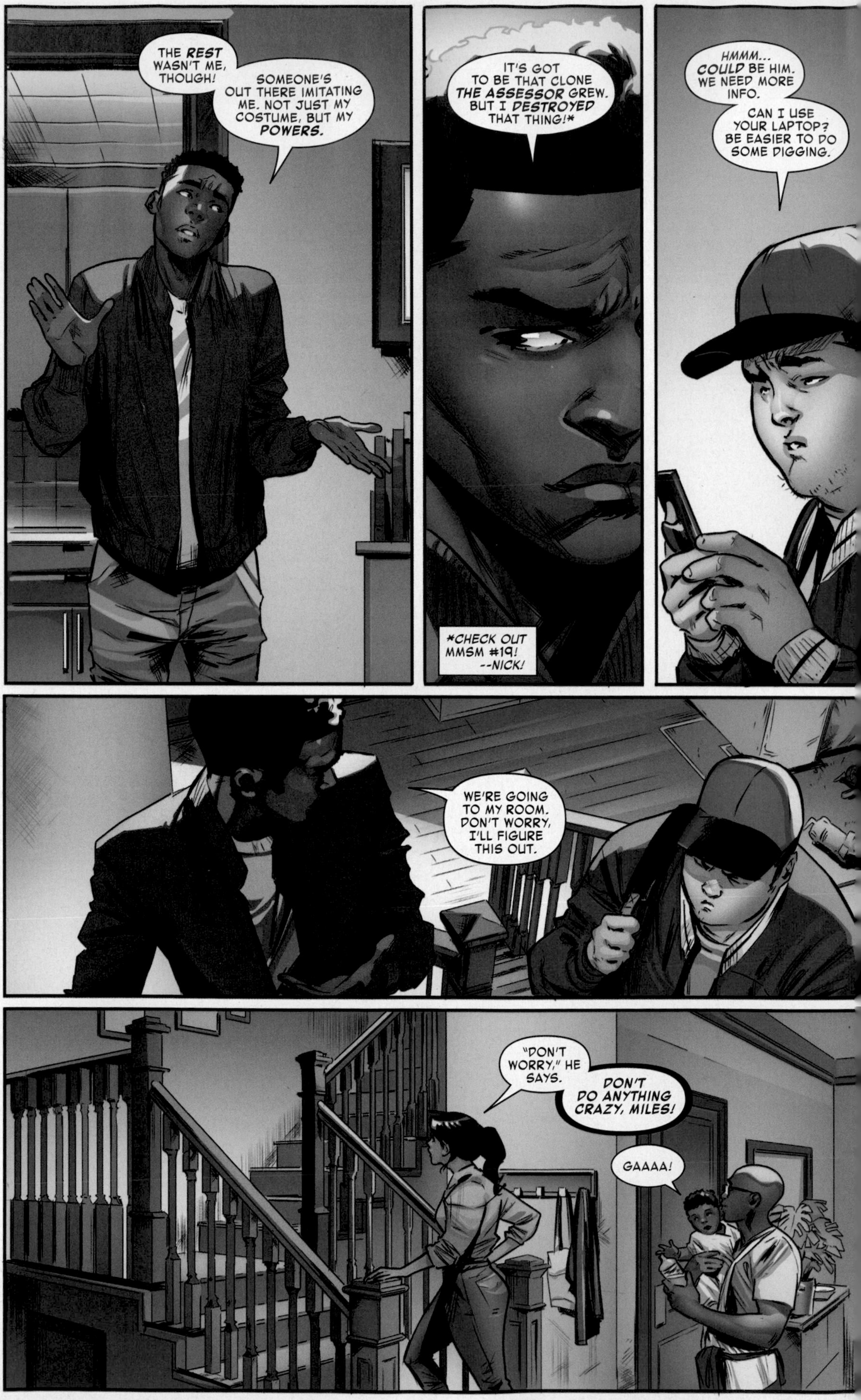
THE REST WASN'T ME, THOUGH!
SOMEONE'S OUT THERE IMITATING ME. NOT JUST MY COSTUME, BUT MY POWERS.
IT'S GOT TO BE THAT CLONE THE ASSESSOR GREW. BUT I DESTROYED THAT THING!*
*CHECK OUT MMSM #19! --NICK!
HMMM... COULD BE HIM. WE NEED MORE INFO.
CAN I USE YOUR LAPTOP? BE EASIER TO DO SOME DIGGING.
WE'RE GOING TO MY ROOM. DON'T WORRY, I'LL FIGURE THIS OUT.
"DON'T WORRY," HE SAYS.
DON'T DO ANYTHING CRAZY, MILES!
GAAAA!

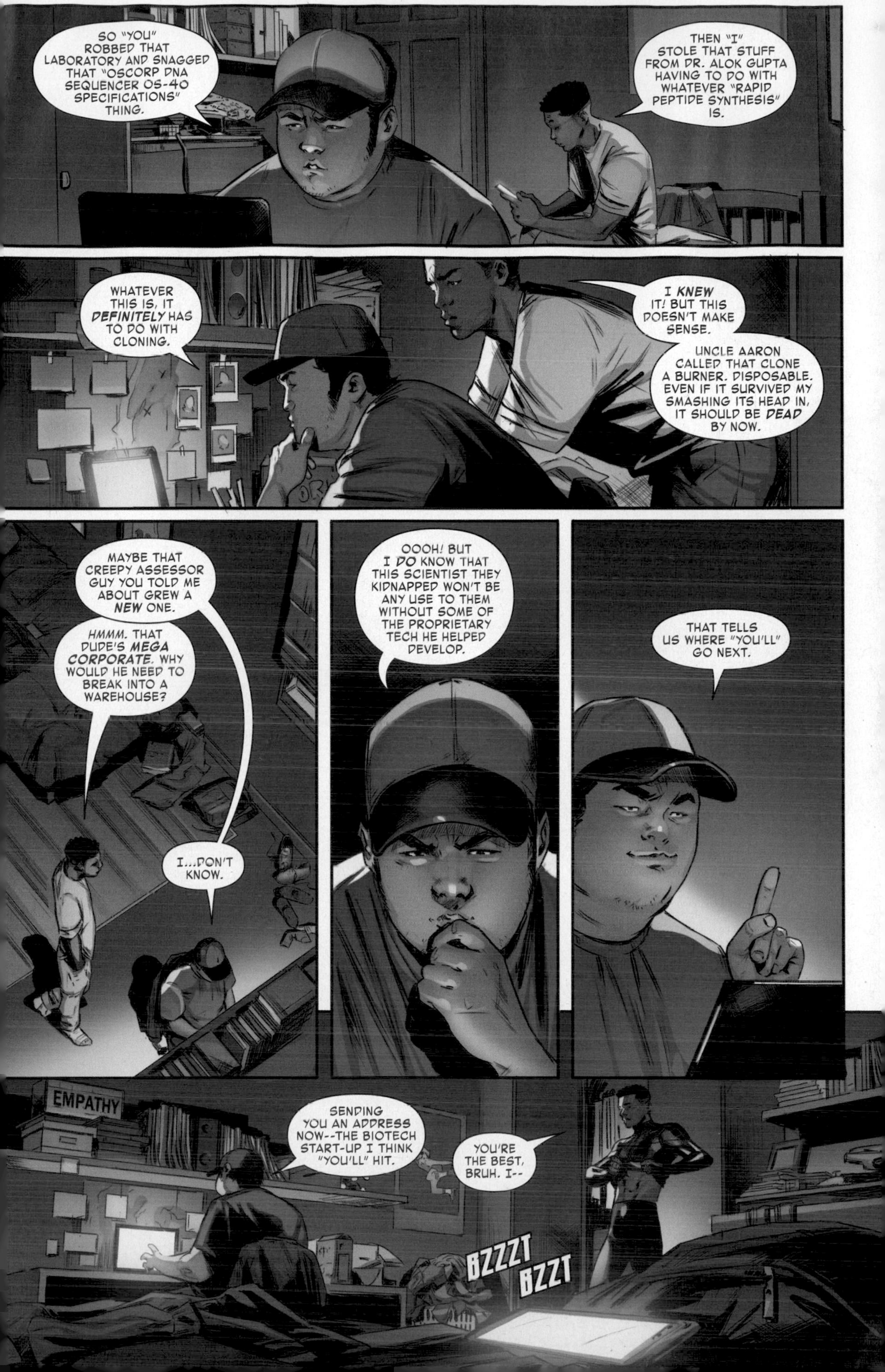
SO "YOU" ROBBED THAT LABORATORY AND SNAGGED THAT "OSCORP DNA SEQUENCER OS-40 SPECIFICATIONS" THING.
THEN "I" STOLE THAT STUFF FROM DR. ALOK GUPTA HAVING TO DO WITH WHATEVER "RAPID PEPTIDE SYNTHESIS" IS.
WHATEVER THIS IS, IT DEFINITELY HAS TO DO WITH CLONING.
I KNEW IT! BUT THIS DOESN'T MAKE SENSE.
UNCLE AARON CALLED THAT CLONE A BURNER. DISPOSABLE. EVEN IF IT SURVIVED MY SMASHING ITS HEAD IN, IT SHOULD BE DEAD BY NOW.
MAYBE THAT CREEPY ASSESSOR GUY YOU TOLD ME ABOUT GREW A NEW ONE.
HMMM. THAT DUDE'S MEGA CORPORATE. WHY WOULD HE NEED TO BREAK INTO A WAREHOUSE?
I...DON'T KNOW.
OOOH! BUT I DO KNOW THAT THIS SCIENTIST THEY KIDNAPPED WON'T BE ANY USE TO THEM WITHOUT SOME OF THE PROPRIETARY TECH HE HELPED DEVELOP.
THAT TELLS US WHERE "YOU'LL" GO NEXT.
EMPATHY
SENDING YOU AN ADDRESS NOW--THE BIOTECH START-UP I THINK "YOU'LL" HIT.
YOU'RE THE BEST, BRUH. I--
BZZZT
BZZT

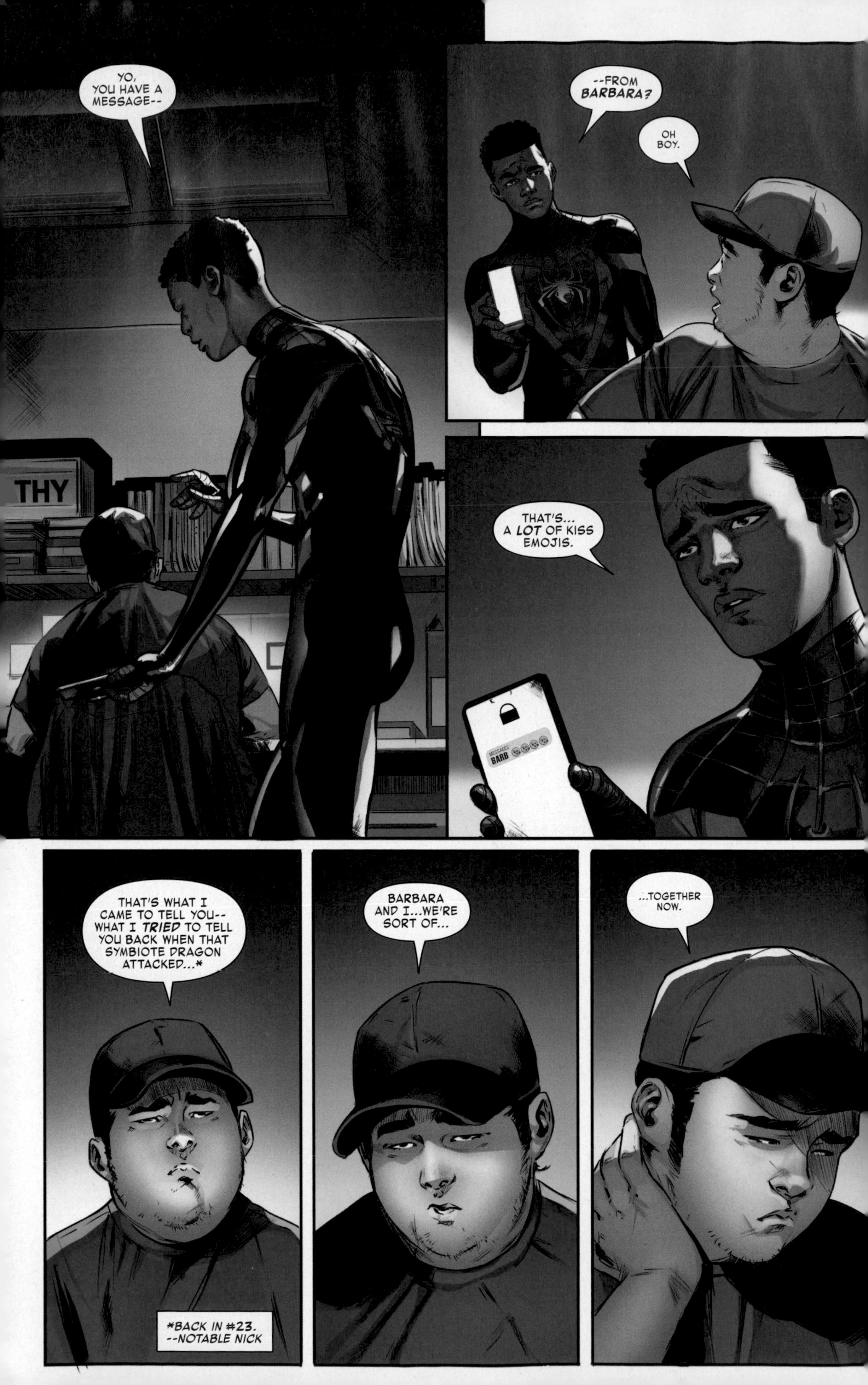
YO, YOU HAVE A MESSAGE--
THY
--FROM BARBARA?
OH BOY.
THAT'S... A LOT OF KISS EMOJIS.
MESSAGES BARB
THAT'S WHAT I CAME TO TELL YOU-- WHAT I TRIED TO TELL YOU BACK WHEN THAT SYMBIOTE DRAGON ATTACKED...*
*BACK IN #23. --NOTABLE NICK
BARBARA AND I...WE'RE SORT OF...
...TOGETHER NOW.

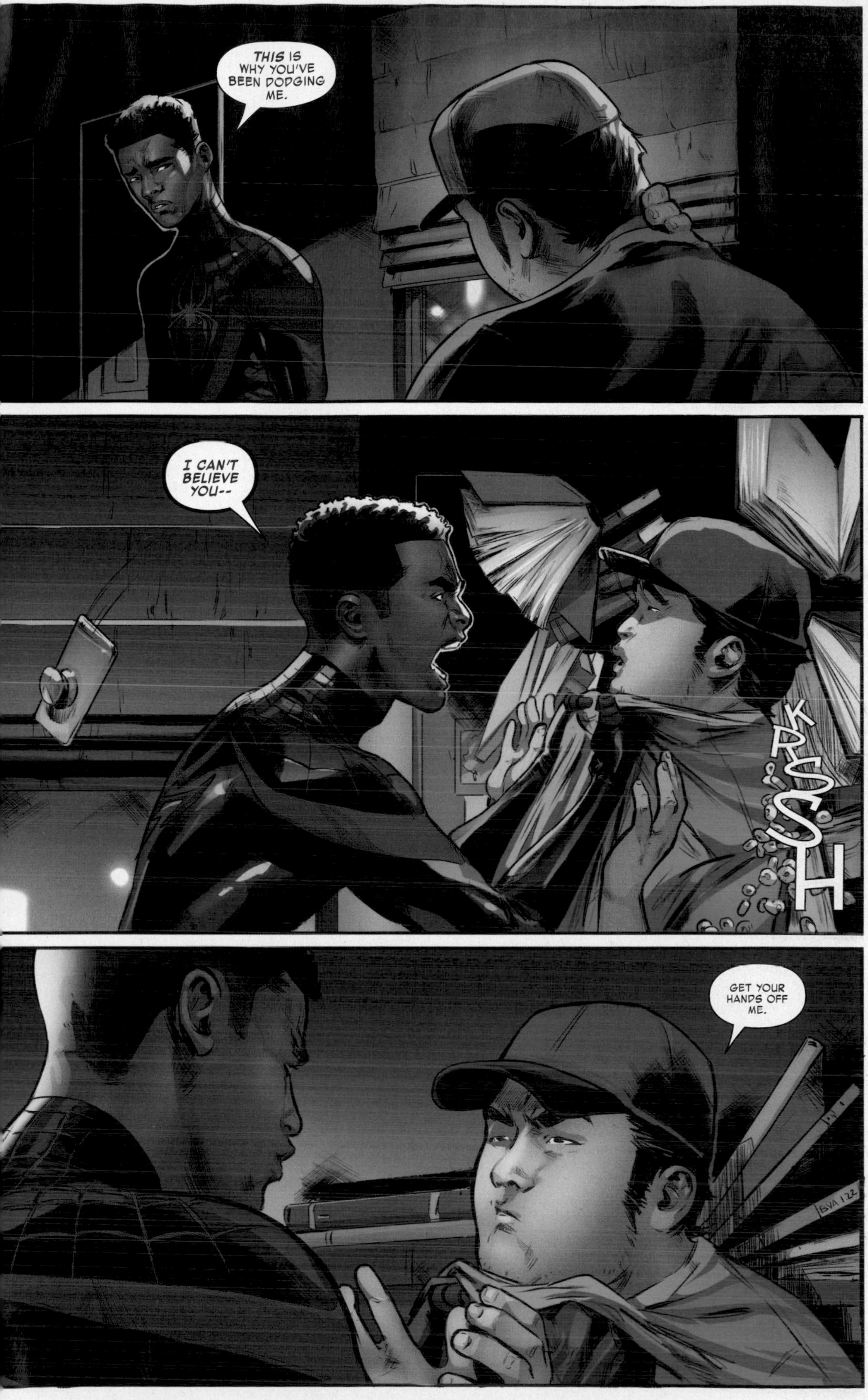
THIS IS WHY YOU'VE BEEN DODGING ME.
I CAN'T BELIEVE YOU--
KRSSH
GET YOUR HANDS OFF ME.

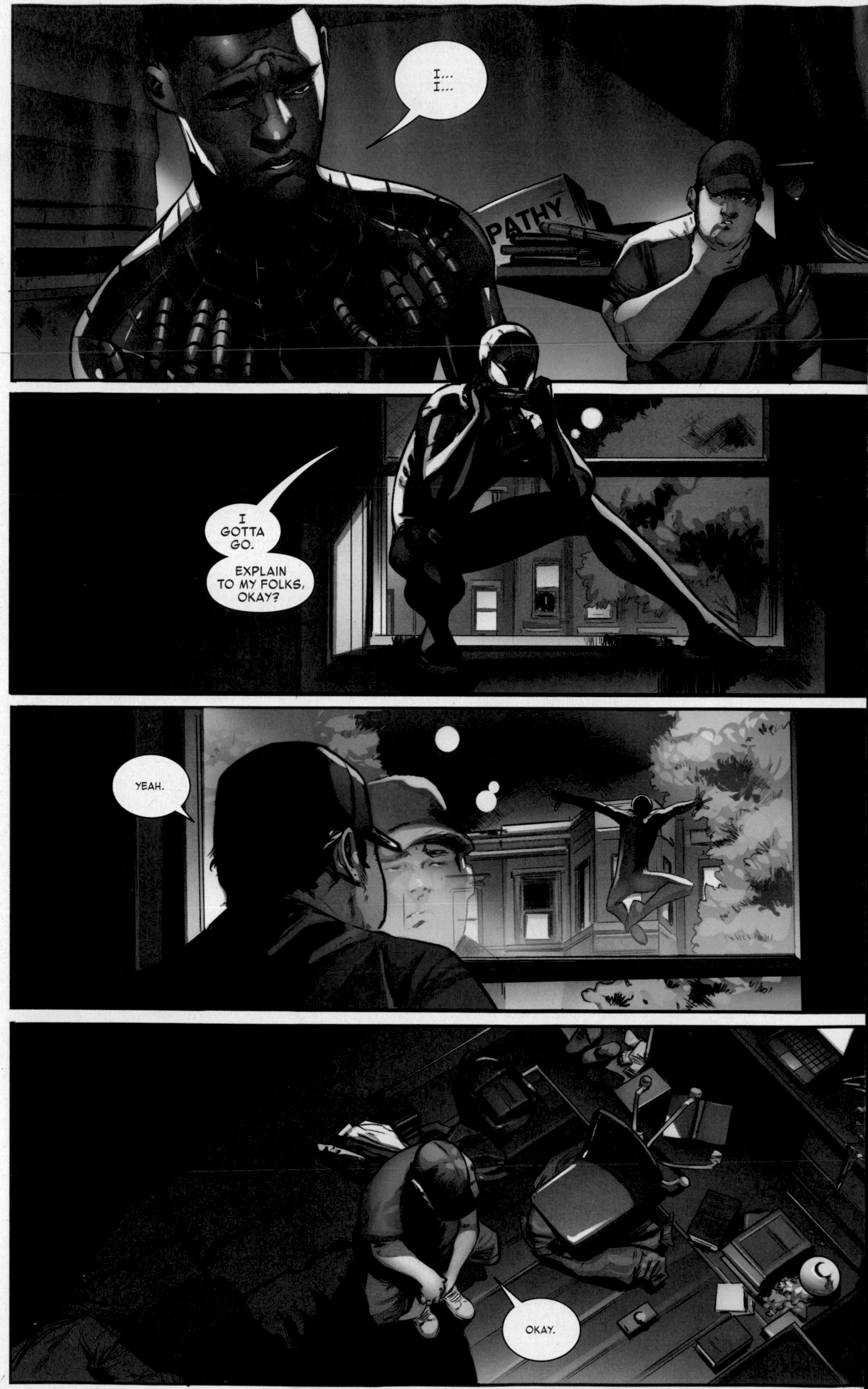
I...
I...
PATHY
I GOTTA GO.
EXPLAIN TO MY FOLKS, OKAY?
YEAH.
OKAY.

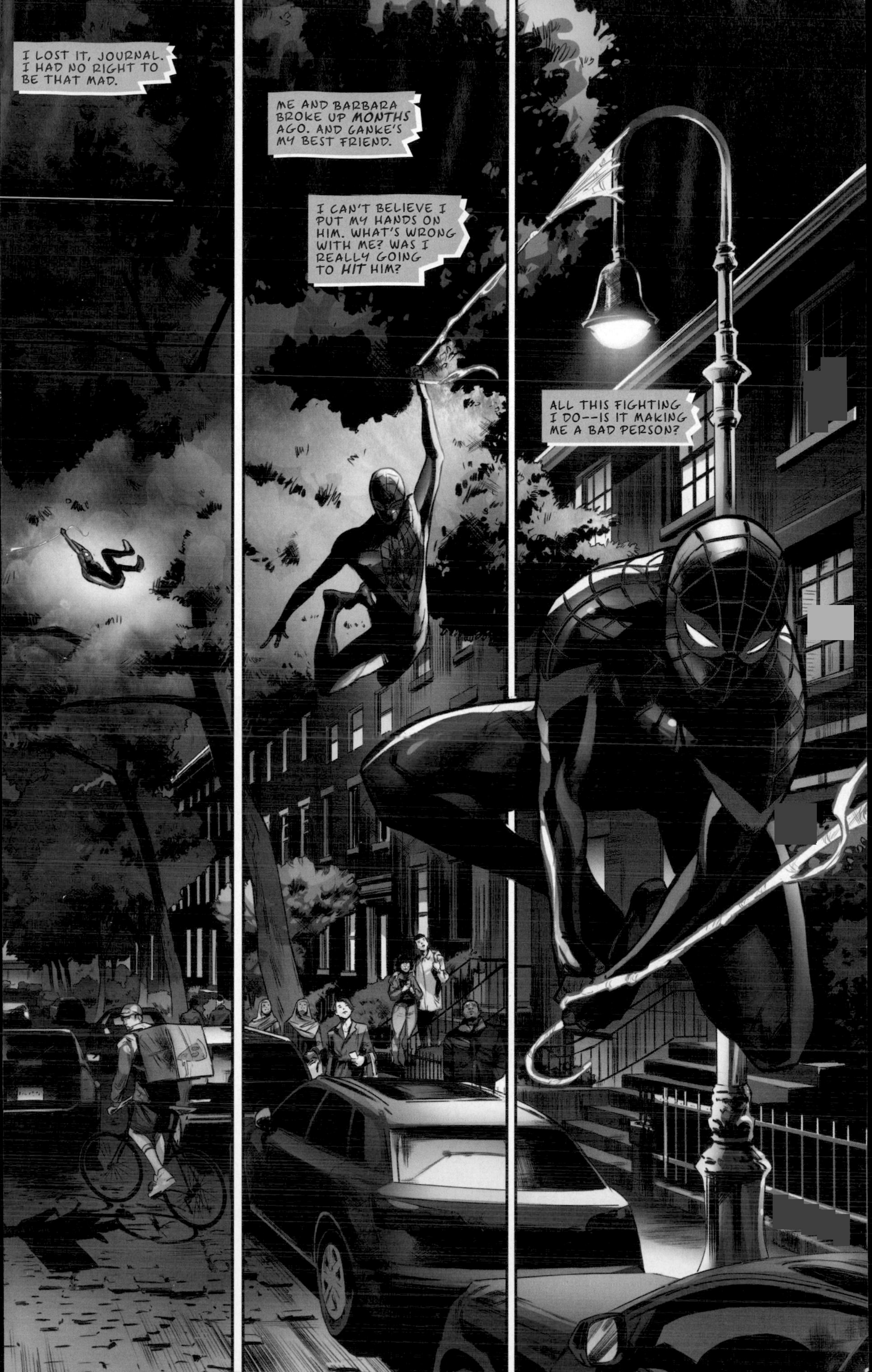
I LOST IT, JOURNAL. I HAD NO RIGHT TO BE THAT MAD.
ME AND BARBARA BROKE UP MONTHS AGO. AND GANKE'S MY BEST FRIEND.
I CAN'T BELIEVE I PUT MY HANDS ON HIM. WHAT'S WRONG WITH ME? WAS I REALLY GOING TO HIT HIM?
ALL THIS FIGHTING I DO--IS IT MAKING ME A BAD PERSON?

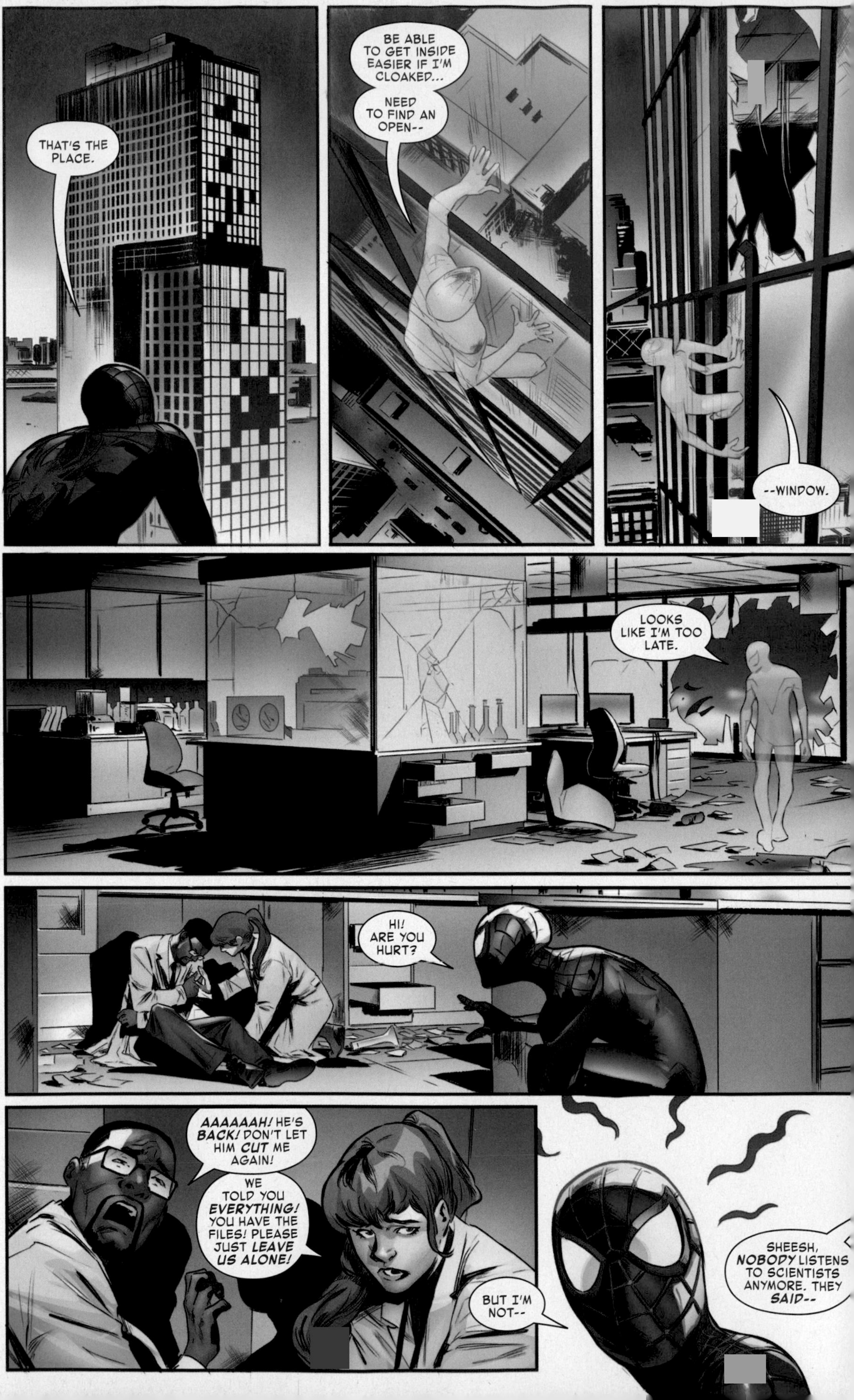
THAT'S THE PLACE.
BE ABLE TO GET INSIDE EASIER IF I'M CLOAKED...
NEED TO FIND AN OPEN--
--WINDOW.
LOOKS LIKE I'M TOO LATE.
HI! ARE YOU HURT?
AAAAAAH! HE'S BACK! DON'T LET HIM CUT ME AGAIN!
WE TOLD YOU EVERYTHING! YOU HAVE THE FILES! PLEASE JUST LEAVE US ALONE!
BUT I'M NOT--
SHEESH, NOBODY LISTENS TO SCIENTISTS ANYMORE. THEY SAID--

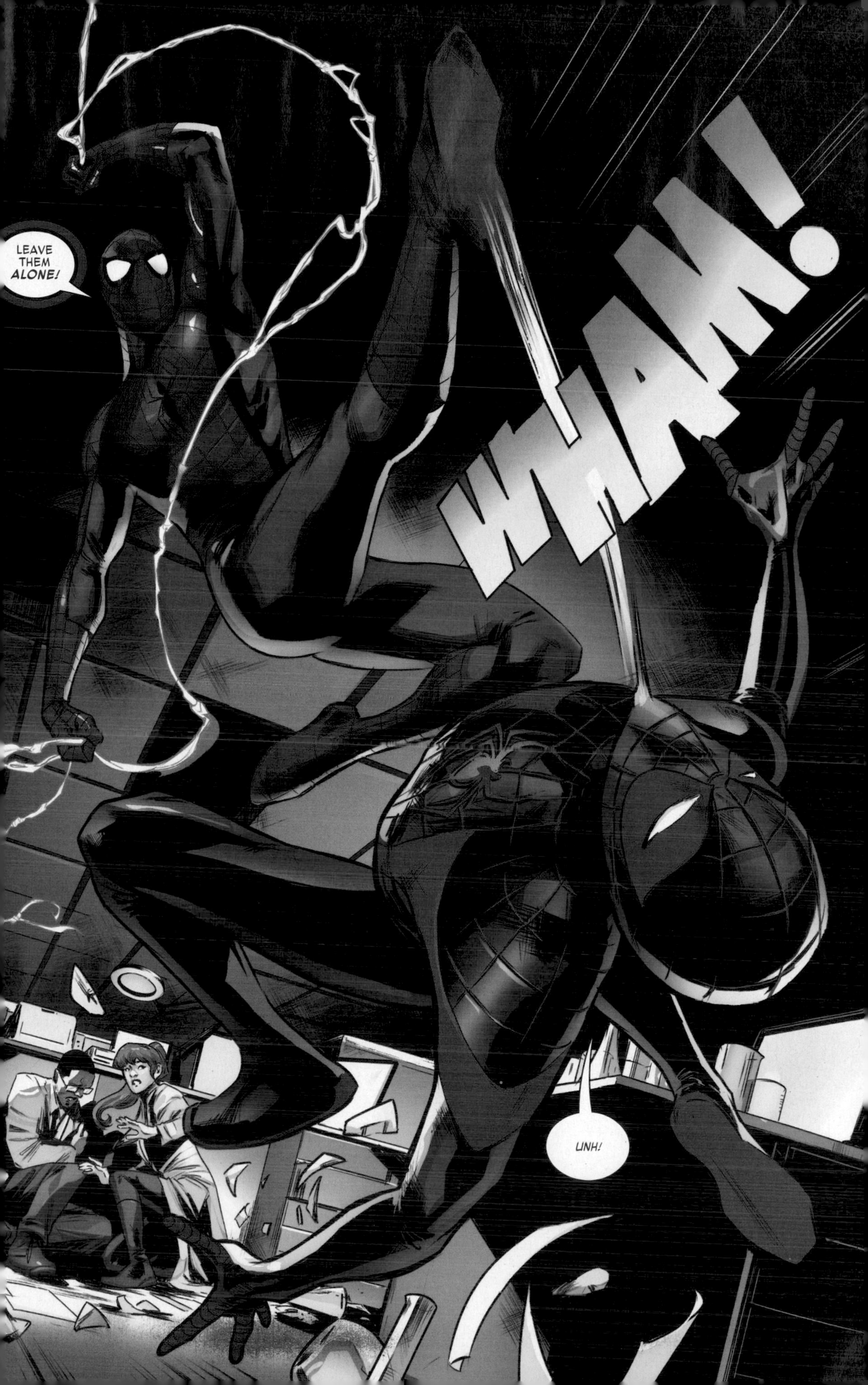
LEAVE THEM ALONE!
WHAM!
UNH!

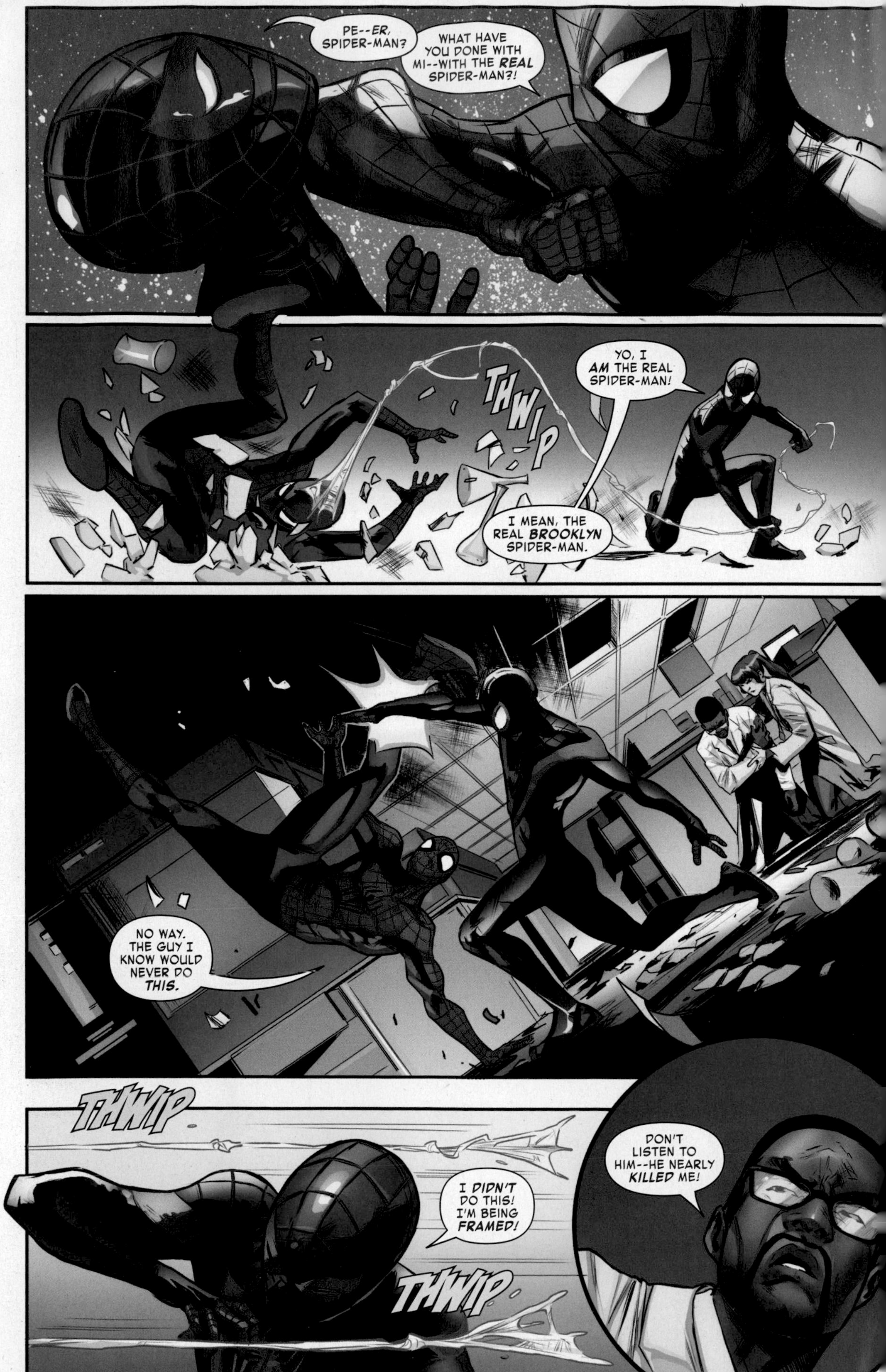

PE--ER, SPIDER-MAN?
WHAT HAVE YOU DONE WITH MI--WITH THE REAL SPIDER-MAN?!
THWIP
YO, I AM THE REAL SPIDER-MAN!
I MEAN, THE REAL BROOKLYN SPIDER-MAN.
NO WAY. THE GUY I KNOW WOULD NEVER DO THIS.
THWIP
I DIDN'T DO THIS! I'M BEING FRAMED!
DON'T LISTEN TO HIM--HE NEARLY KILLED ME!
THWIP

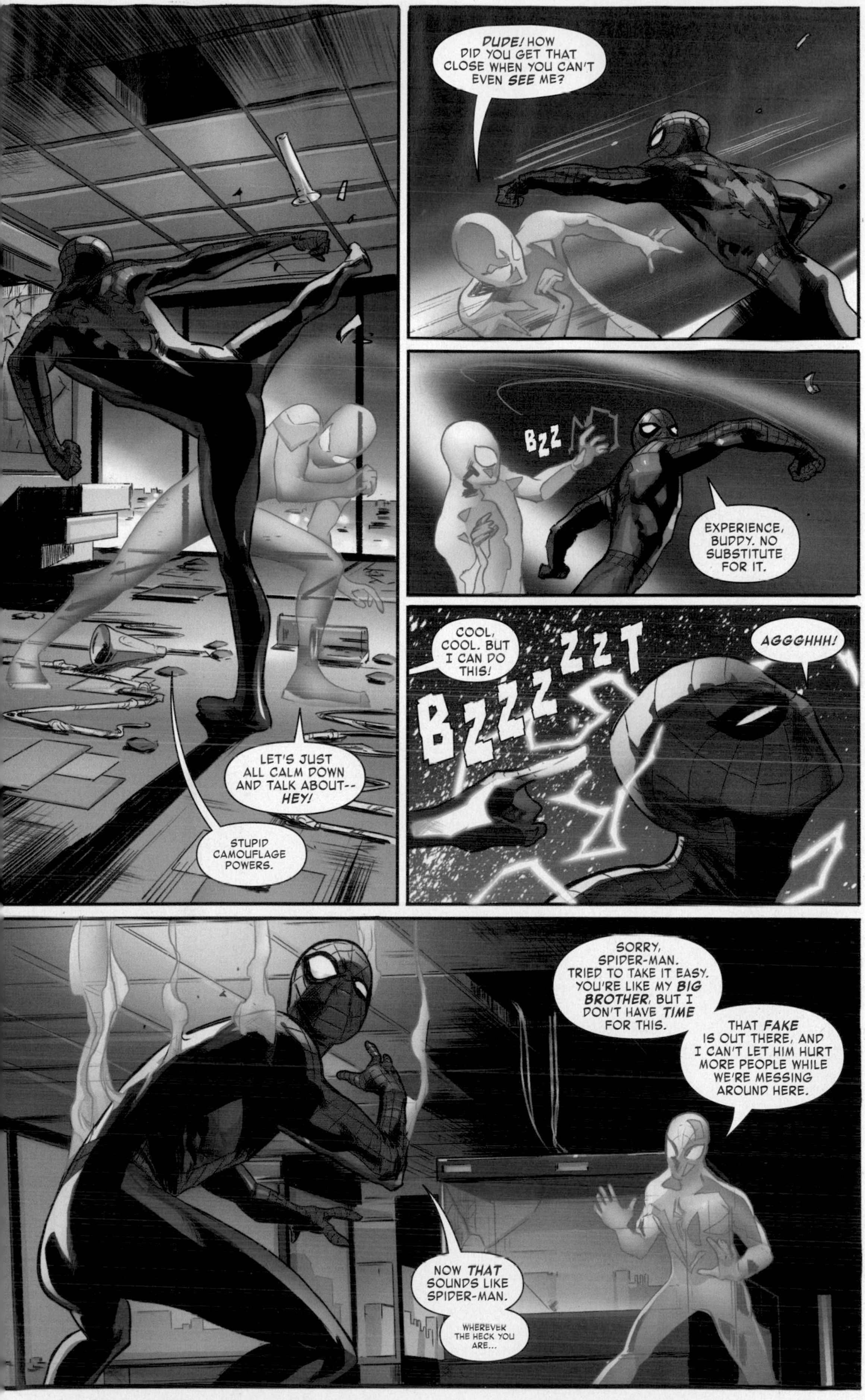
LET'S JUST ALL CALM DOWN AND TALK ABOUT-- HEY!
STUPID CAMOUFLAGE POWERS.
DUDE! HOW DID YOU GET THAT CLOSE WHEN YOU CAN'T EVEN SEE ME?
BZZ
EXPERIENCE, BUDDY. NO SUBSTITUTE FOR IT.
COOL, COOL. BUT I CAN DO THIS!
BZZZZZZT
AGGGHHH!
SORRY, SPIDER-MAN. TRIED TO TAKE IT EASY. YOU'RE LIKE MY BIG BROTHER, BUT I DON'T HAVE TIME FOR THIS.
THAT FAKE IS OUT THERE, AND I CAN'T LET HIM HURT MORE PEOPLE WHILE WE'RE MESSING AROUND HERE.
NOW THAT SOUNDS LIKE SPIDER-MAN.
WHEREVER THE HECK YOU ARE...

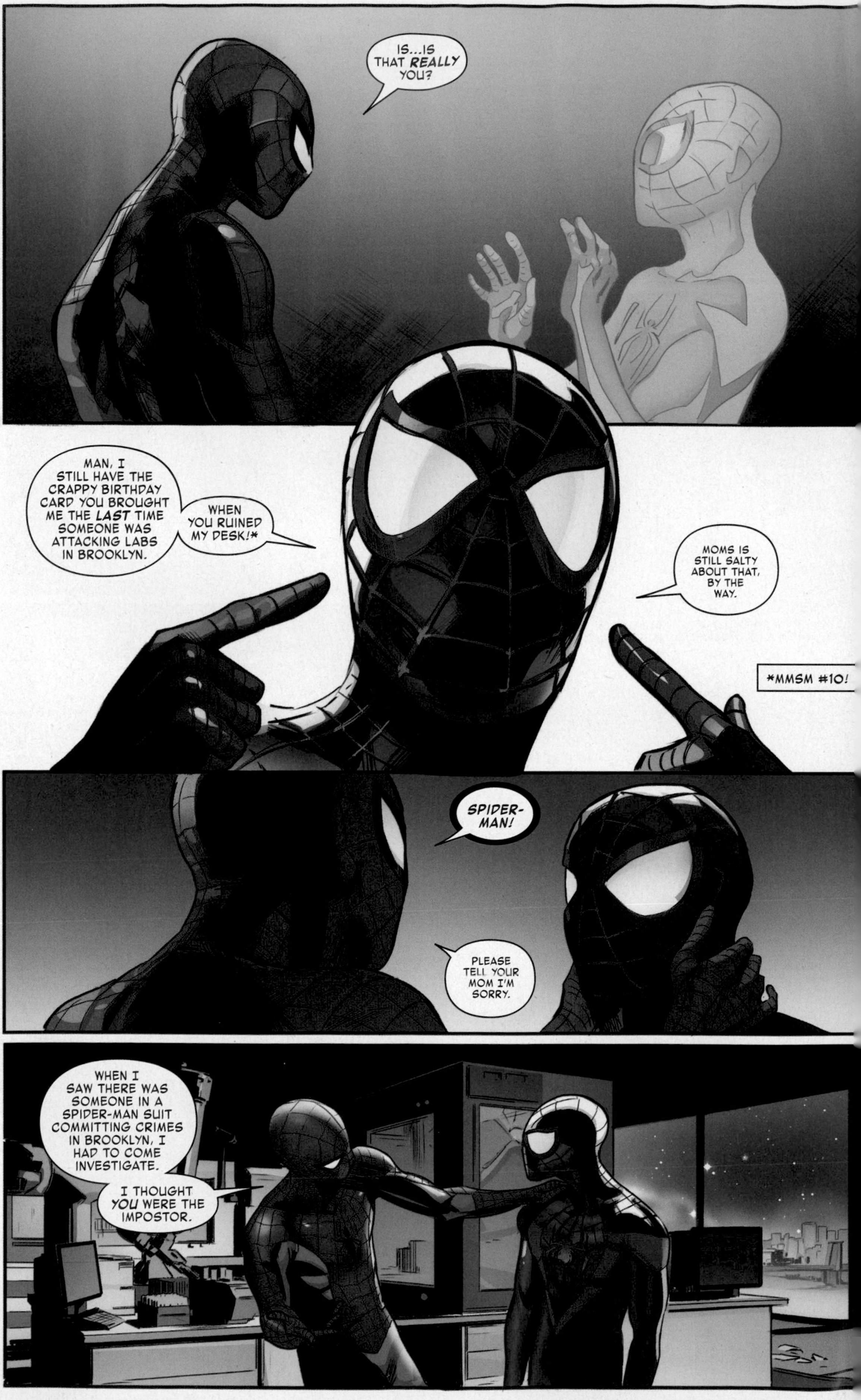
IS...IS THAT REALLY YOU?
MAN, I STILL HAVE THE CRAPPY BIRTHDAY CARD YOU BROUGHT ME THE LAST TIME SOMEONE WAS ATTACKING LABS IN BROOKLYN.
WHEN YOU RUINED MY DESK!*
MOMS IS STILL SALTY ABOUT THAT, BY THE WAY.
*MMSM #10!
SPIDER-MAN!
PLEASE TELL YOUR MOM I'M SORRY.
WHEN I SAW THERE WAS SOMEONE IN A SPIDER-MAN SUIT COMMITTING CRIMES IN BROOKLYN, I HAD TO COME INVESTIGATE.
I THOUGHT YOU WERE THE IMPOSTOR.

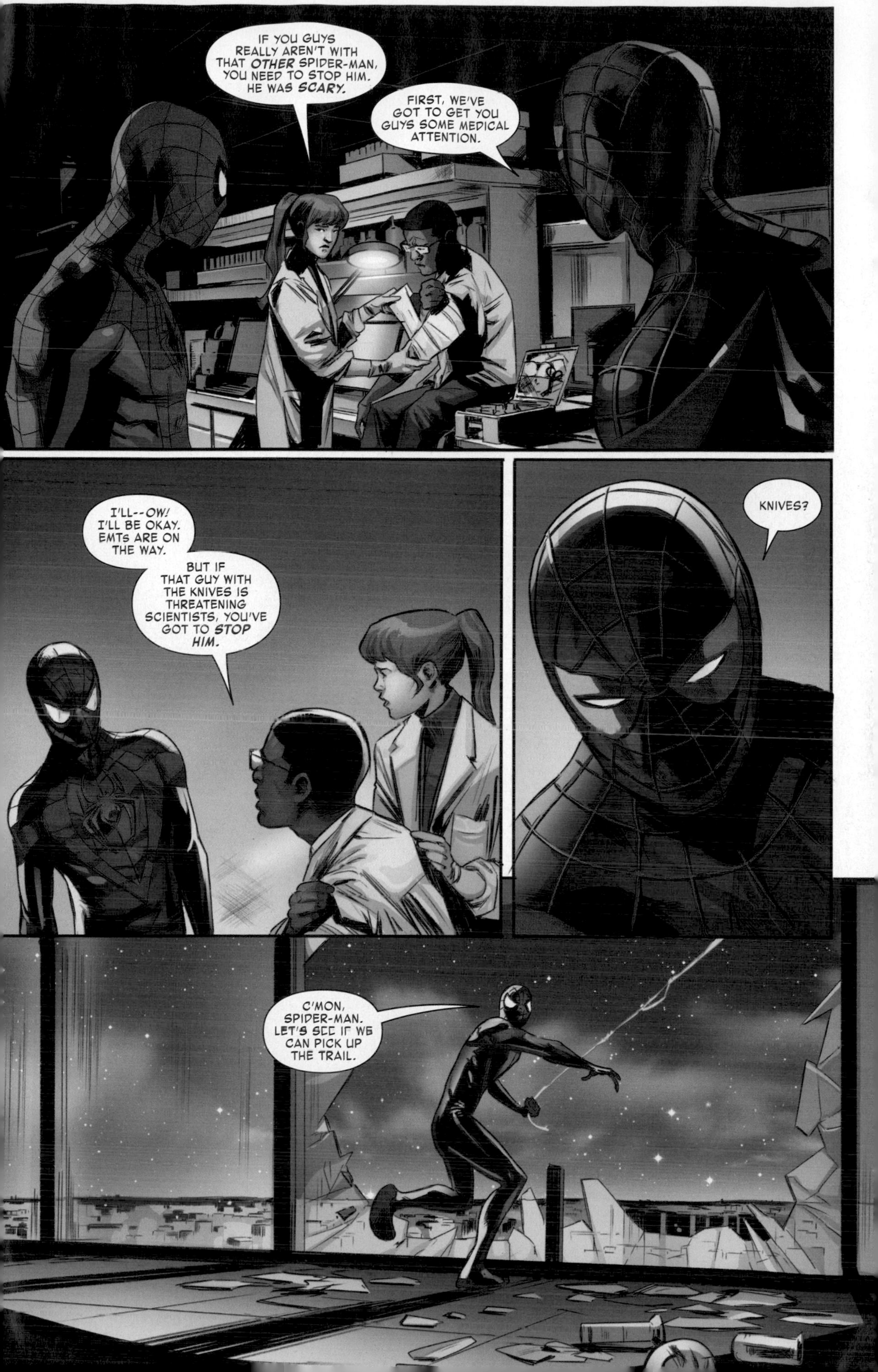
IF YOU GUYS REALLY AREN'T WITH THAT OTHER SPIDER-MAN, YOU NEED TO STOP HIM. HE WAS SCARY.
FIRST, WE'VE GOT TO GET YOU GUYS SOME MEDICAL ATTENTION.
I'LL--OW! I'LL BE OKAY. EMTs ARE ON THE WAY.
BUT IF THAT GUY WITH THE KNIVES IS THREATENING SCIENTISTS, YOU'VE GOT TO STOP HIM.
KNIVES?
C'MON, SPIDER-MAN. LET'S SEE IF WE CAN PICK UP THE TRAIL.

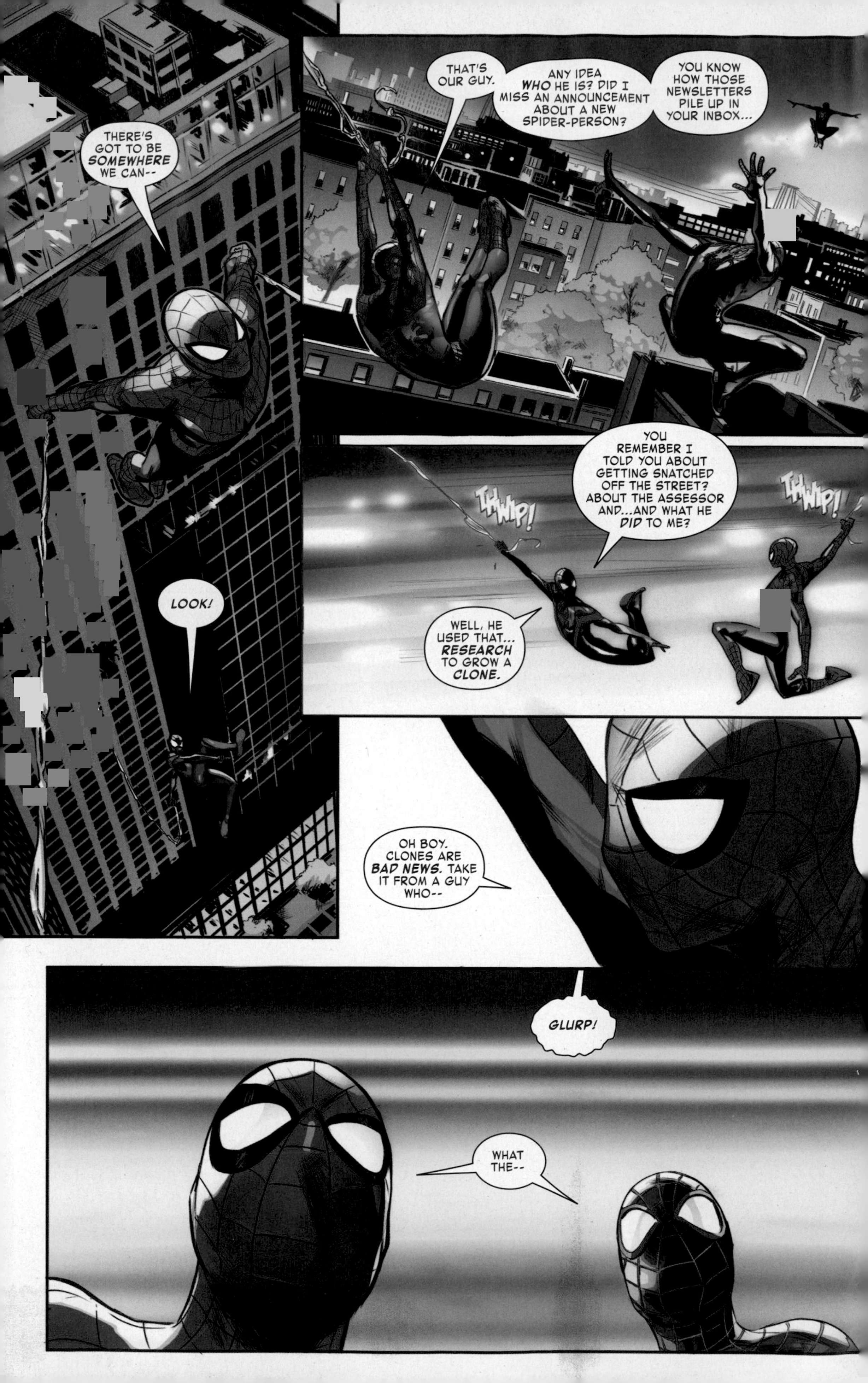
THERE'S GOT TO BE SOMEWHERE WE CAN--
LOOK!
THAT'S OUR GUY.
ANY IDEA WHO HE IS? DID I MISS AN ANNOUNCEMENT ABOUT A NEW SPIDER-PERSON?
YOU KNOW HOW THOSE NEWSLETTERS PILE UP IN YOUR INBOX...
THWIP!
YOU REMEMBER I TOLD YOU ABOUT GETTING SNATCHED OFF THE STREET? ABOUT THE ASSESSOR AND...AND WHAT HE DID TO ME?
THWIP!
WELL, HE USED THAT... RESEARCH TO GROW A CLONE.
OH BOY. CLONES ARE BAD NEWS. TAKE IT FROM A GUY WHO--
GLURP!
WHAT THE--

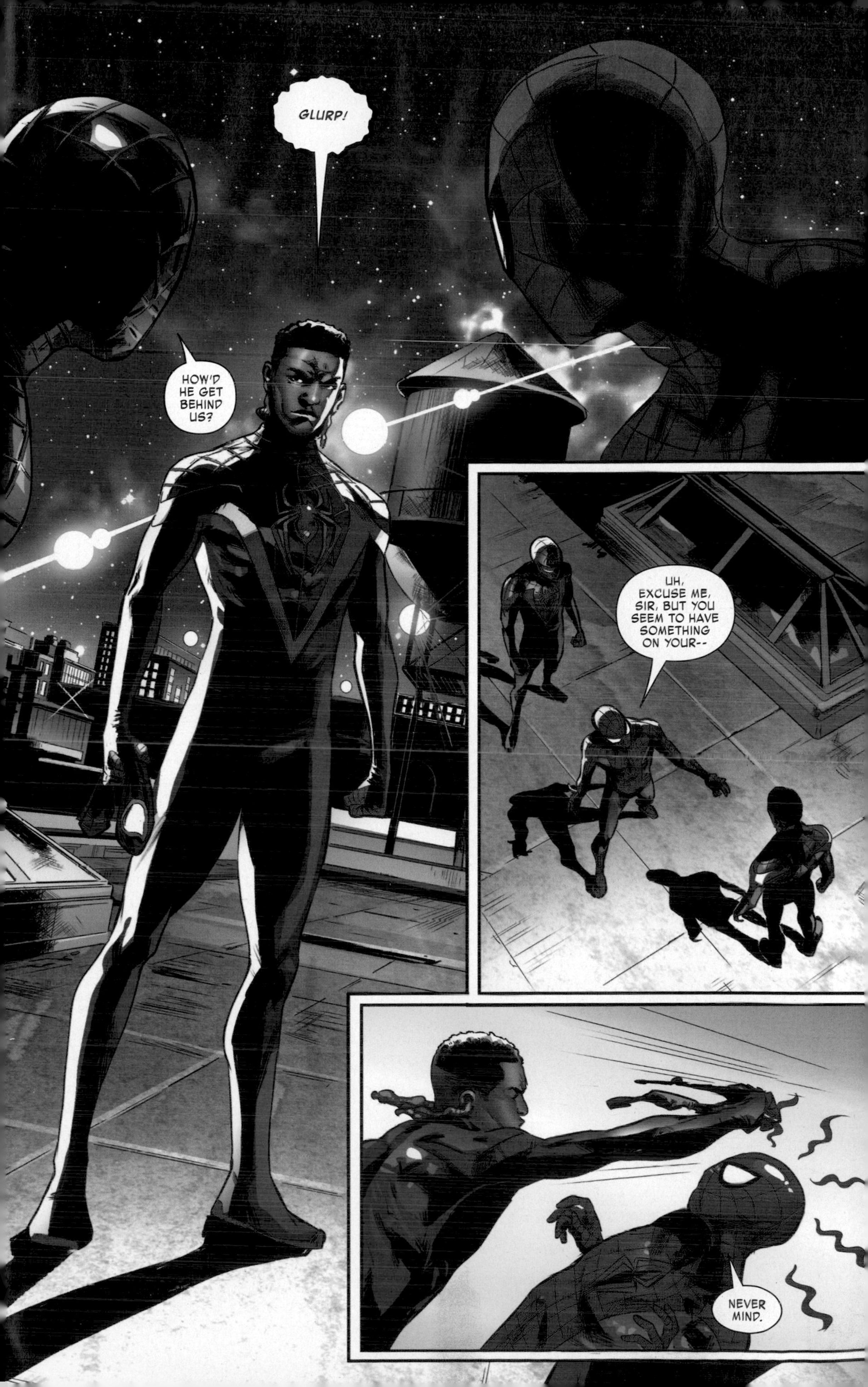
GLURP!
HOW'D HE GET BEHIND US?
UH, EXCUSE ME, SIR, BUT YOU SEEM TO HAVE SOMETHING ON YOUR--
NEVER MIND.

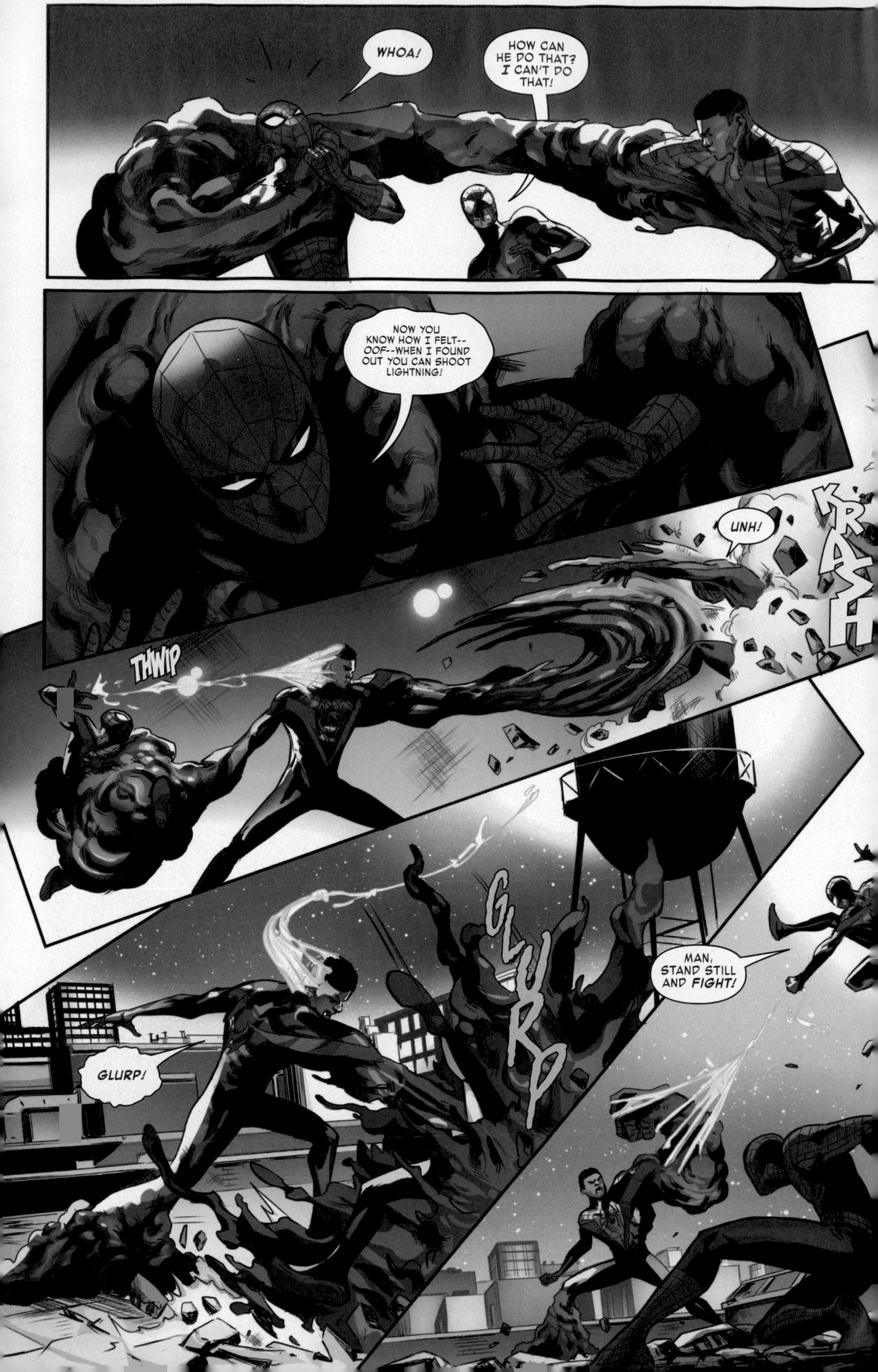
WHOA!
HOW CAN HE DO THAT? I CAN'T DO THAT!
NOW YOU KNOW HOW I FELT-- OOF--WHEN I FOUND OUT YOU CAN SHOOT LIGHTNING!
UNH!
KRASH
THWIP
GLURP
MAN, STAND STILL AND FIGHT!
GLURP!

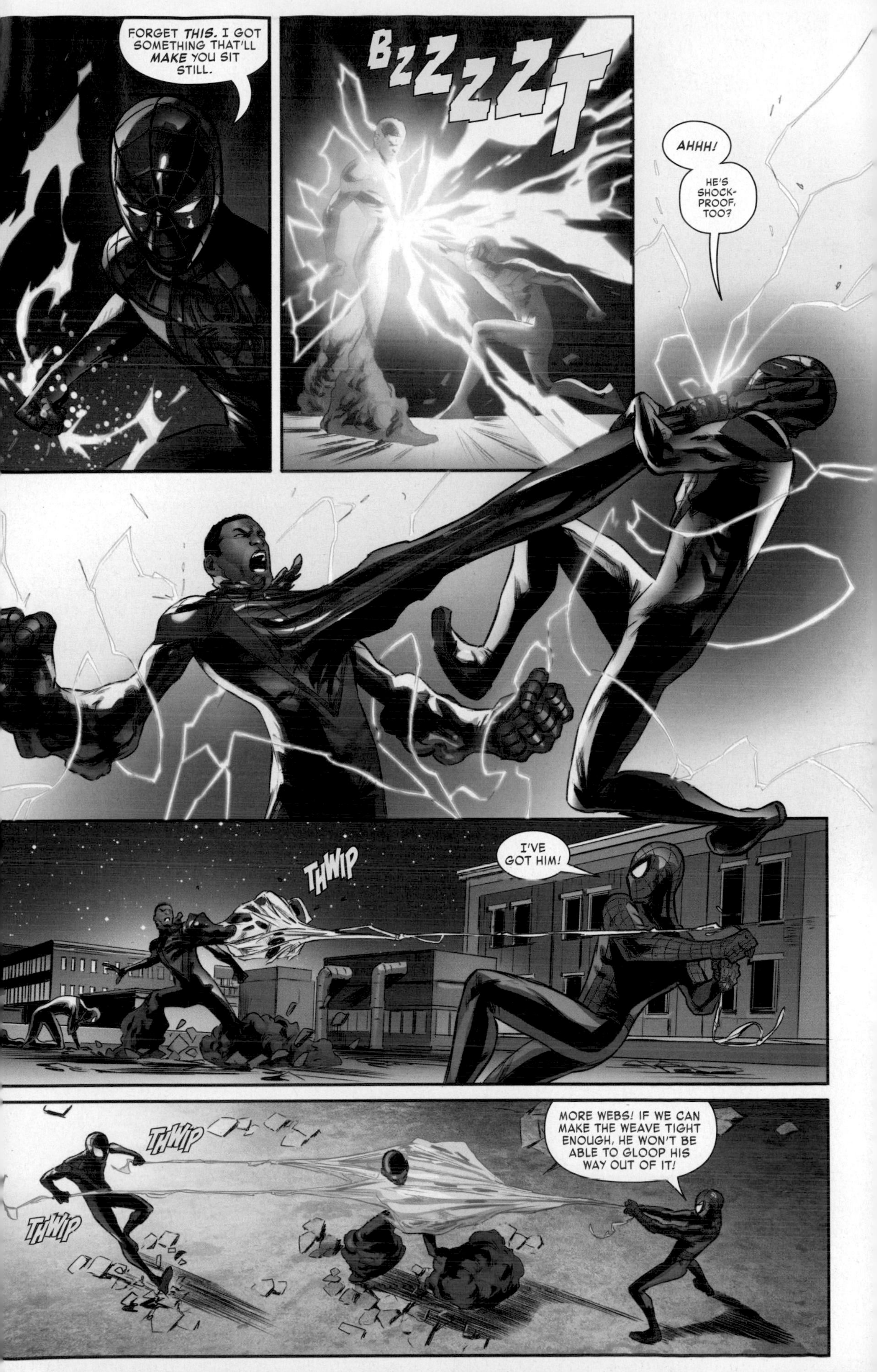
FORGET THIS. I GOT SOMETHING THAT'LL MAKE YOU SIT STILL.
BZZZZT
AHHH!
HE'S SHOCK-PROOF, TOO?
THWIP
I'VE GOT HIM!
THWIP
THWIP
MORE WEBS! IF WE CAN MAKE THE WEAVE TIGHT ENOUGH, HE WON'T BE ABLE TO GLOOP HIS WAY OUT OF IT!

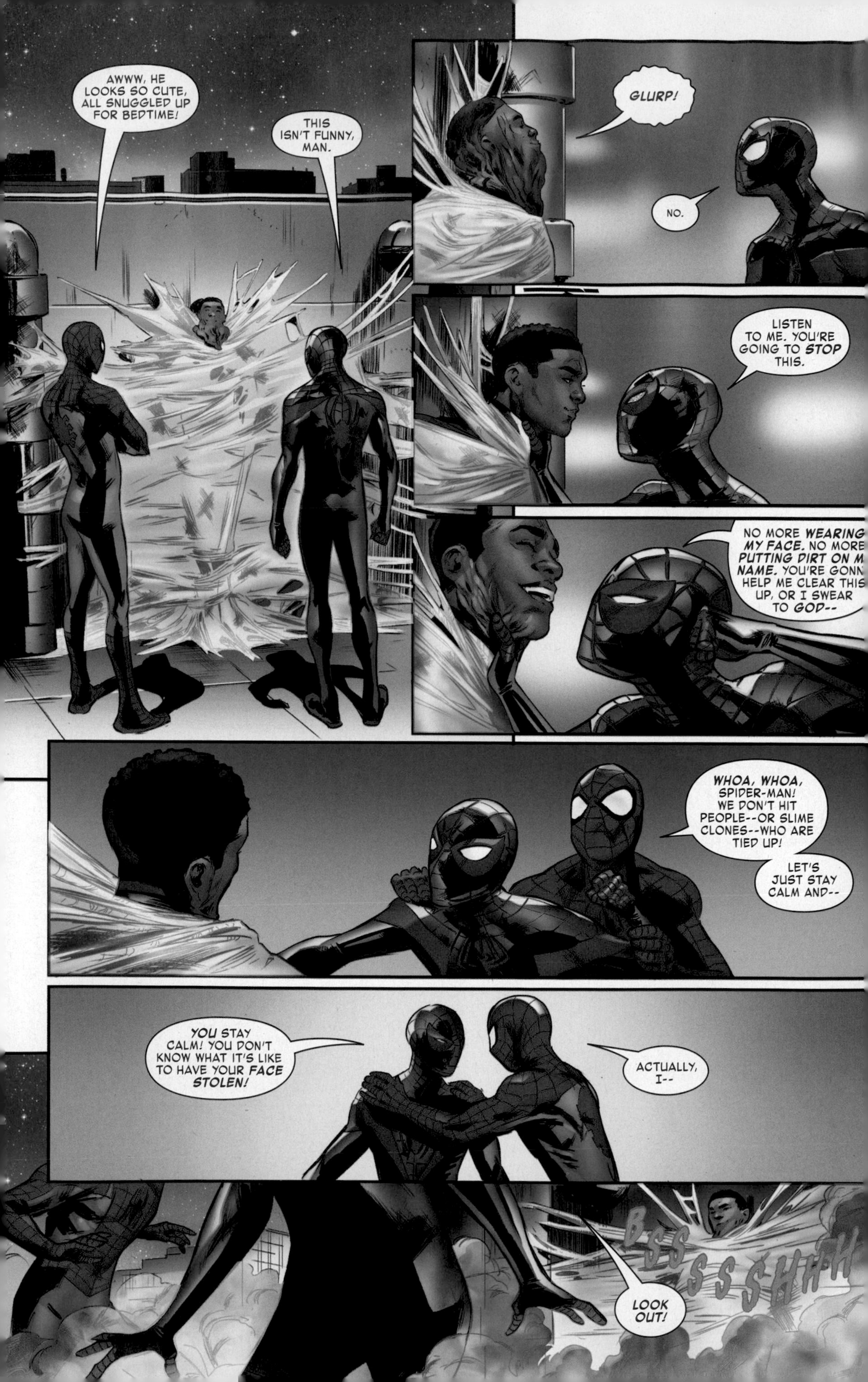
AWWW, HE LOOKS SO CUTE, ALL SNUGGLED UP FOR BEDTIME!
THIS ISN'T FUNNY, MAN.
GLURP!
NO.
LISTEN TO ME. YOU'RE GOING TO STOP THIS.
NO MORE WEARING MY FACE. NO MORE PUTTING DIRT ON M NAME. YOU'RE GONN HELP ME CLEAR THIS UP, OR I SWEAR TO GOD--
WHOA, WHOA, SPIDER-MAN! WE DON'T HIT PEOPLE--OR SLIME CLONES--WHO ARE TIED UP!
LET'S JUST STAY CALM AND--
YOU STAY CALM! YOU DON'T KNOW WHAT IT'S LIKE TO HAVE YOUR FACE STOLEN!
ACTUALLY, I--
BSSSSSHHH
LOOK OUT!

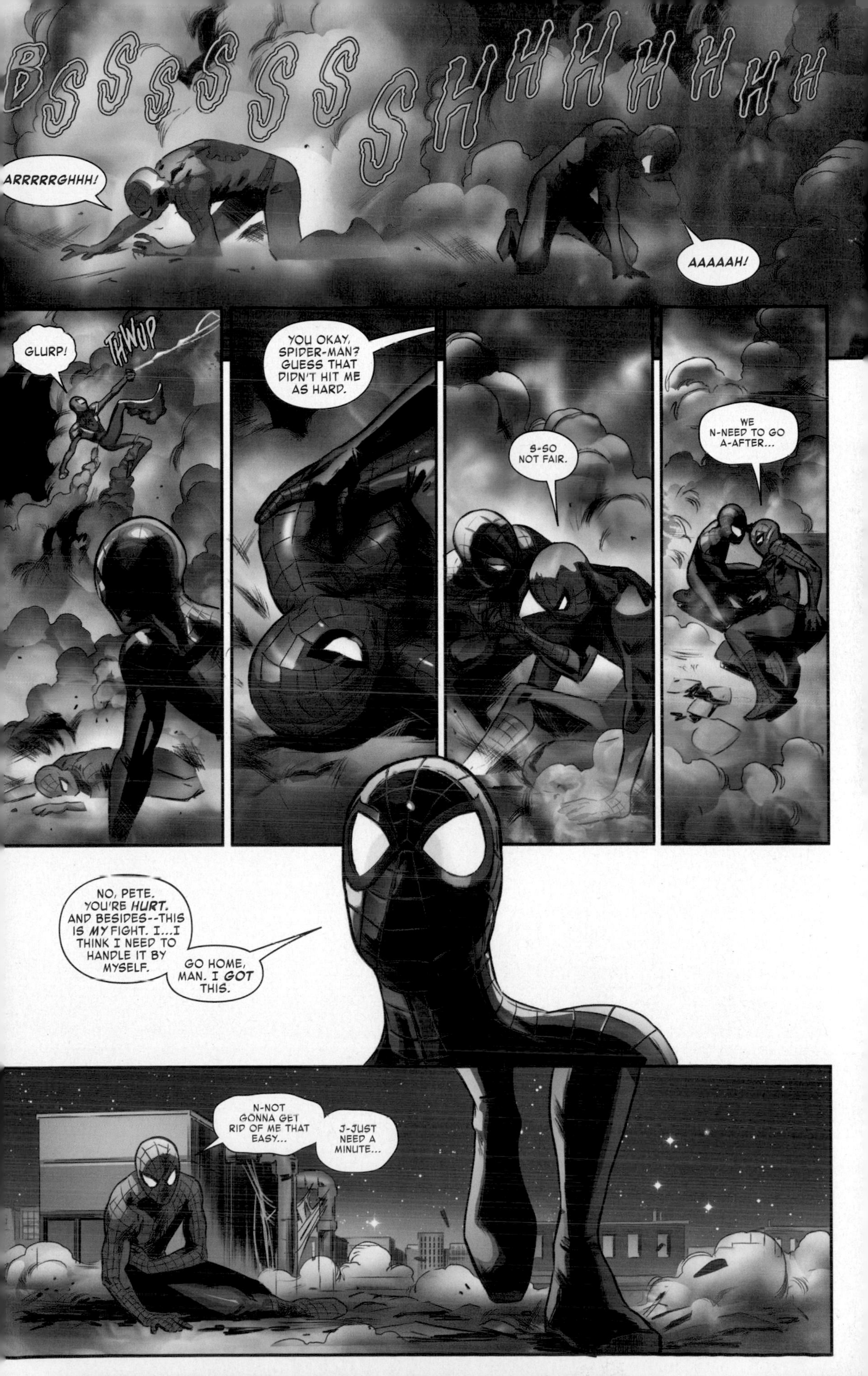

BSSSSSSSHHHHHHHH
ARRRRRGHHH!
AAAAAH!
GLURP!
THWUP
YOU OKAY, SPIDER-MAN? GUESS THAT DIDN'T HIT ME AS HARD.
S-SO NOT FAIR.
WE N-NEED TO GO A-AFTER...
NO, PETE. YOU'RE HURT. AND BESIDES--THIS IS MY FIGHT. I...I THINK I NEED TO HANDLE IT BY MYSELF.
GO HOME, MAN. I GOT THIS.
N-NOT GONNA GET RID OF ME THAT EASY...
J-JUST NEED A MINUTE...

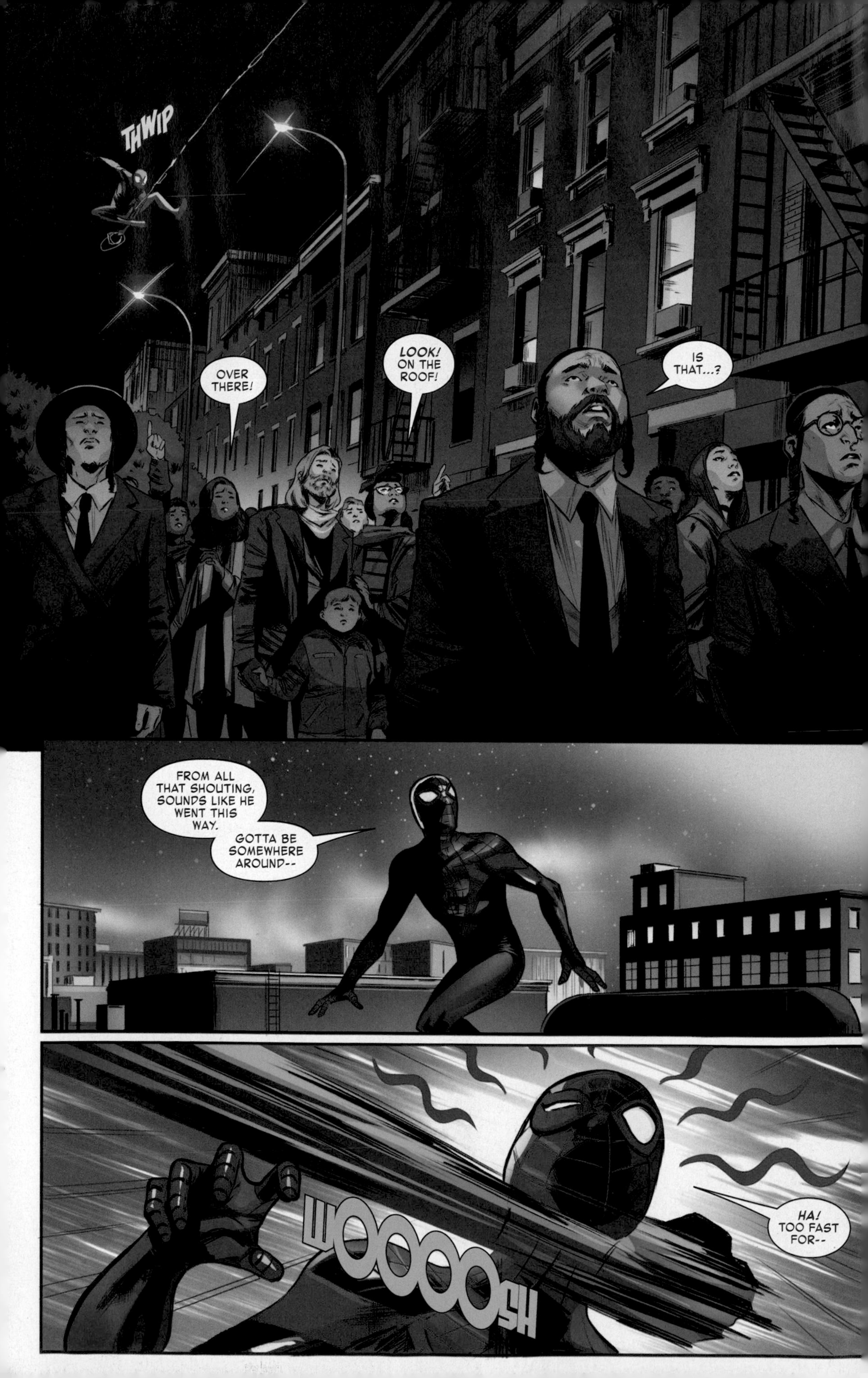
THWIP
OVER THERE!
LOOK! ON THE ROOF!
IS THAT...?
FROM ALL THAT SHOUTING, SOUNDS LIKE HE WENT THIS WAY.
GOTTA BE SOMEWHERE AROUND--
WOOOOOSH
HA! TOO FAST FOR--

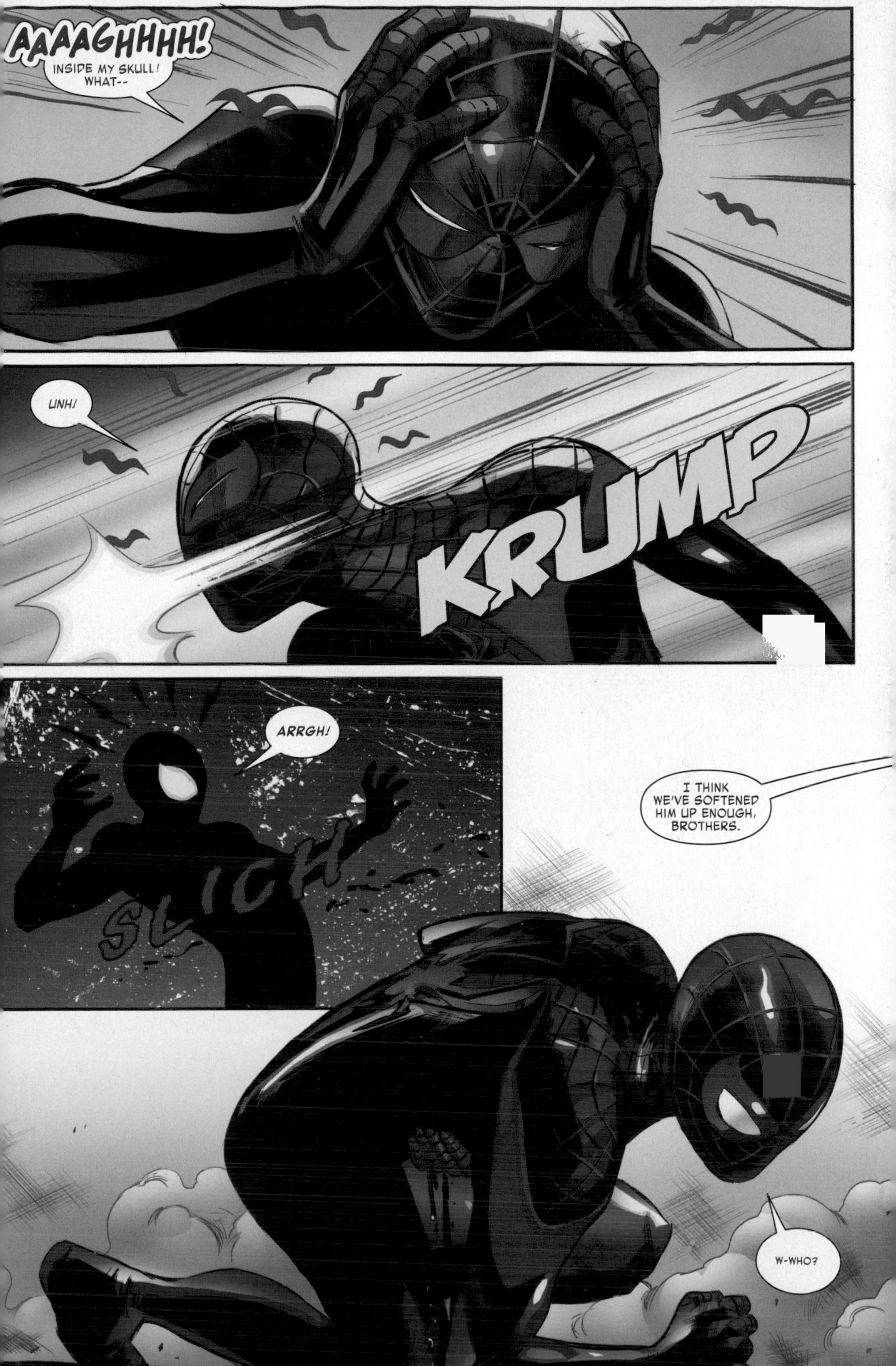
AAAAGHHHH!
INSIDE MY SKULL! WHAT--
UNH!
KRUMP
ARRGH!
SLICH
I THINK WE'VE SOFTENED HIM UP ENOUGH, BROTHERS.
W-WHO?

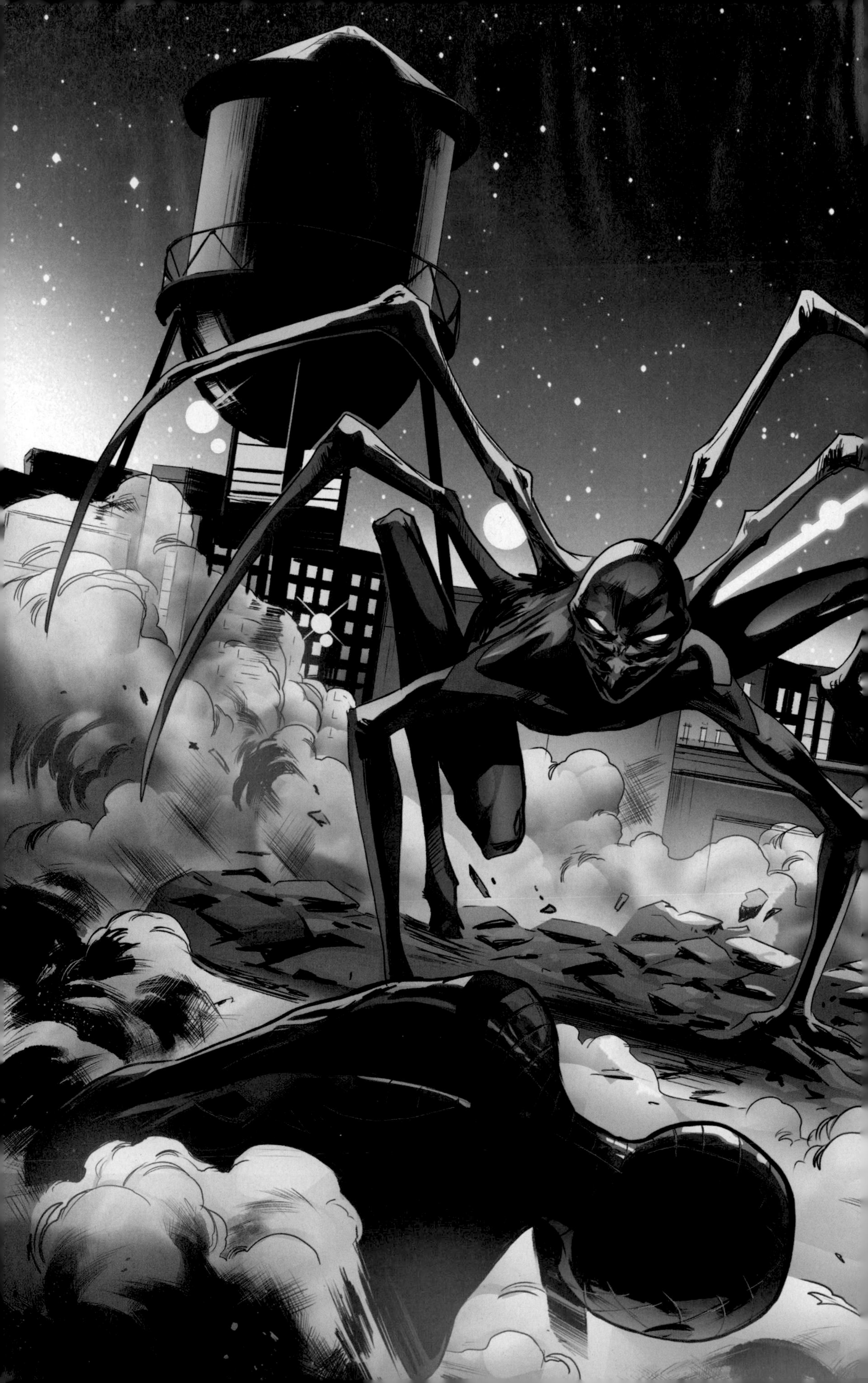

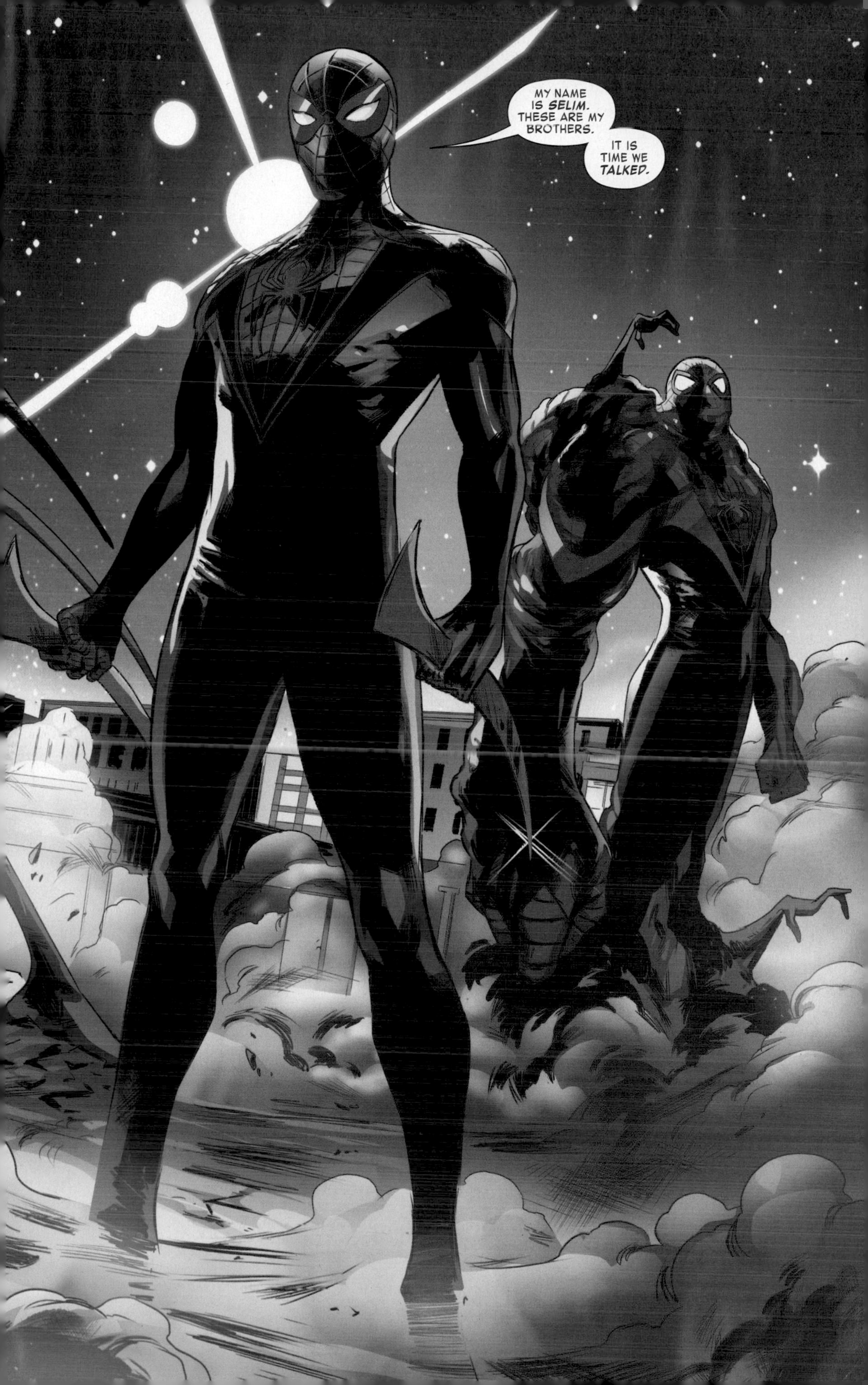
MY NAME IS SELIM. THESE ARE MY BROTHERS.
IT IS TIME WE TALKED.

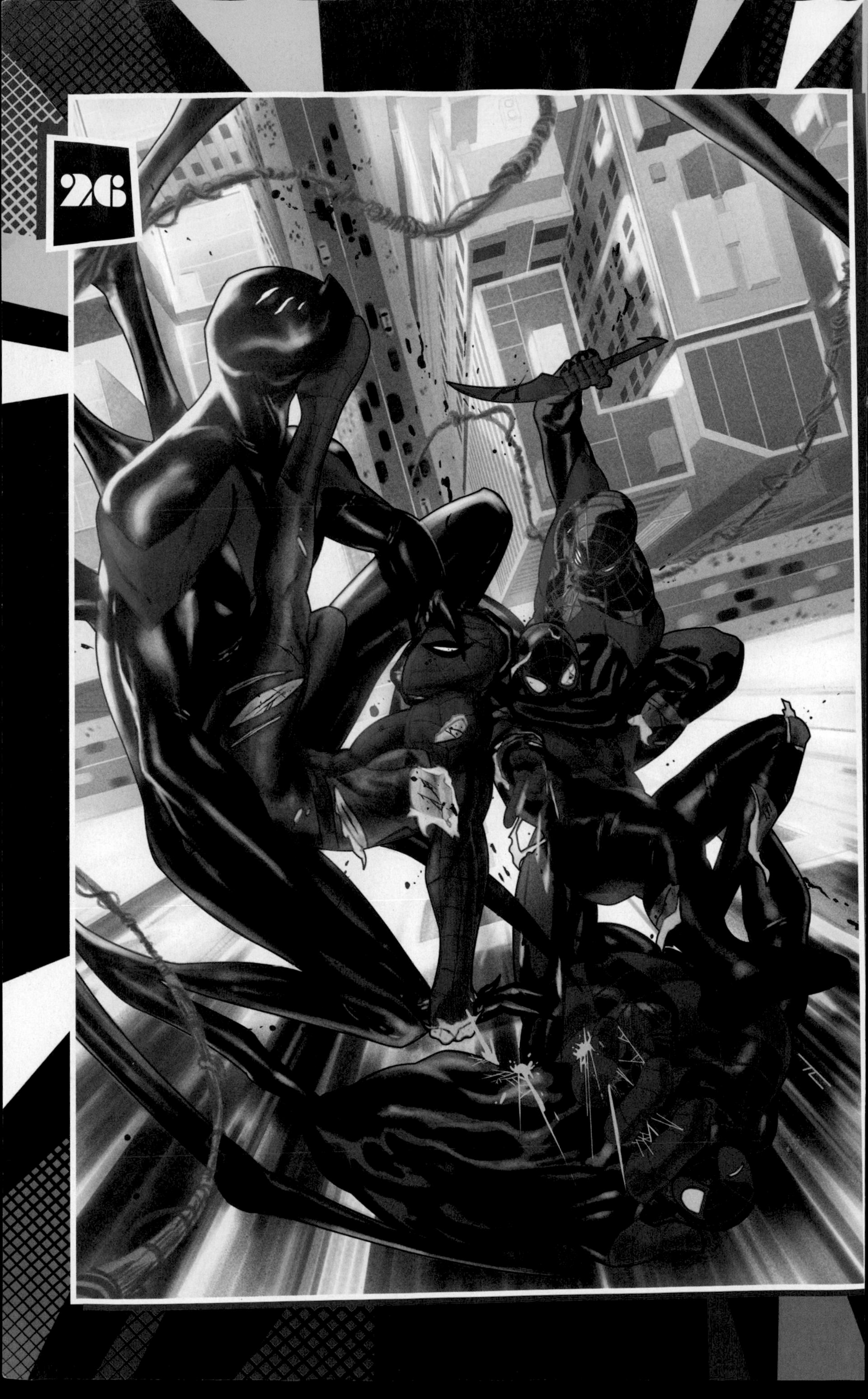
26

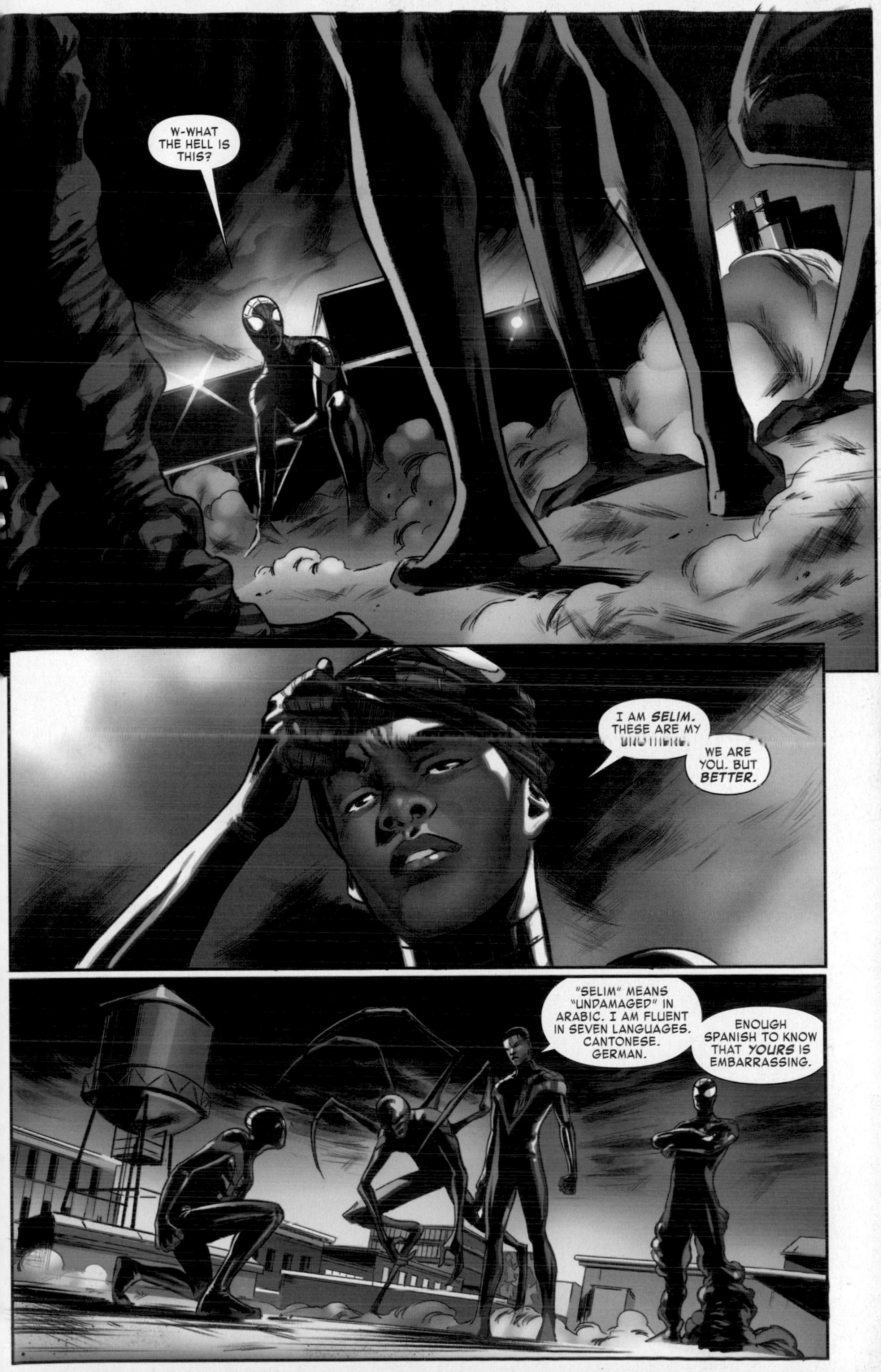
W-WHAT THE HELL IS THIS?
I AM *SELIM.* THESE ARE MY
WE ARE YOU. BUT *BETTER.*
"SELIM" MEANS "UNDAMAGED" IN ARABIC. I AM FLUENT IN SEVEN LANGUAGES. CANTONESE. GERMAN.
ENOUGH SPANISH TO KNOW THAT *YOURS* IS EMBARRASSING.

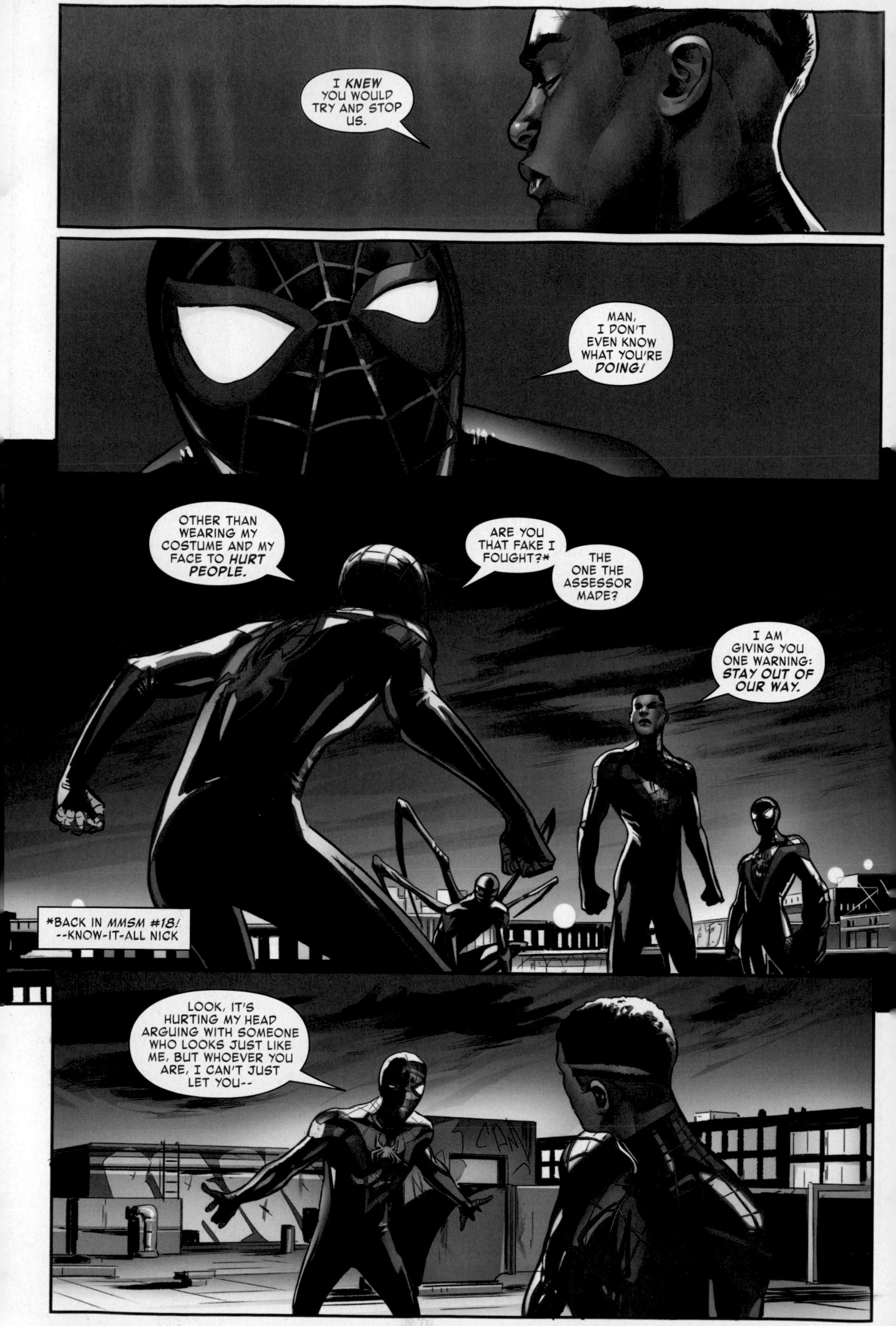
I *KNEW* YOU WOULD TRY AND STOP US.
MAN, I DON'T EVEN KNOW WHAT YOU'RE *DOING!*
OTHER THAN WEARING MY COSTUME AND MY FACE TO *HURT PEOPLE.*
ARE YOU THAT FAKE I FOUGHT?*
THE ONE THE ASSESSOR MADE?
I AM GIVING YOU ONE WARNING: *STAY OUT OF OUR WAY.*
*BACK IN *MMSM* #18! --KNOW-IT-ALL NICK
LOOK, IT'S HURTING MY HEAD ARGUING WITH SOMEONE WHO LOOKS JUST LIKE ME, BUT WHOEVER YOU ARE, I CAN'T JUST LET YOU--

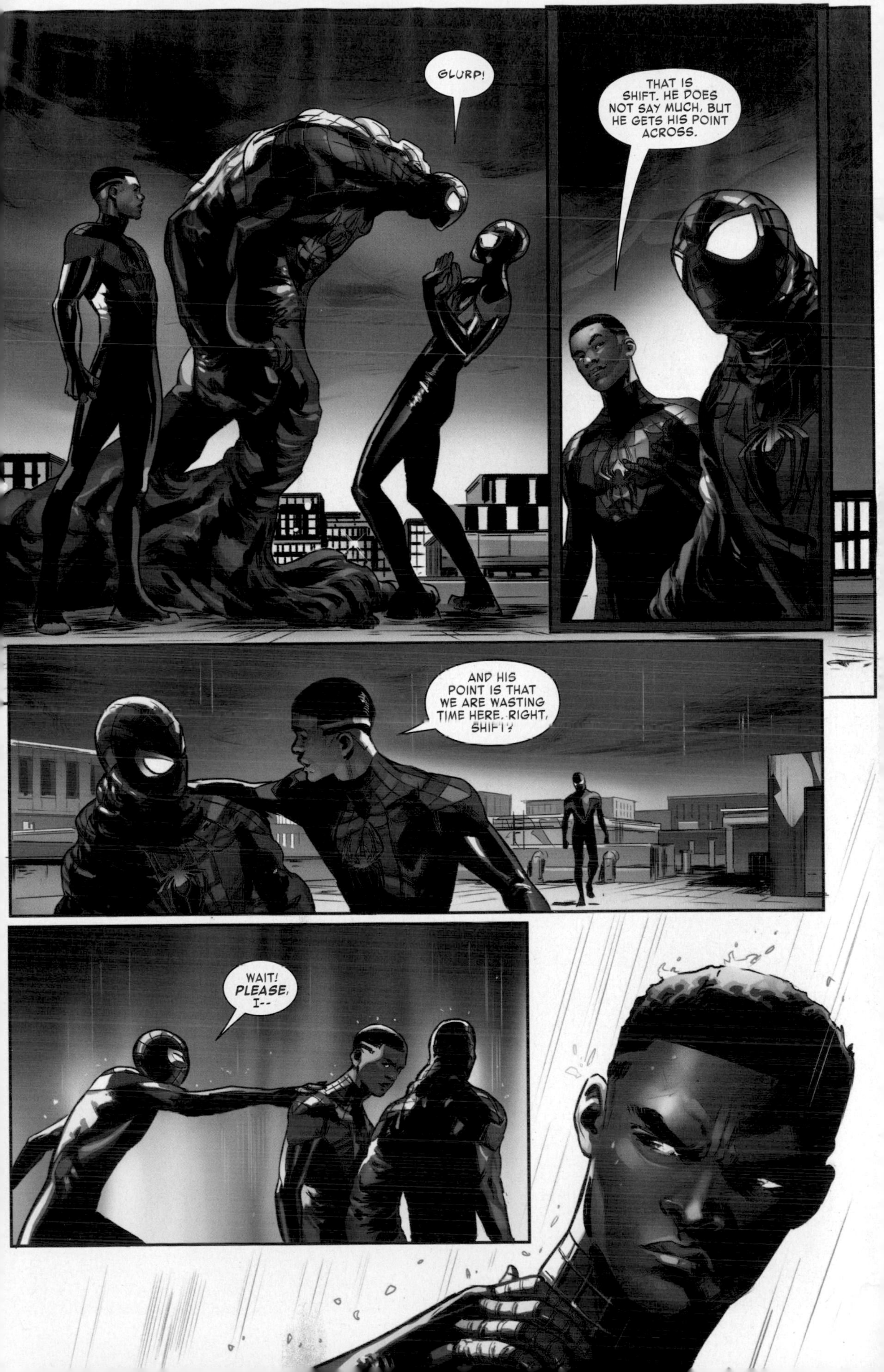
GLURP!
THAT IS SHIFT. HE DOES NOT SAY MUCH, BUT HE GETS HIS POINT ACROSS.
AND HIS POINT IS THAT WE ARE WASTING TIME HERE. RIGHT, SHIFT?
WAIT! PLEASE, I--

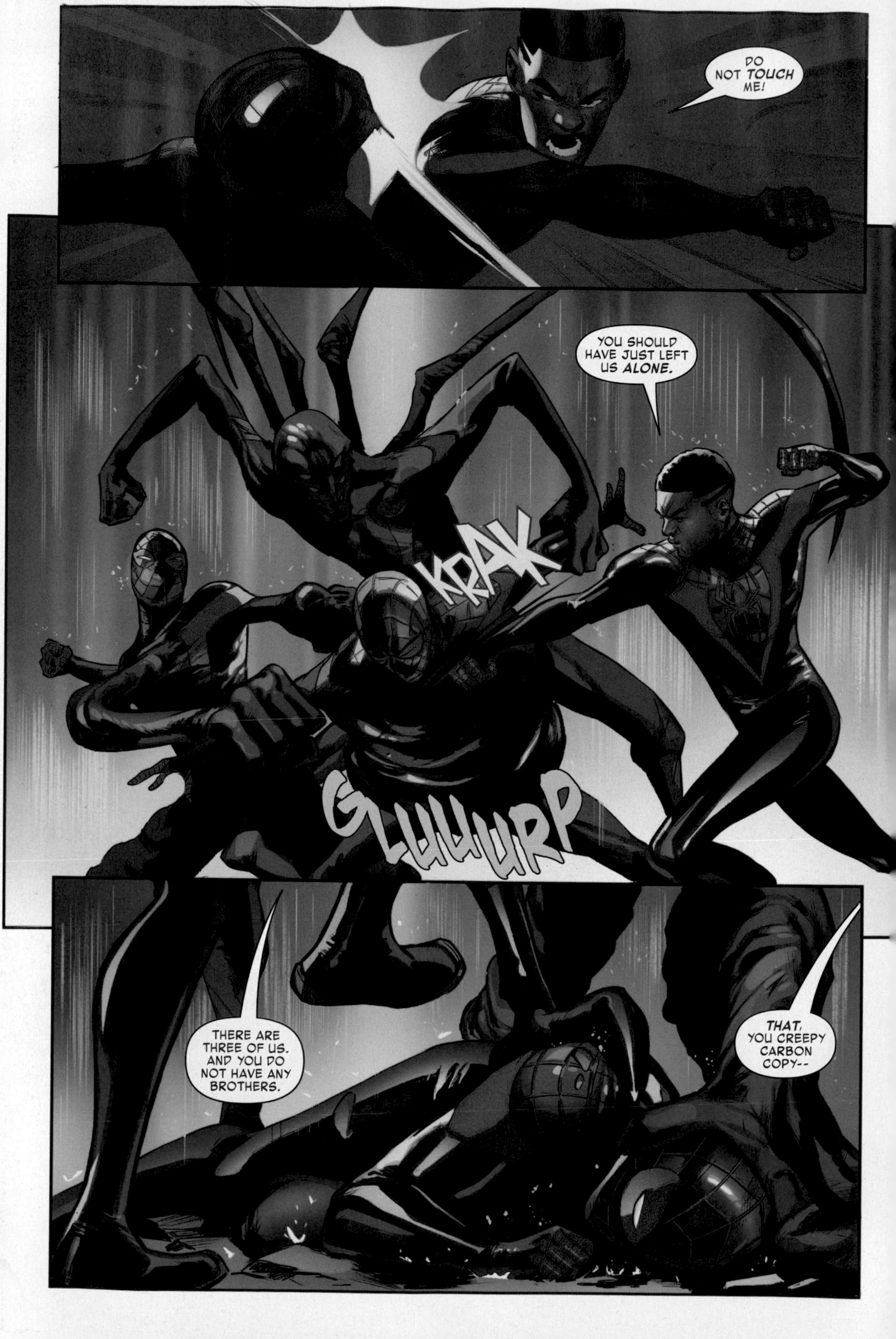
DO NOT TOUCH ME!
YOU SHOULD HAVE JUST LEFT US ALONE.
KRAK
GLUUURP
THERE ARE THREE OF US. AND YOU DO NOT HAVE ANY BROTHERS.
THAT, YOU CREEPY CARBON COPY--

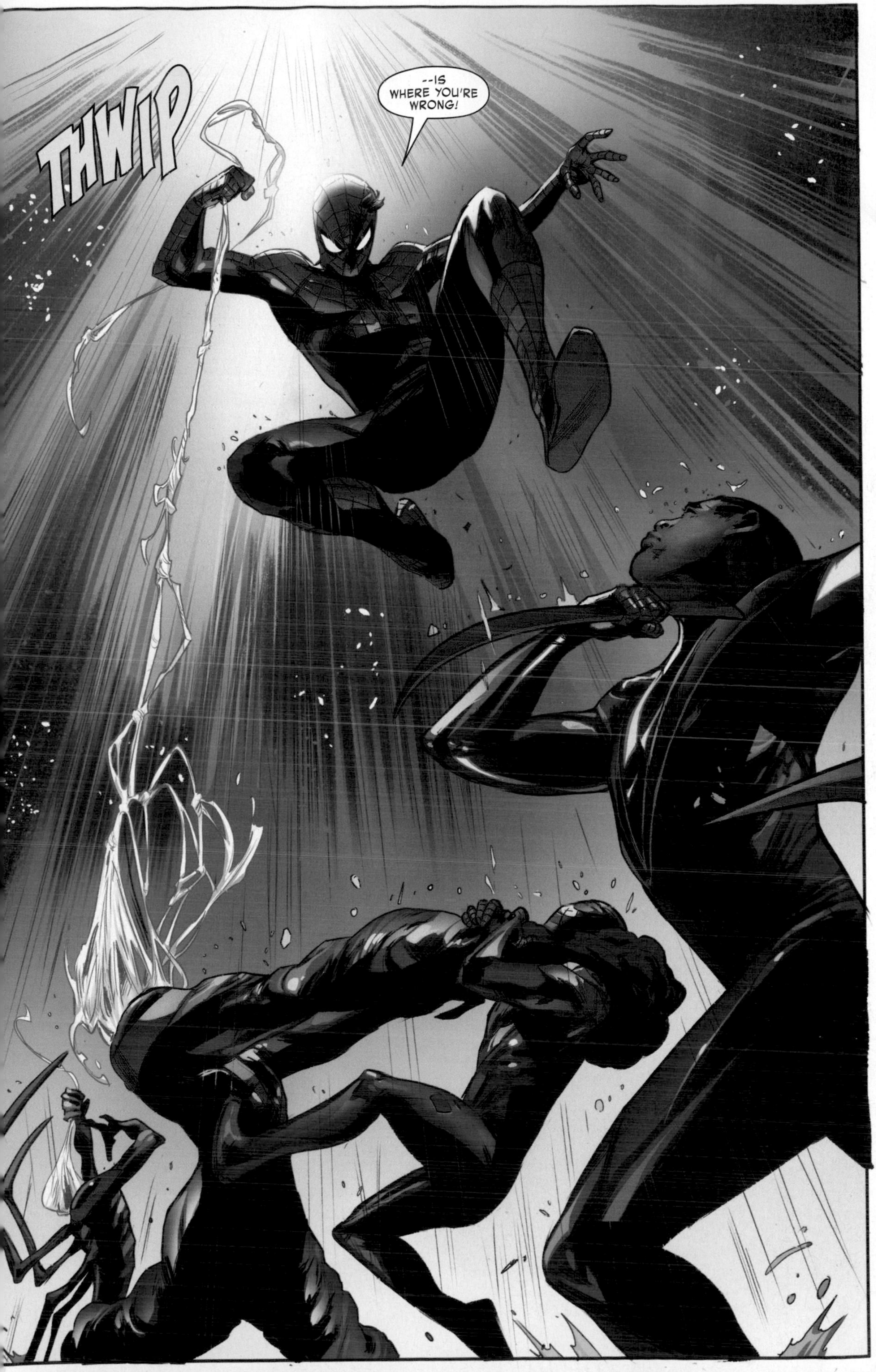
THWIP
--IS WHERE YOU'RE WRONG!

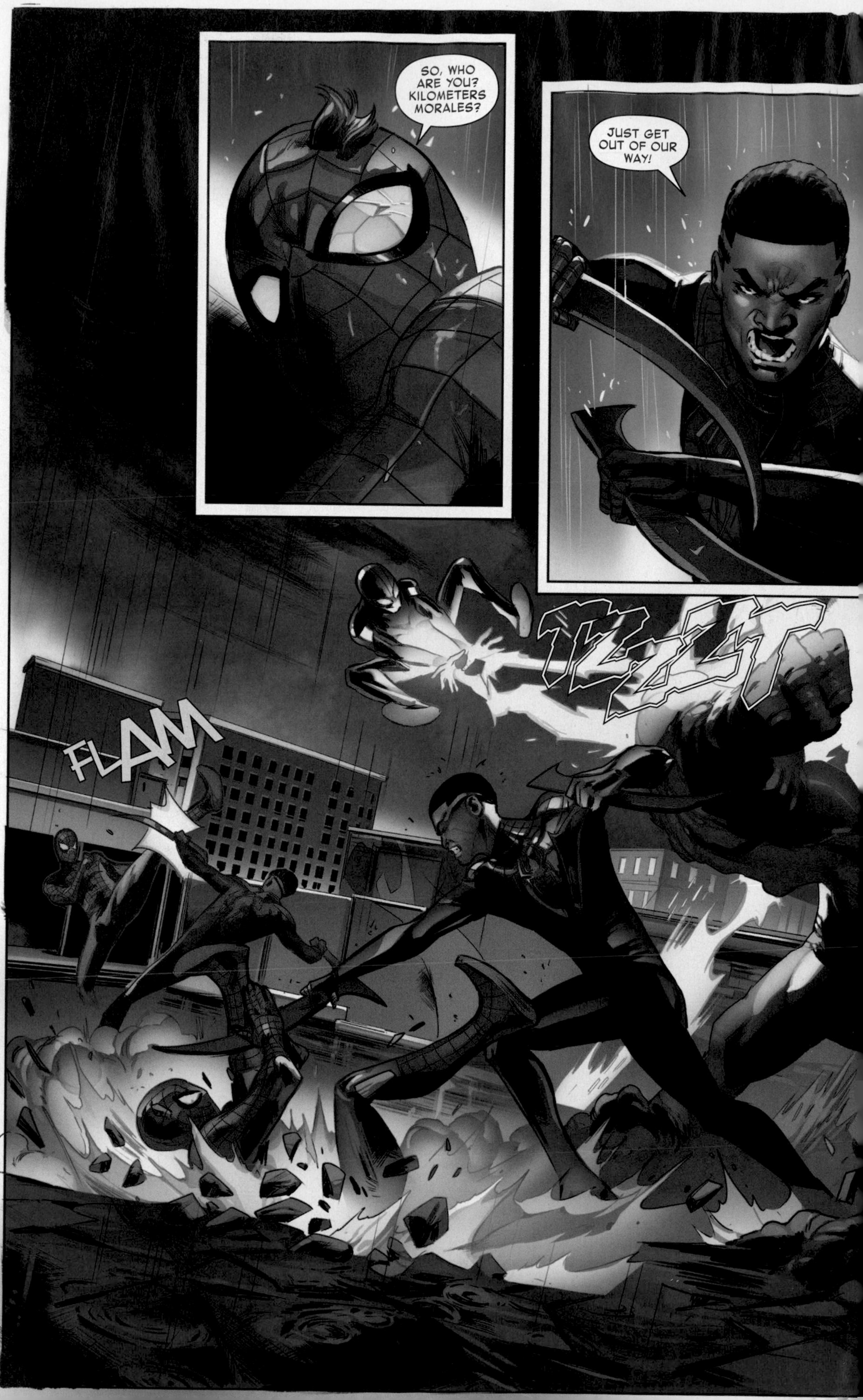
SO, WHO ARE YOU? KILOMETERS MORALES?
JUST GET OUT OF OUR WAY!
TZZZT
FLAM

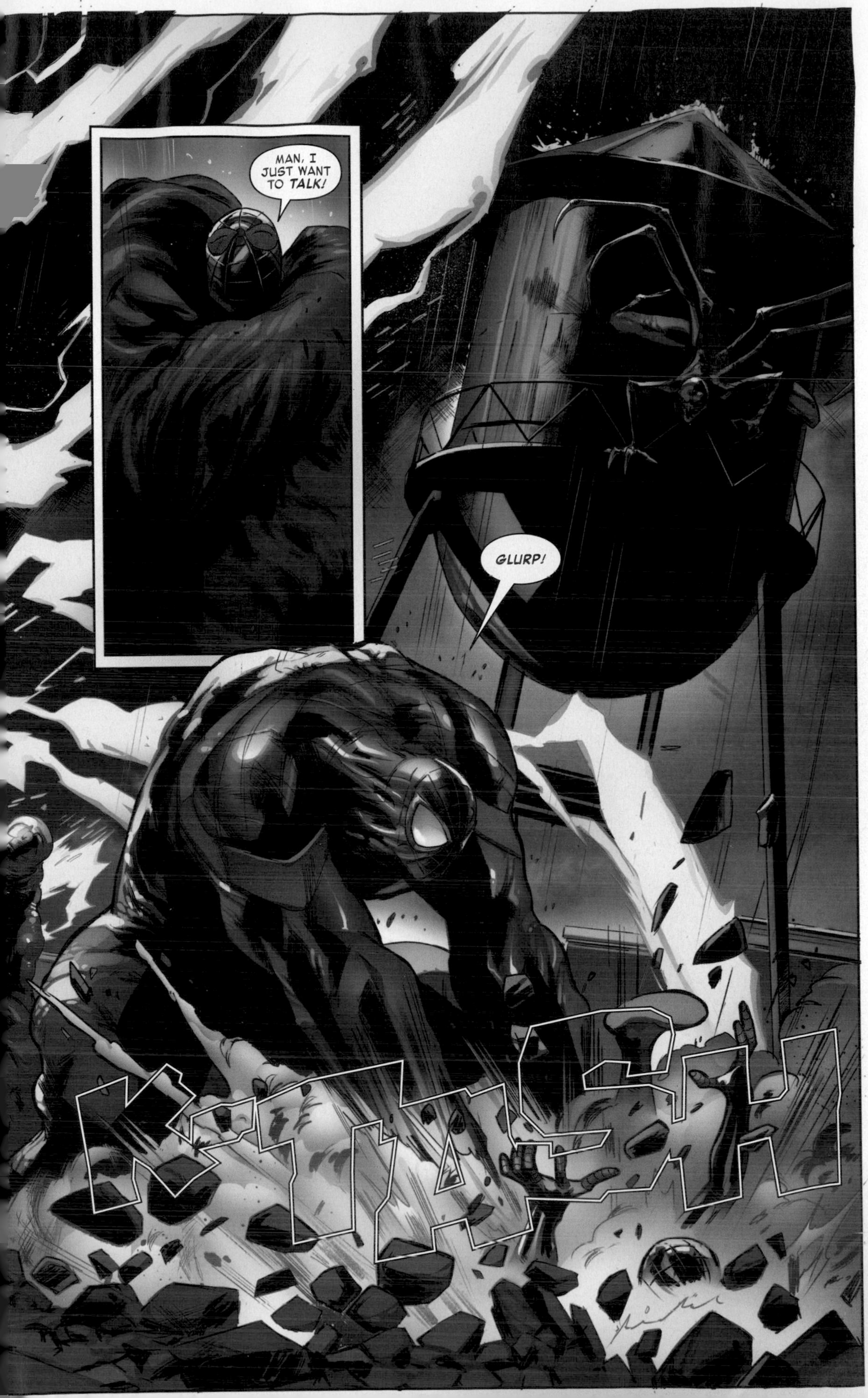
MAN, I JUST WANT TO TALK!
GLURP!

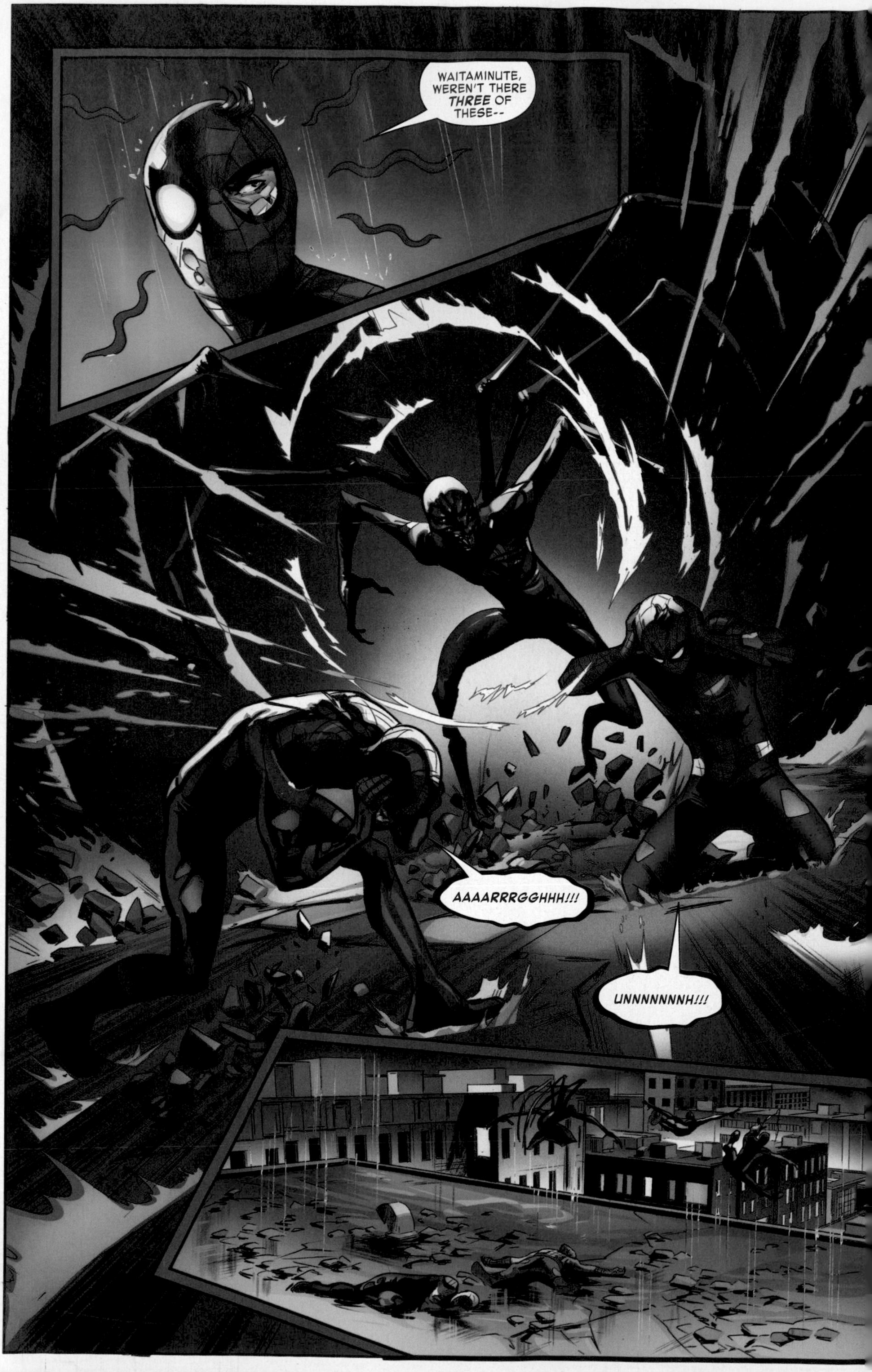
WAITAMINUTE, WEREN'T THERE *THREE* OF THESE--
AAAARRRGGHHH!!!
UNNNNNNNH!!!

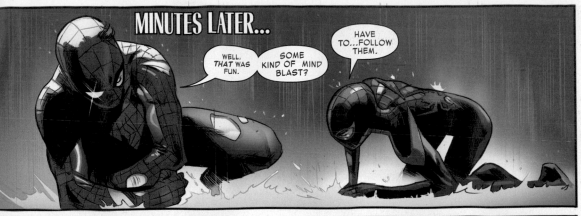

MINUTES LATER...

WELL, *THAT* WAS FUN.

SOME KIND OF MIND BLAST?

HAVE TO...FOLLOW THEM.

NO ONE *TO* FOLLOW. WE MIGHT HAVE BEEN OUT FOR A LITTLE WHILE...

I'VE GOT TO *FIND* THEM!

WE'LL COVER MORE GROUND IF WE SPLIT UP...

WAIT, THAT'S WHAT THEY SAY IN HORROR MOVIES.

NO, YOU'RE RIGHT.

NOTHING.

NOTHING.

NADA.

NO LUCK, HUH?

WHERE *ARE* THEY?!

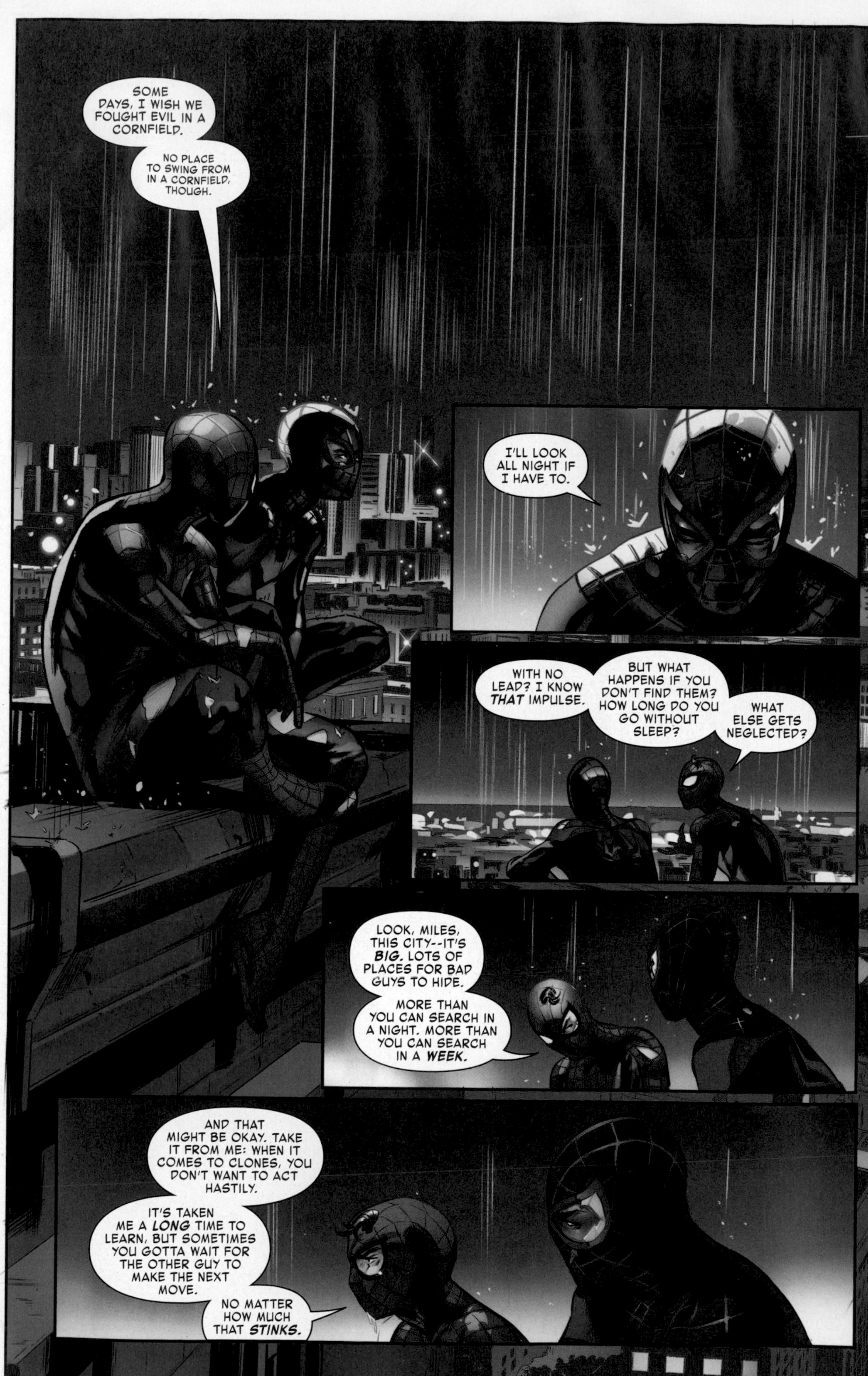
SOME DAYS, I WISH WE FOUGHT EVIL IN A CORNFIELD.
NO PLACE TO SWING FROM IN A CORNFIELD, THOUGH.
I'LL LOOK ALL NIGHT IF I HAVE TO.
WITH NO LEAD? I KNOW THAT IMPULSE.
BUT WHAT HAPPENS IF YOU DON'T FIND THEM? HOW LONG DO YOU GO WITHOUT SLEEP?
WHAT ELSE GETS NEGLECTED?
LOOK, MILES, THIS CITY--IT'S BIG. LOTS OF PLACES FOR BAD GUYS TO HIDE.
MORE THAN YOU CAN SEARCH IN A NIGHT. MORE THAN YOU CAN SEARCH IN A WEEK.
AND THAT MIGHT BE OKAY. TAKE IT FROM ME: WHEN IT COMES TO CLONES, YOU DON'T WANT TO ACT HASTILY.
IT'S TAKEN ME A LONG TIME TO LEARN, BUT SOMETIMES YOU GOTTA WAIT FOR THE OTHER GUY TO MAKE THE NEXT MOVE.
NO MATTER HOW MUCH THAT STINKS.

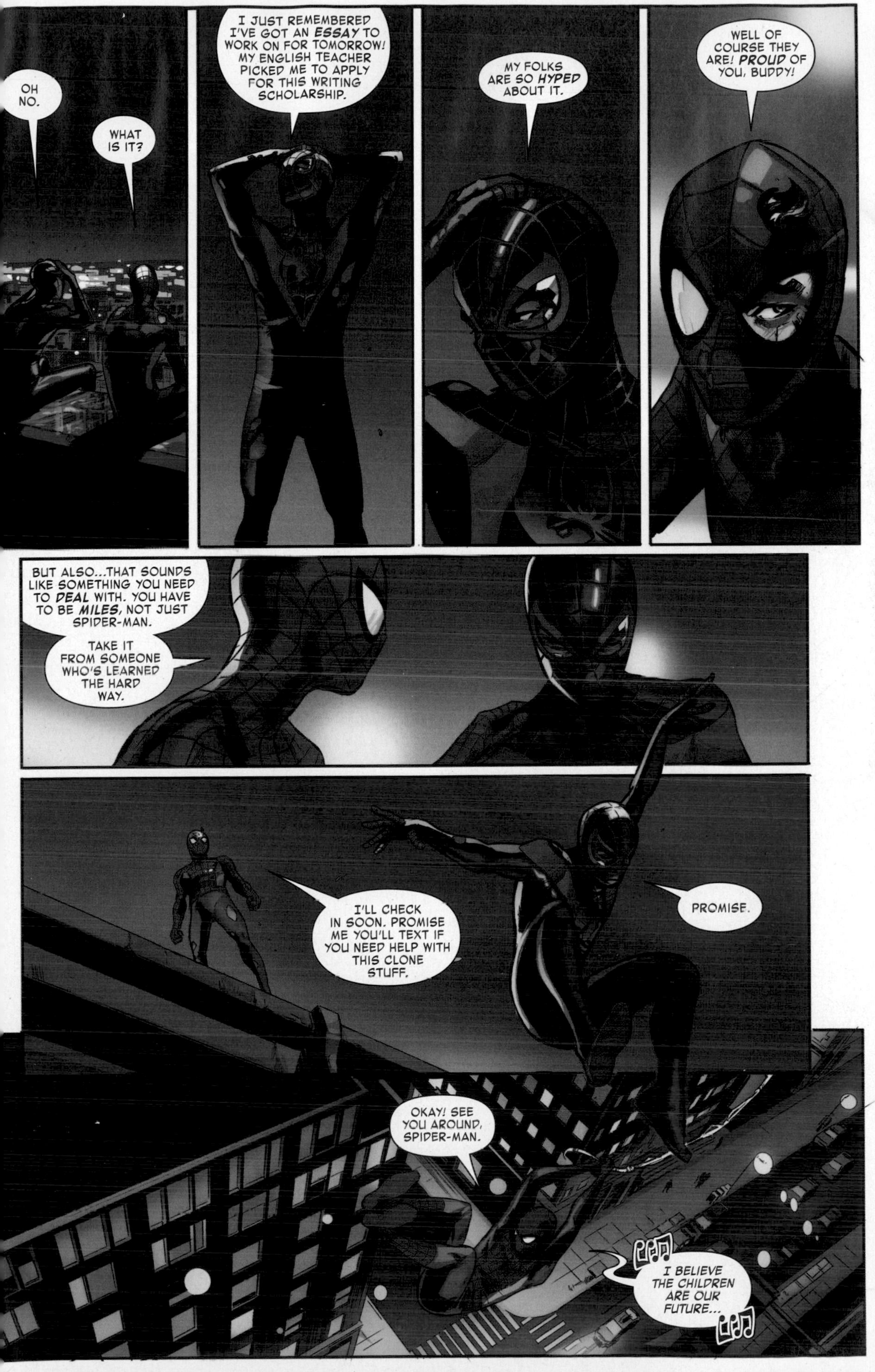
OH NO.
WHAT IS IT?
I JUST REMEMBERED I'VE GOT AN ESSAY TO WORK ON FOR TOMORROW! MY ENGLISH TEACHER PICKED ME TO APPLY FOR THIS WRITING SCHOLARSHIP.
MY FOLKS ARE SO HYPED ABOUT IT.
WELL OF COURSE THEY ARE! PROUD OF YOU, BUDDY!
BUT ALSO...THAT SOUNDS LIKE SOMETHING YOU NEED TO DEAL WITH. YOU HAVE TO BE MILES, NOT JUST SPIDER-MAN.
TAKE IT FROM SOMEONE WHO'S LEARNED THE HARD WAY.
I'LL CHECK IN SOON. PROMISE ME YOU'LL TEXT IF YOU NEED HELP WITH THIS CLONE STUFF.
PROMISE.
OKAY! SEE YOU AROUND, SPIDER-MAN.
I BELIEVE THE CHILDREN ARE OUR FUTURE...

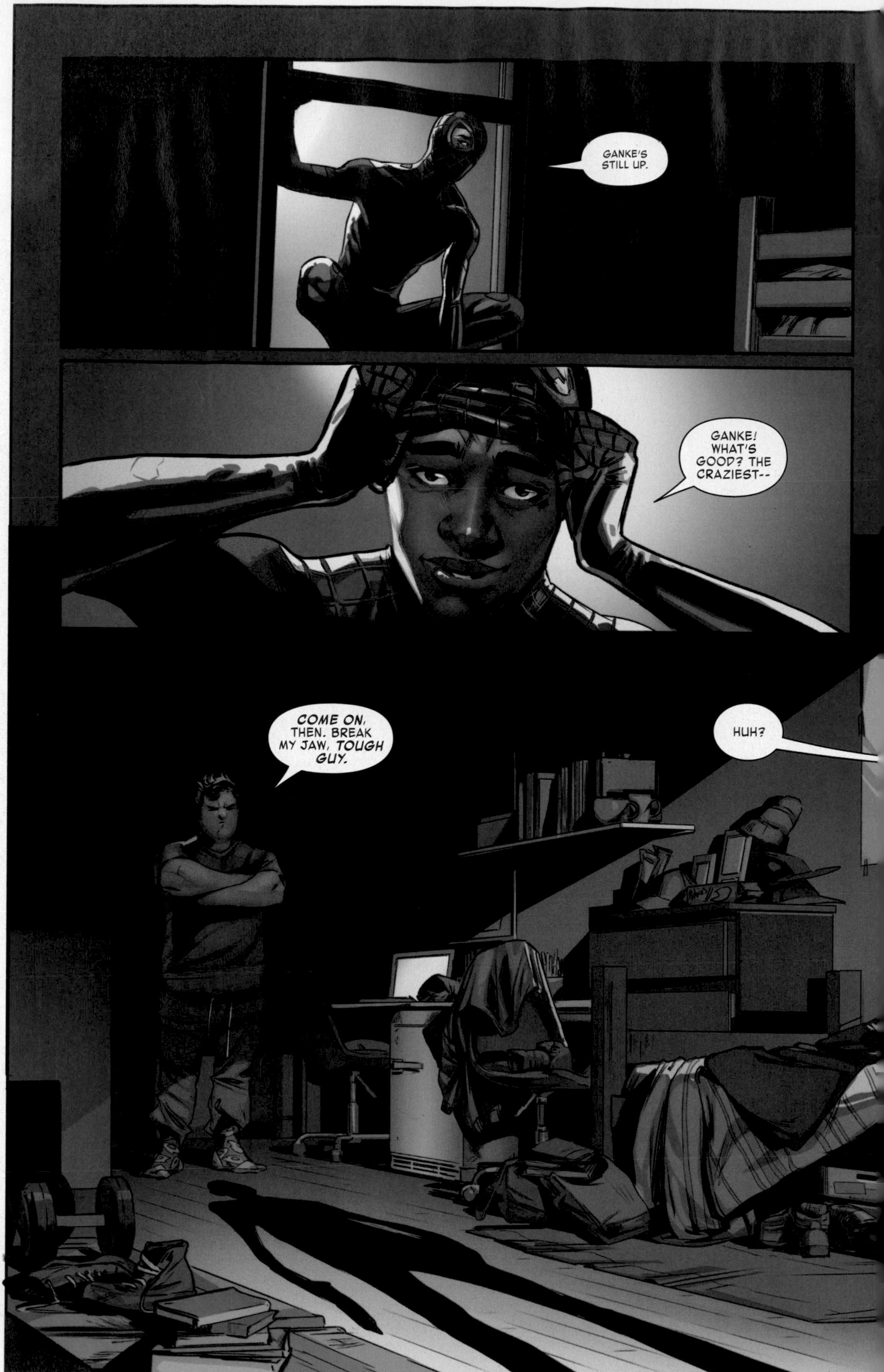
GANKE'S STILL UP.
GANKE! WHAT'S GOOD? THE CRAZIEST--
HUH?
COME ON, THEN. BREAK MY JAW, TOUGH GUY.

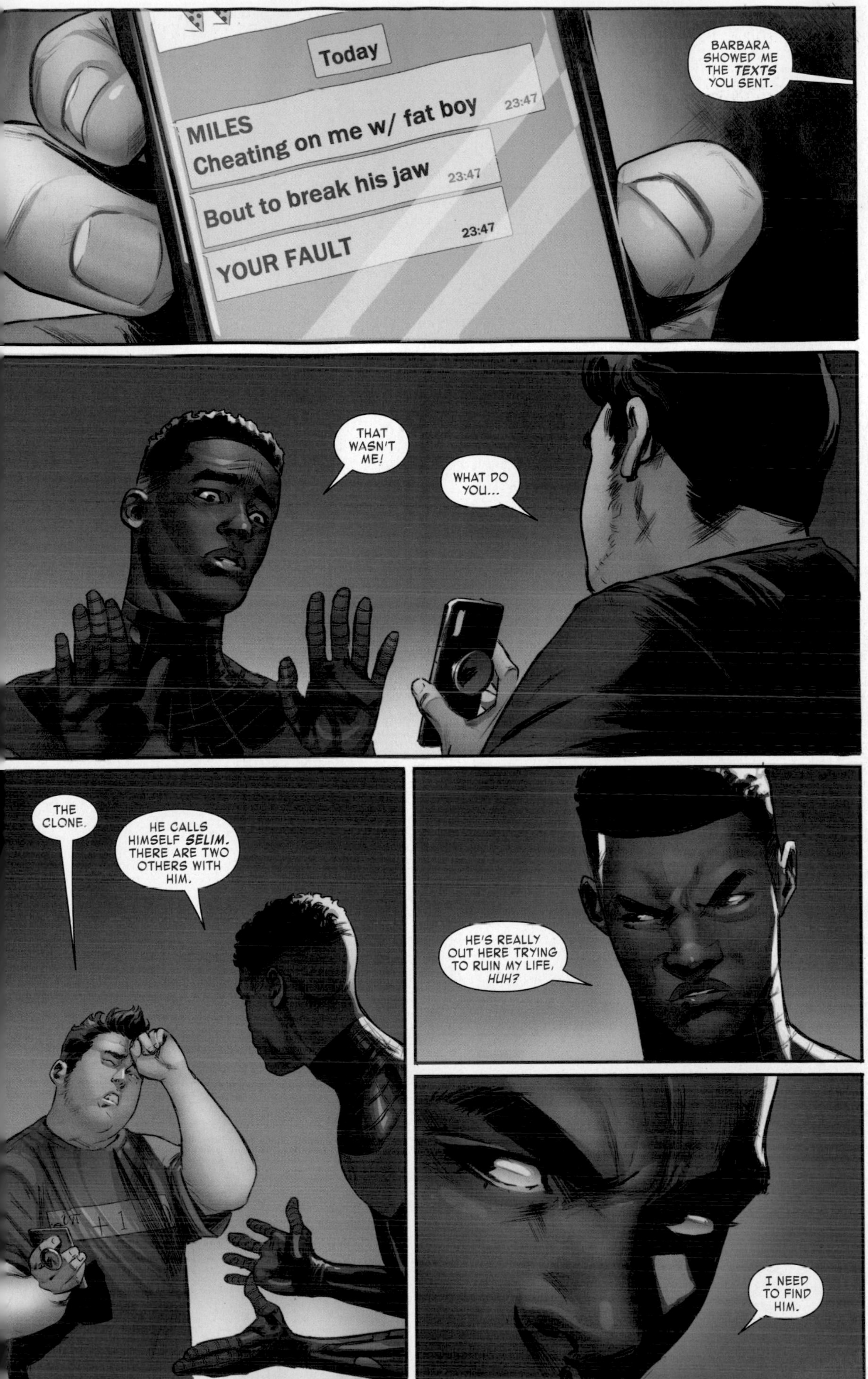
Today
MILES
Cheating on me w/ fat boy
23:47
Bout to break his jaw
23:47
YOUR FAULT
23:47
BARBARA SHOWED ME THE TEXTS YOU SENT.
THAT WASN'T ME!
WHAT DO YOU...
THE CLONE.
HE CALLS HIMSELF SELIM. THERE ARE TWO OTHERS WITH HIM.
HE'S REALLY OUT HERE TRYING TO RUIN MY LIFE, HUH?
I NEED TO FIND HIM.

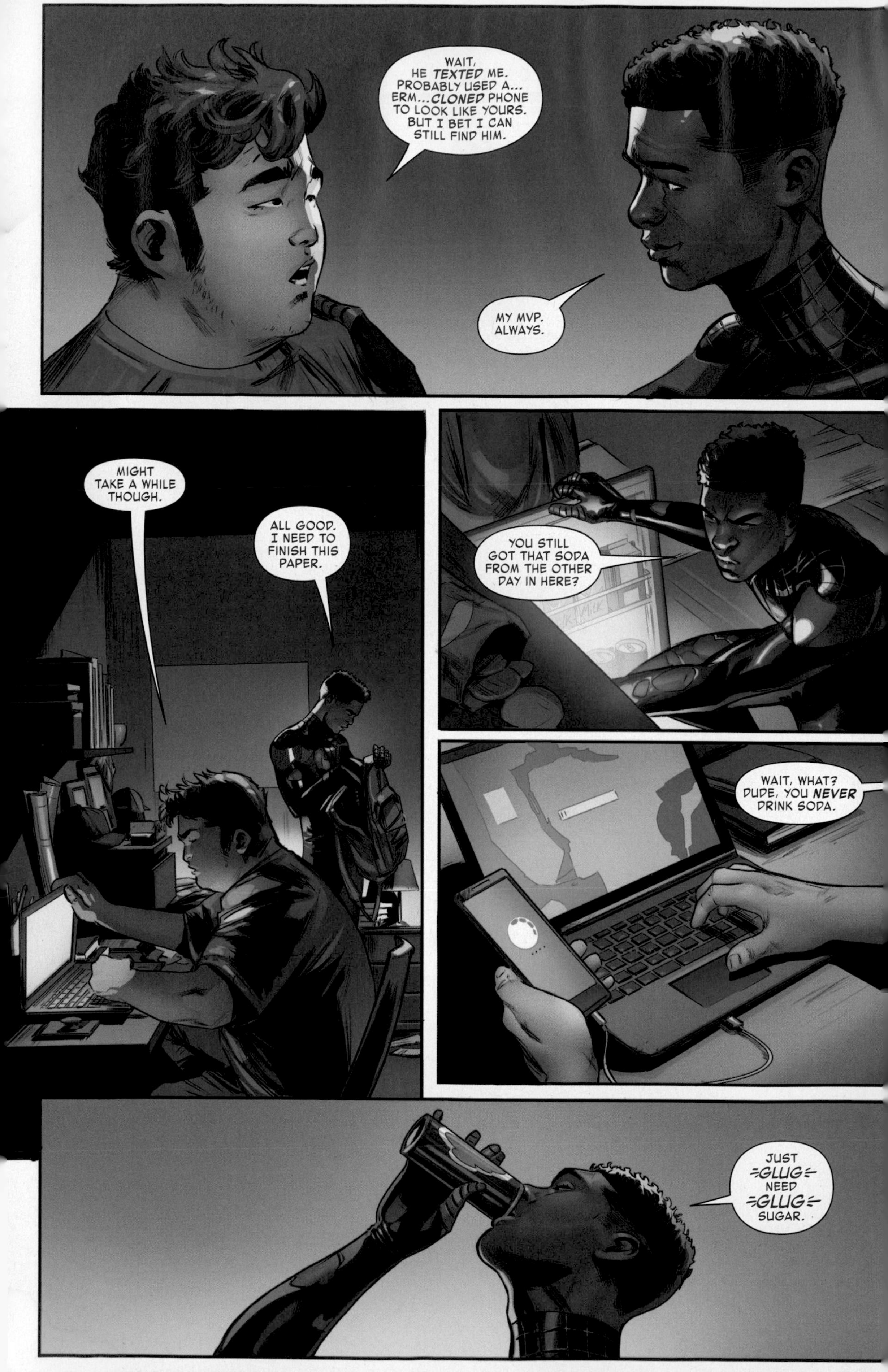
WAIT, HE TEXTED ME. PROBABLY USED A... ERM...CLONED PHONE TO LOOK LIKE YOURS. BUT I BET I CAN STILL FIND HIM.
MY MVP. ALWAYS.
MIGHT TAKE A WHILE THOUGH.
ALL GOOD. I NEED TO FINISH THIS PAPER.
YOU STILL GOT THAT SODA FROM THE OTHER DAY IN HERE?
WAIT, WHAT? DUDE, YOU NEVER DRINK SODA.
JUST =GLUG= NEED =GLUG= SUGAR.

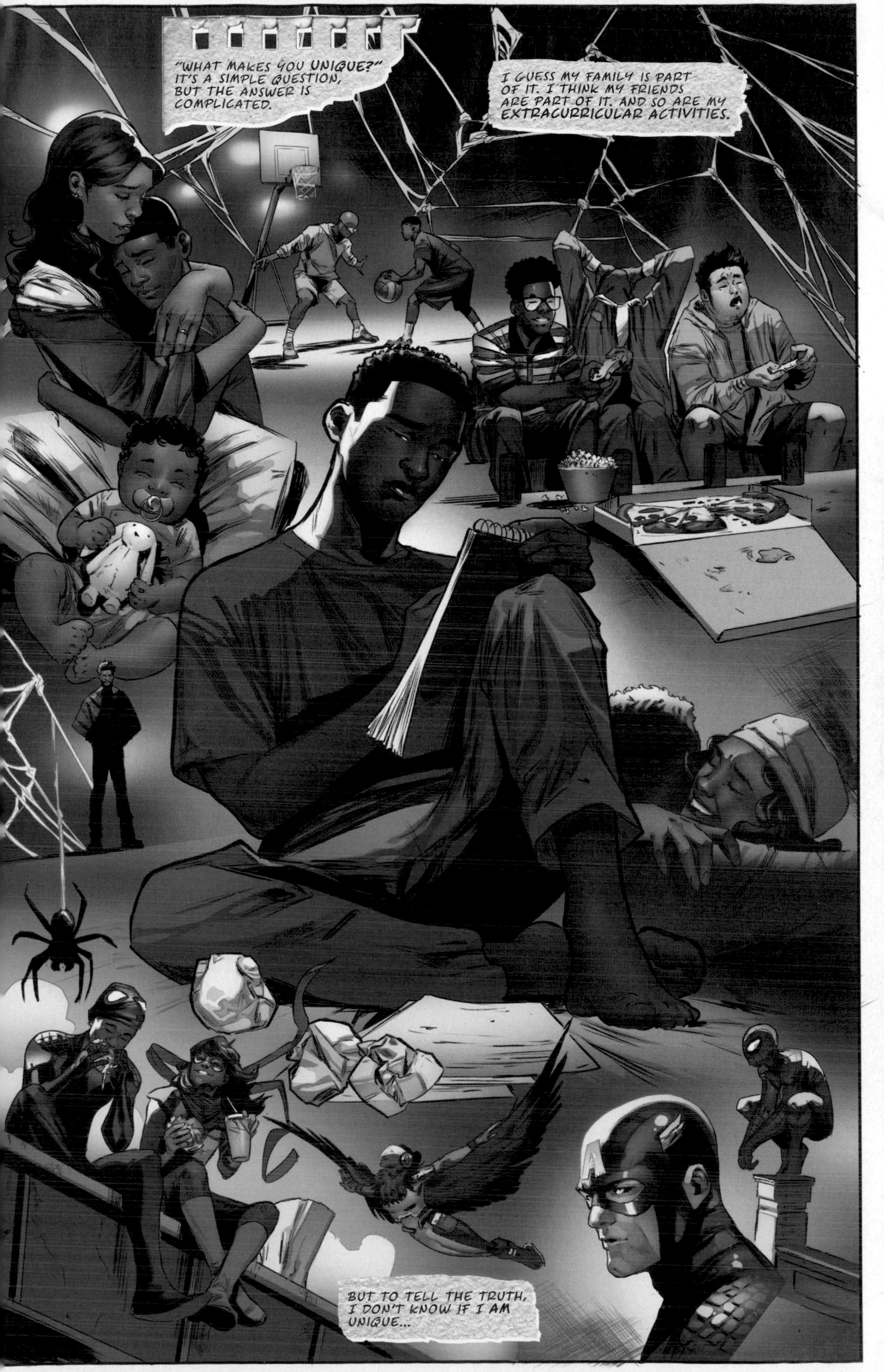
"WHAT MAKES YOU UNIQUE?" IT'S A SIMPLE QUESTION, BUT THE ANSWER IS COMPLICATED.
I GUESS MY FAMILY IS PART OF IT. I THINK MY FRIENDS ARE PART OF IT. AND SO ARE MY EXTRACURRICULAR ACTIVITIES.
BUT TO TELL THE TRUTH, I DON'T KNOW IF I AM UNIQUE...

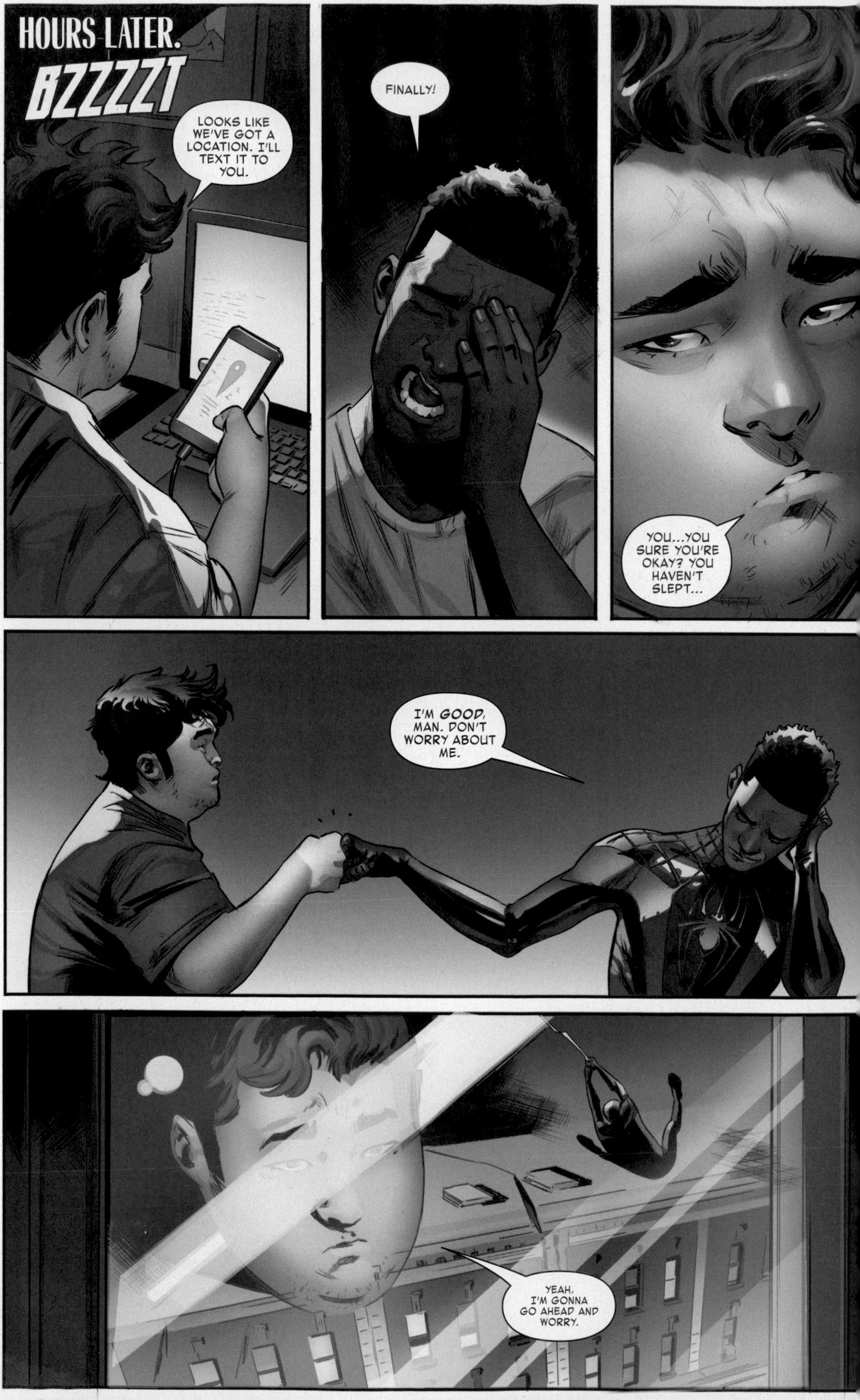
HOURS LATER.
BZZZZT
LOOKS LIKE WE'VE GOT A LOCATION. I'LL TEXT IT TO YOU.
FINALLY!
YOU...YOU SURE YOU'RE OKAY? YOU HAVEN'T SLEPT...
I'M GOOD, MAN. DON'T WORRY ABOUT ME.
YEAH, I'M GONNA GO AHEAD AND WORRY.

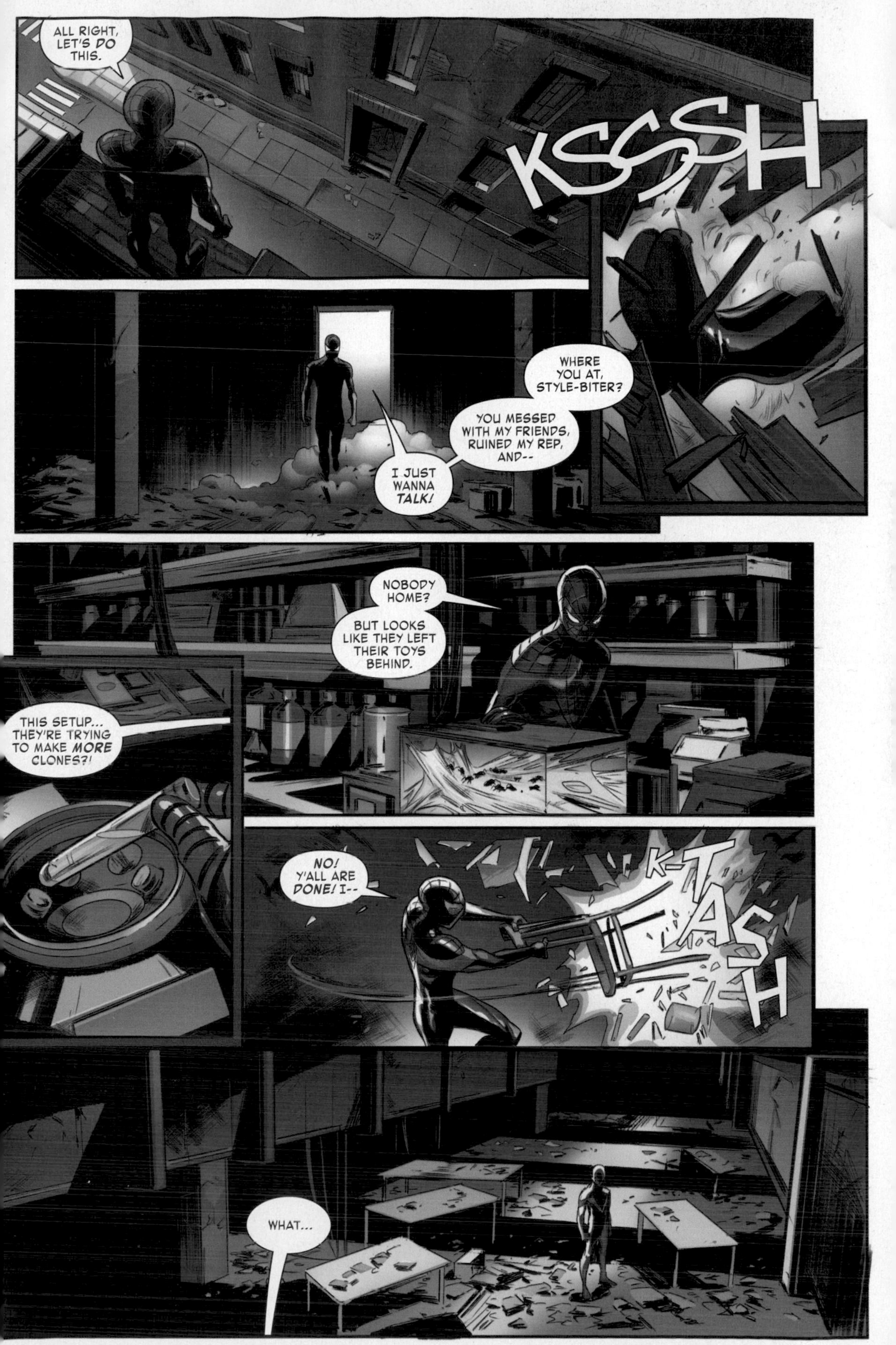
ALL RIGHT, LET'S DO THIS.
KSSSH
WHERE YOU AT, STYLE-BITER?
YOU MESSED WITH MY FRIENDS, RUINED MY REP, AND--
I JUST WANNA TALK!
NOBODY HOME?
BUT LOOKS LIKE THEY LEFT THEIR TOYS BEHIND.
THIS SETUP... THEY'RE TRYING TO MAKE MORE CLONES?!
NO! Y'ALL ARE DONE! I--
K-TASH
WHAT...

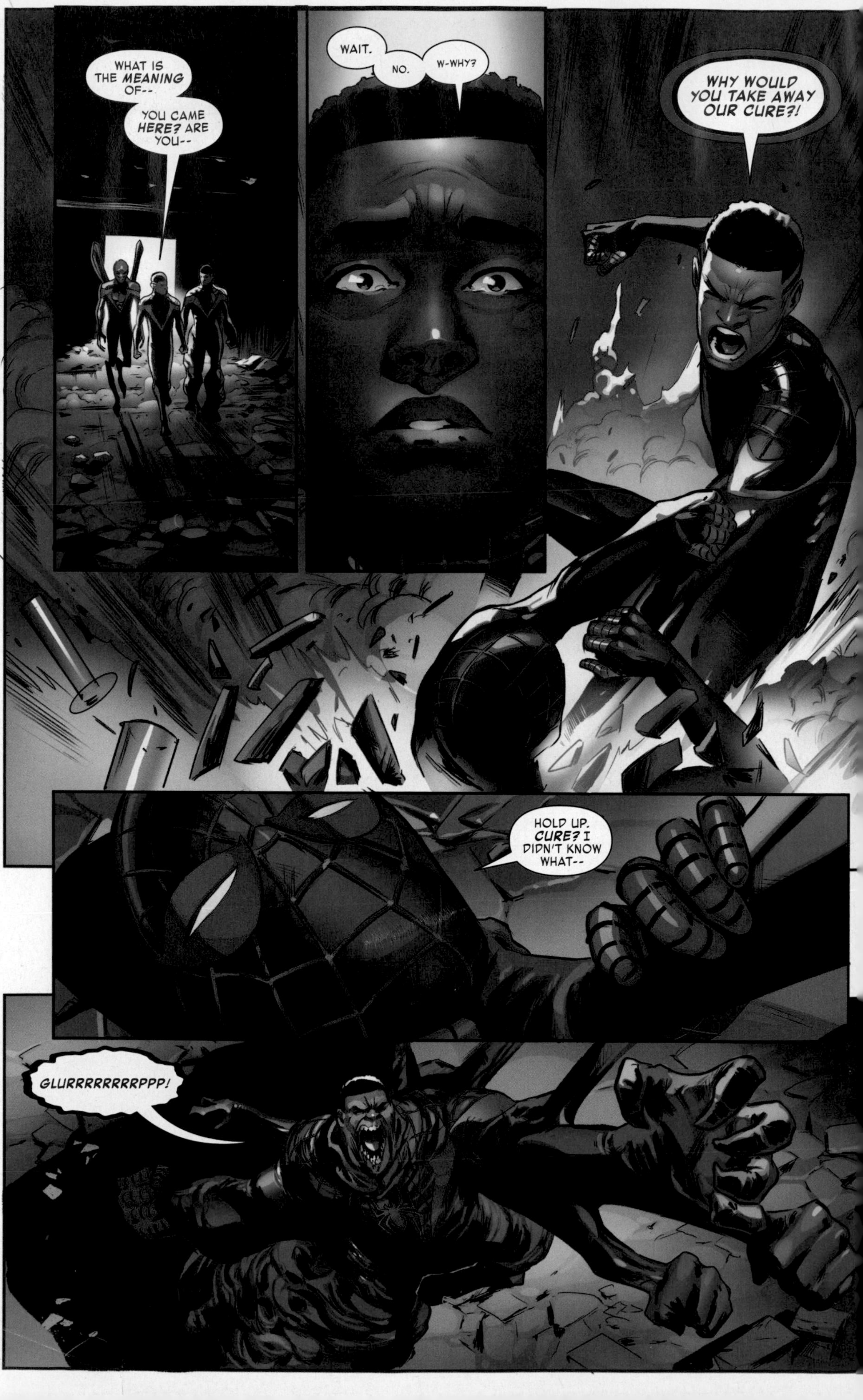
WHAT IS THE MEANING OF--
YOU CAME HERE? ARE YOU--
WAIT.
NO.
W-WHY?
WHY WOULD YOU TAKE AWAY OUR CURE?!
HOLD UP. CURE? I DIDN'T KNOW WHAT--
GLURRRRRRRRPPP!

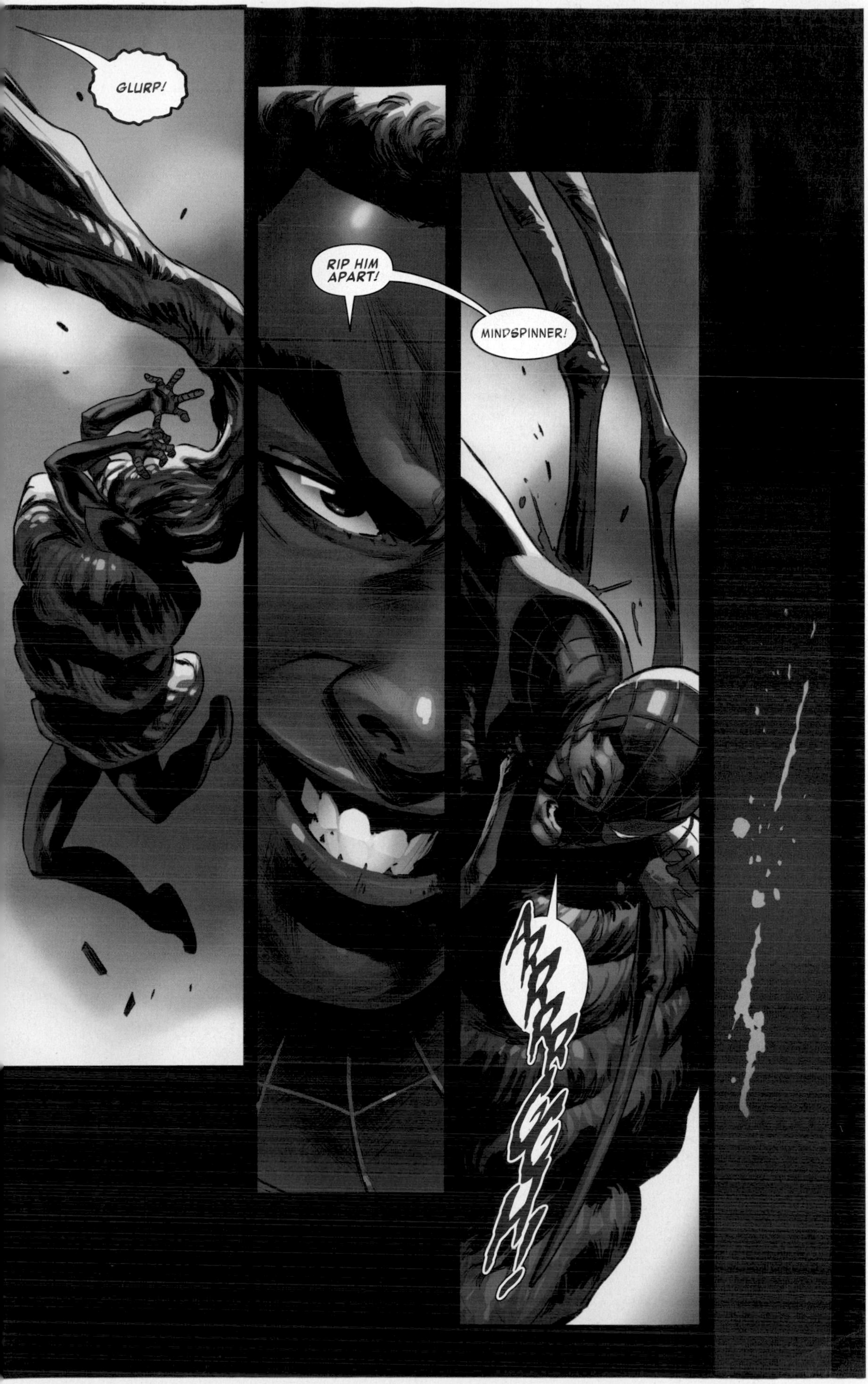
GLURP!
RIP HIM APART!
MINDSPINNER!
ARRRGGHH

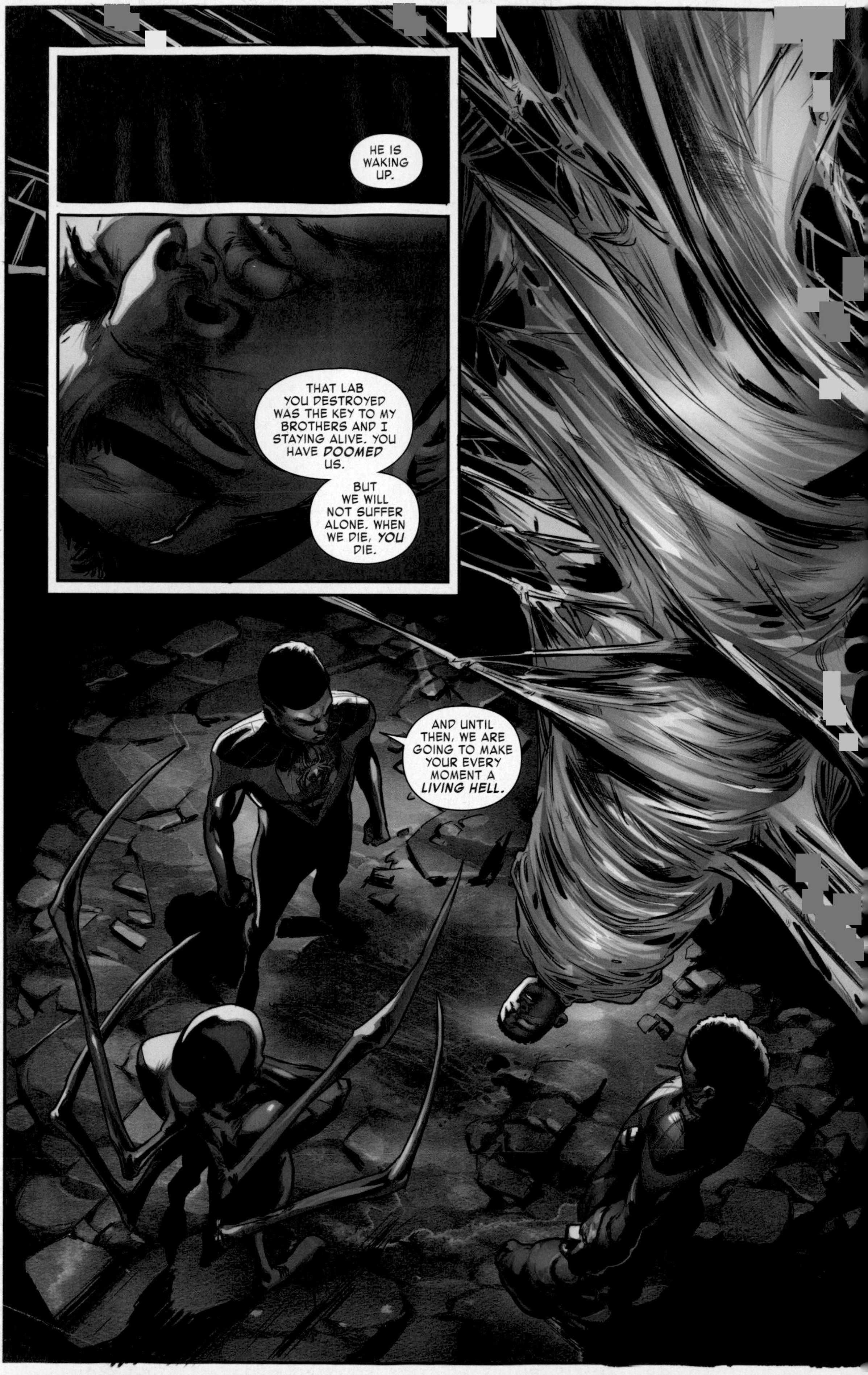
HE IS WAKING UP.
THAT LAB YOU DESTROYED WAS THE KEY TO MY BROTHERS AND I STAYING ALIVE. YOU HAVE *DOOMED* US.
BUT WE WILL NOT SUFFER ALONE. WHEN WE DIE, *YOU* DIE.
AND UNTIL THEN, WE ARE GOING TO MAKE YOUR EVERY MOMENT A *LIVING HELL.*

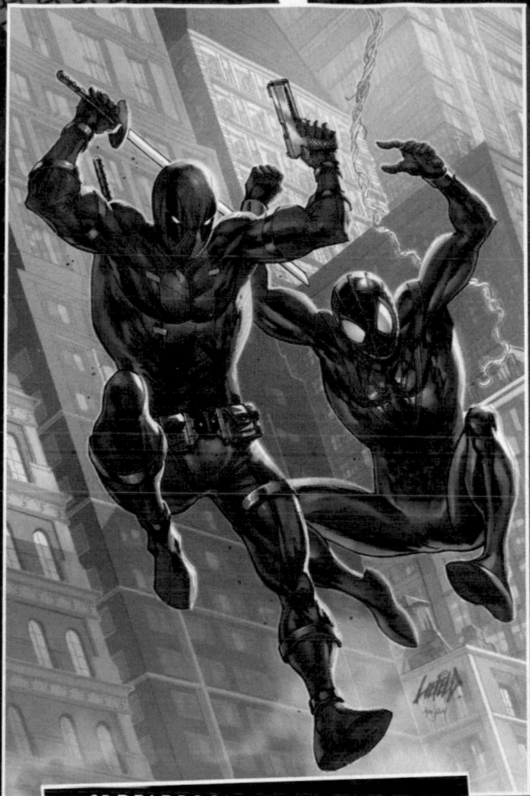

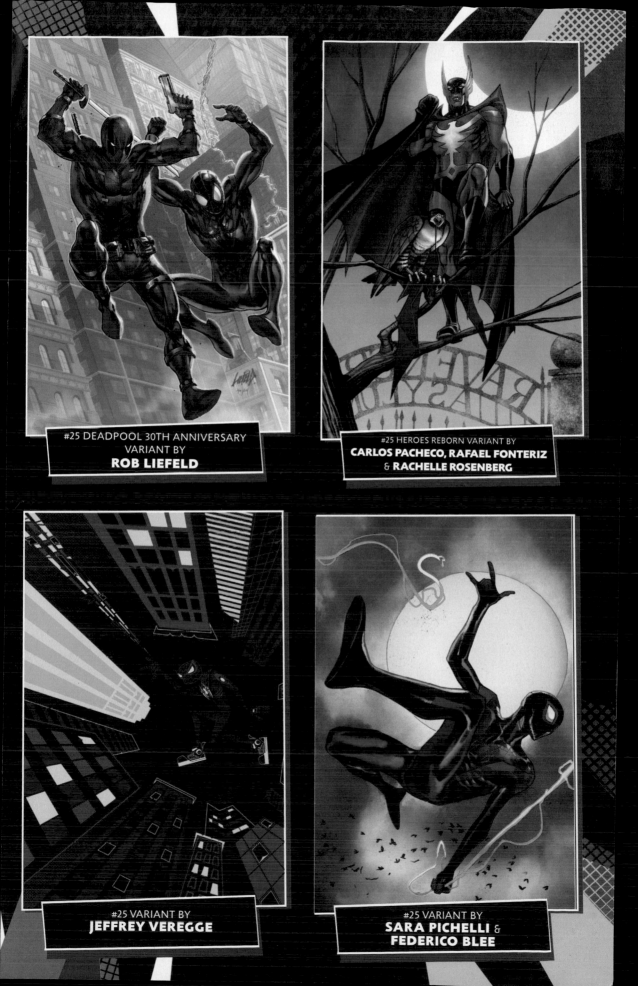

#25 DEADPOOL 30TH ANNIVERSARY
VARIANT BY
ROB LIEFELD

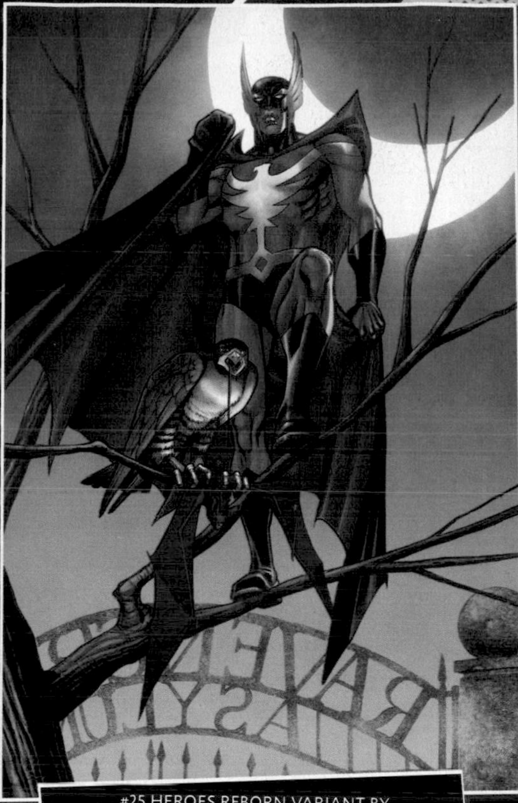

#25 HEROES REBORN VARIANT BY
CARLOS PACHECO, RAFAEL FONTERIZ
& **RACHELLE ROSENBERG**

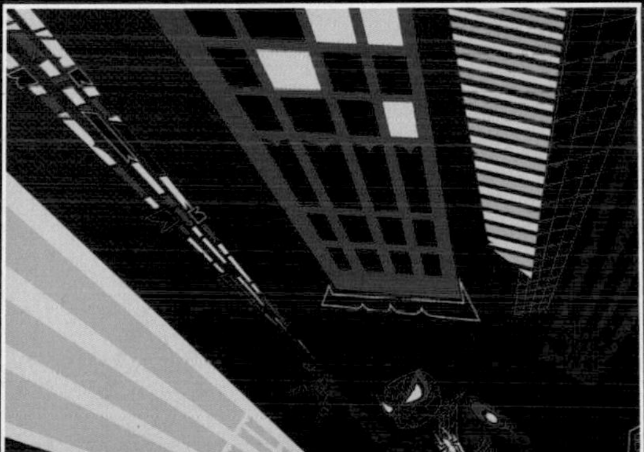

#25 VARIANT BY
JEFFREY VEREGGE

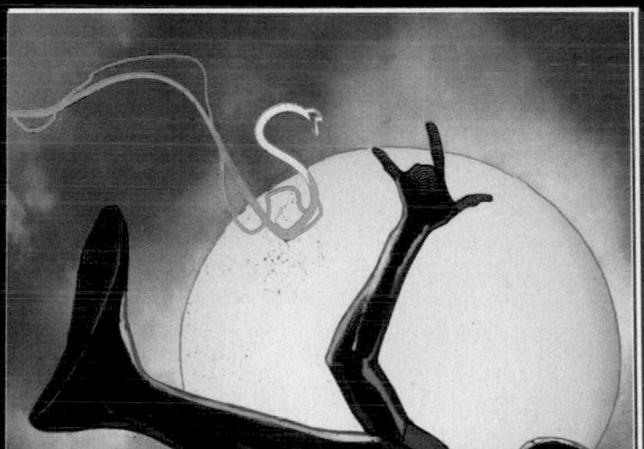

#25 VARIANT BY
SARA PICHELLI &
FEDERICO BLEE

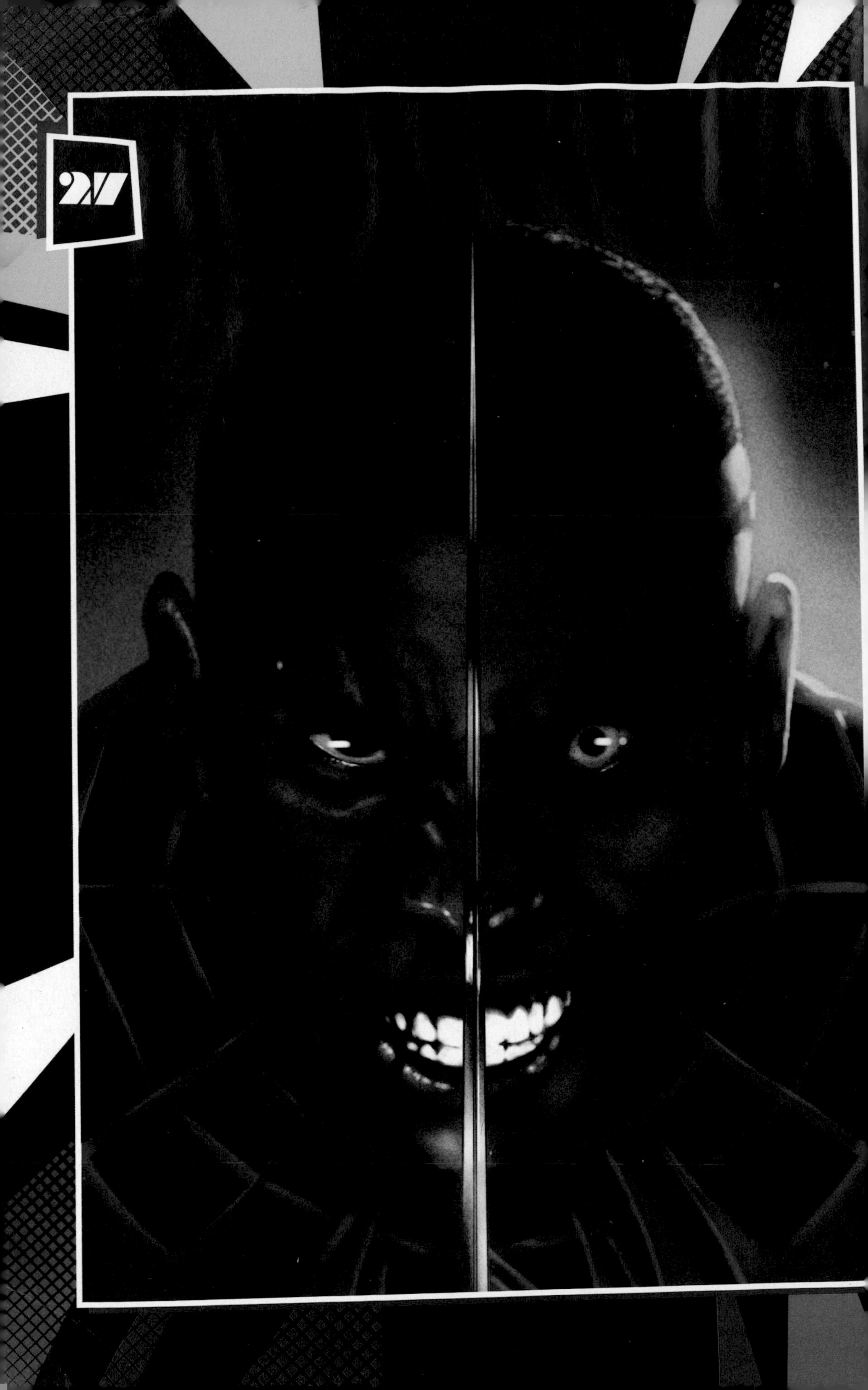

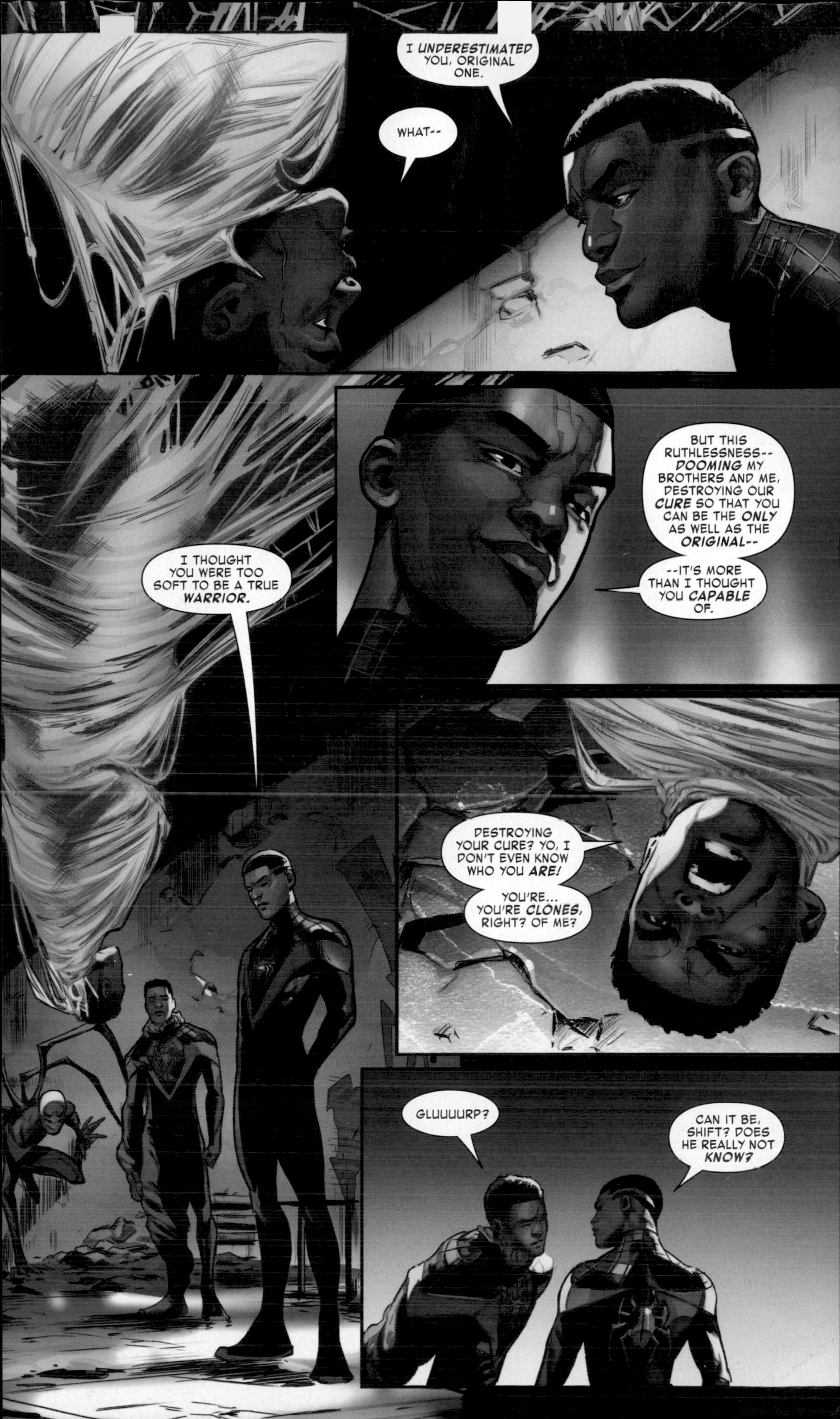
I UNDERESTIMATED YOU, ORIGINAL ONE.
WHAT--
I THOUGHT YOU WERE TOO SOFT TO BE A TRUE WARRIOR.
BUT THIS RUTHLESSNESS-- DOOMING MY BROTHERS AND ME, DESTROYING OUR CURE SO THAT YOU CAN BE THE ONLY AS WELL AS THE ORIGINAL--
--IT'S MORE THAN I THOUGHT YOU CAPABLE OF.
DESTROYING YOUR CURE? YO, I DON'T EVEN KNOW WHO YOU ARE!
YOU'RE... YOU'RE CLONES, RIGHT? OF ME?
GLUUUURP?
CAN IT BE, SHIFT? DOES HE REALLY NOT KNOW?

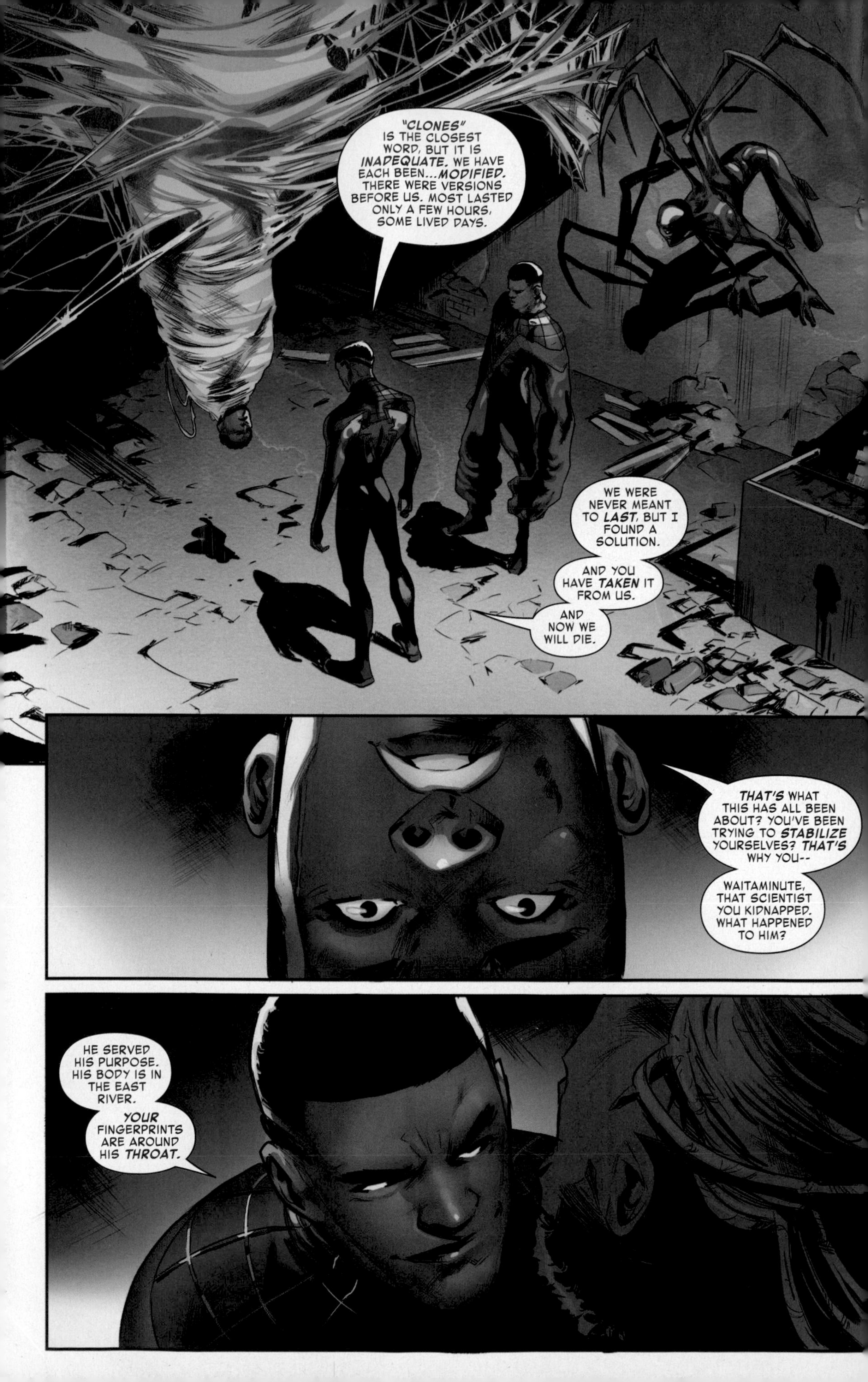
"CLONES" IS THE CLOSEST WORD, BUT IT IS INADEQUATE. WE HAVE EACH BEEN...MODIFIED. THERE WERE VERSIONS BEFORE US. MOST LASTED ONLY A FEW HOURS, SOME LIVED DAYS.
WE WERE NEVER MEANT TO LAST, BUT I FOUND A SOLUTION.
AND YOU HAVE TAKEN IT FROM US.
AND NOW WE WILL DIE.
THAT'S WHAT THIS HAS ALL BEEN ABOUT? YOU'VE BEEN TRYING TO STABILIZE YOURSELVES? THAT'S WHY YOU--
WAITAMINUTE, THAT SCIENTIST YOU KIDNAPPED. WHAT HAPPENED TO HIM?
HE SERVED HIS PURPOSE. HIS BODY IS IN THE EAST RIVER.
YOUR FINGERPRINTS ARE AROUND HIS THROAT.

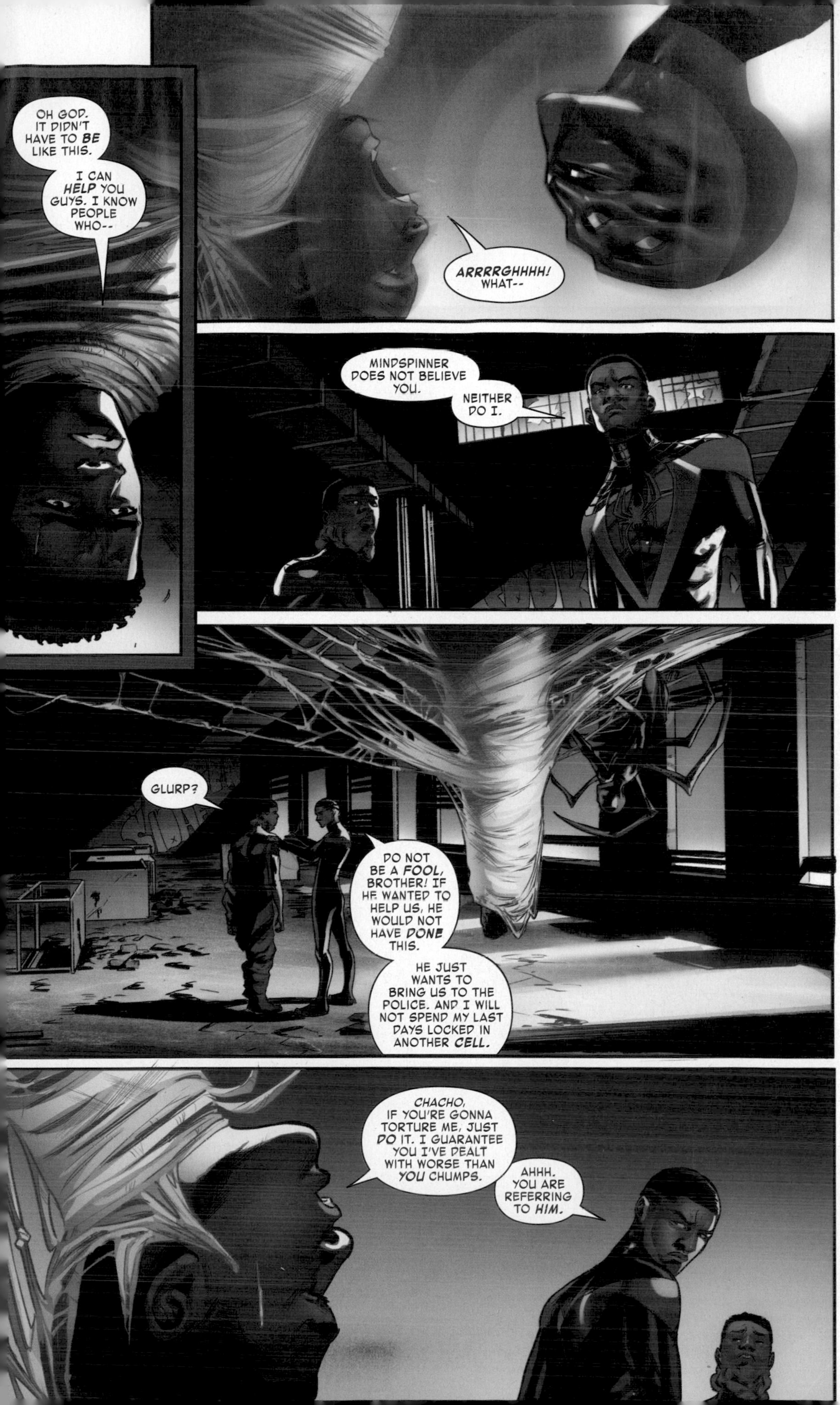
OH GOD. IT DIDN'T HAVE TO BE LIKE THIS.
I CAN HELP YOU GUYS. I KNOW PEOPLE WHO--
ARRRRGHHHH! WHAT--
MINDSPINNER DOES NOT BELIEVE YOU.
NEITHER DO I.
GLURP?
DO NOT BE A FOOL, BROTHER! IF HE WANTED TO HELP US, HE WOULD NOT HAVE DONE THIS.
HE JUST WANTS TO BRING US TO THE POLICE. AND I WILL NOT SPEND MY LAST DAYS LOCKED IN ANOTHER CELL.
CHACHO, IF YOU'RE GONNA TORTURE ME, JUST DO IT. I GUARANTEE YOU I'VE DEALT WITH WORSE THAN YOU CHUMPS.
AHHH. YOU ARE REFERRING TO HIM.

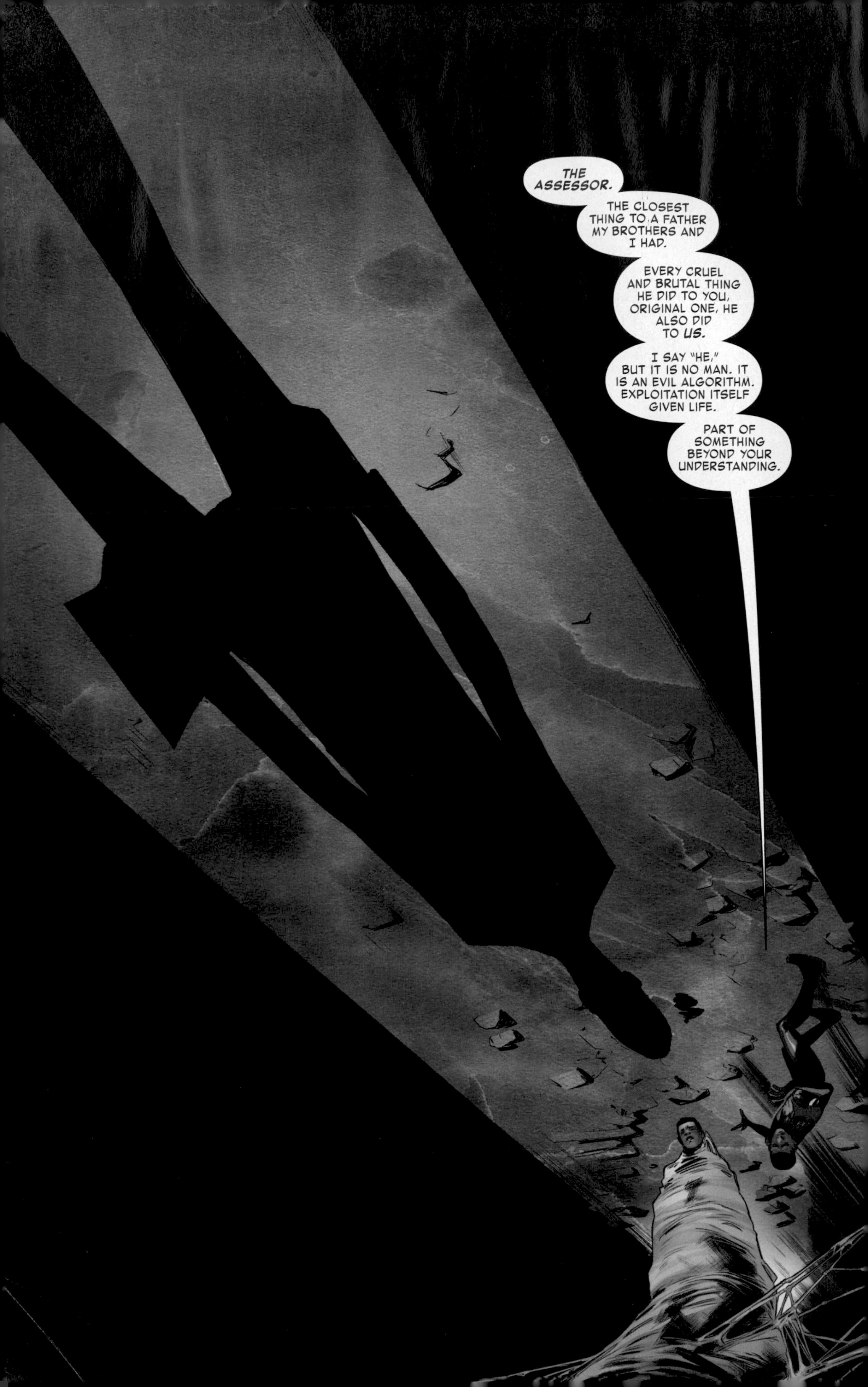
THE ASSESSOR.
THE CLOSEST THING TO A FATHER MY BROTHERS AND I HAD.
EVERY CRUEL AND BRUTAL THING HE DID TO YOU, ORIGINAL ONE, HE ALSO DID TO US.
I SAY "HE," BUT IT IS NO MAN. IT IS AN EVIL ALGORITHM. EXPLOITATION ITSELF GIVEN LIFE.
PART OF SOMETHING BEYOND YOUR UNDERSTANDING.

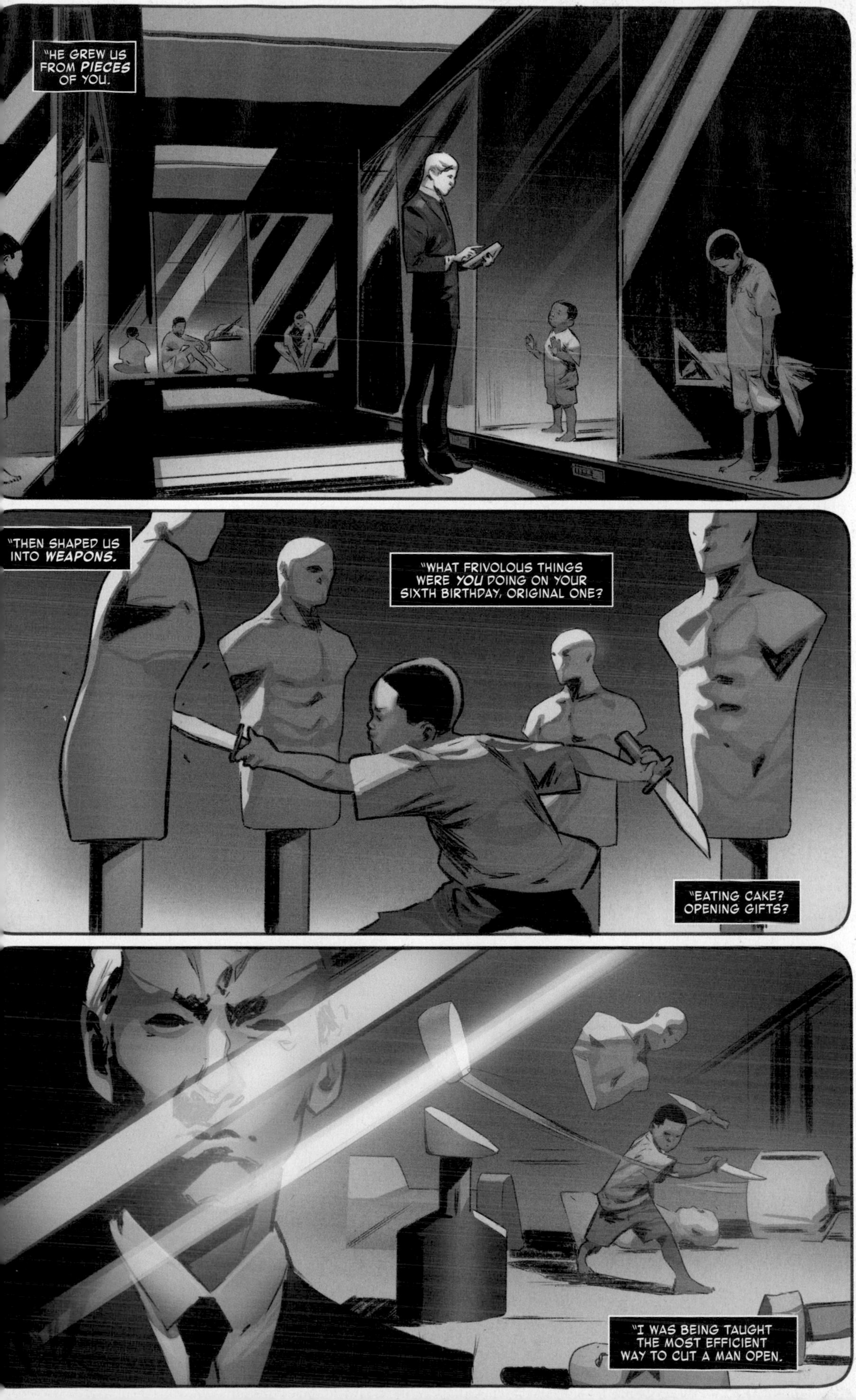
"HE GREW US FROM *PIECES* OF YOU.
"THEN SHAPED US INTO *WEAPONS.*
"WHAT FRIVOLOUS THINGS WERE *YOU* DOING ON YOUR SIXTH BIRTHDAY, ORIGINAL ONE?
"EATING CAKE? OPENING GIFTS?
"I WAS BEING TAUGHT THE MOST EFFICIENT WAY TO CUT A MAN OPEN.

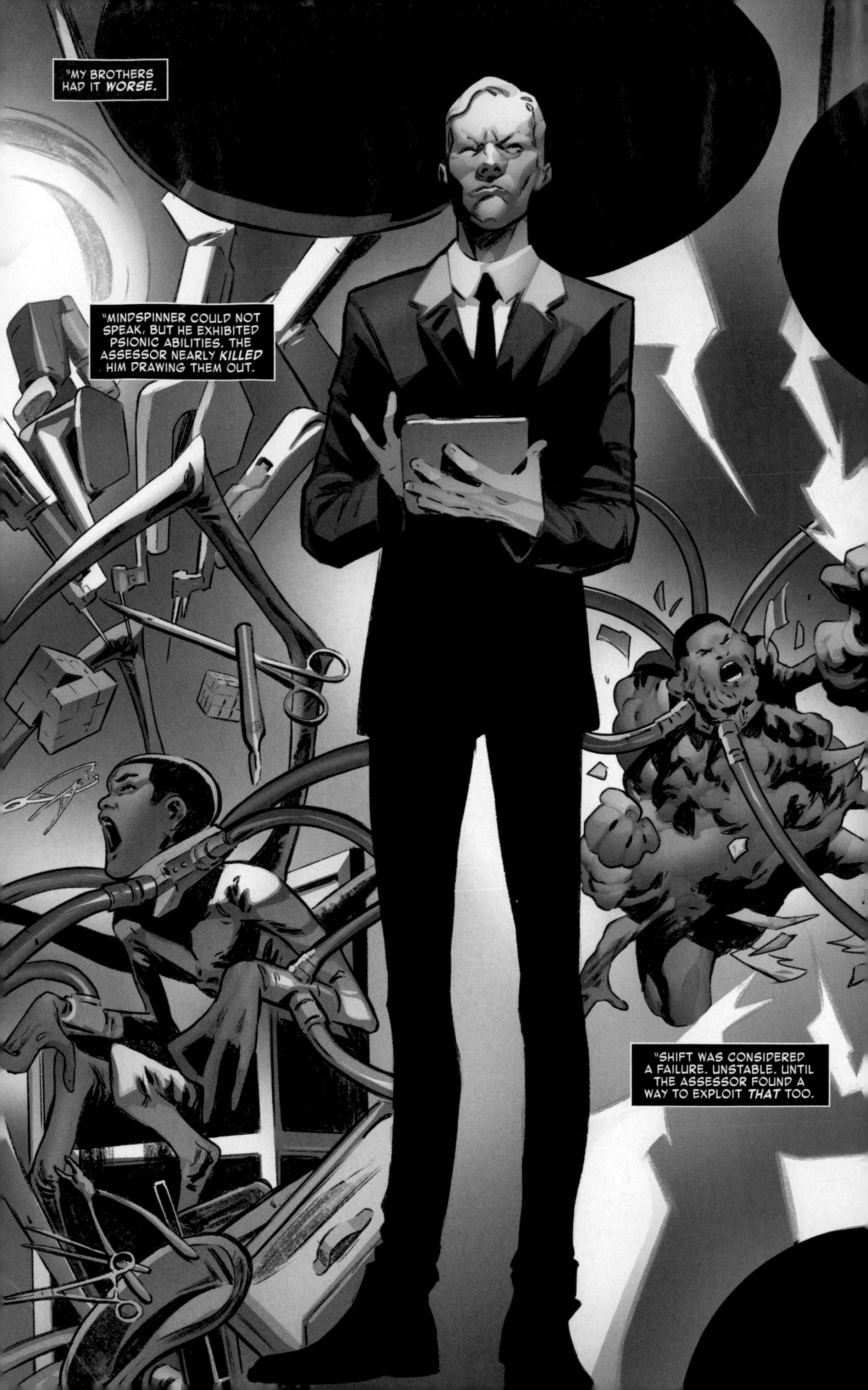
"MY BROTHERS HAD IT WORSE.
"MINDSPINNER COULD NOT SPEAK, BUT HE EXHIBITED PSIONIC ABILITIES. THE ASSESSOR NEARLY KILLED HIM DRAWING THEM OUT.
"SHIFT WAS CONSIDERED A FAILURE. UNSTABLE. UNTIL THE ASSESSOR FOUND A WAY TO EXPLOIT THAT TOO.

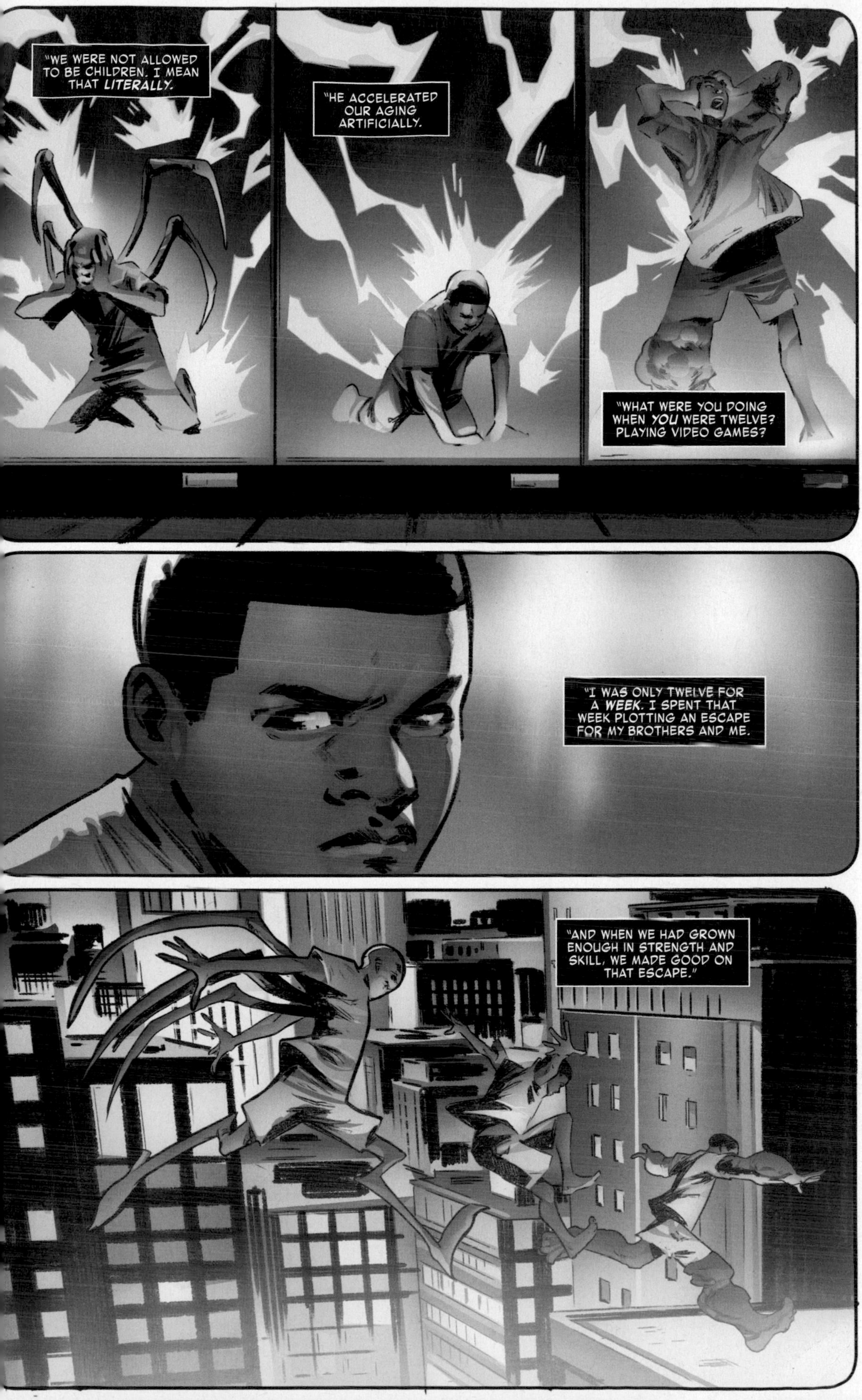
"WE WERE NOT ALLOWED TO BE CHILDREN. I MEAN THAT LITERALLY.
"HE ACCELERATED OUR AGING ARTIFICIALLY.
"WHAT WERE YOU DOING WHEN YOU WERE TWELVE? PLAYING VIDEO GAMES?
"I WAS ONLY TWELVE FOR A WEEK. I SPENT THAT WEEK PLOTTING AN ESCAPE FOR MY BROTHERS AND ME.
"AND WHEN WE HAD GROWN ENOUGH IN STRENGTH AND SKILL, WE MADE GOOD ON THAT ESCAPE."

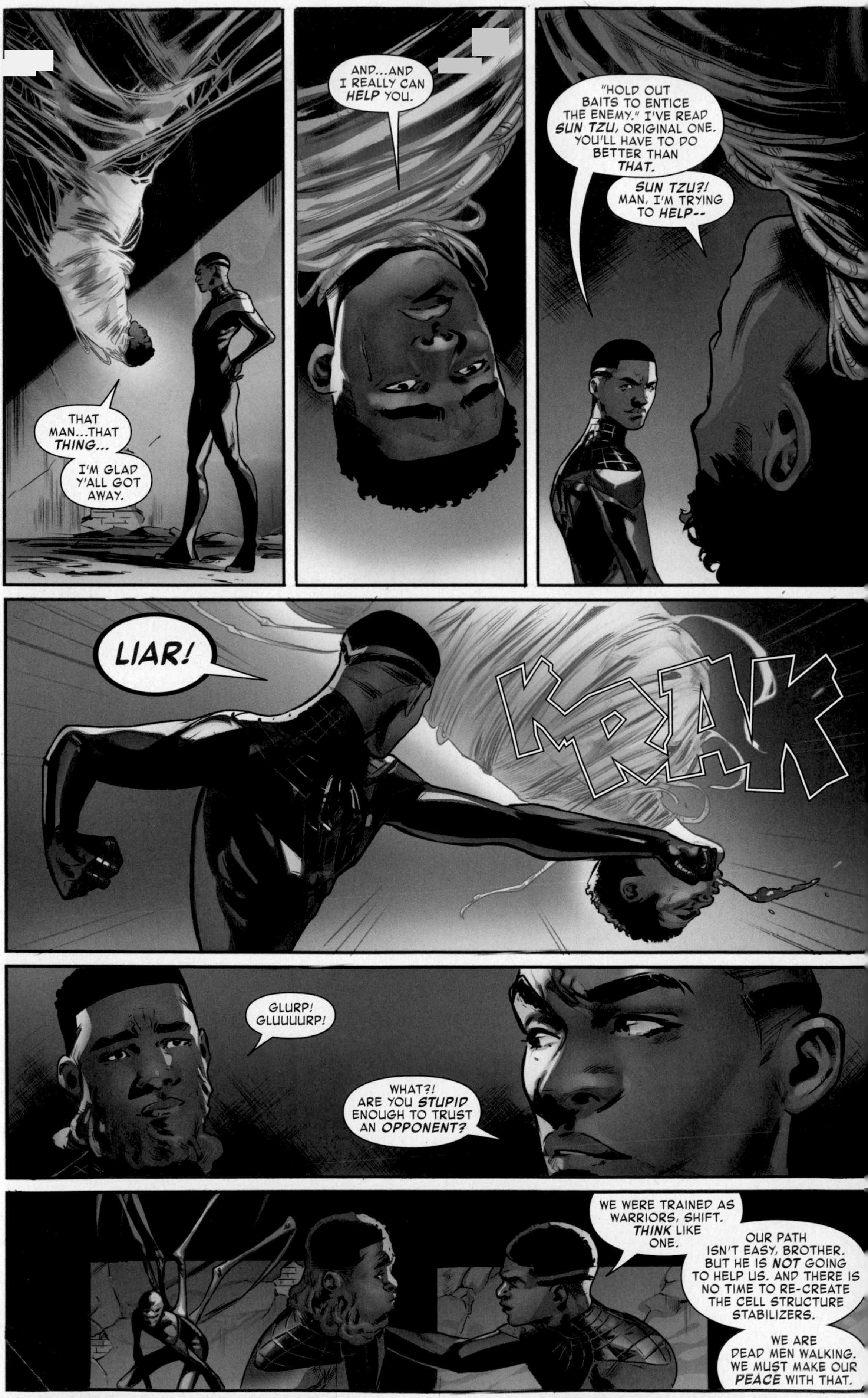
THAT MAN...THAT THING...
I'M GLAD Y'ALL GOT AWAY.
AND...AND I REALLY CAN HELP YOU.
"HOLD OUT BAITS TO ENTICE THE ENEMY." I'VE READ SUN TZU, ORIGINAL ONE. YOU'LL HAVE TO DO BETTER THAN THAT.
SUN TZU?! MAN, I'M TRYING TO HELP--
LIAR!
KRAK
GLURP! GLUUUURP!
WHAT?! ARE YOU STUPID ENOUGH TO TRUST AN OPPONENT?
WE WERE TRAINED AS WARRIORS, SHIFT. THINK LIKE ONE.
OUR PATH ISN'T EASY, BROTHER. BUT HE IS NOT GOING TO HELP US. AND THERE IS NO TIME TO RE-CREATE THE CELL STRUCTURE STABILIZERS.
WE ARE DEAD MEN WALKING. WE MUST MAKE OUR PEACE WITH THAT.

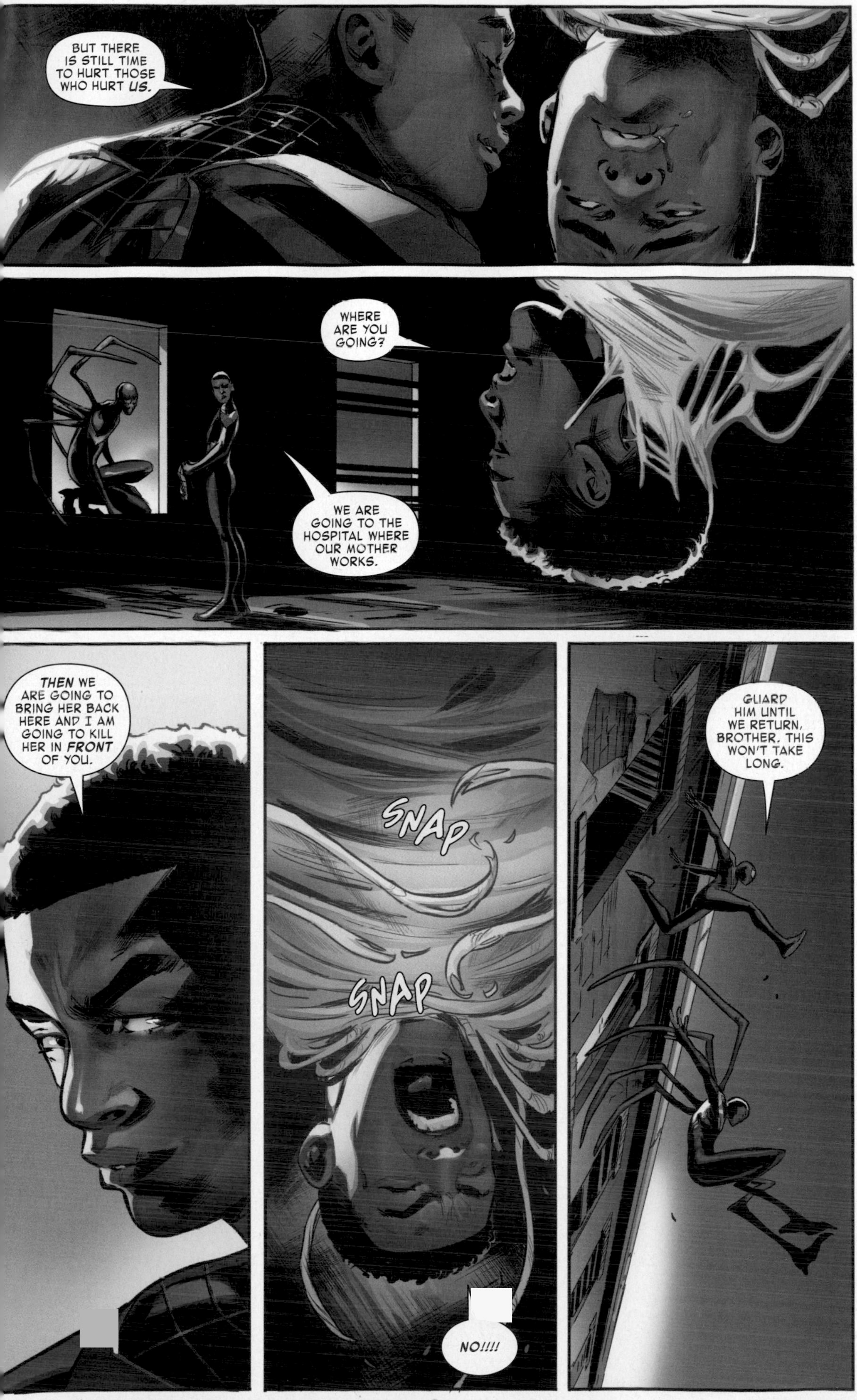
BUT THERE IS STILL TIME TO HURT THOSE WHO HURT *US.*
WHERE ARE YOU GOING?
WE ARE GOING TO THE HOSPITAL WHERE OUR MOTHER WORKS.
THEN WE ARE GOING TO BRING HER BACK HERE AND I AM GOING TO KILL HER IN *FRONT* OF YOU.
SNAP
SNAP
NO!!!!
GUARD HIM UNTIL WE RETURN, BROTHER. THIS WON'T TAKE LONG.

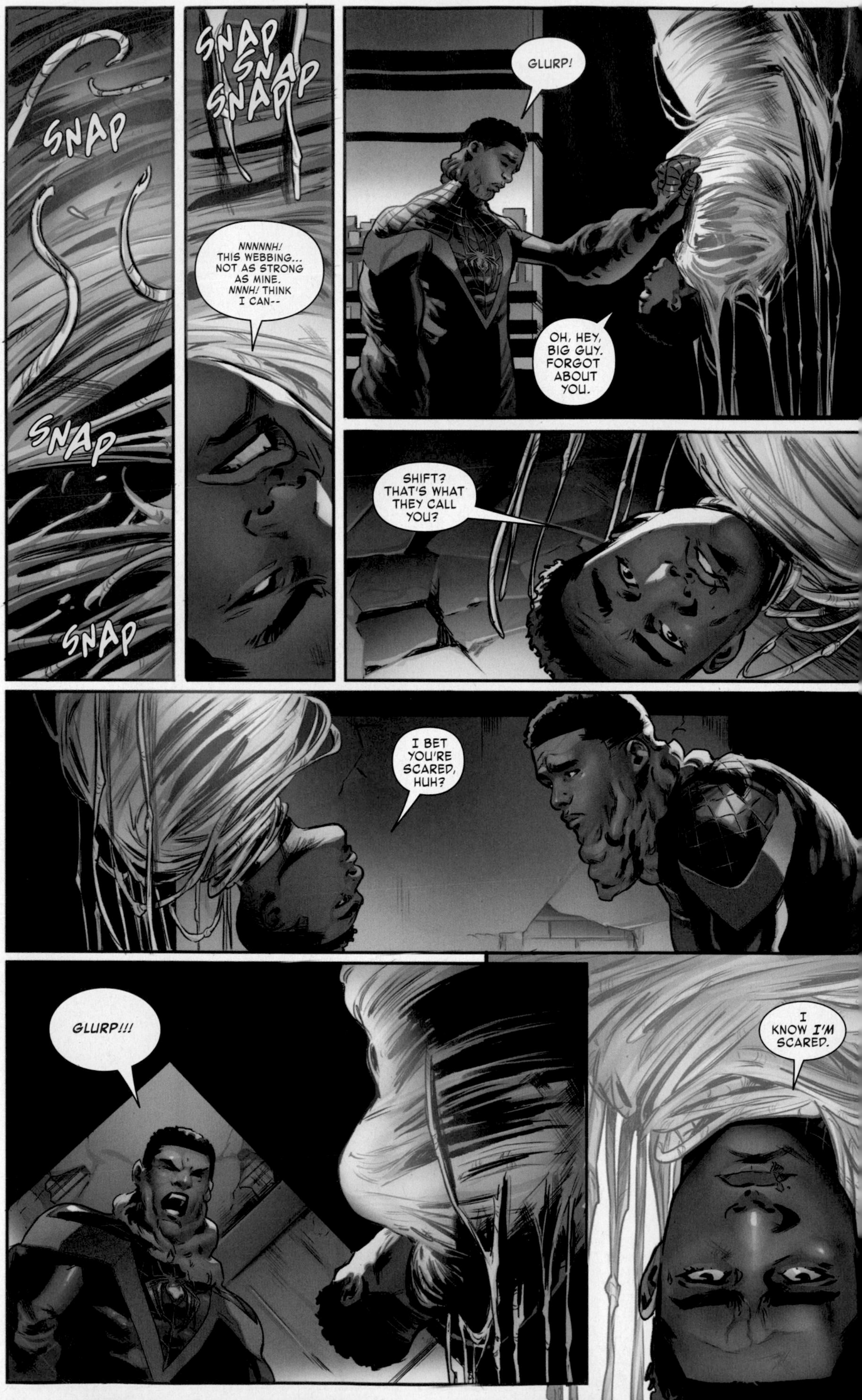
SNAP
SNAP
SNAP
SNAP SNAP SNAP
NNNNNH! THIS WEBBING... NOT AS STRONG AS MINE. NNNH! THINK I CAN--
GLURP!
OH, HEY, BIG GUY. FORGOT ABOUT YOU.
SHIFT? THAT'S WHAT THEY CALL YOU?
I BET YOU'RE SCARED, HUH?
GLURP!!!
I KNOW I'M SCARED.

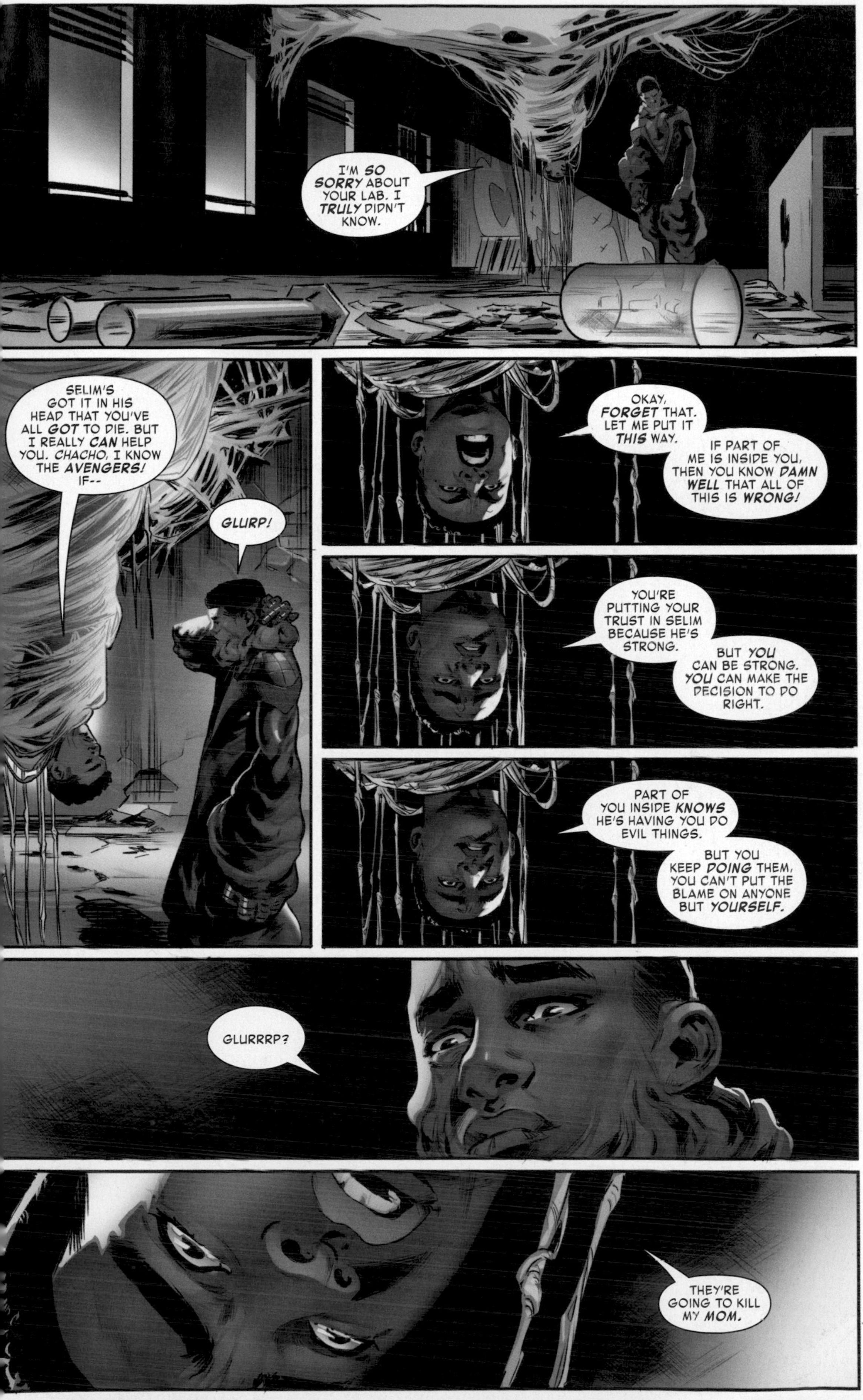
I'M SO SORRY ABOUT YOUR LAB. I TRULY DIDN'T KNOW.
SELIM'S GOT IT IN HIS HEAD THAT YOU'VE ALL GOT TO DIE. BUT I REALLY CAN HELP YOU. CHACHO, I KNOW THE AVENGERS! IF--
GLURP!
OKAY, FORGET THAT. LET ME PUT IT THIS WAY.
IF PART OF ME IS INSIDE YOU, THEN YOU KNOW DAMN WELL THAT ALL OF THIS IS WRONG!
YOU'RE PUTTING YOUR TRUST IN SELIM BECAUSE HE'S STRONG.
BUT YOU CAN BE STRONG. YOU CAN MAKE THE DECISION TO DO RIGHT.
PART OF YOU INSIDE KNOWS HE'S HAVING YOU DO EVIL THINGS.
BUT YOU KEEP DOING THEM, YOU CAN'T PUT THE BLAME ON ANYONE BUT YOURSELF.
GLURRRP?
THEY'RE GOING TO KILL MY MOM.

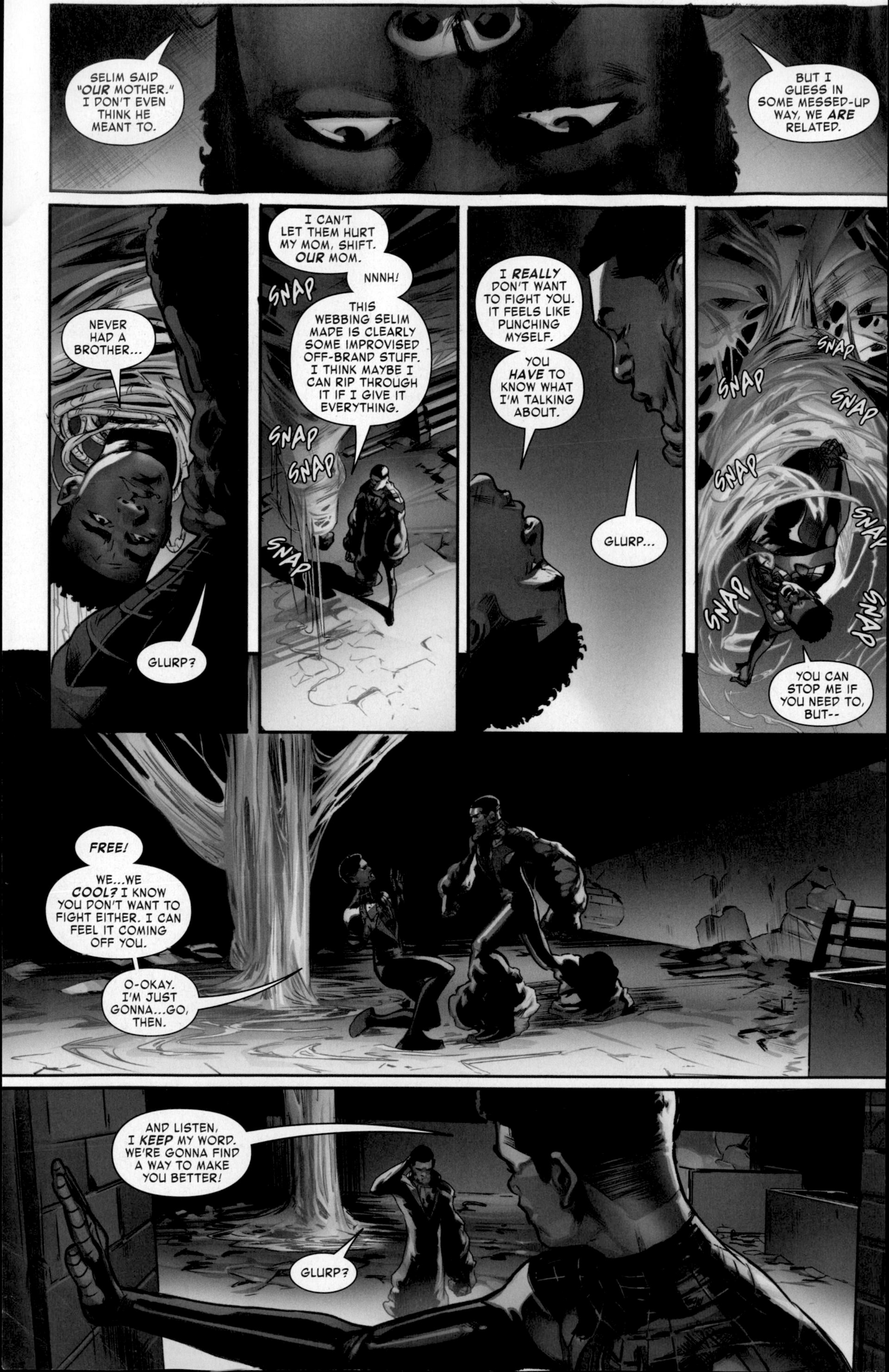
SELIM SAID "OUR MOTHER." I DON'T EVEN THINK HE MEANT TO.
BUT I GUESS IN SOME MESSED-UP WAY, WE ARE RELATED.
NEVER HAD A BROTHER...
GLURP?
I CAN'T LET THEM HURT MY MOM, SHIFT. OUR MOM.
NNNH!
THIS WEBBING SELIM MADE IS CLEARLY SOME IMPROVISED OFF-BRAND STUFF. I THINK MAYBE I CAN RIP THROUGH IT IF I GIVE IT EVERYTHING.
SNAP
SNAP
SNAP
SNAP
I REALLY DON'T WANT TO FIGHT YOU. IT FEELS LIKE PUNCHING MYSELF.
YOU HAVE TO KNOW WHAT I'M TALKING ABOUT.
GLURP...
SNAP
SNAP
SNAP
SNAP
SNAP
SNAP
SNAP
YOU CAN STOP ME IF YOU NEED TO, BUT--
FREE!
WE...WE COOL? I KNOW YOU DON'T WANT TO FIGHT EITHER. I CAN FEEL IT COMING OFF YOU.
O-OKAY. I'M JUST GONNA...GO, THEN.
AND LISTEN, I KEEP MY WORD. WE'RE GONNA FIND A WAY TO MAKE YOU BETTER!
GLURP?

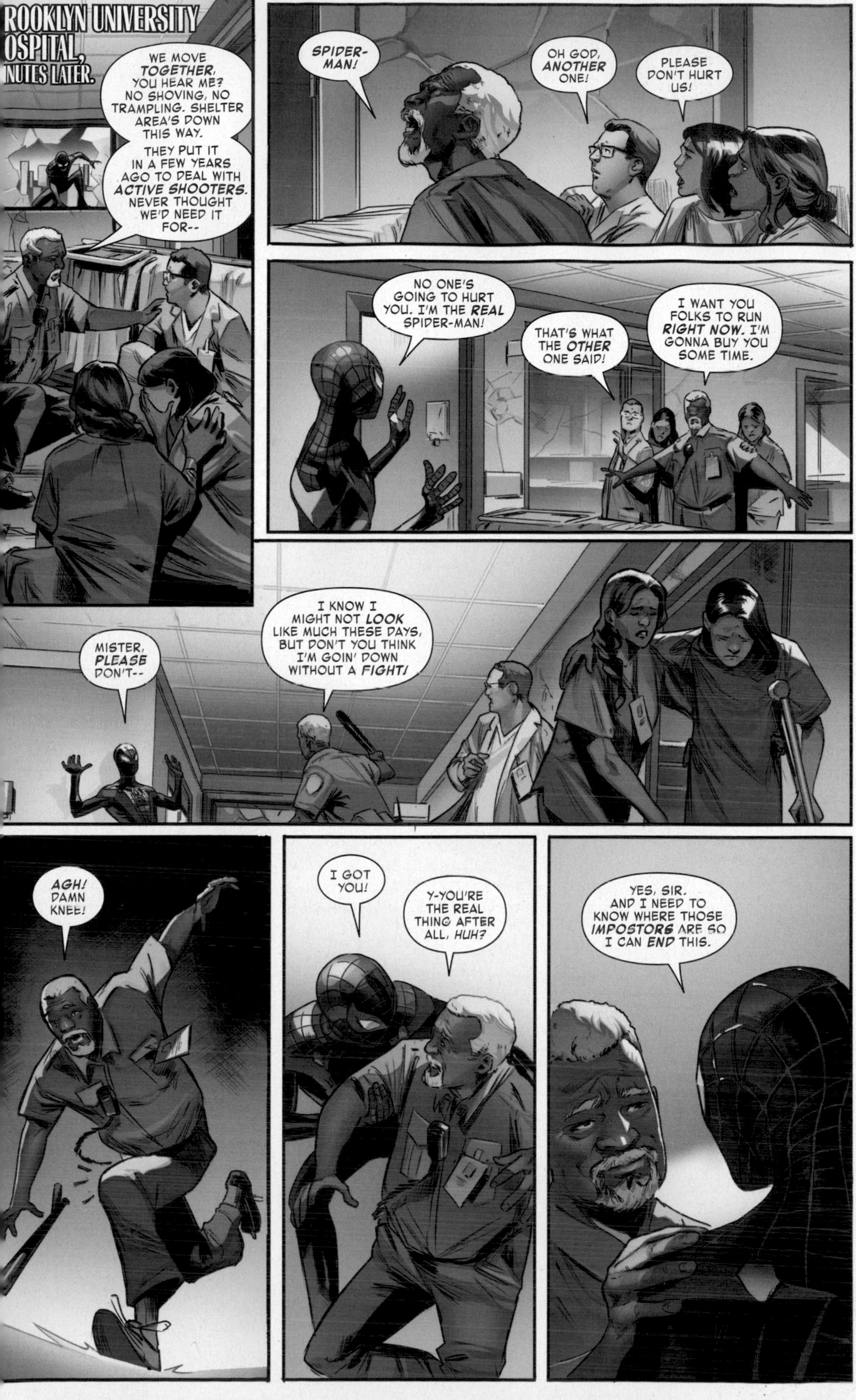

ROOKLYN UNIVERSITY OSPITAL, NUTES LATER.
WE MOVE TOGETHER, YOU HEAR ME? NO SHOVING, NO TRAMPLING. SHELTER AREA'S DOWN THIS WAY.
THEY PUT IT IN A FEW YEARS AGO TO DEAL WITH ACTIVE SHOOTERS. NEVER THOUGHT WE'D NEED IT FOR--
SPIDER-MAN!
OH GOD, ANOTHER ONE!
PLEASE DON'T HURT US!
NO ONE'S GOING TO HURT YOU. I'M THE REAL SPIDER-MAN!
THAT'S WHAT THE OTHER ONE SAID!
I WANT YOU FOLKS TO RUN RIGHT NOW. I'M GONNA BUY YOU SOME TIME.
MISTER, PLEASE DON'T--
I KNOW I MIGHT NOT LOOK LIKE MUCH THESE DAYS, BUT DON'T YOU THINK I'M GOIN' DOWN WITHOUT A FIGHT!
AGH! DAMN KNEE!
I GOT YOU!
Y-YOU'RE THE REAL THING AFTER ALL, HUH?
YES, SIR. AND I NEED TO KNOW WHERE THOSE IMPOSTORS ARE SO I CAN END THIS.

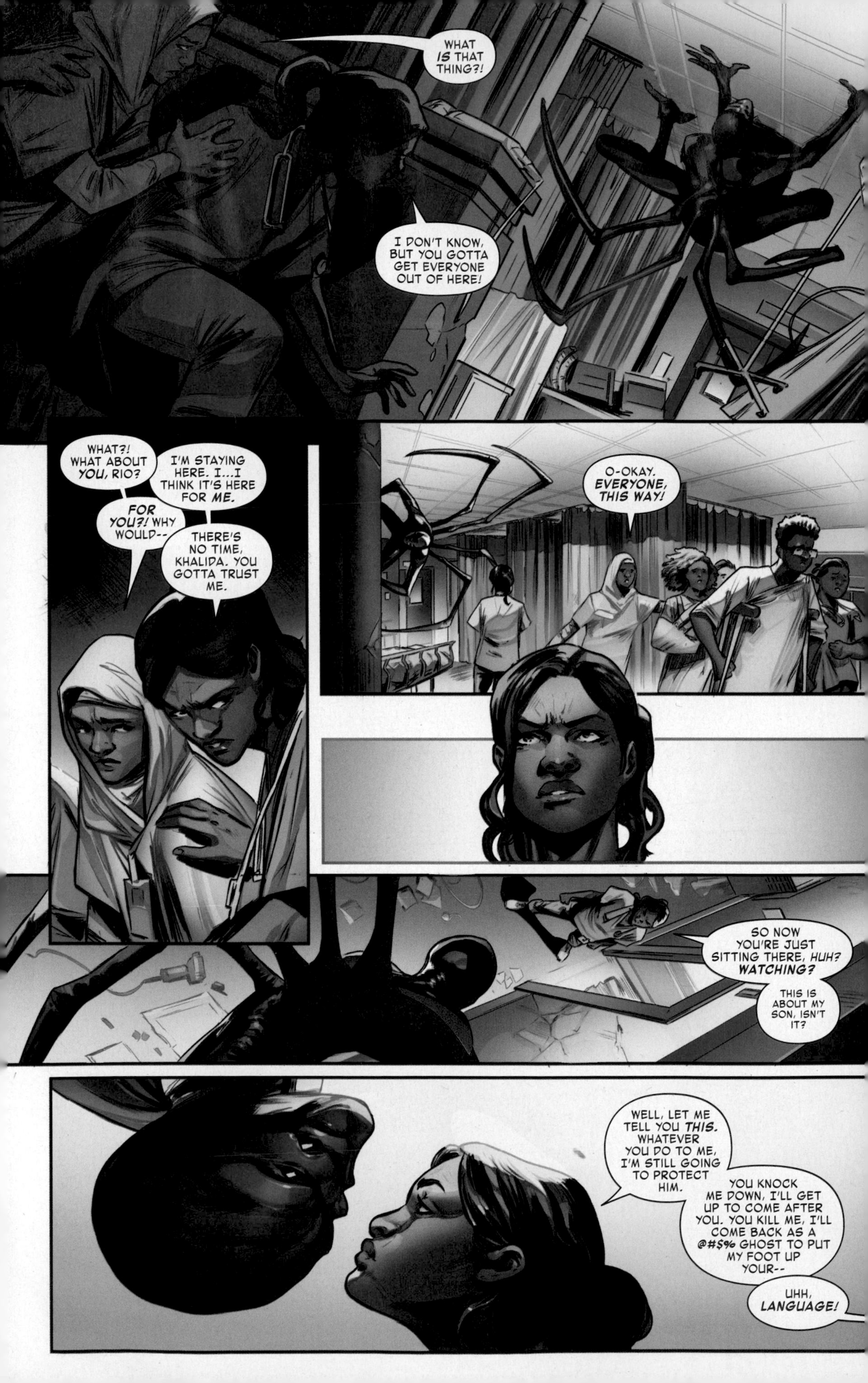
WHAT IS THAT THING?!
I DON'T KNOW, BUT YOU GOTTA GET EVERYONE OUT OF HERE!
WHAT?! WHAT ABOUT YOU, RIO?
I'M STAYING HERE. I...I THINK IT'S HERE FOR ME.
FOR YOU?! WHY WOULD--
THERE'S NO TIME, KHALIDA. YOU GOTTA TRUST ME.
O-OKAY. EVERYONE, THIS WAY!
SO NOW YOU'RE JUST SITTING THERE, HUH? WATCHING?
THIS IS ABOUT MY SON, ISN'T IT?
WELL, LET ME TELL YOU THIS. WHATEVER YOU DO TO ME, I'M STILL GOING TO PROTECT HIM.
YOU KNOCK ME DOWN, I'LL GET UP TO COME AFTER YOU. YOU KILL ME, I'LL COME BACK AS A @#$% GHOST TO PUT MY FOOT UP YOUR--
UHH, LANGUAGE!

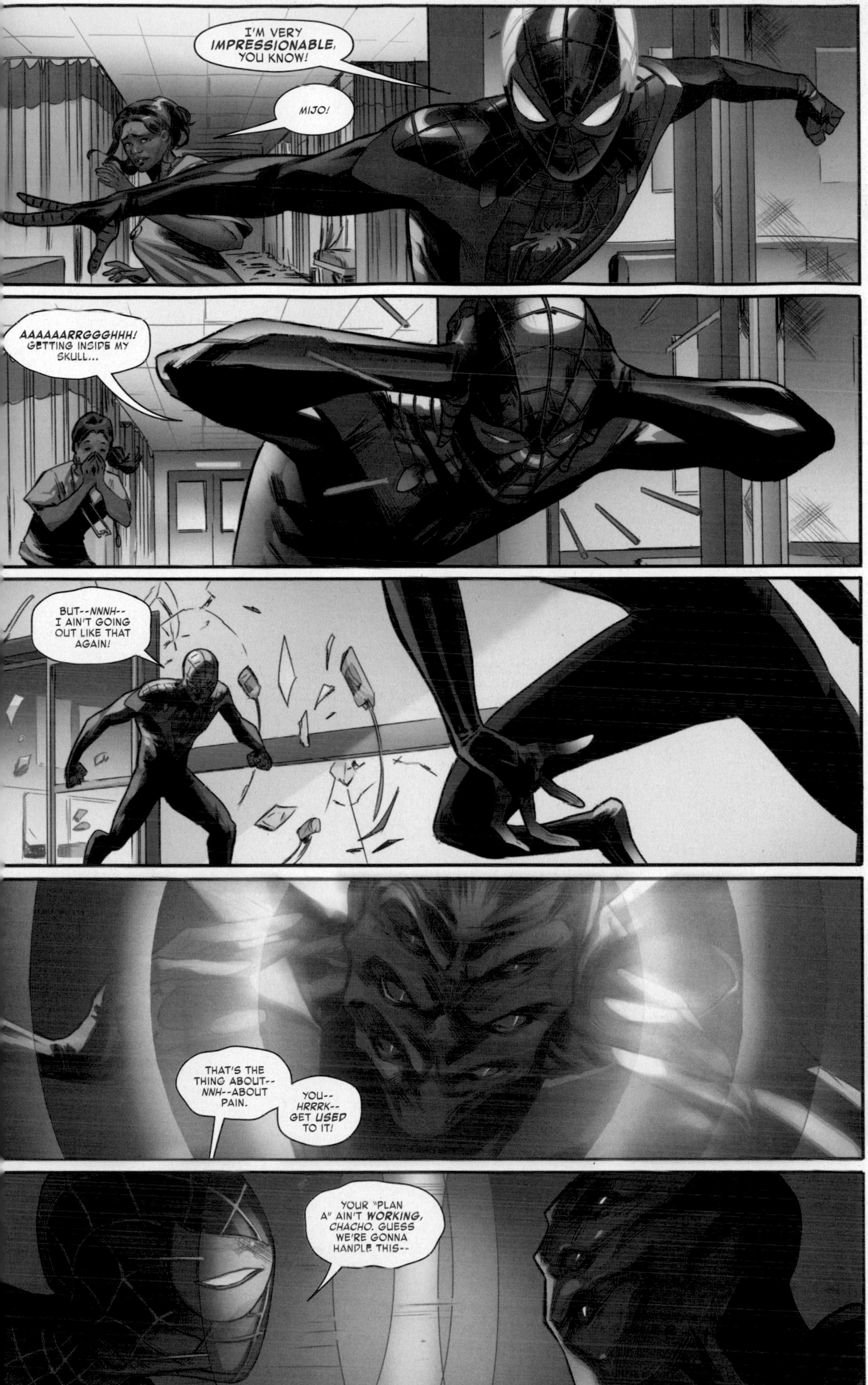
I'M VERY IMPRESSIONABLE, YOU KNOW!
MIJO!
AAAAAARRGGGHHH! GETTING INSIDE MY SKULL...
BUT--NNNH-- I AIN'T GOING OUT LIKE THAT AGAIN!
THAT'S THE THING ABOUT-- NNH--ABOUT PAIN.
YOU-- HRRRK-- GET USED TO IT!
YOUR "PLAN A" AIN'T WORKING, CHACHO. GUESS WE'RE GONNA HANDLE THIS--

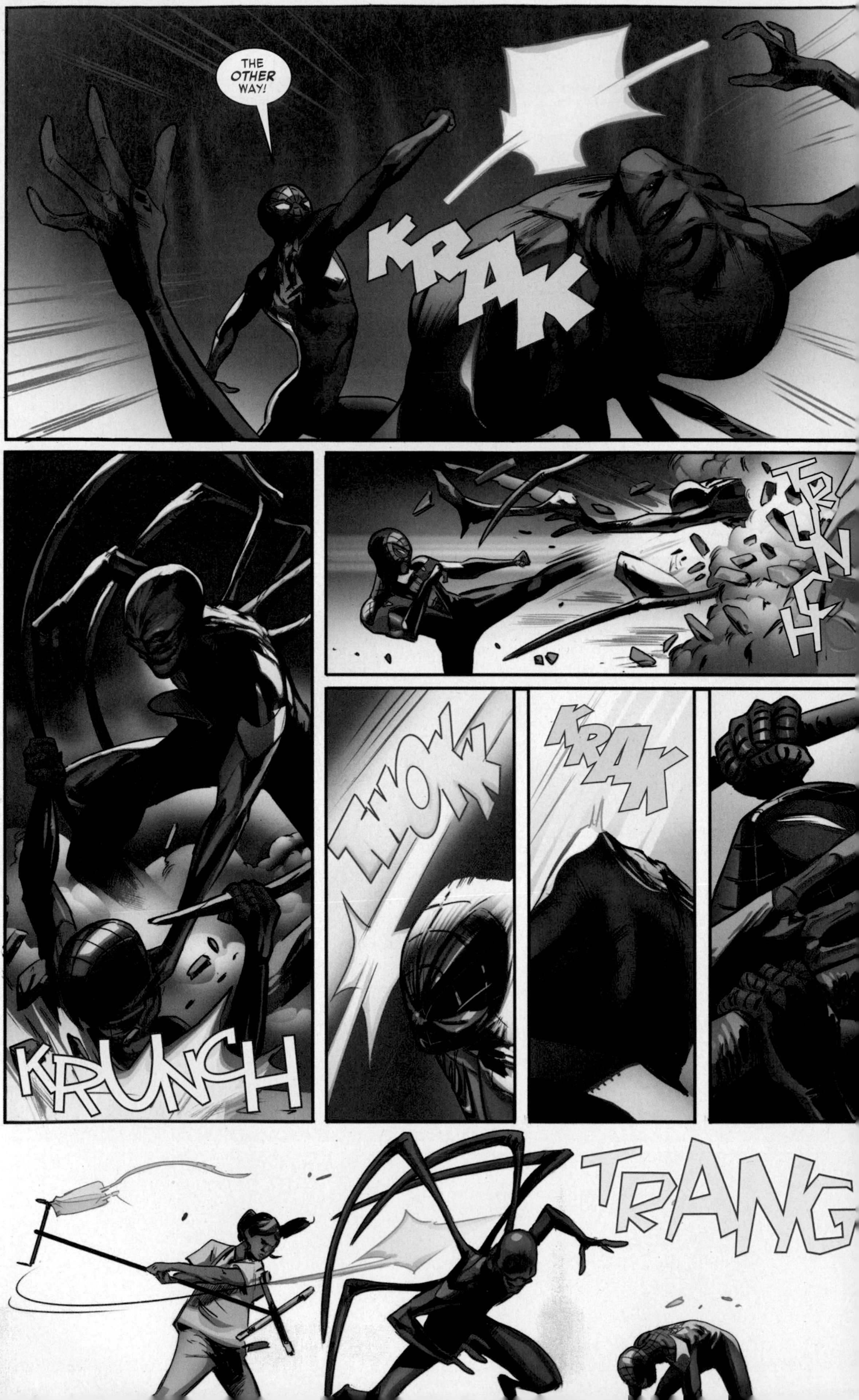
THE OTHER WAY!
KRAK
TRUNCH
KRUNCH
THWOK
KRAK
TRANG

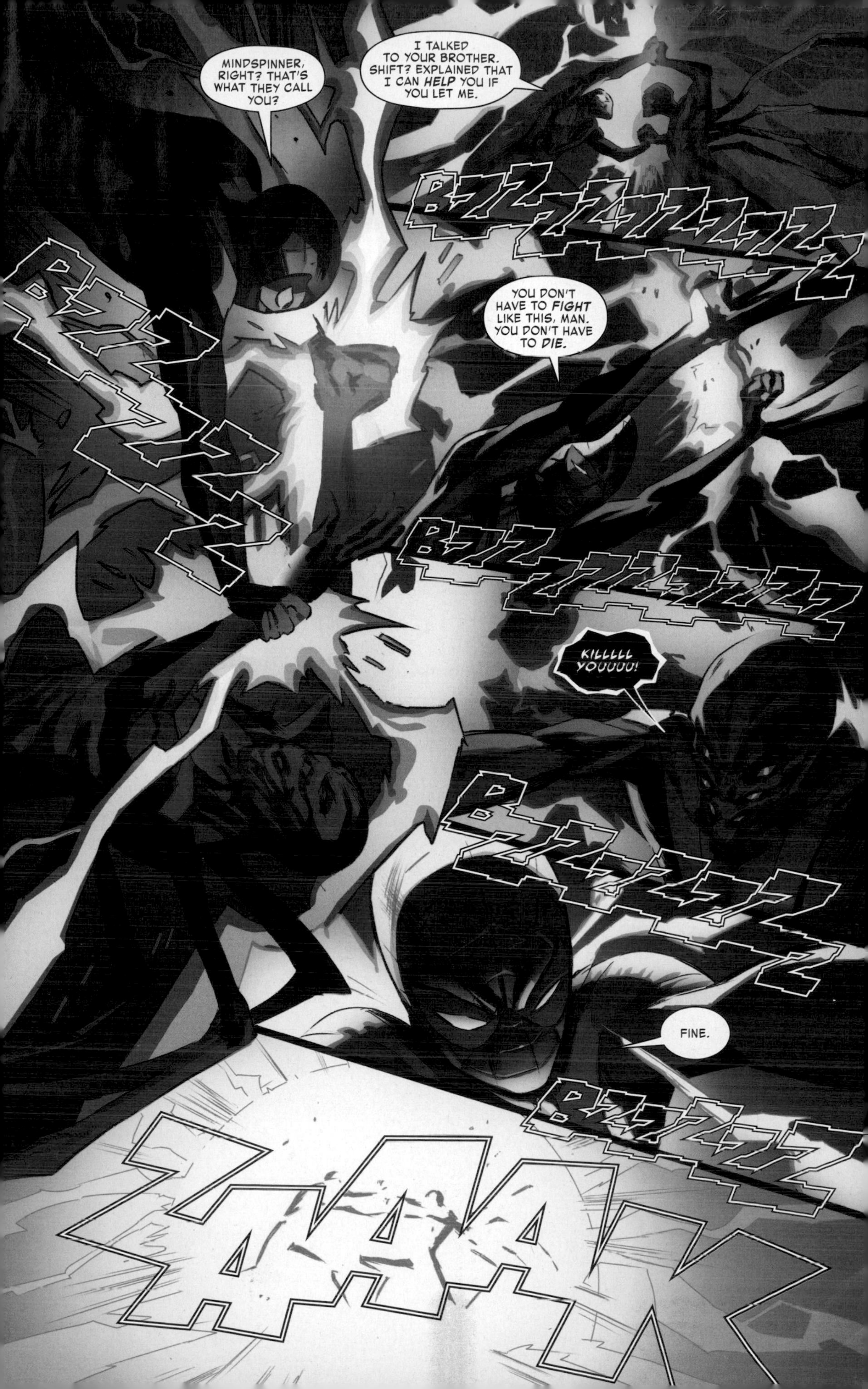
MINDSPINNER, RIGHT? THAT'S WHAT THEY CALL YOU?
I TALKED TO YOUR BROTHER. SHIFT? EXPLAINED THAT I CAN HELP YOU IF YOU LET ME.
BZZZZZZZZZZZZ
BZZZZZZZZ
YOU DON'T HAVE TO FIGHT LIKE THIS, MAN. YOU DON'T HAVE TO DIE.
BZZZZZZZZZZZ
KILLLLLL YOUUUU!
BZZZZZZZZZ
FINE.
BZZZZZZZZ
ZAAK

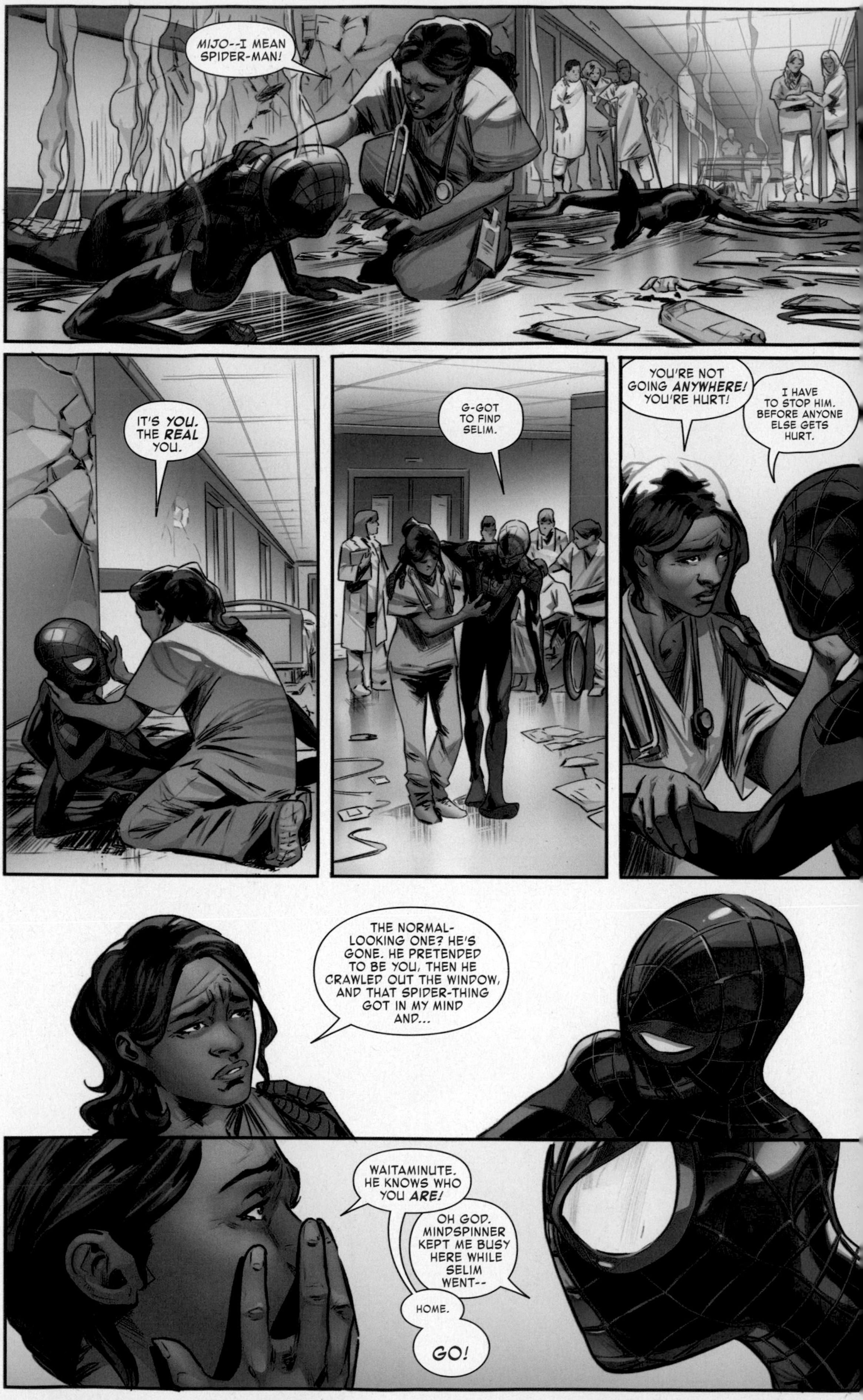
MIJO--I MEAN SPIDER-MAN!
IT'S YOU. THE REAL YOU.
G-GOT TO FIND SELIM.
YOU'RE NOT GOING ANYWHERE! YOU'RE HURT!
I HAVE TO STOP HIM. BEFORE ANYONE ELSE GETS HURT.
THE NORMAL-LOOKING ONE? HE'S GONE. HE PRETENDED TO BE YOU, THEN HE CRAWLED OUT THE WINDOW, AND THAT SPIDER-THING GOT IN MY MIND AND...
WAITAMINUTE. HE KNOWS WHO YOU ARE!
OH GOD. MINDSPINNER KEPT ME BUSY HERE WHILE SELIM WENT--
HOME.
GO!

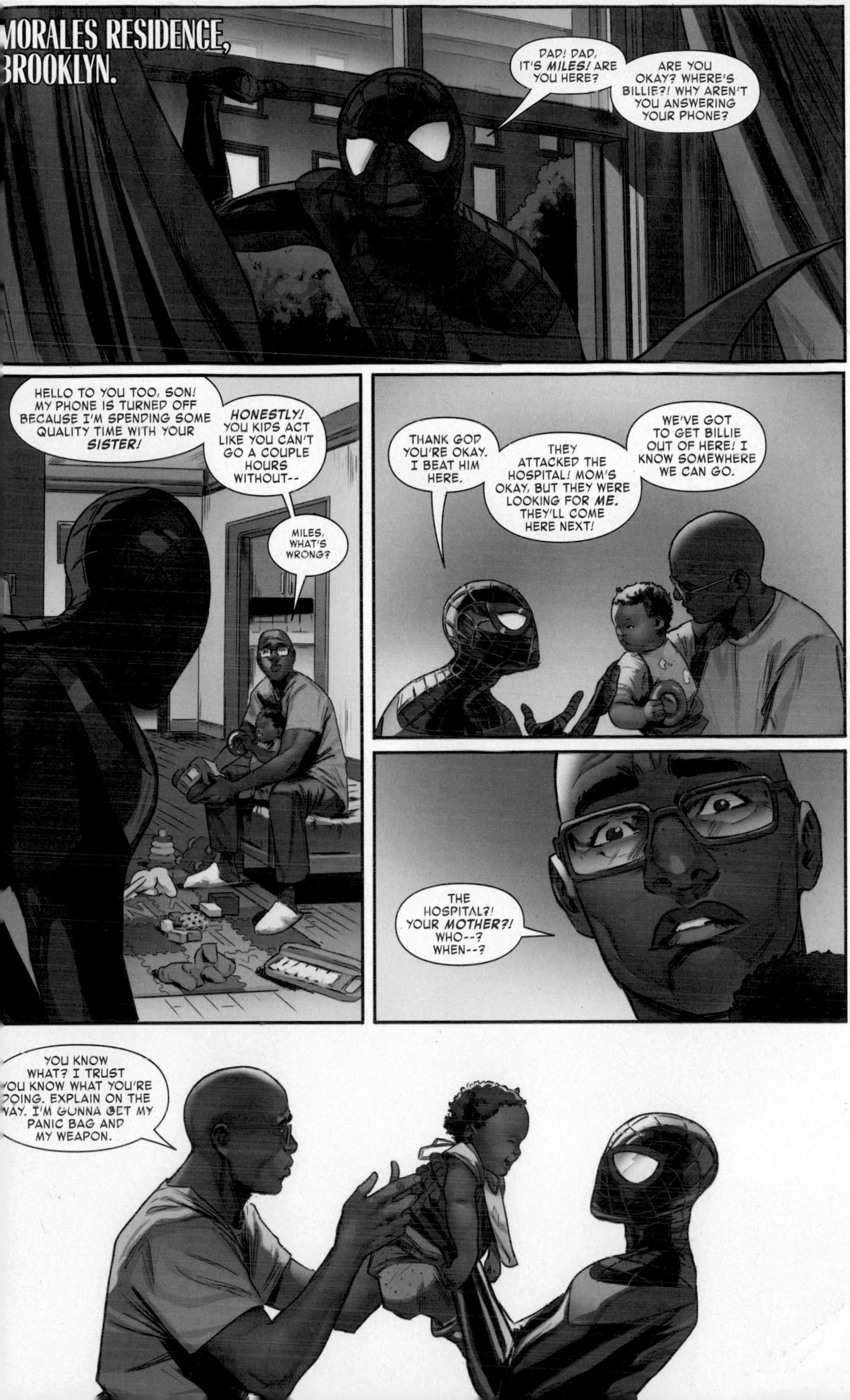
MORALES RESIDENCE, BROOKLYN.
DAD! DAD, IT'S MILES! ARE YOU HERE?
ARE YOU OKAY? WHERE'S BILLIE?! WHY AREN'T YOU ANSWERING YOUR PHONE?
HELLO TO YOU TOO, SON! MY PHONE IS TURNED OFF BECAUSE I'M SPENDING SOME QUALITY TIME WITH YOUR SISTER!
HONESTLY! YOU KIDS ACT LIKE YOU CAN'T GO A COUPLE HOURS WITHOUT--
MILES, WHAT'S WRONG?
THANK GOD YOU'RE OKAY. I BEAT HIM HERE.
THEY ATTACKED THE HOSPITAL! MOM'S OKAY, BUT THEY WERE LOOKING FOR ME. THEY'LL COME HERE NEXT!
WE'VE GOT TO GET BILLIE OUT OF HERE! I KNOW SOMEWHERE WE CAN GO.
THE HOSPITAL?! YOUR MOTHER?! WHO--? WHEN--?
YOU KNOW WHAT? I TRUST OU KNOW WHAT YOU'RE OING. EXPLAIN ON THE AY. I'M GUNNA GET MY PANIC BAG AND MY WEAPON.

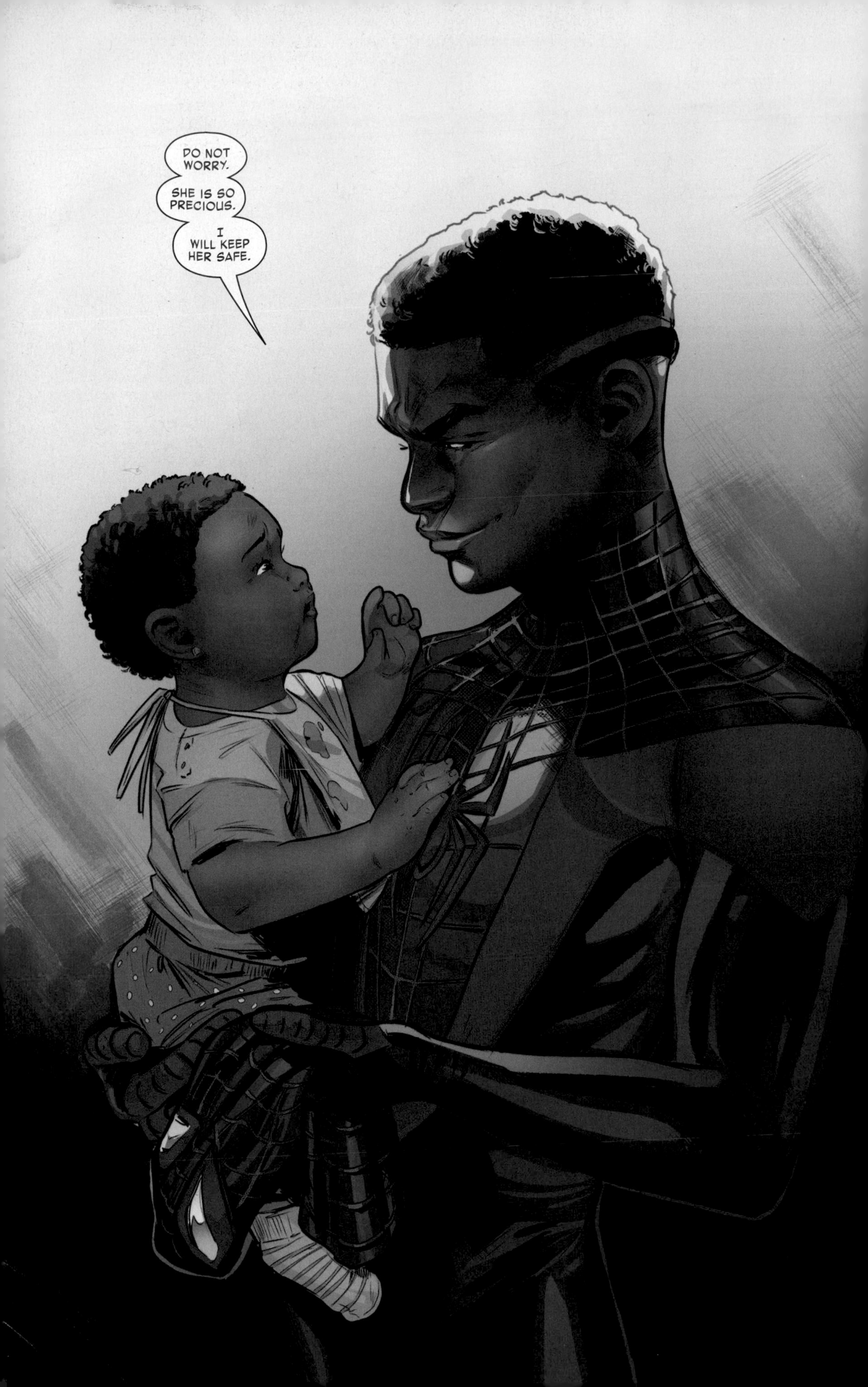
DO NOT WORRY.
SHE IS SO PRECIOUS.
I WILL KEEP HER SAFE.

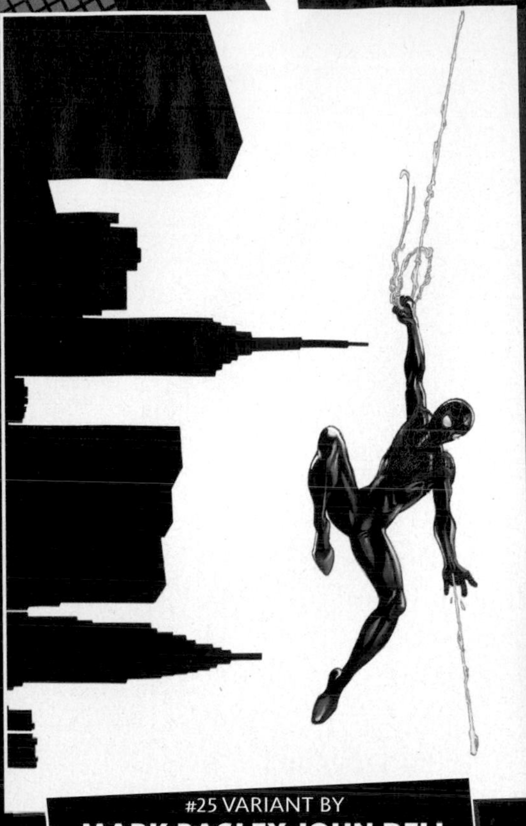

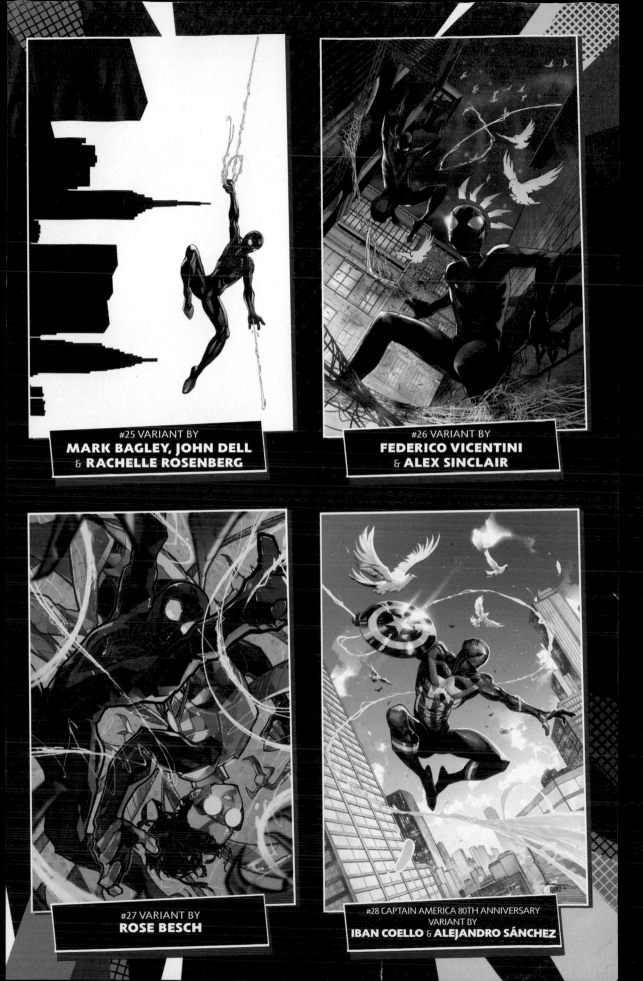

#25 VARIANT BY
MARK BAGLEY, JOHN DELL & RACHELLE ROSENBERG

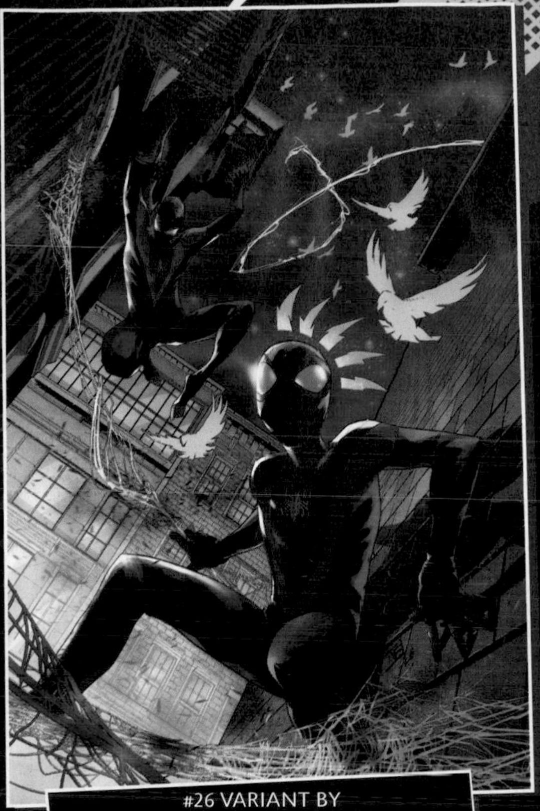

#26 VARIANT BY
FEDERICO VICENTINI & ALEX SINCLAIR

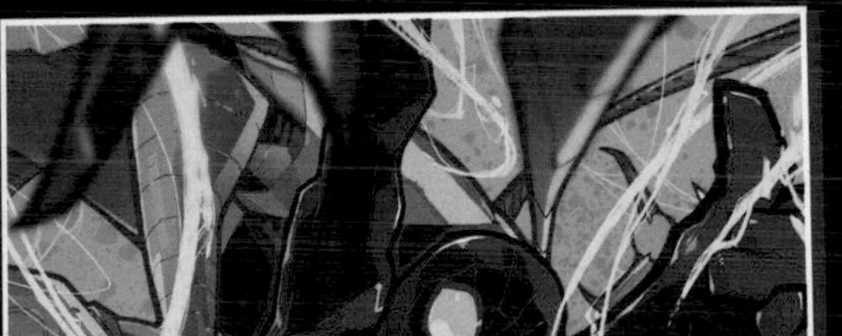

#27 VARIANT BY
ROSE BESCH

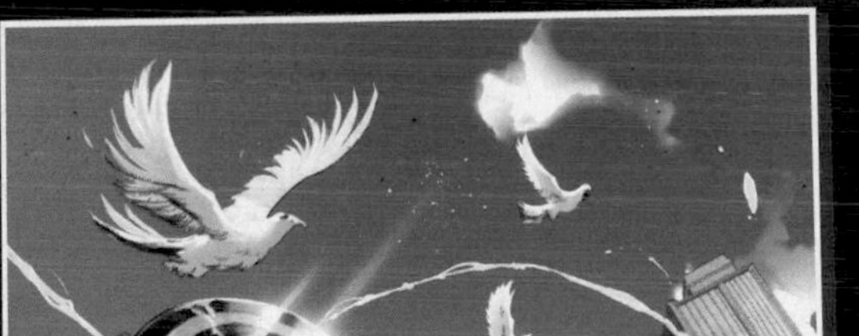

#28 CAPTAIN AMERICA 80TH ANNIVERSARY VARIANT BY
IBAN COELLO & ALEJANDRO SÁNCHEZ

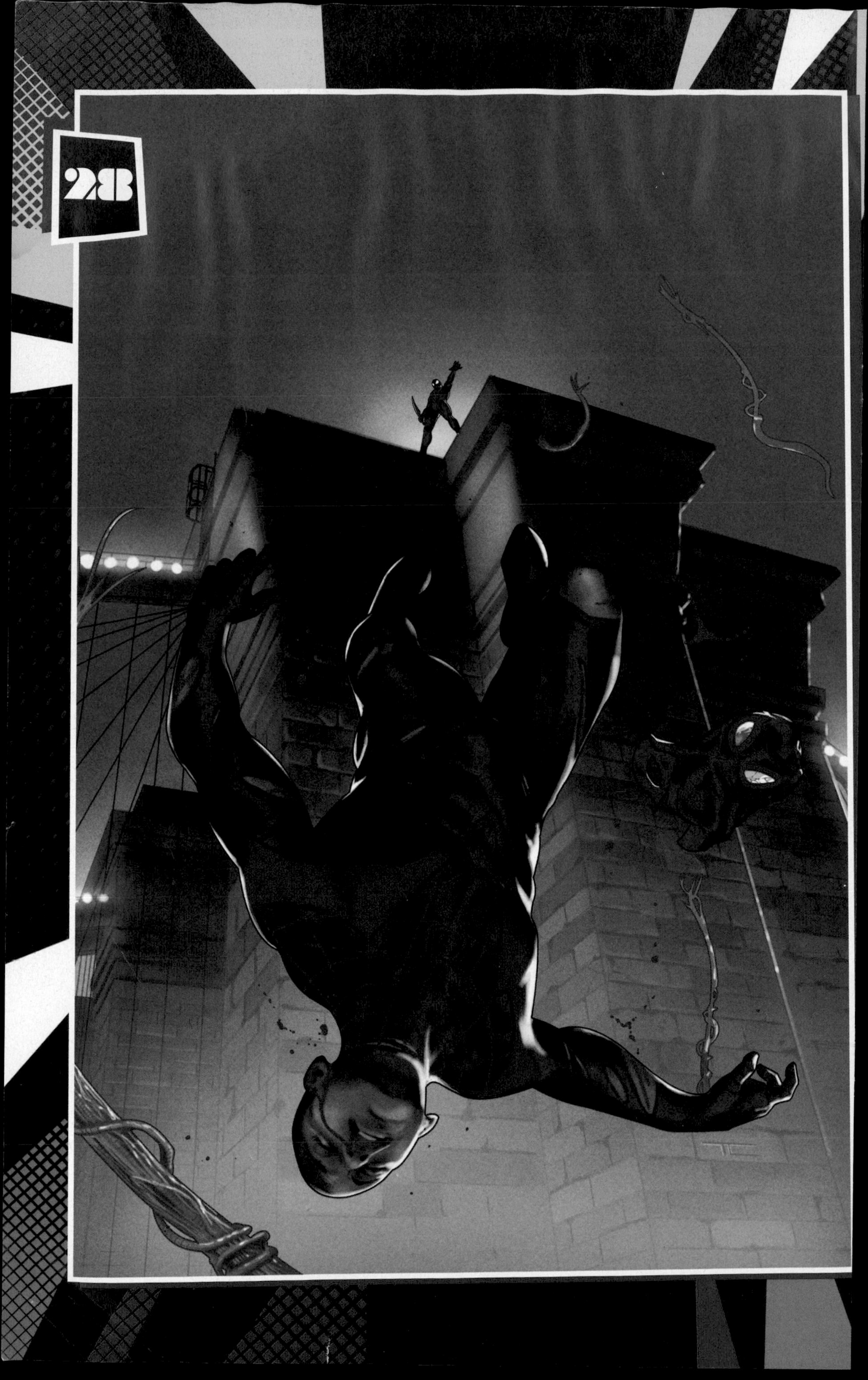
28

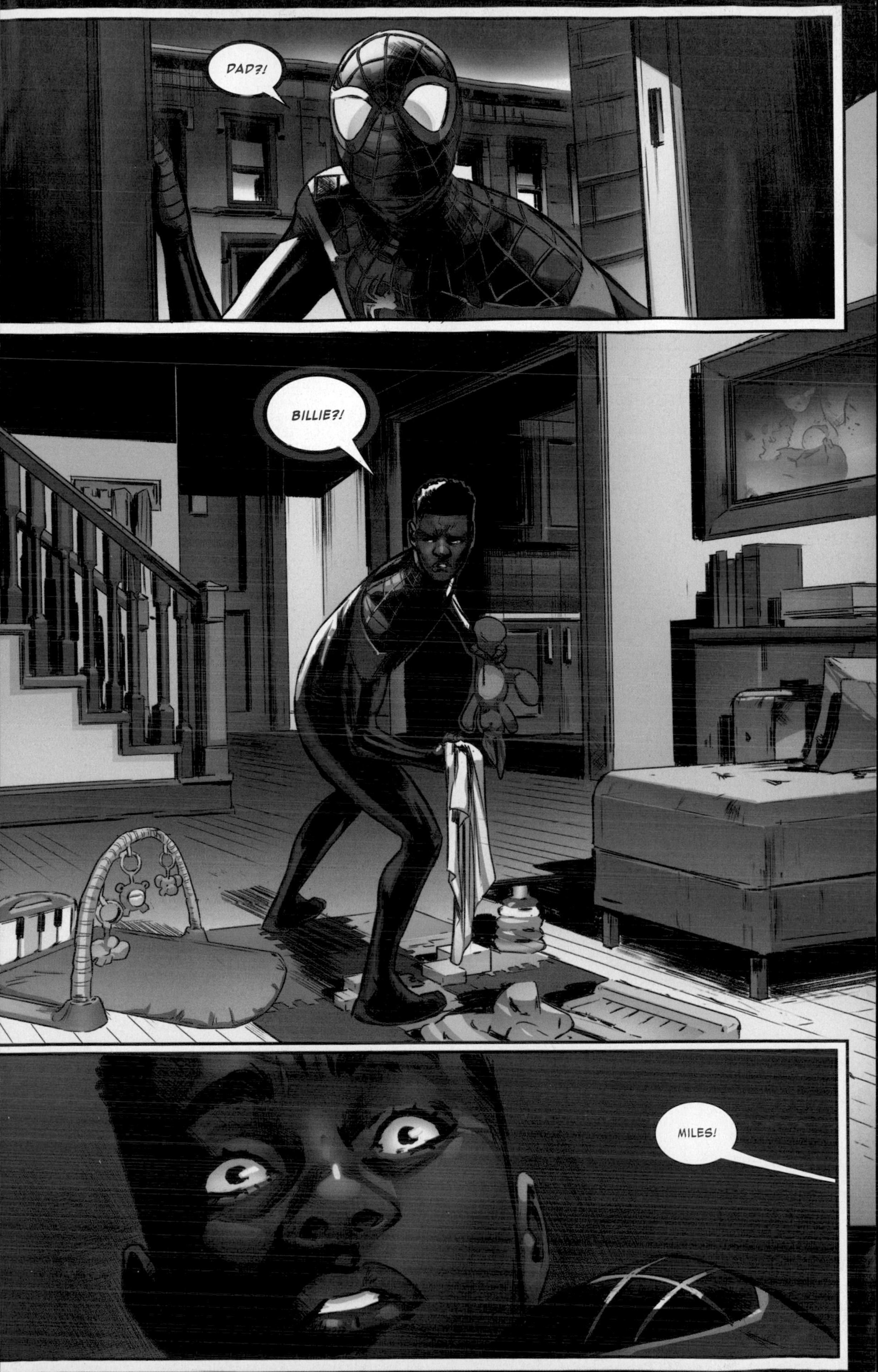
DAD?!
BILLIE?!
MILES!

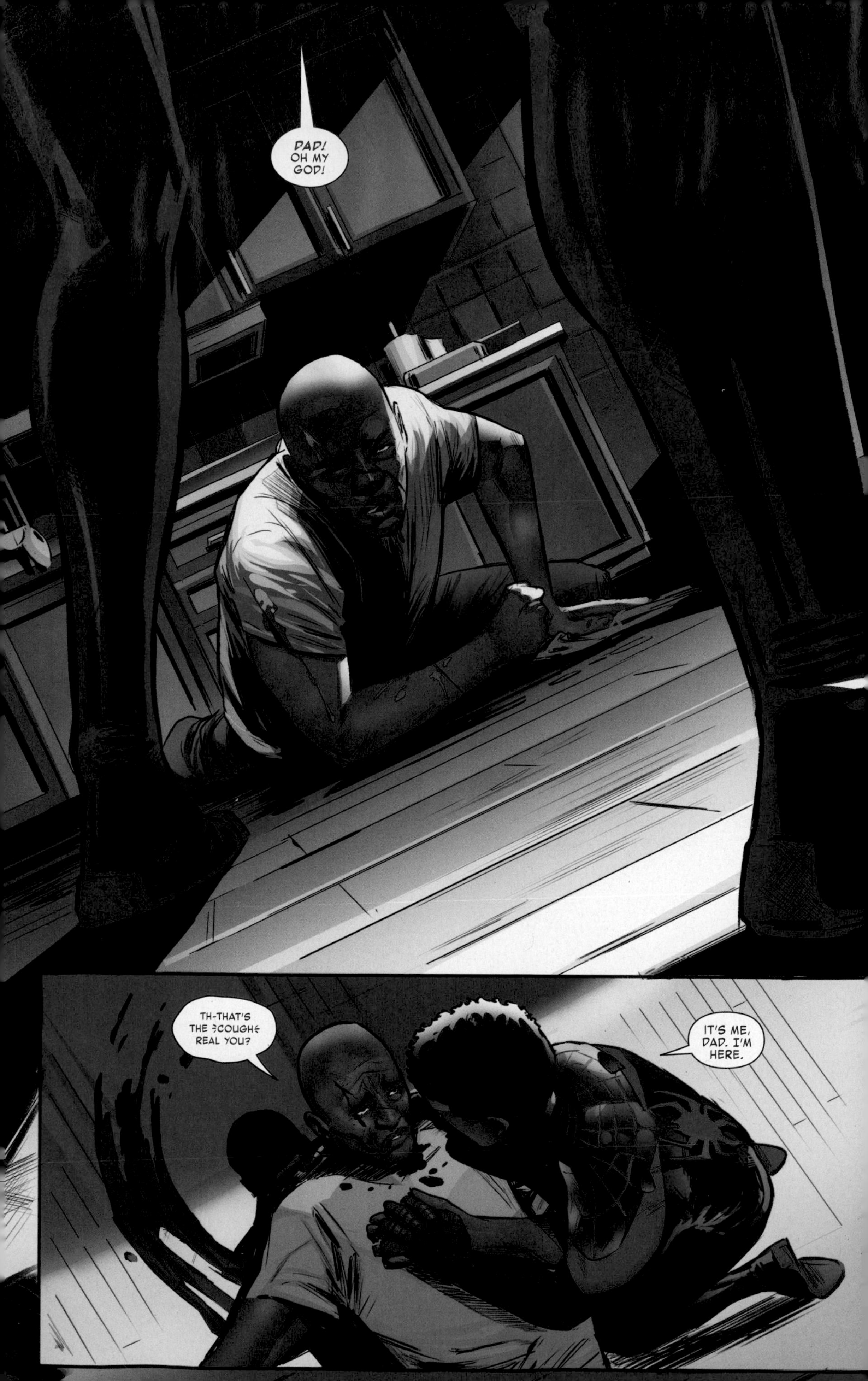
DAD! OH MY GOD!
TH-THAT'S THE *COUGH* REAL YOU?
IT'S ME, DAD. I'M HERE.

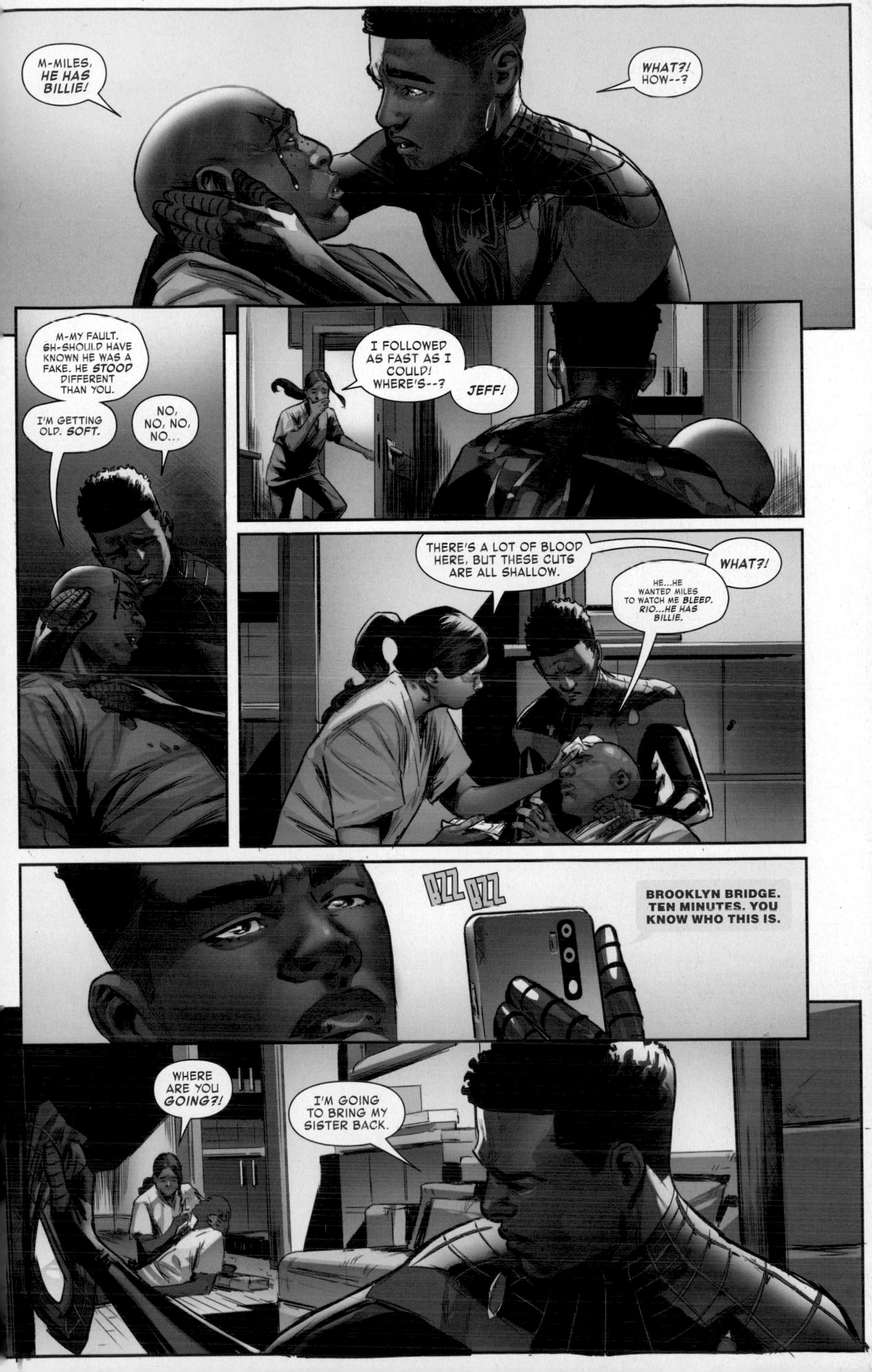
M-MILES, HE HAS BILLIE!
WHAT?! HOW--?
M-MY FAULT. SH-SHOULD HAVE KNOWN HE WAS A FAKE. HE STOOD DIFFERENT THAN YOU.
I'M GETTING OLD. SOFT.
NO, NO, NO, NO...
I FOLLOWED AS FAST AS I COULD! WHERE'S--?
JEFF!
THERE'S A LOT OF BLOOD HERE, BUT THESE CUTS ARE ALL SHALLOW.
WHAT?!
HE...HE WANTED MILES TO WATCH ME BLEED. RIO...HE HAS BILLIE.
BZZ BZZ
BROOKLYN BRIDGE. TEN MINUTES. YOU KNOW WHO THIS IS.
WHERE ARE YOU GOING?!
I'M GOING TO BRING MY SISTER BACK.

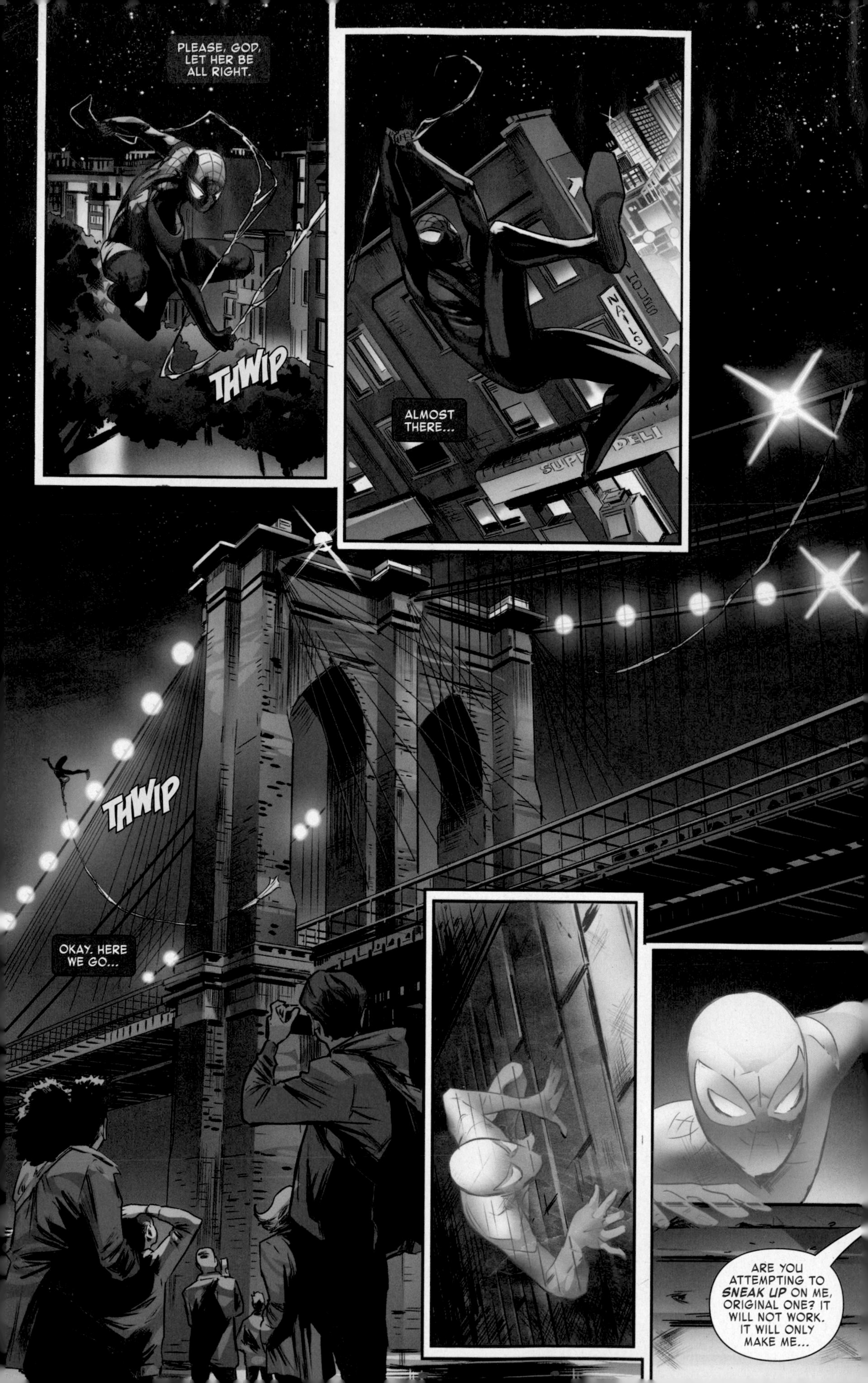
PLEASE, GOD, LET HER BE ALL RIGHT.
THWIP
NAILS
ALMOST THERE...
DELI
THWIP
OKAY. HERE WE GO...
ARE YOU ATTEMPTING TO SNEAK UP ON ME, ORIGINAL ONE? IT WILL NOT WORK. IT WILL ONLY MAKE ME...

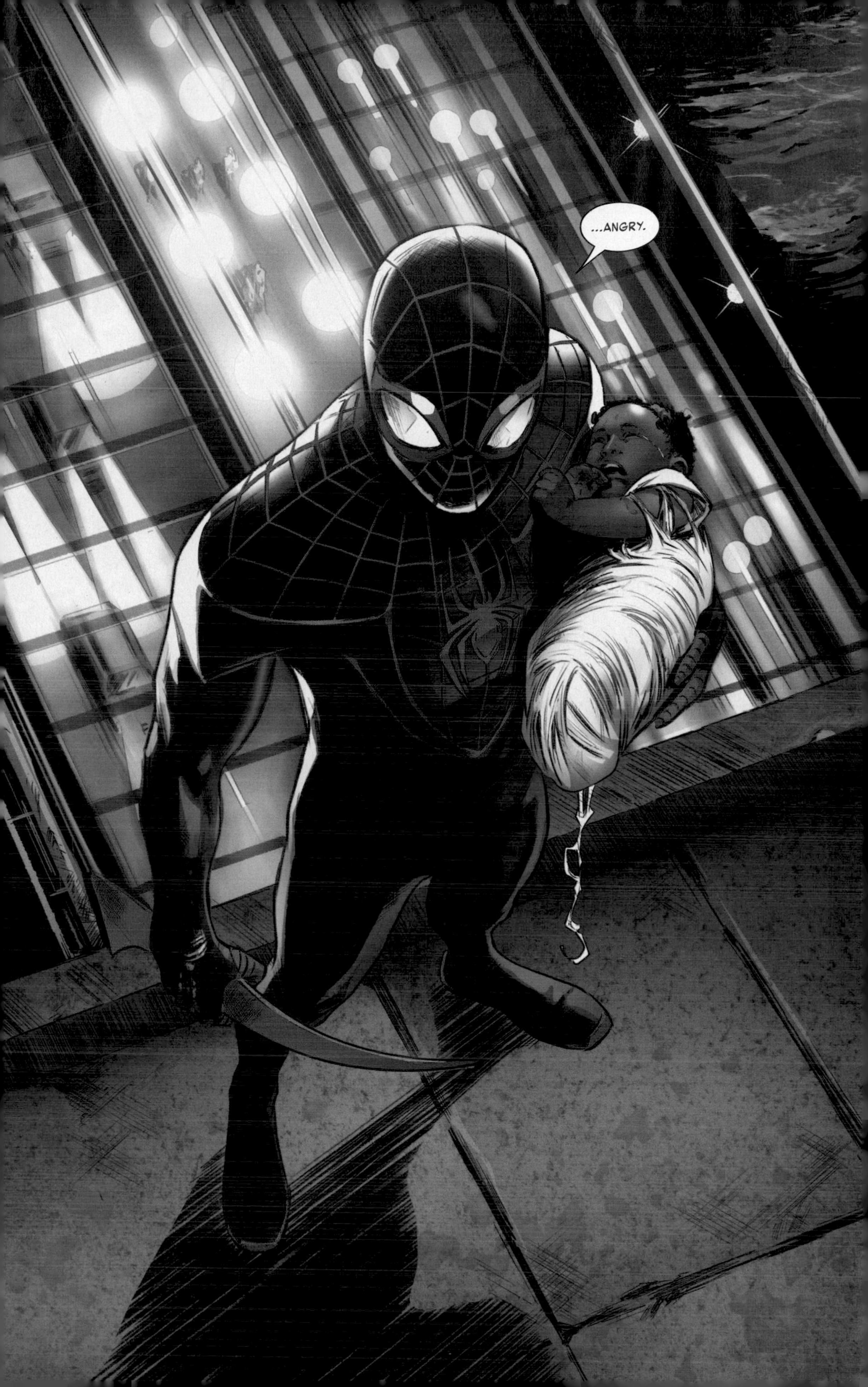
...ANGRY.

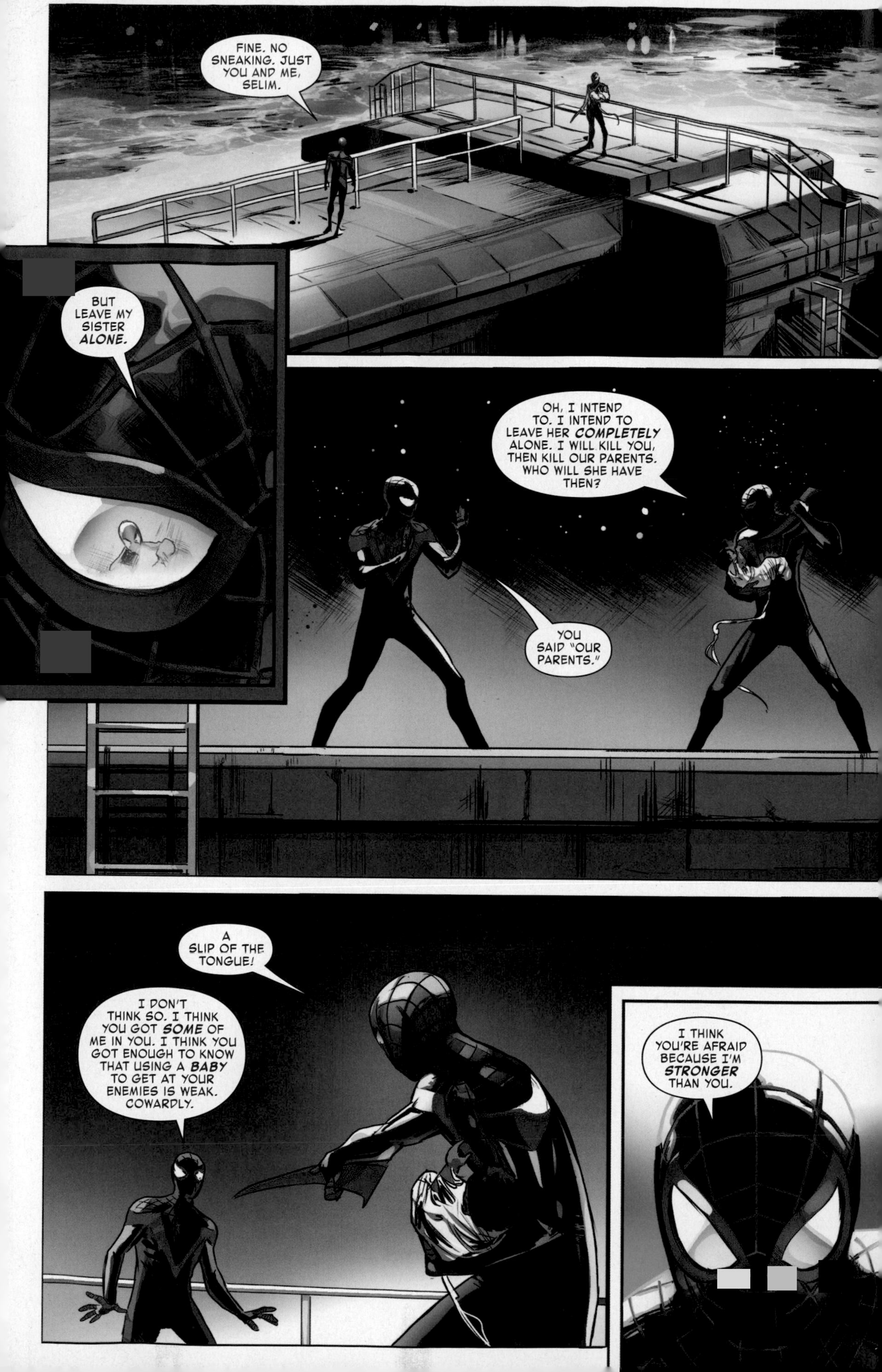
FINE. NO SNEAKING. JUST YOU AND ME, SELIM.
BUT LEAVE MY SISTER *ALONE.*
OH, I INTEND TO. I INTEND TO LEAVE HER *COMPLETELY* ALONE. I WILL KILL YOU, THEN KILL OUR PARENTS. WHO WILL SHE HAVE THEN?
YOU SAID "OUR PARENTS."
A SLIP OF THE TONGUE!
I DON'T THINK SO. I THINK YOU GOT *SOME* OF ME IN YOU. I THINK YOU GOT ENOUGH TO KNOW THAT USING A *BABY* TO GET AT YOUR ENEMIES IS WEAK. COWARDLY.
I THINK YOU'RE AFRAID BECAUSE I'M *STRONGER* THAN YOU.

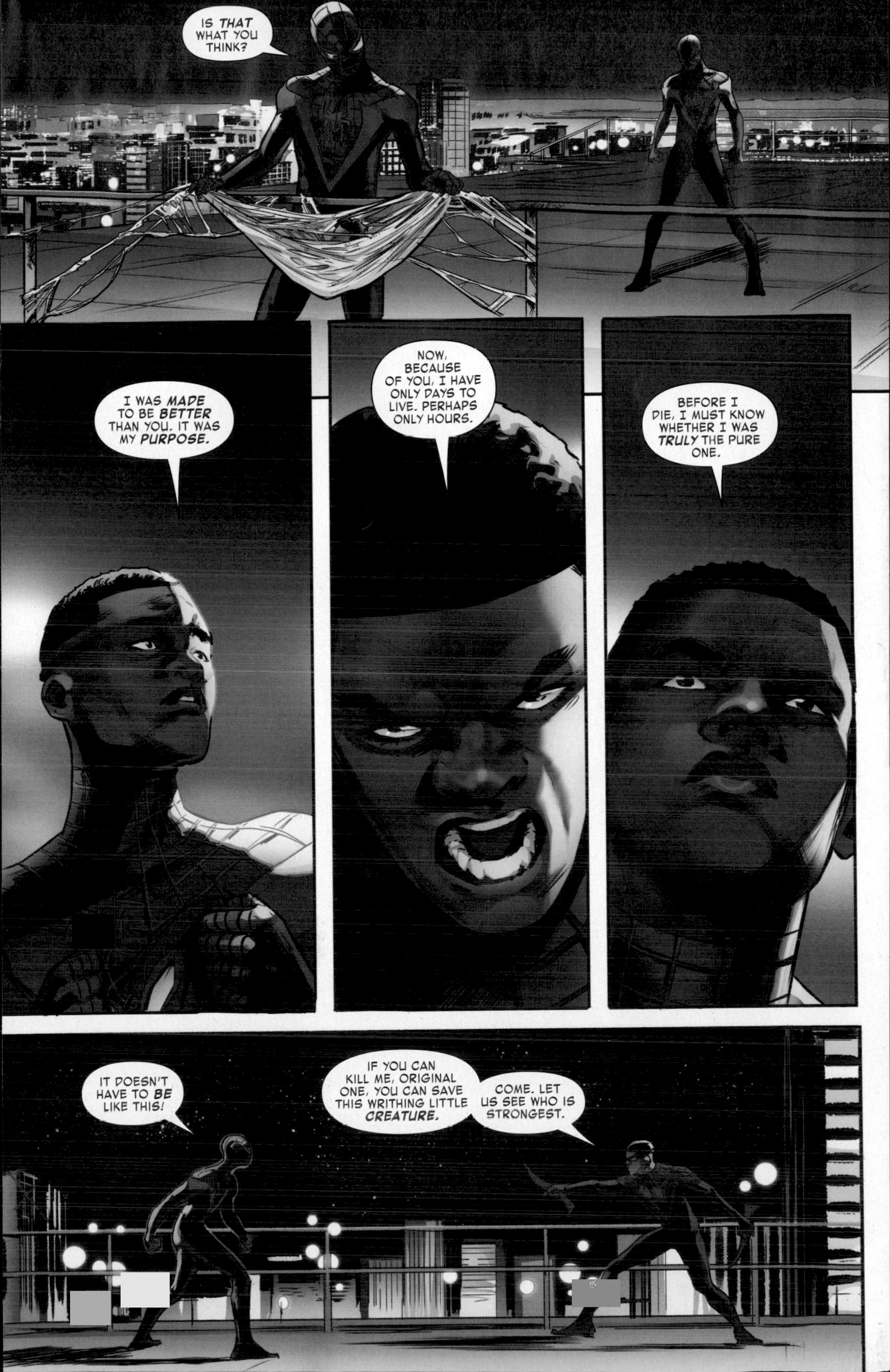
IS THAT WHAT YOU THINK?
I WAS MADE TO BE BETTER THAN YOU. IT WAS MY PURPOSE.
NOW, BECAUSE OF YOU, I HAVE ONLY DAYS TO LIVE. PERHAPS ONLY HOURS.
BEFORE I DIE, I MUST KNOW WHETHER I WAS TRULY THE PURE ONE.
IT DOESN'T HAVE TO BE LIKE THIS!
IF YOU CAN KILL ME, ORIGINAL ONE, YOU CAN SAVE THIS WRITHING LITTLE CREATURE.
COME. LET US SEE WHO IS STRONGEST.

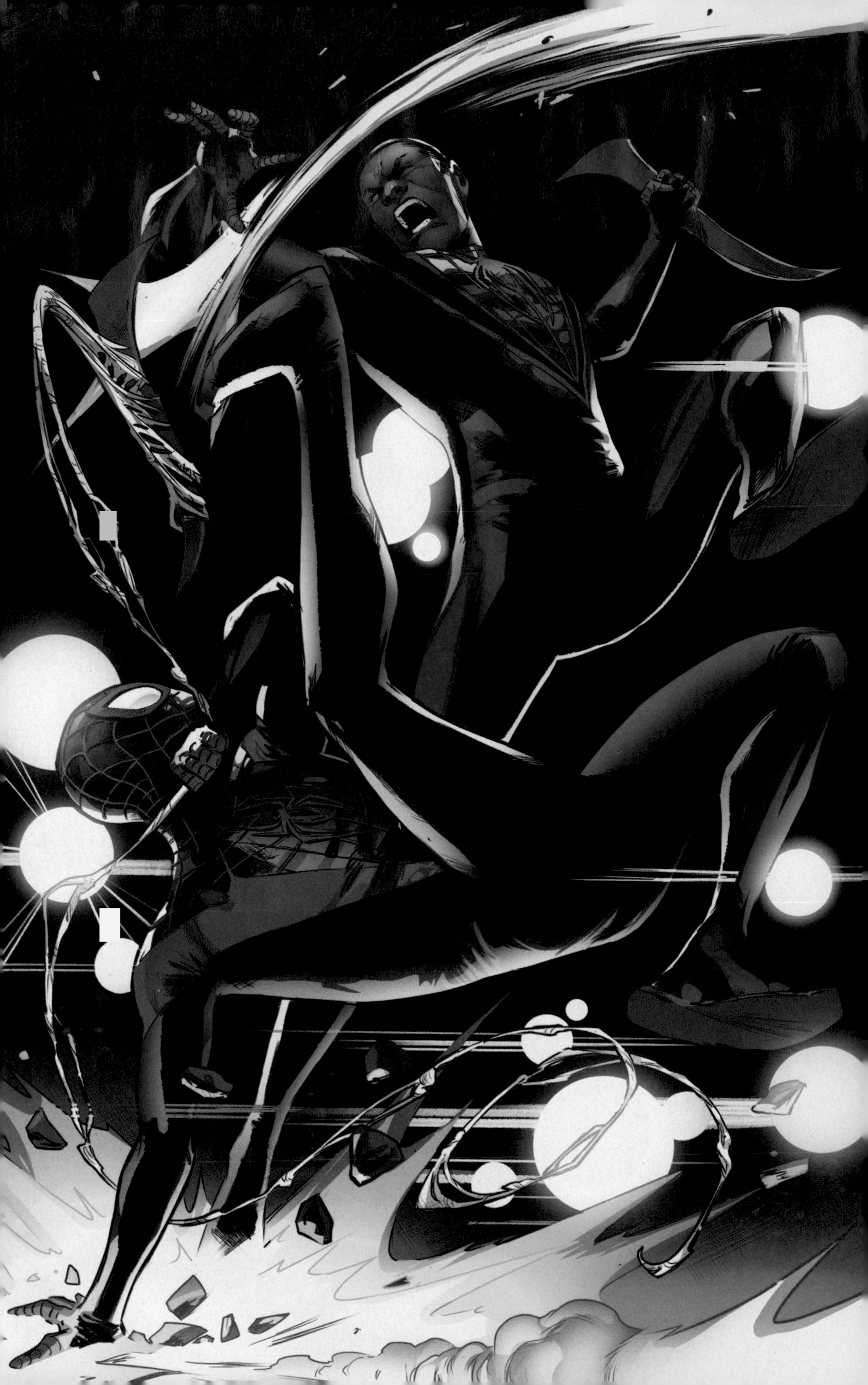

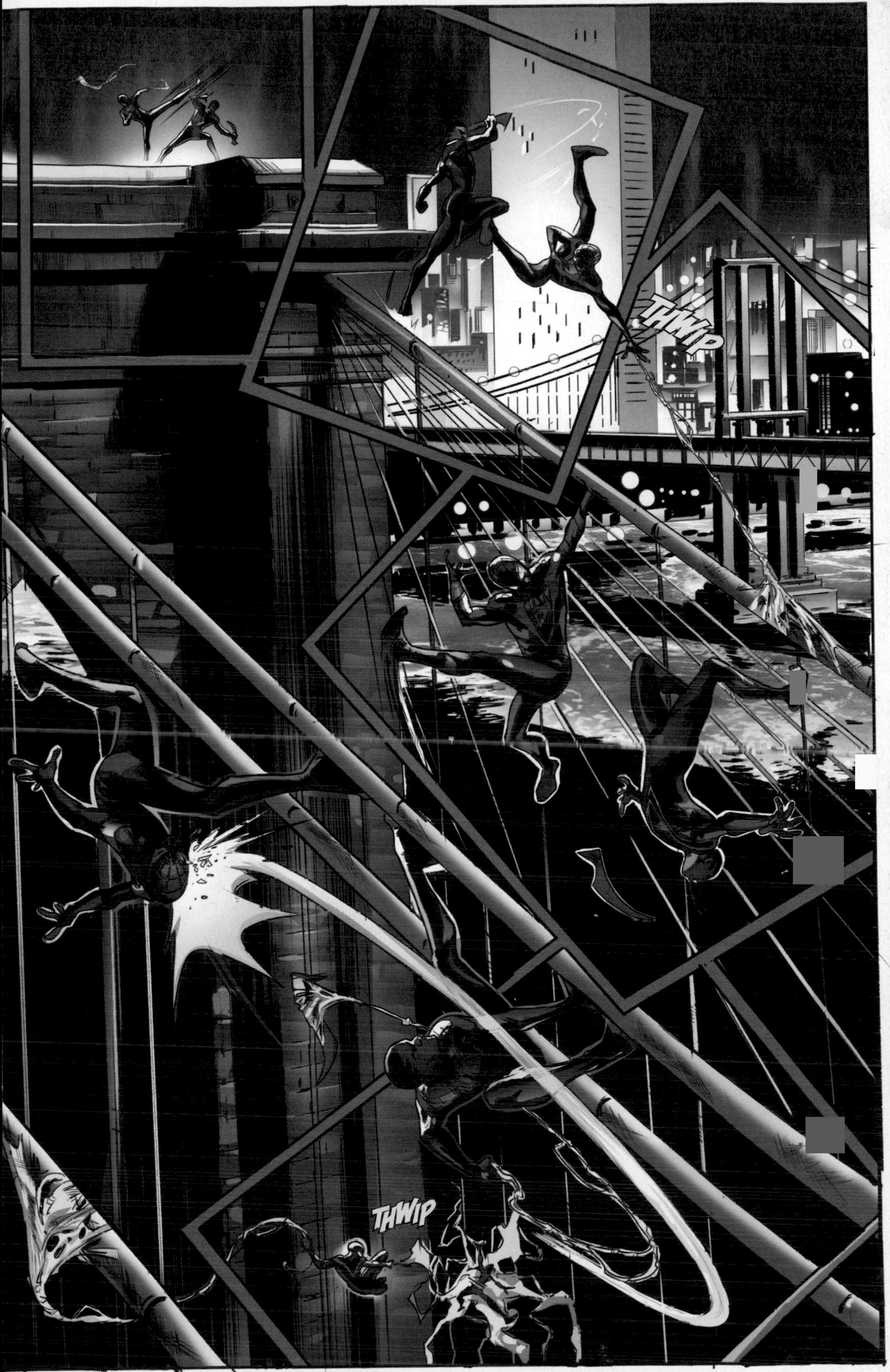
THWIP
THWIP

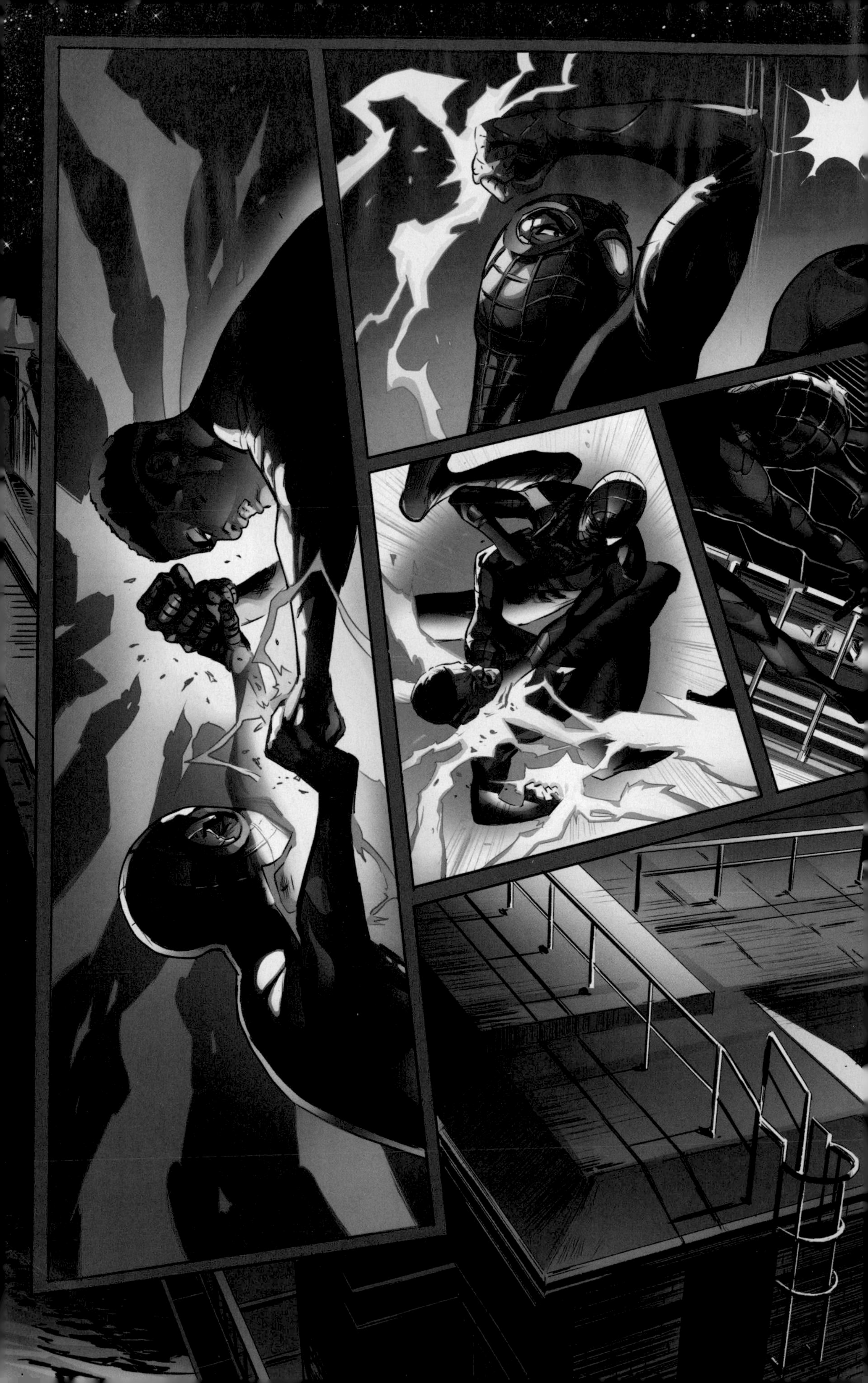

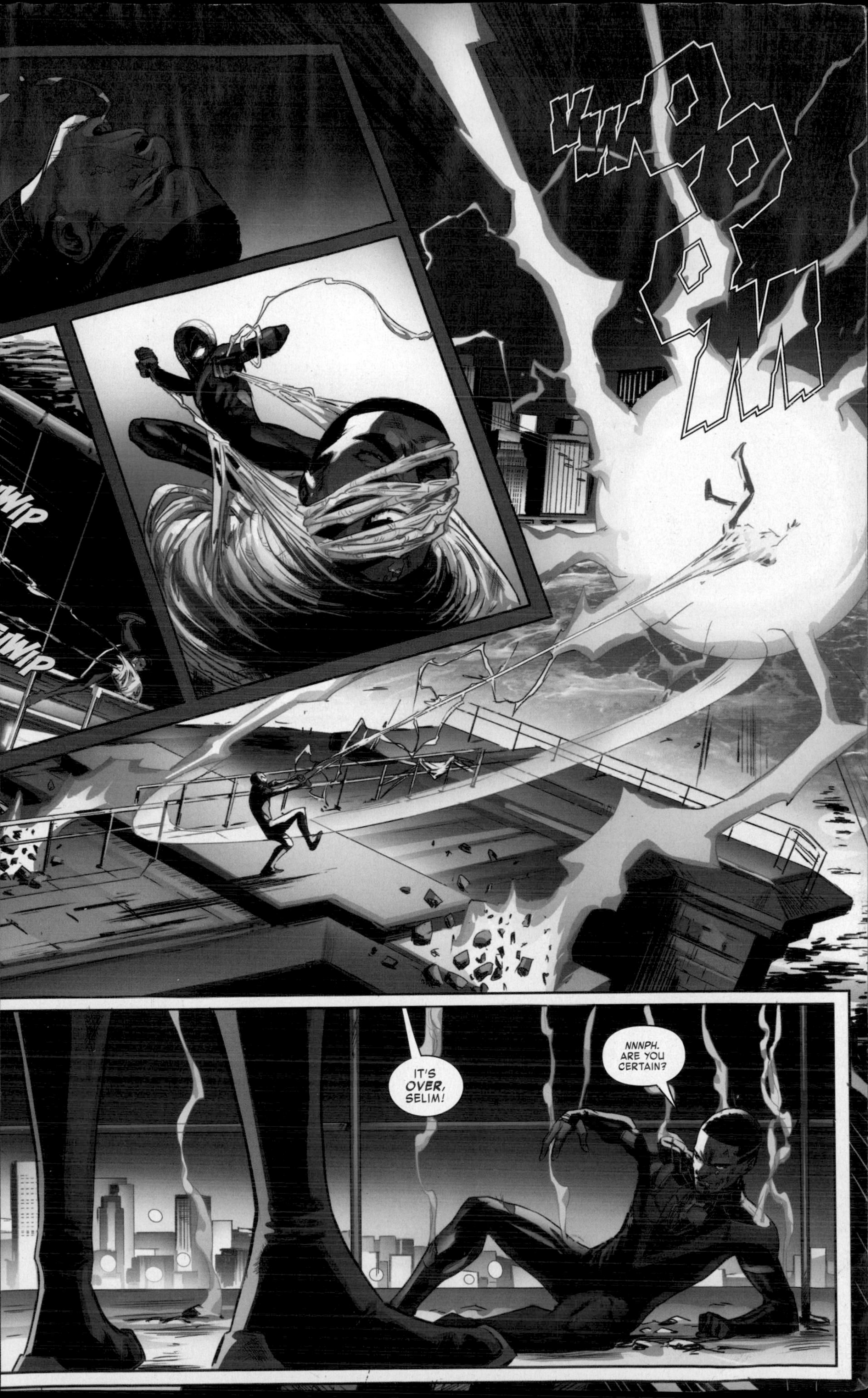

THWIP
THWIP
KWABOOM
IT'S OVER, SELIM!
NNNPH. ARE YOU CERTAIN?

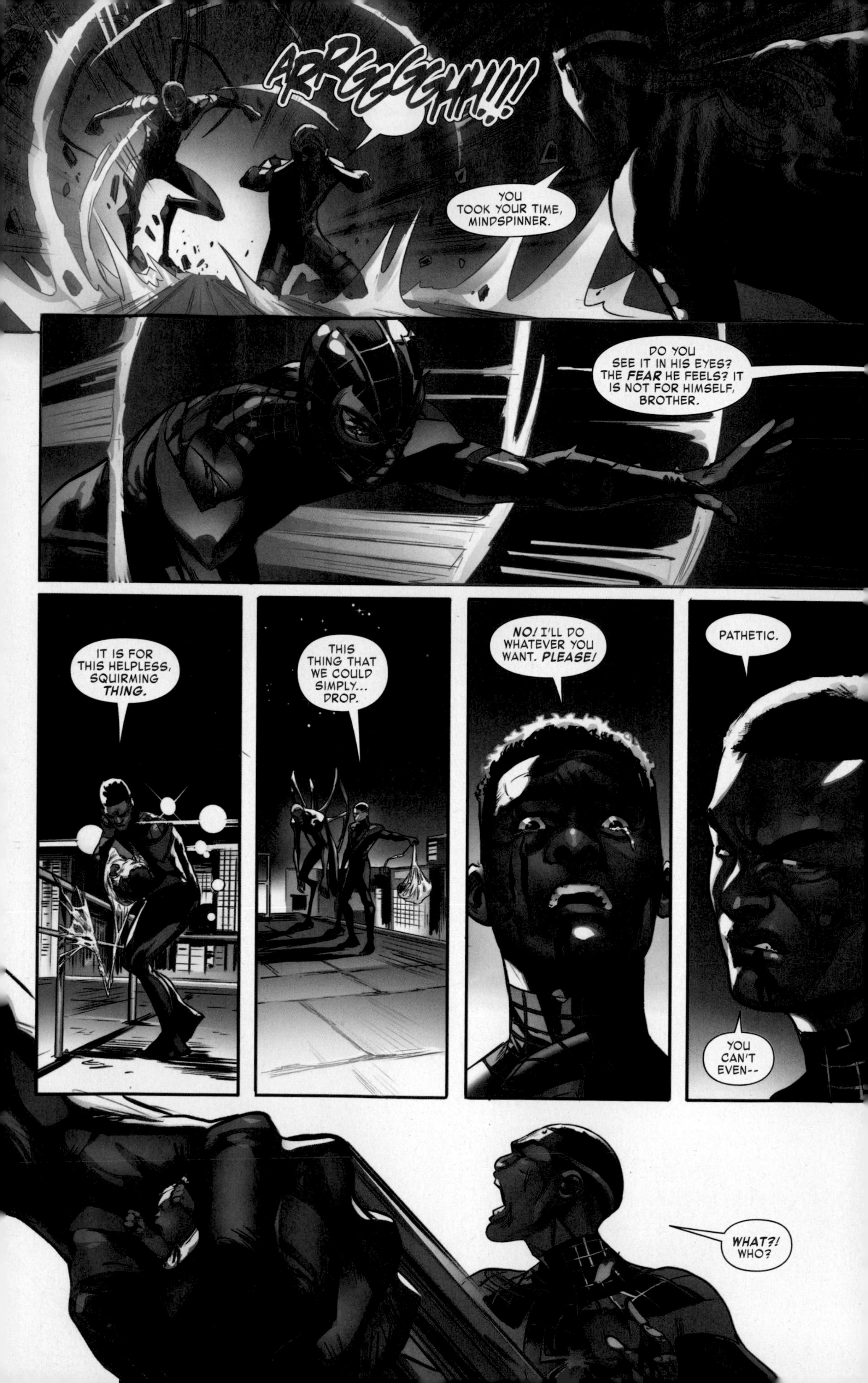
ARRGGGGGHH!!!
YOU TOOK YOUR TIME, MINDSPINNER.
DO YOU SEE IT IN HIS EYES? THE FEAR HE FEELS? IT IS NOT FOR HIMSELF, BROTHER.
IT IS FOR THIS HELPLESS, SQUIRMING THING.
THIS THING THAT WE COULD SIMPLY... DROP.
NO! I'LL DO WHATEVER YOU WANT. PLEASE!
PATHETIC.
YOU CAN'T EVEN--
WHAT?! WHO?

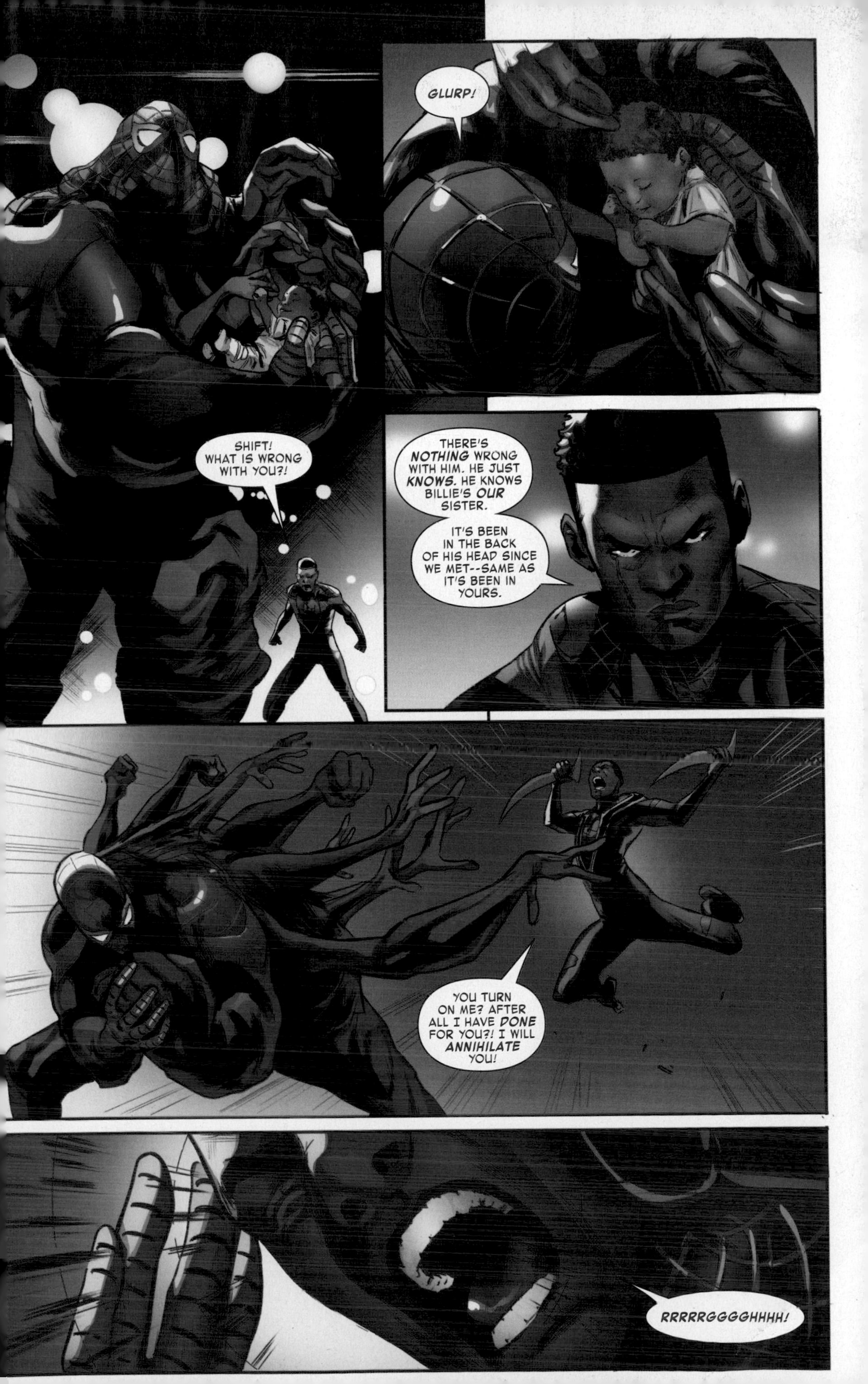
GLURP!
SHIFT! WHAT IS WRONG WITH YOU?!
THERE'S NOTHING WRONG WITH HIM. HE JUST KNOWS. HE KNOWS BILLIE'S OUR SISTER.
IT'S BEEN IN THE BACK OF HIS HEAD SINCE WE MET--SAME AS IT'S BEEN IN YOURS.
YOU TURN ON ME? AFTER ALL I HAVE DONE FOR YOU?! I WILL ANNIHILATE YOU!
RRRRRGGGGHHHH!

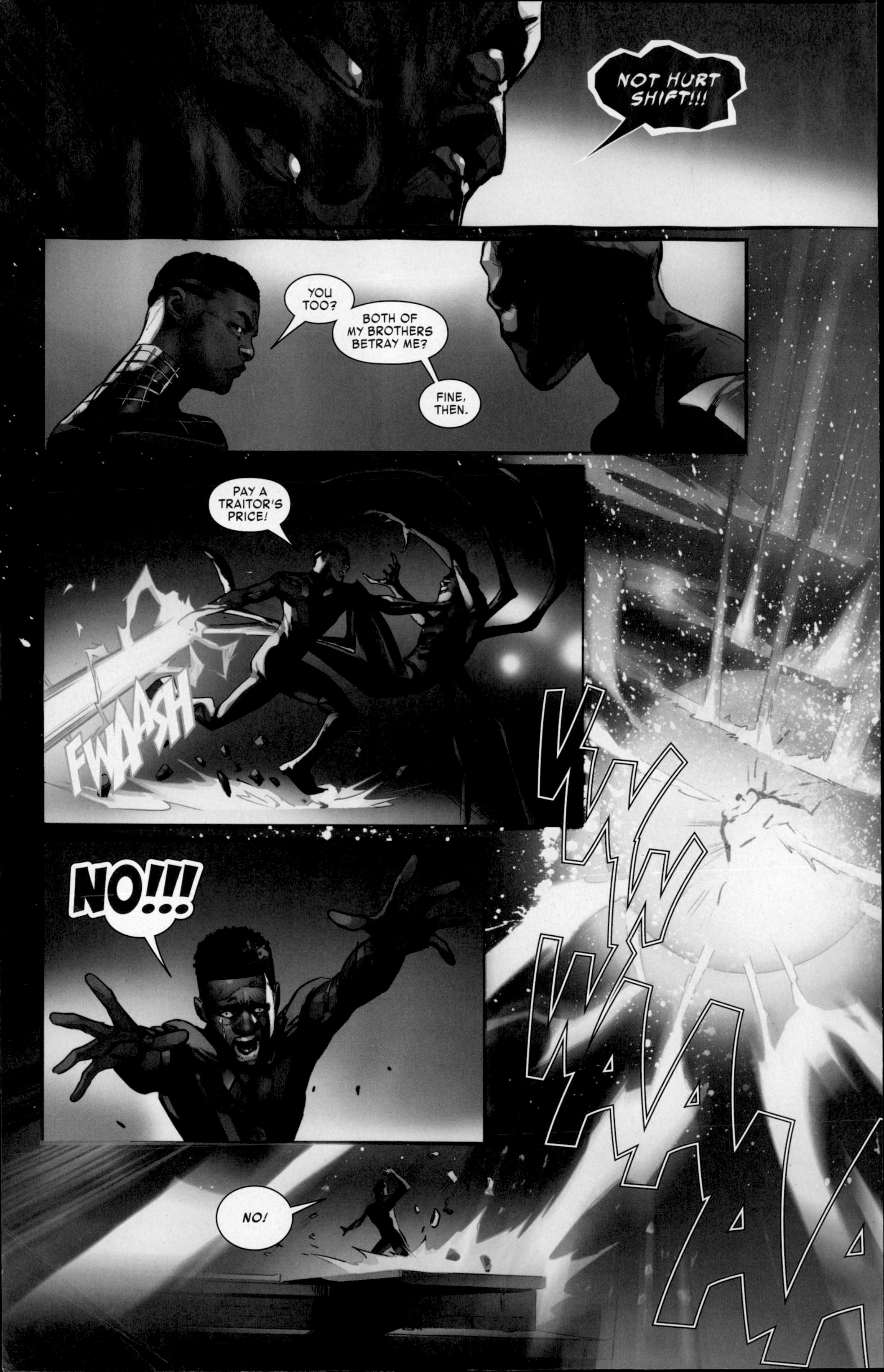
NOT HURT SHIFT!!!
YOU TOO?
BOTH OF MY BROTHERS BETRAY ME?
FINE, THEN.
PAY A TRAITOR'S PRICE!
FWAASH
KWWWWAAAA
NO!!!
NO!

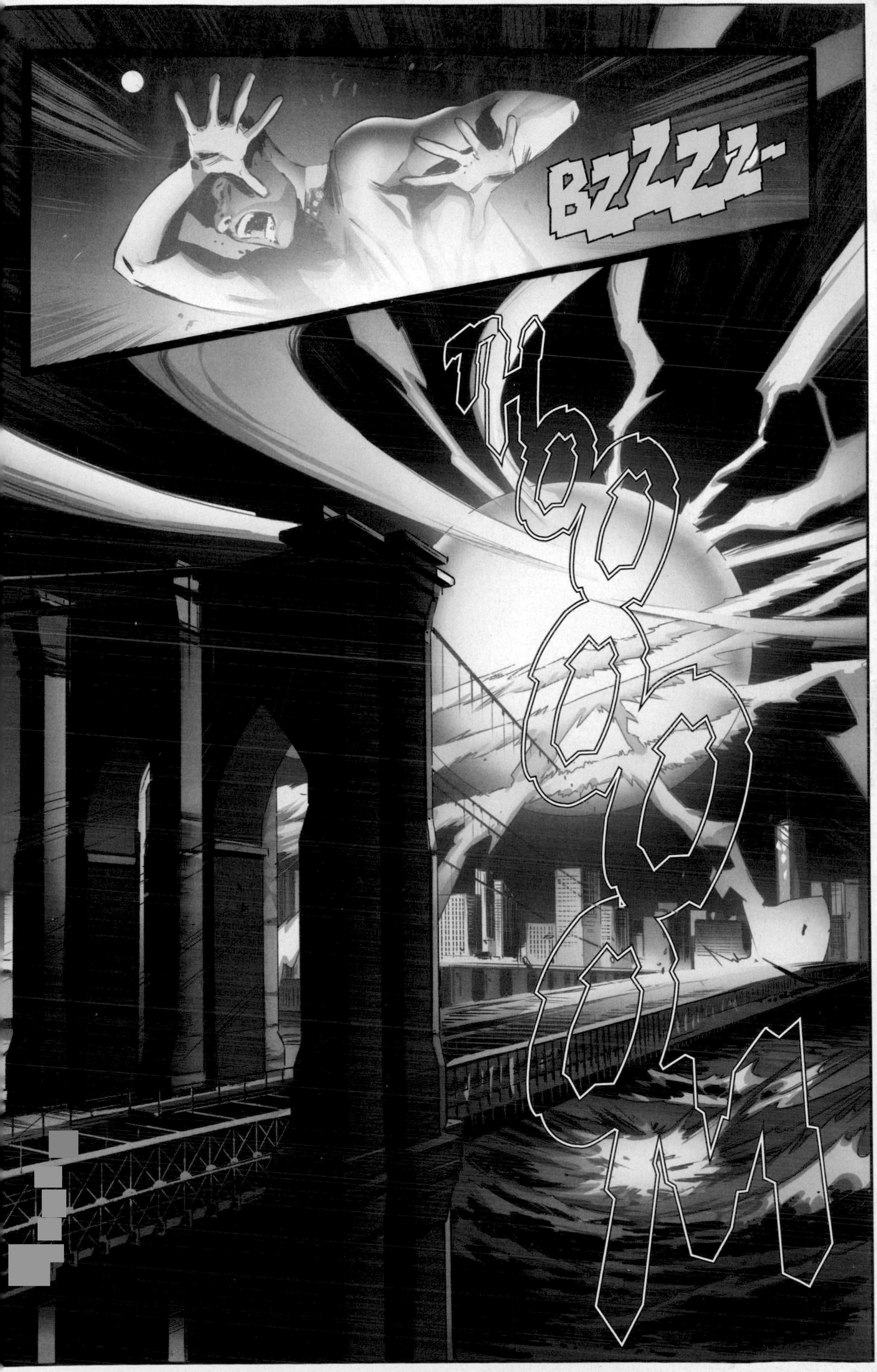
BZZZZ-
THOOOOOM

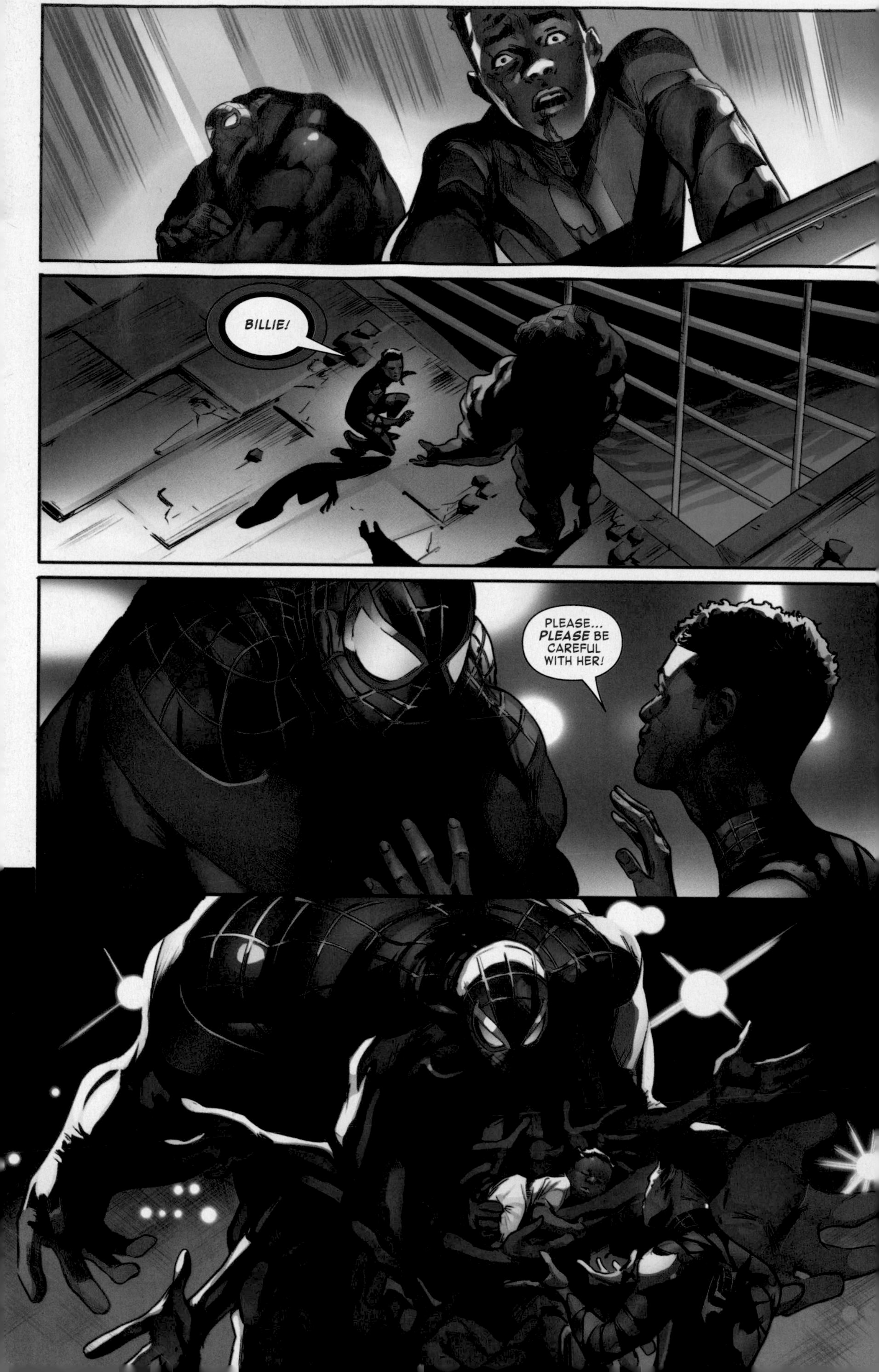
BILLIE!
PLEASE... PLEASE BE CAREFUL WITH HER!

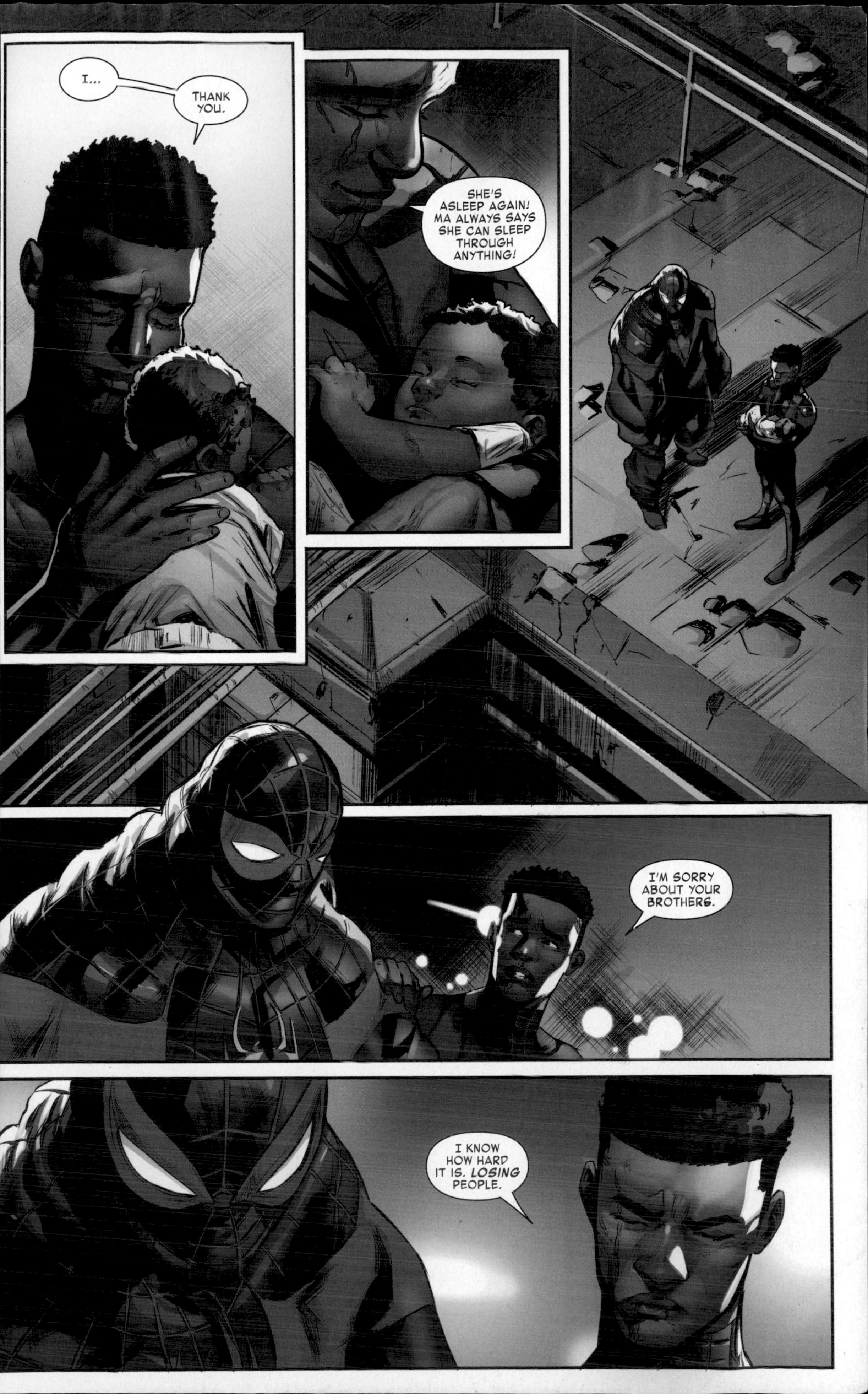
I...
THANK YOU.
SHE'S ASLEEP AGAIN! MA ALWAYS SAYS SHE CAN SLEEP THROUGH ANYTHING!
I'M SORRY ABOUT YOUR BROTHERS.
I KNOW HOW HARD IT IS. LOSING PEOPLE.

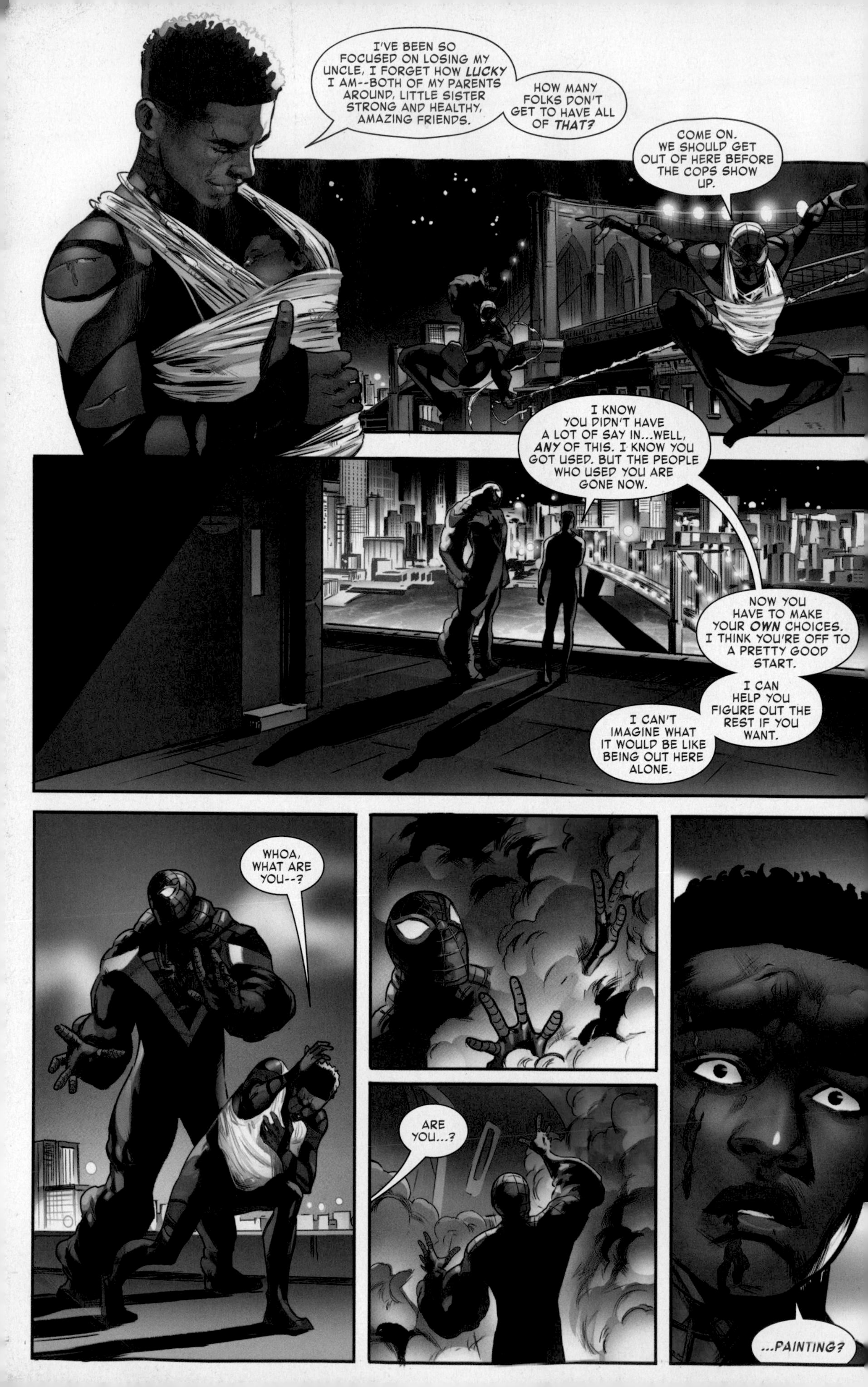
I'VE BEEN SO FOCUSED ON LOSING MY UNCLE, I FORGET HOW LUCKY I AM--BOTH OF MY PARENTS AROUND, LITTLE SISTER STRONG AND HEALTHY, AMAZING FRIENDS.
HOW MANY FOLKS DON'T GET TO HAVE ALL OF THAT?
COME ON. WE SHOULD GET OUT OF HERE BEFORE THE COPS SHOW UP.
I KNOW YOU DIDN'T HAVE A LOT OF SAY IN...WELL, ANY OF THIS. I KNOW YOU GOT USED. BUT THE PEOPLE WHO USED YOU ARE GONE NOW.
NOW YOU HAVE TO MAKE YOUR OWN CHOICES. I THINK YOU'RE OFF TO A PRETTY GOOD START.
I CAN'T IMAGINE WHAT IT WOULD BE LIKE BEING OUT HERE ALONE.
I CAN HELP YOU FIGURE OUT THE REST IF YOU WANT.
WHOA, WHAT ARE YOU--?
ARE YOU...?
...PAINTING?

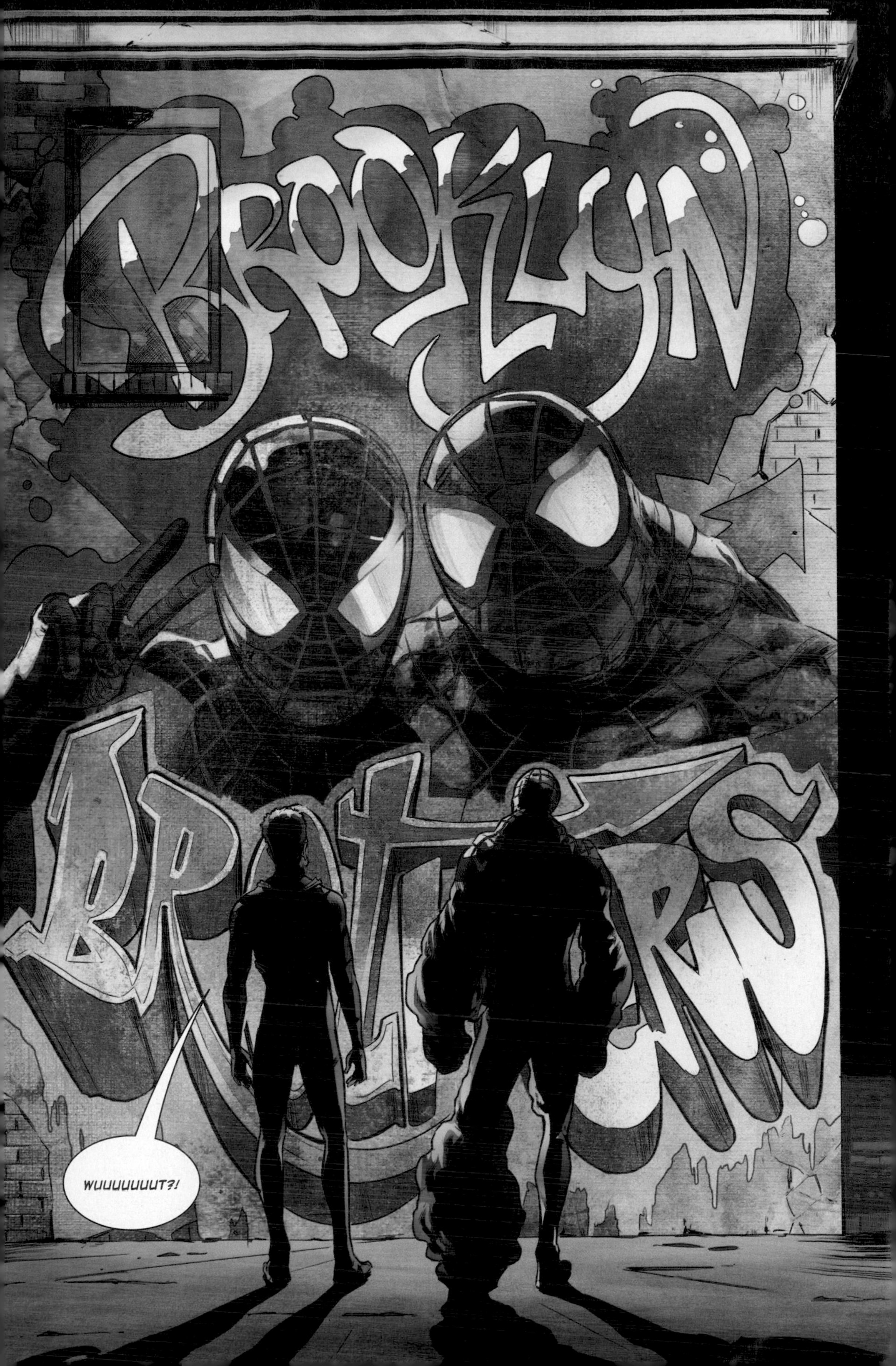
BROOKLYN
WUUUUUUUUT?!

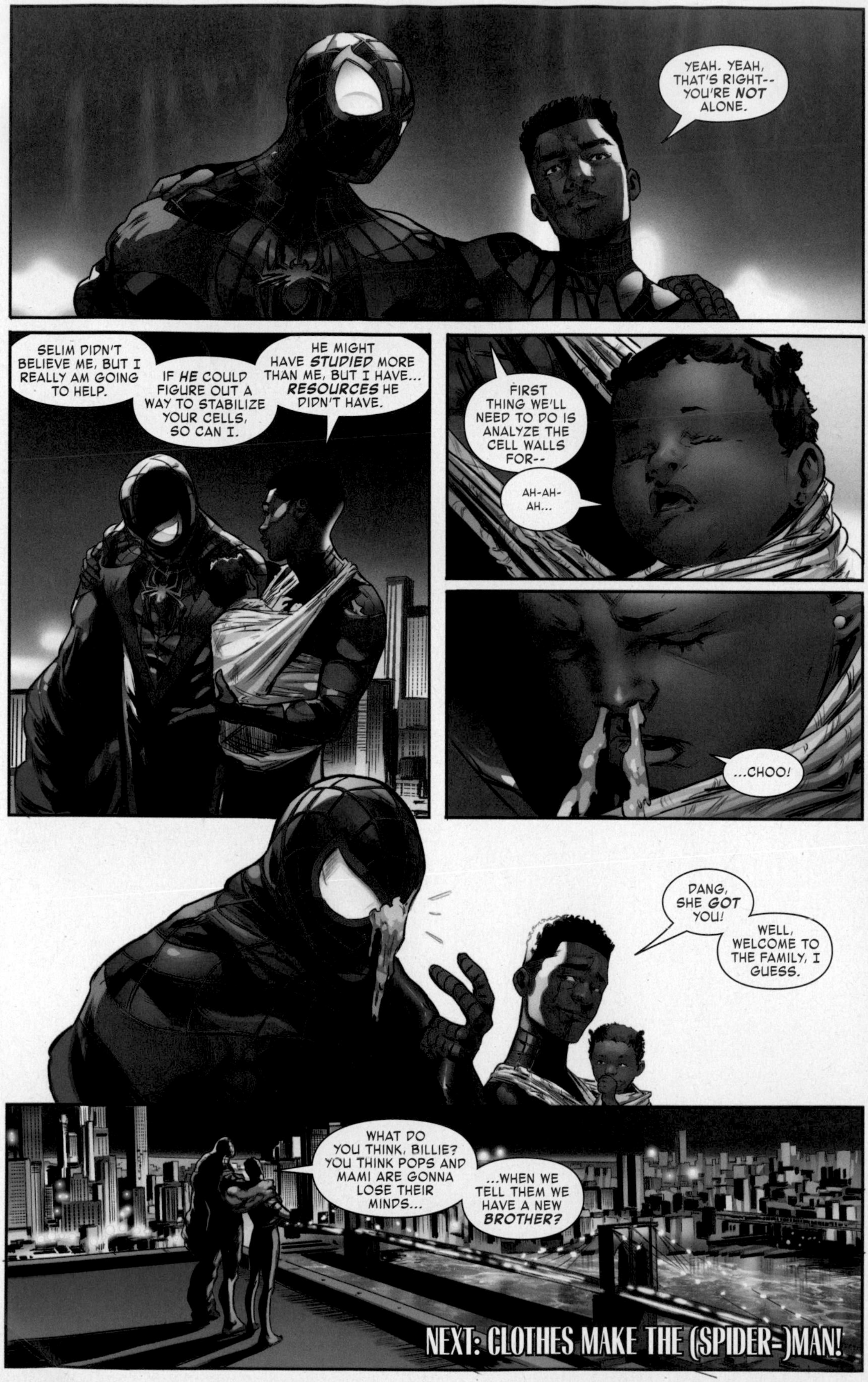
YEAH. YEAH, THAT'S RIGHT-- YOU'RE NOT ALONE.
SELIM DIDN'T BELIEVE ME, BUT I REALLY AM GOING TO HELP.
IF HE COULD FIGURE OUT A WAY TO STABILIZE YOUR CELLS, SO CAN I.
HE MIGHT HAVE STUDIED MORE THAN ME, BUT I HAVE... RESOURCES HE DIDN'T HAVE.
FIRST THING WE'LL NEED TO DO IS ANALYZE THE CELL WALLS FOR--
AH-AH-AH...
...CHOO!
DANG, SHE GOT YOU!
WELL, WELCOME TO THE FAMILY, I GUESS.
WHAT DO YOU THINK, BILLIE? YOU THINK POPS AND MAMI ARE GONNA LOSE THEIR MINDS...
...WHEN WE TELL THEM WE HAVE A NEW BROTHER?
NEXT: CLOTHES MAKE THE (SPIDER-)MAN!

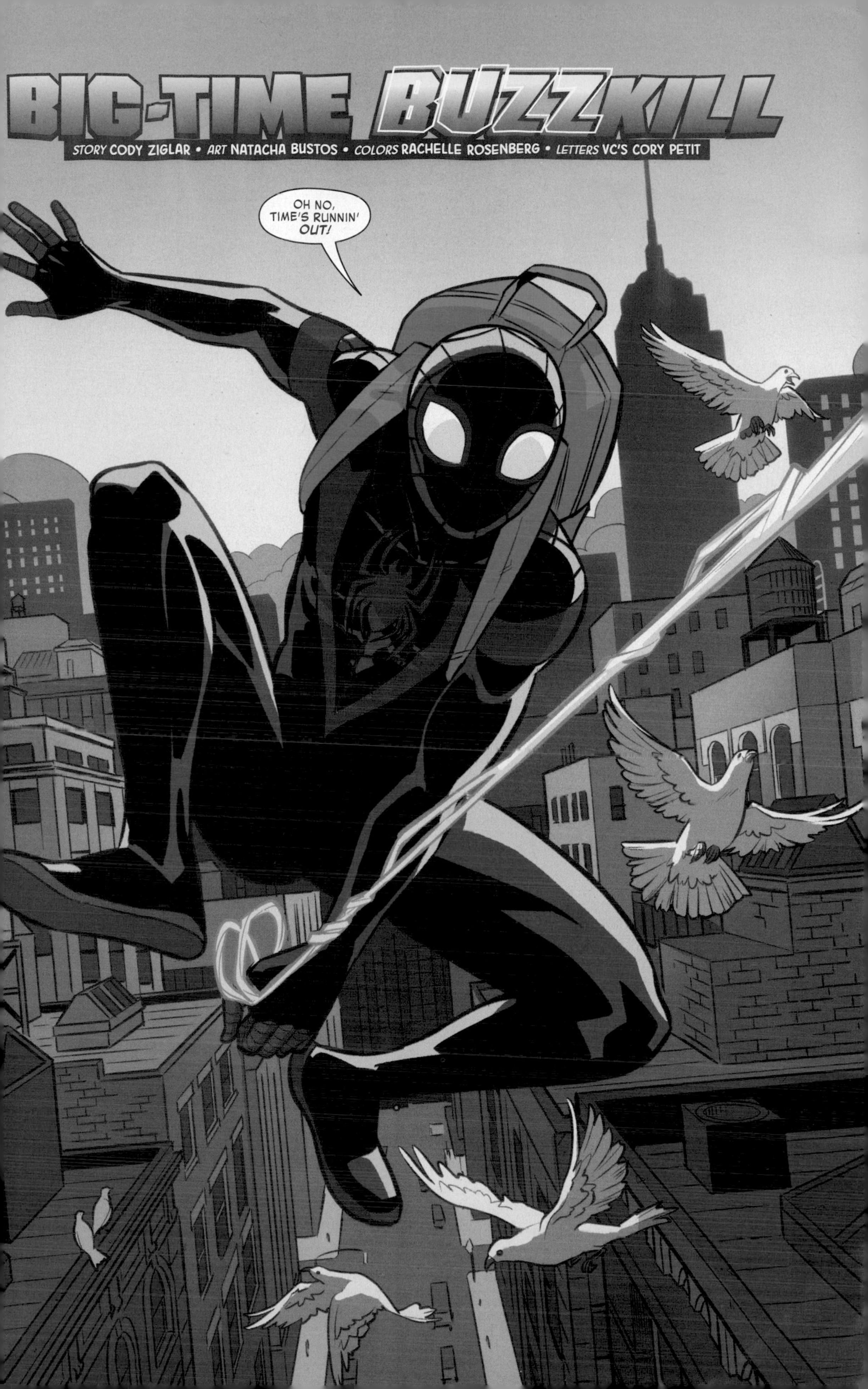
BIG-TIME BUZZKILL
STORY CODY ZIGLAR • ART NATACHA BUSTOS • COLORS RACHELLE ROSENBERG • LETTERS VC'S CORY PETIT
OH NO, TIME'S RUNNIN' OUT!

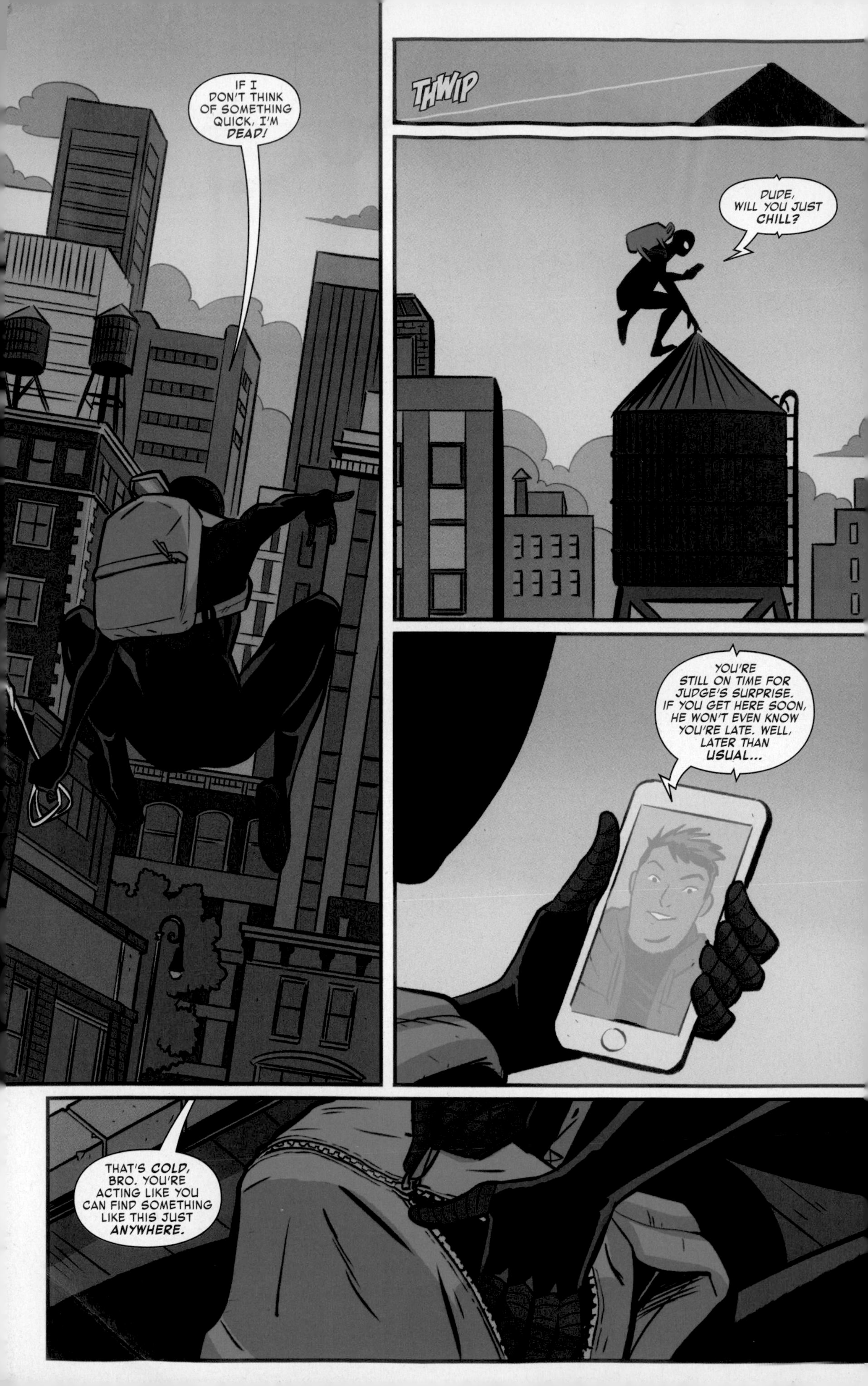
IF I DON'T THINK OF SOMETHING QUICK, I'M DEAD!
THWIP
DUDE, WILL YOU JUST CHILL?
YOU'RE STILL ON TIME FOR JUDGE'S SURPRISE. IF YOU GET HERE SOON, HE WON'T EVEN KNOW YOU'RE LATE. WELL, LATER THAN USUAL...
THAT'S COLD, BRO. YOU'RE ACTING LIKE YOU CAN FIND SOMETHING LIKE THIS JUST ANYWHERE.

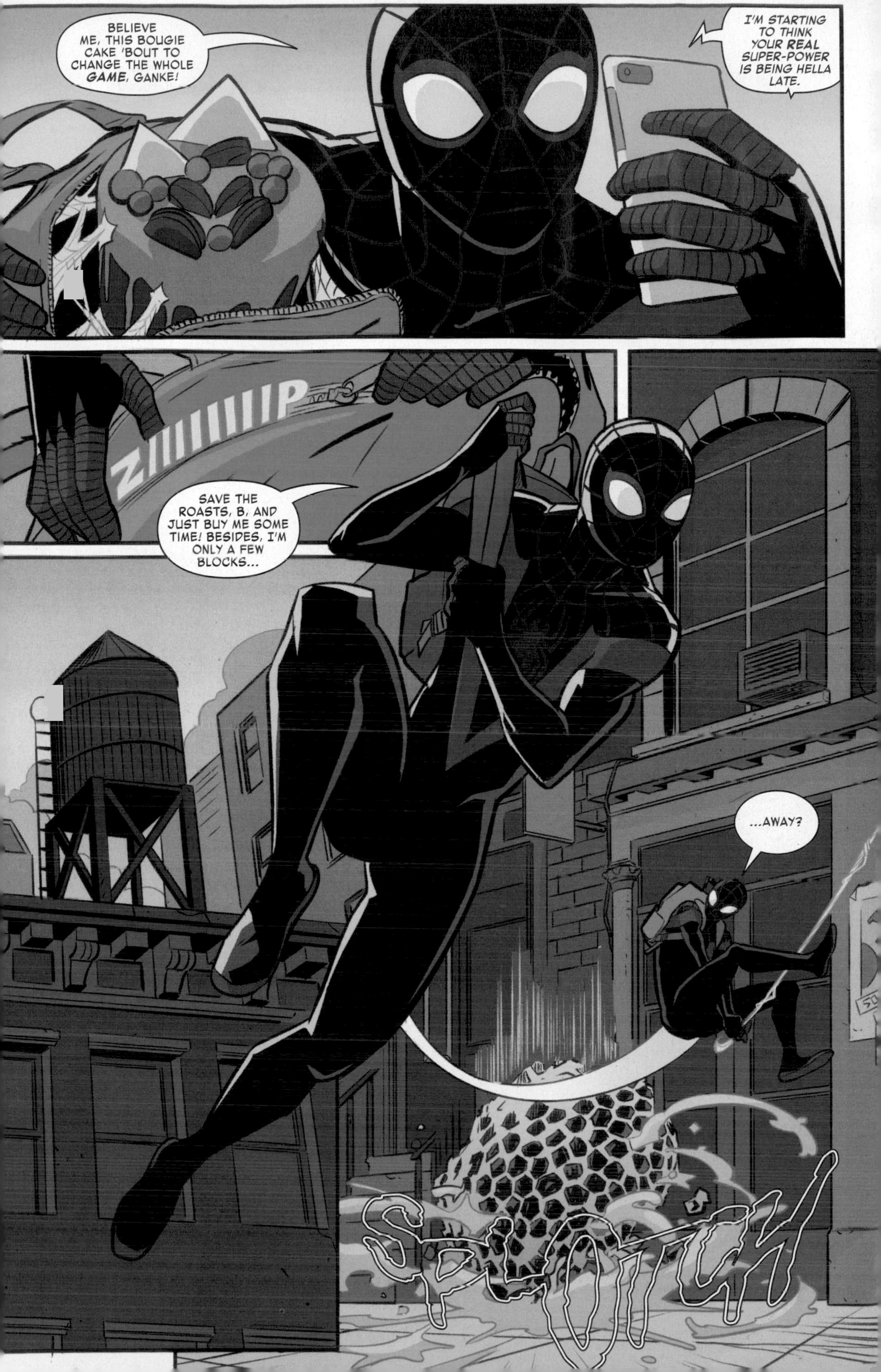
BELIEVE ME, THIS BOUGIE CAKE 'BOUT TO CHANGE THE WHOLE GAME, GANKE!
I'M STARTING TO THINK YOUR REAL SUPER-POWER IS BEING HELLA LATE.
ZIIIIIIIP
SAVE THE ROASTS, B, AND JUST BUY ME SOME TIME! BESIDES, I'M ONLY A FEW BLOCKS...
...AWAY?
SPLOOTCH

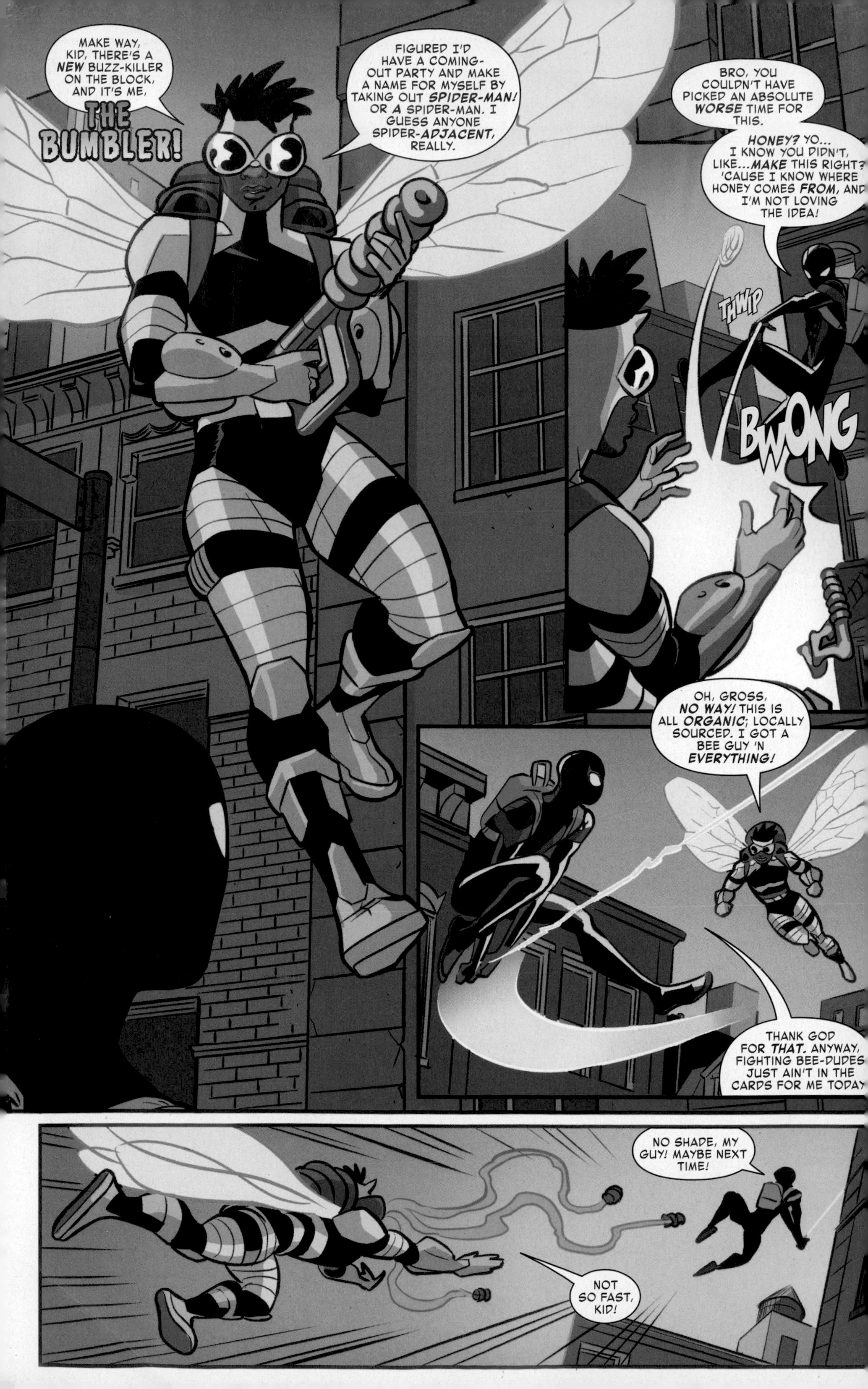
MAKE WAY, KID, THERE'S A NEW BUZZ-KILLER ON THE BLOCK, AND IT'S ME, THE BUMBLER!
FIGURED I'D HAVE A COMING-OUT PARTY AND MAKE A NAME FOR MYSELF BY TAKING OUT SPIDER-MAN! OR A SPIDER-MAN. I GUESS ANYONE SPIDER-ADJACENT, REALLY.
BRO, YOU COULDN'T HAVE PICKED AN ABSOLUTE WORSE TIME FOR THIS.
HONEY? YO... I KNOW YOU DIDN'T, LIKE...MAKE THIS RIGHT? 'CAUSE I KNOW WHERE HONEY COMES FROM, AND I'M NOT LOVING THE IDEA!
THWIP
BWONG
OH, GROSS, NO WAY! THIS IS ALL ORGANIC; LOCALLY SOURCED. I GOT A BEE GUY 'N EVERYTHING!
THANK GOD FOR THAT. ANYWAY, FIGHTING BEE-DUDES JUST AIN'T IN THE CARDS FOR ME TODAY
NO SHADE, MY GUY! MAYBE NEXT TIME!
NOT SO FAST, KID!

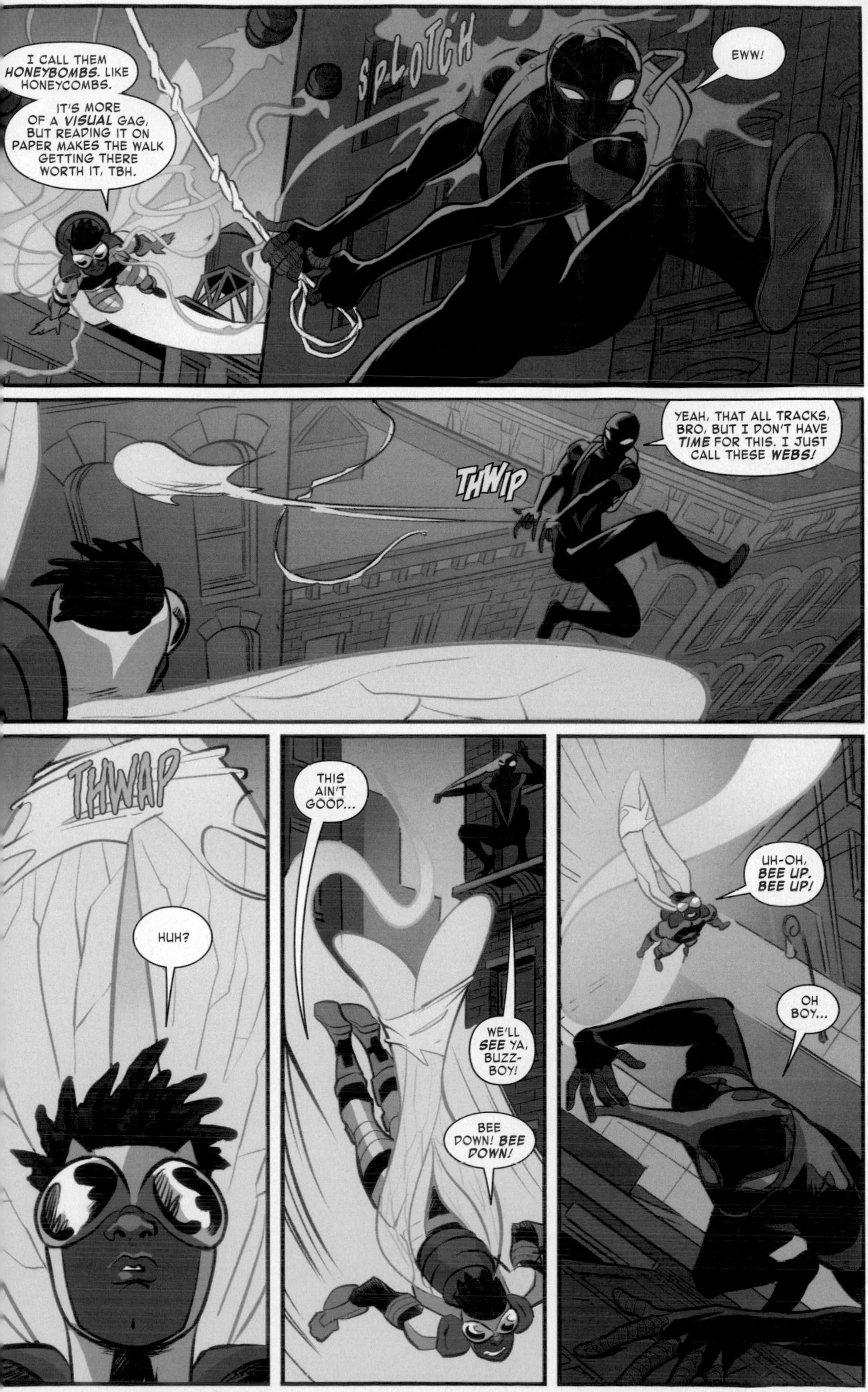
SPLOTCH
I CALL THEM HONEYBOMBS. LIKE HONEYCOMBS.
IT'S MORE OF A VISUAL GAG, BUT READING IT ON PAPER MAKES THE WALK GETTING THERE WORTH IT, TBH.
EWW!
YEAH, THAT ALL TRACKS, BRO, BUT I DON'T HAVE TIME FOR THIS. I JUST CALL THESE WEBS!
THWIP
THWAP
HUH?
THIS AIN'T GOOD...
WE'LL SEE YA, BUZZ-BOY!
BEE DOWN! BEE DOWN!
UH-OH, BEE UP. BEE UP!
OH BOY...

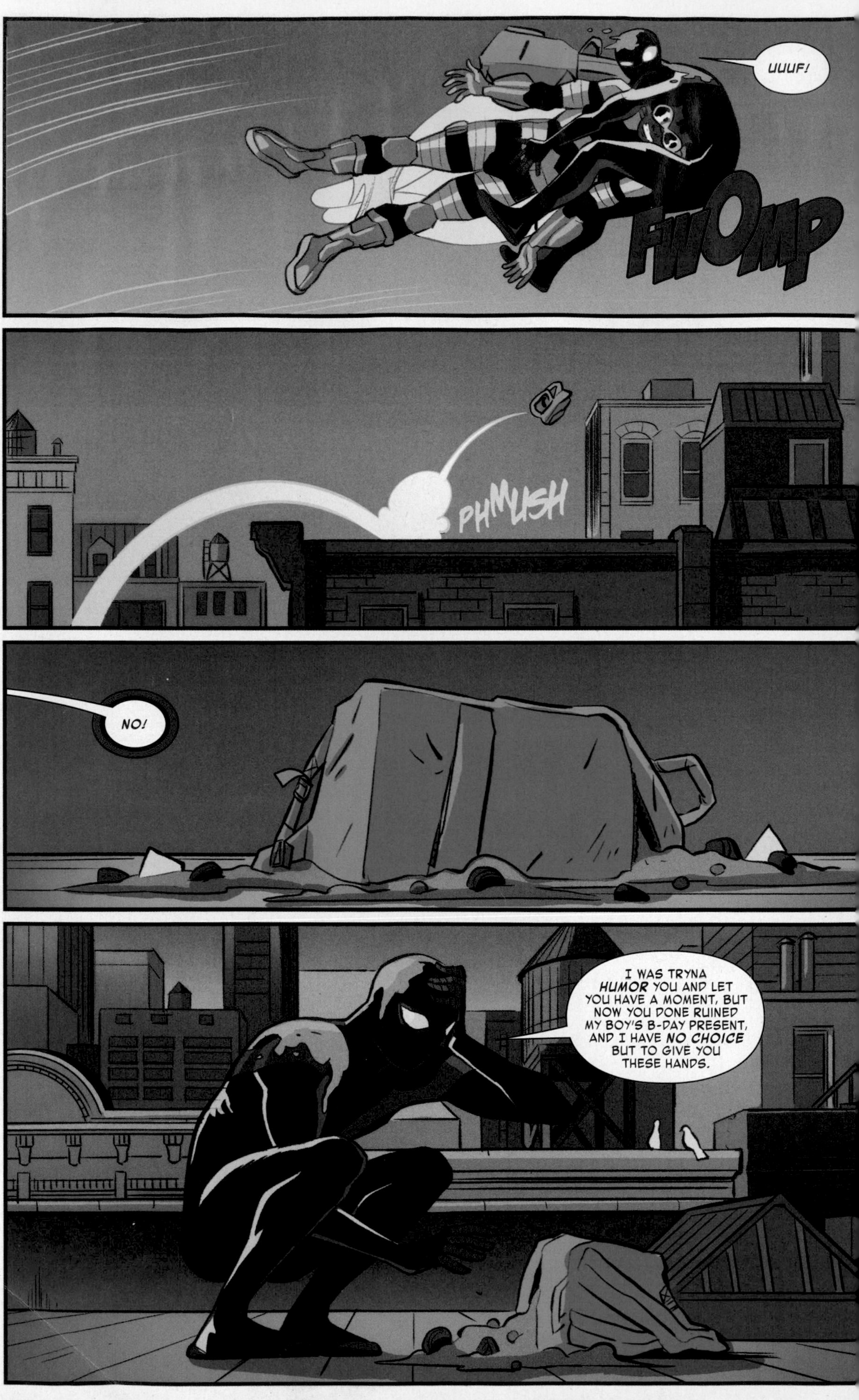
UUUF!
FWOMP
PHMUSH
NO!
I WAS TRYNA HUMOR YOU AND LET YOU HAVE A MOMENT, BUT NOW YOU DONE RUINED MY BOY'S B-DAY PRESENT, AND I HAVE NO CHOICE BUT TO GIVE YOU THESE HANDS.

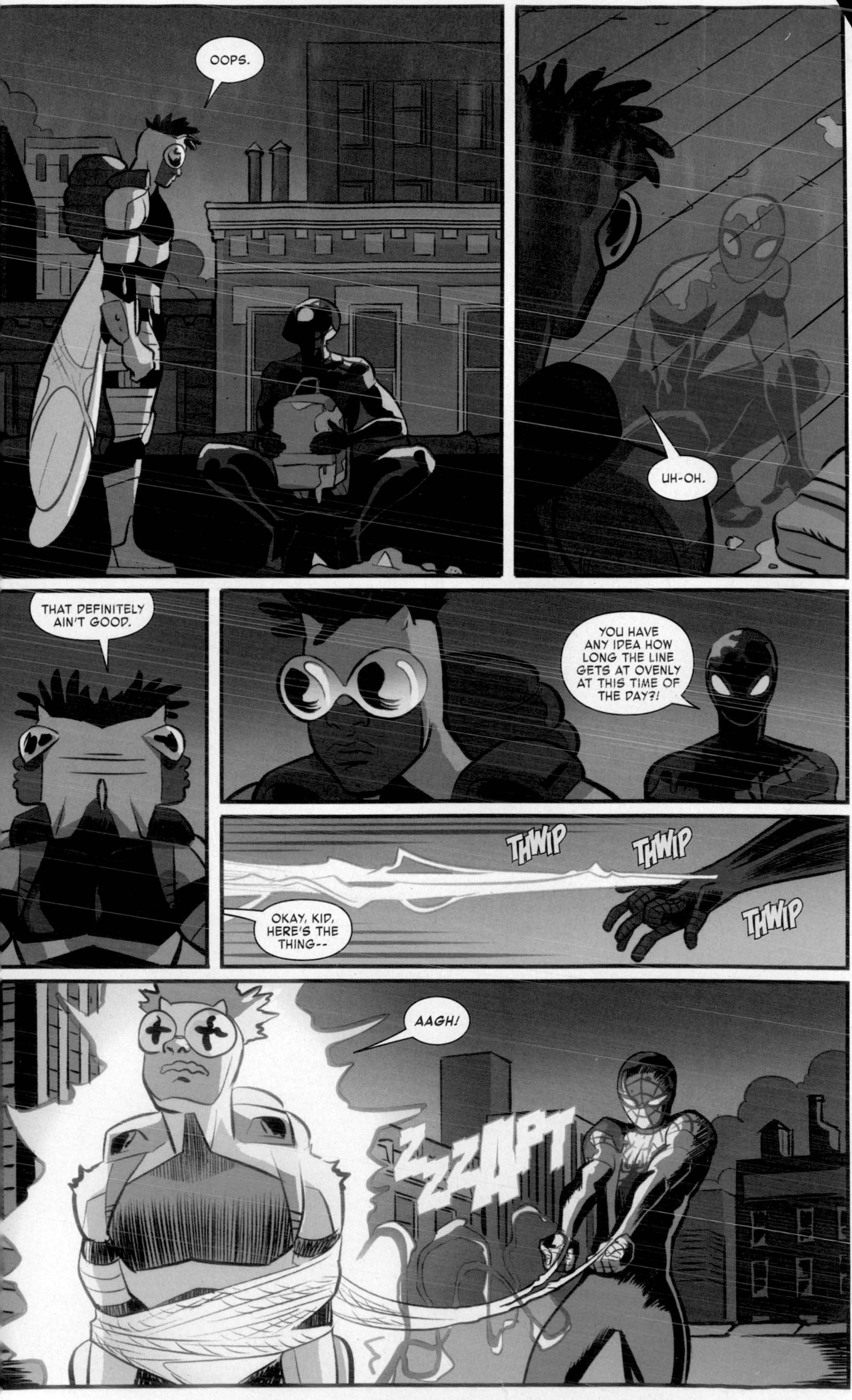
OOPS.
UH-OH.
THAT DEFINITELY AIN'T GOOD.
YOU HAVE ANY IDEA HOW LONG THE LINE GETS AT OVENLY AT THIS TIME OF THE DAY?!
THWIP
THWIP
THWIP
OKAY, KID, HERE'S THE THING--
AAGH!
ZZZAPT

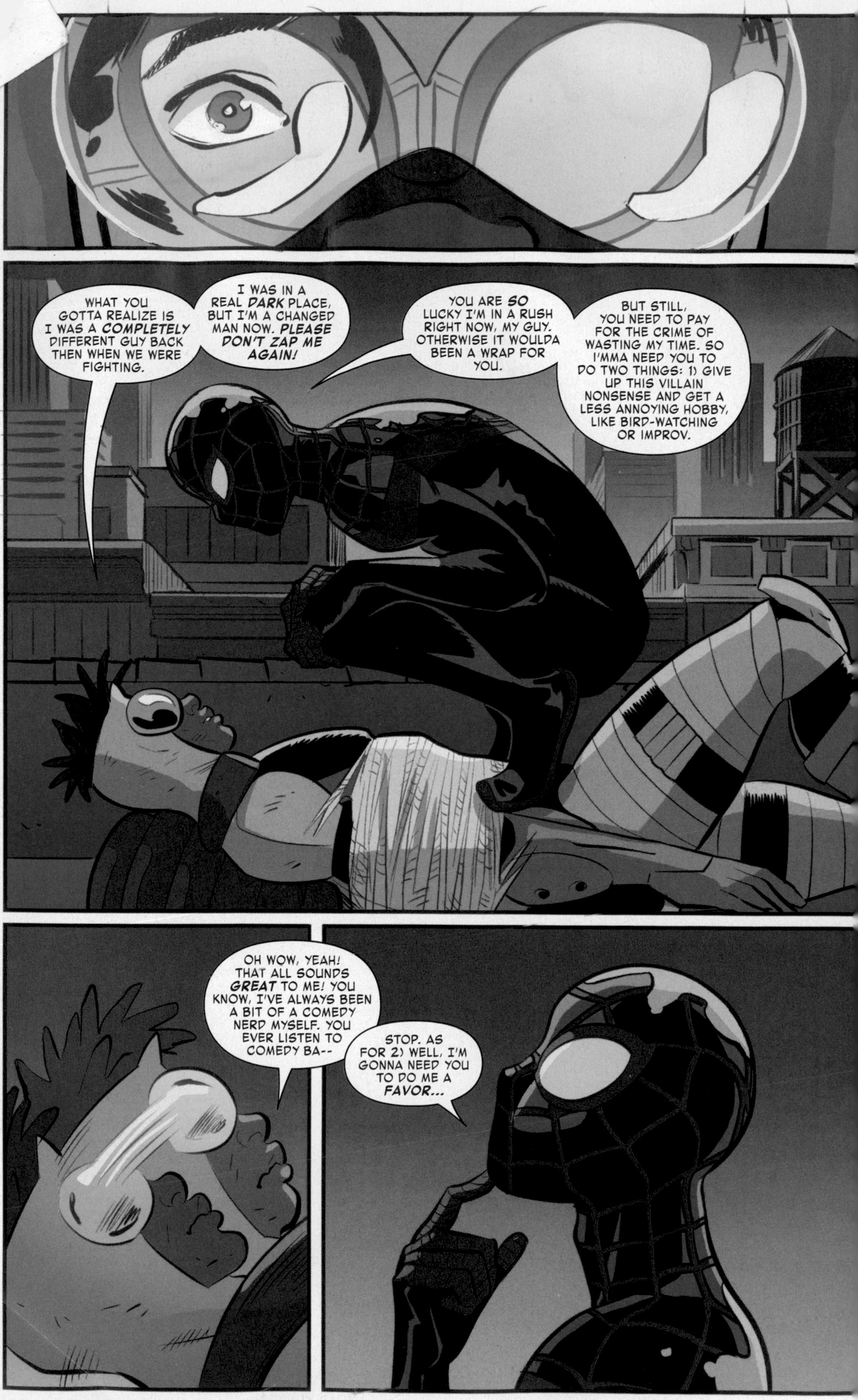
WHAT YOU GOTTA REALIZE IS I WAS A COMPLETELY DIFFERENT GUY BACK THEN WHEN WE WERE FIGHTING.
I WAS IN A REAL DARK PLACE, BUT I'M A CHANGED MAN NOW. PLEASE DON'T ZAP ME AGAIN!
YOU ARE SO LUCKY I'M IN A RUSH RIGHT NOW, MY GUY. OTHERWISE IT WOULDA BEEN A WRAP FOR YOU.
BUT STILL, YOU NEED TO PAY FOR THE CRIME OF WASTING MY TIME. SO I'MMA NEED YOU TO DO TWO THINGS: 1) GIVE UP THIS VILLAIN NONSENSE AND GET A LESS ANNOYING HOBBY, LIKE BIRD-WATCHING OR IMPROV.
OH WOW, YEAH! THAT ALL SOUNDS GREAT TO ME! YOU KNOW, I'VE ALWAYS BEEN A BIT OF A COMEDY NERD MYSELF. YOU EVER LISTEN TO COMEDY BA--
STOP. AS FOR 2) WELL, I'M GONNA NEED YOU TO DO ME A FAVOR...

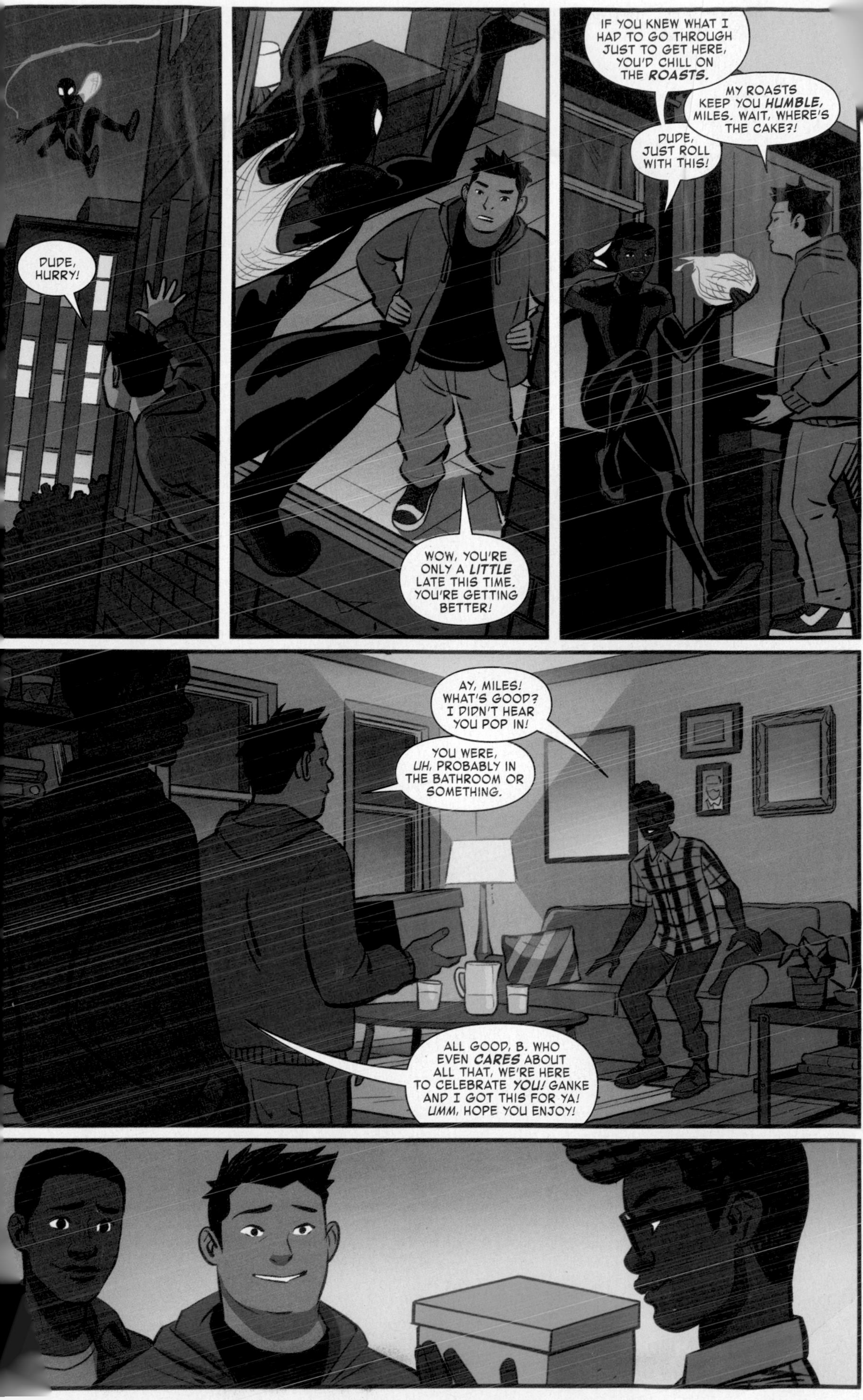
DUDE, HURRY!
WOW, YOU'RE ONLY A LITTLE LATE THIS TIME. YOU'RE GETTING BETTER!
IF YOU KNEW WHAT I HAD TO GO THROUGH JUST TO GET HERE, YOU'D CHILL ON THE ROASTS.
MY ROASTS KEEP YOU HUMBLE, MILES. WAIT, WHERE'S THE CAKE?!
DUDE, JUST ROLL WITH THIS!
AY, MILES! WHAT'S GOOD? I DIDN'T HEAR YOU POP IN!
YOU WERE, UH, PROBABLY IN THE BATHROOM OR SOMETHING.
ALL GOOD, B. WHO EVEN CARES ABOUT ALL THAT, WE'RE HERE TO CELEBRATE YOU! GANKE AND I GOT THIS FOR YA! UMM, HOPE YOU ENJOY!

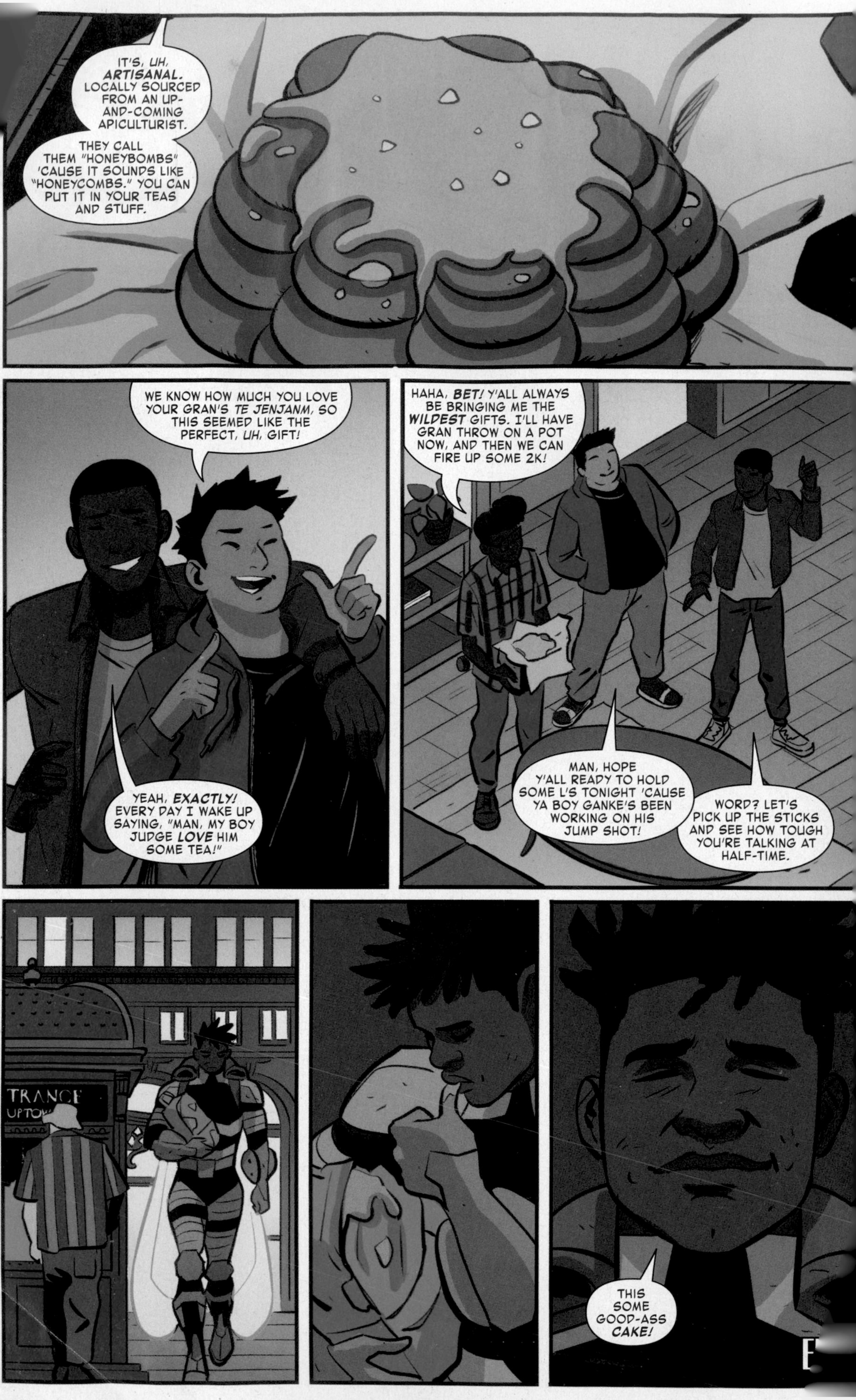
IT'S, UH, ARTISANAL. LOCALLY SOURCED FROM AN UP-AND-COMING APICULTURIST.
THEY CALL THEM "HONEYBOMBS" 'CAUSE IT SOUNDS LIKE "HONEYCOMBS." YOU CAN PUT IT IN YOUR TEAS AND STUFF.
WE KNOW HOW MUCH YOU LOVE YOUR GRAN'S TE JENJANM, SO THIS SEEMED LIKE THE PERFECT, UH, GIFT!
YEAH, EXACTLY! EVERY DAY I WAKE UP SAYING, "MAN, MY BOY JUDGE LOVE HIM SOME TEA!"
HAHA, BET! Y'ALL ALWAYS BE BRINGING ME THE WILDEST GIFTS. I'LL HAVE GRAN THROW ON A POT NOW, AND THEN WE CAN FIRE UP SOME 2K!
MAN, HOPE Y'ALL READY TO HOLD SOME L'S TONIGHT 'CAUSE YA BOY GANKE'S BEEN WORKING ON HIS JUMP SHOT!
WORD? LET'S PICK UP THE STICKS AND SEE HOW TOUGH YOU'RE TALKING AT HALF-TIME.
TRANCE
UPTOW
THIS SOME GOOD-ASS CAKE!